Critical Essays on William Faulkner: The McCaslin Family

William Faulkner in the 1940s.
Photograph © 1978 by Jack Cofield.

Critical Essays on William Faulkner: The McCaslin Family

Arthur F. Kinney

G. K. Hall & Co. • Boston, Massachusetts

First published 1990.
10 9 8 7 6 5 4 3 2 1

Library of Congress Cataloging-in-Publication Data
Critical essays on William Faulkner—the McCaslin family / [edited by]
  Arthur F. Kinney.
      p.   cm. — (Critical essays on American literature)
    Includes bibliographical references.
    ISBN 0-8161-8895-5 (alk. paper)
    1. Faulkner, William, 1897–1962—Characters—McCaslin family.
  2. McCaslin family (Fictitious characters)   I. Kinney, Arthur F.,
  1933– .   II. Series.
  PS3511.A86Z7777 1990
  813'.52—dc20   90-33661
                                                             CIP

The paper used in this publication meets the minimum requirements
of American National Standard for Information Sciences—Permanence
of Paper for Printed Library Materials, ANSI Z39.48-1984. ∞™

Printed and bound in the United States of America

CRITICAL ESSAYS ON AMERICAN LITERATURE

This series seeks to anthologize the most important criticism on a wide variety of topics and writers in American literature. Our readers will find in various volumes not only a generous selection of reprinted articles and reviews but original essays, bibliographies, manuscript sections, and other materials brought to public attention for the first time. This volume provides a historical record of critical reaction to one of William Faulkner's most important fictional families, the McCaslins. The book contains a section on the resources Faulkner used in creating his characters, a number of reprinted essays about the family, and an important appendix containing Faulkner's genealogy for the family and related documents. Among the authors of reprinted essays are Booker T. Washington, Charles V. Chesnutt, John Faulkner, Thadious M. Davis, Lee Jenkins, and Walter Taylor. In addition to Arthur F. Kinney's survey of criticism in the introduction, there are also six original essays commissioned specifically for publication in this volume, new studies by Mick Gidley, Panthea Reid Broughton, Albert J. Devlin, Elisabeth Muhlenfeld, Bernard W. Bell, and Richard H. King. We are confident that this book will make a permanent and significant contribution to American literary study.

JAMES NAGEL, GENERAL EDITOR

Northeastern University

For the George Ivan Mudge Family:
Thelma and Dorothy
and in memory of Ivan and Gertie

and for
Frank Childrey, Jr., of Richmond, Martha Cofield,
of Oxford, and the late William Lamar Wilder, of Pontotoc,
for sharing local legend and local history,
the best of all breathing and forever the best
of all listening

"Q.   This genealogy with all these people that were connected with each other, McCaslins and everybody—was that
made up before the books were written or as each one was
written?

A.   No, that came along as these people appeared. I
would think of one character to write a story about and suddenly he would drag in a lot of people I never saw or heard of
before, and so the genealogy developed itself.

—William Faulkner with students
at the University of Virginia, 27 April 1957

Of what was Faulkner writing in . . . *Go Down, Moses* but the
haunted mind of the South—and of the nation—its house still
divided by racial nightmares?

—Eric J. Sundquist,
"Faulkner, Race, and the Forms of American Fiction"

It's all *now* you see. Yesterday wont be over until tomorrow and
tomorrow began ten thousand years ago.

—Gavin Stevens to Chick Mallison
in *Intruder in the Dust*

CONTENTS

INTRODUCTION

Clan rather than class forms the basic social unit in Faulkner's world. Pride in family and reverence for ancestors are far more powerful motives in behavior than any involvement with class. . . . It is through [the] breakup of the clans that Faulkner charts the decay of the traditional South. Though the Compsons, Sartorises, and McCaslins, all landowners of prominence, begin roughly on the same social level, their histories from the Civil war serve radically different purposes. Their responses to modern life seem to illustrate the various moral courses that are, or were, open to the South: the chivalric recklessness and self-destruction of the Sartorises, the more extreme and tragic disintegration of the Compsons and, by way of resolution, the heroic expiation for the evil of the past upon which Isaac McCaslin decides. . . . The Yoknapatawpha story is to be read more as a chronicle than as a group of novels. It is concerned less with the struggle of the classes than with the rise and fall of the clans, and through its history of the clans it elaborates a moral fable whose source is Southern life.

—Irving Howe[1]

For one swift but splendidly memorable moment in the whole of Faulkner's work we find a Sartoris, a Compson, and a McCaslin together—a community of the clans that constitutes the triumphs and tragedies of Yoknapatawpha. This moment comes in the big woods, in a hunt after bear and deer. It is celebrated by young Isaac (whose full name, joining his father's and mother's lines, is Isaac Beauchamp McCaslin), who in "The Bear" recalls that this gathering of aristocracy in the woods spawns a larger community drawn from even the poorest and most vagrant in the county.

There were five guests in camp that night, from Jefferson: Mr Bayard Sartoris and his son and General Compson's son and two others. And the next morning he looked out the window, into the gray thin drizzle of daybreak which Ash had predicted, and there they were, standing and

1

squatting beneath the thin rain, almost two dozen of them who had fed Old
Ben corn and shoats and even calves for ten years. . . . While they ate
breakfast a dozen more arrived, mounted and on foot: loggers from the
camp thirteen miles below and sawmill men from Hoke's. . . . The little
yard would not hold them.[2]

The little yard would not hold them: The crowd, gathering in size and
momentum, reminds Isaac, looking back in time as usual, of glorious Confederate forces coming together, knowing they are outnumbered and destined
to defeat. But his mind, like theirs, imposes on the forces at the hunting
camp only the anticipation and hope of victory.

Irving Howe is correct in seeing the history of Yoknapatawpha as the
efforts and accomplishments of its clans; and Faulkner seems to want to
reinforce that understanding here by bringing the chief families together.
But this moment is just as surely *not* a moment of "heroic expiation for the
evil of the past." Quite clearly, it is the reverse. If this crowd gathering for
the kill reminds Isaac of historic troops challenging Union forces, for us, able
to look forward, it is equally evocative, and grimly resonant, of the gathering
white mob which, led by the Gowries, fills the square of Jefferson to lynch
Lucas Beauchamp or, much earlier, the raucous crowd which comes on a
mid-week afternoon to Parsham, Tennessee, to watch a backwoods horse
race, the outcome of which will mean freedom or continuing bondage of the
black Bobo Beauchamp to the white Mr. van Tosch. Such relatively easy
analogues of hunt as battle, lynching, and race reveal suddenly and starkly
how easily exchanged such terms and concepts can be in the Yoknapatawpha
of the McCaslins and of the Beauchamp, Edmonds, and Priest families they
breed. Worse yet, when we learn later in "The Bear" segment of *Go Down,
Moses* of the McCaslin lineage, we are caught up once more, just as suddenly
and starkly, as we witness how these concepts are used to contain and even
excuse issues and deeds that are, at root, racial. The hunt for the legendary
bear, Old Ben, at the center of *Go Down, Moses* is a necessary—but
momentary—displacement of the more serious, more lasting hunts that surround it (as Zora Neale Hurston found in a black folktale): the chase of Buck
and Buddy McCaslin for their unacknowledged and enslaved half-brother
(and the anxious hunt of Miss Sophonsiba for a husband and children) in the
opening section entitled "Was," and the deadly manhunt by white justice for
the black Samuel Worsham Beauchamp in the closing section entitled "Go
Down, Moses." Throughout the McCaslin family history, the urgent needs
are for justice, love, and peace—for the end of hunting, battling, lynching,
and subordinating men and women which nonetheless survive in stubborn
and subtle ways, continually reinforced by frustration, hatred, fear, guilt,
and shame. David Minter is surely right when he notes that "*Go Down,
Moses* is primarily the story of what it means to be a descendant and an
inheritor,"[3] and to find there, in "the largest and most complexly entangled of
all Yoknapatawpha families, the McCaslins," all of Faulkner's abiding and

"familiar preoccupations, including such explicitly moral ones as slavery and the land and man's hunger for possession and power" (p. 186). What distinguishes the McCaslin family and its various branches from every other family in Faulkner's work, however, is its persistent recognition of and confrontation with matters of race: what the Sutpens deny in horror, the McCaslins can also grieve. While the complexity and entanglement are not reduced—they are, after all, the very consequences of such matters as rape, incest, and miscegenation—they are all manifest since nearly every family member (as well as Faulkner himself) is obsessed with the family not simply in terms of genealogy but, more specifically, in terms of racial heritage and composition and their resulting moral obligations and responsibilities. Again and again Faulkner's characters (most commonly Ike, Cass, and Lucas) recall—cannot escape—their racial lineage. The concern of the McCaslins for their past spills into the present reality as well. Its power and urgency are reinforced when Faulkner borrows Ike's sentiments for his own Nobel Prize address and takes Gavin Stevens's actual phrases to Chick Mallison regarding Lucas Beauchamp for his public speeches and letters to the Southern (and Northern) press. The McCaslin family legacy starts almost as early as the founding of Yoknapatawpha; and its debts have yet to be paid.

The fundamental facts of the McCaslin family, restated in *Intruder in the Dust* (1948) and extended through the collateral Priest line in *The Reivers* (1962), are set out most fully in *Go Down, Moses* (1942). But this is not our first introduction to certain members of the family. Ike McCaslin had already appeared in "A Bear Hunt," *The Hamlet*, and "Fool About a Horse," where he was first conceived as a landowner and where he works in a hardware store in Jefferson. He is also a character in *Big Woods, Intruder in the Dust, The Mansion, The Reivers*, "Delta Autumn," "Lion," "The Old People," and "Race at Morning." His father, Uncle Buck, briefly enters *Absalom, Absalom!*, is mentioned in *The Hamlet*, and reappears in *Big Woods, The Reivers*, "Raid," "Retreat," "The Unvanquished," and "Vendée," while the method he and his twin brother uncle Buddy invent to free their slaves is first announced in *The Unvanquished*. Ike's Uncle Buddy also appears in "Was," "The Bear," "Vendée," and "The Fire and the Hearth"; his mother Sophonsiba (Sibbey) appears in "Was" and "The Bear"; his grandfather Lucius Quintus Carothers McCaslin is in "The Bear" and "The Old People"; and a distant cousin Ned, the son of Tennie and a black slave, the husband of the Priests' family cook, and the coachman for "Boss" Priest, is introduced in Faulkner's last work, *The Reivers*.

There are, then, essentially three generations of McCaslins in the Yoknapatawpha saga, Lucius, Buck and Buddy, and Ike; but there are five generations of Edmondses and six of Beauchamps. Of these three lines, we know least about the Edmondses. This "female branch" of the McCaslin family originates with the marriage of Carothers's daughter to an unidentified Edmonds (Faulkner's holograph genealogy names her Mary); her grandson is McCaslin (Cass) Edmonds, who is a part of "Was," "The Fire and the Hearth," "The Bear," "Delta Autumn," and "The Old People." Cass rears Isaac and has one son, Zack ("The Fire and the Hearth," and *The Reivers*) who in turn has a lone son named Carothers and nicknamed Roth (*Intruder in the Dust, The Town,* "Go Down, Moses," "Delta Autumn" "Race at Morning," "Gold Is Not Always," and "A Point of Law"). Roth, too, sires a single son who appears, newborn and unnamed, in "Delta Autumn."

Thus the most populous and complicated line in the family is that of the mulatto Beauchamps who take their name not from Hubert but from his wife on whose plantation Tennie, if not Eunice, lives. This branch of the McCaslin family begins in the complexities of rape and incest; with Eunice, a slave he has purchased in New Orleans for Thucydus, Lucius Quintus Carothers McCaslin sires Tomasina or Tomey ("The Bear") and then by her has a son named Terrel (or Tomey's Terrel) corrupted, after the Civil War, to Tomey's Turl ("The Bear," and "Was"). Together Terrel and Tennie have six children, three of whom reach adulthood: James Thucydides (named for his grandfather) who appears in *Big Woods,* "The Bear," "The Old People," and "Delta Autumn"; Sophonsiba (or Fonsiba), named for Ike's mother as the nominal origin of the Beauchamp line ("The Bear"); and Lucius Quintus Carothers McCaslin Beauchamp, which he changes to Lucas (*Intruder in the Dust, The Reivers,* "The Fire and the Hearth," "Pantaloon in Black," "The Bear," "Gold Is Not Always," and "A Point of Law"). Those identified in the fourth generation are both Lucas's children by Molly (later Mollie): Henry, who in turn fathers Samuel Worsham Beauchamp ("The Fire and the Hearth," and "Go Down, Moses") and Nat, who marries George Wilkins ("The Fire and the Hearth"). The sole identified member of the fifth generation of Beauchamps is Samuel Worsham Beauchamp ("Go Down, Moses"); the sole identified member of the sixth Beauchamp generation is the unnamed son of Roth Edmonds by an unnamed mulatto from Chicago ("Delta Autumn").

Lucius McCaslin (1772–1837) begins the main line of the family; Lucius ("Boss") Priest (born around 1850) begins the most distant branch of it one generation later. Like McCaslin he too was born in Carolina and migrated to Mississippi before his marriage to Sarah Edmonds, "a McCaslin, too," in 1869 (*The Reivers*). This union produces one son, Maury, who eventually owns the livery stable in Jefferson and, by marriage to Alison Lessep, has four sons: Lucius, Lessep, Maury, and Alexander (*The Reivers*). This last Lucius, the protagonist of *The Reivers,* is also the novel's narrator and the last of the Priest line who is identified, although the novel is his gift to his own (unnamed) grandson.[4]

During the crucial commissary scene in part 4 of "The Bear," Ike attempts to reorder and make sense of the complex McCaslin heritage with scriptural direction. He sees himself descended from the prototypical Issac of Genesis who, apparently meant to be a sacrificial lamb, was at the last moment spared by God Himself. This astonishing (and presumptuous) reach for identification, however, by which Lucius Quintus Carothers McCaslin is made a kind of Abraham, is not wholly without point or purpose, as our own tracing of the biblical story will show.

The account given us in Genesis tells that Abram (later Abraham), under God's command, left the country of his father and with his wife Sarai and his nephew Lot went into the land of Canaan where he heard the Lord promise that his seed would multiply until his progeny would be as numerous as the dust of the earth or the stars in the sky and that the land as far as he could see would be his (12:5–6; 13:15–16; 15:5). After a journey into Egypt, he returned to Canaan where he was "very rich in cattle, in silver, and in gold" and he and Lot possessed "great substance" (13:2, 6). Sarai, in turn, was served by a bond-woman, and there were in his house slaves (the text reads men bought with money from a stranger, 17:27; 21:10). Similarly, we learn through Ike that Carothers McCaslin, chief progenitor of his line, journeyed out of Carolina to Mississippi with his wife and slaves; there he acquired a handsome estate—a large plantation, cattle, and additional slaves.

Sarai, however, was barren, and she gave to Abram in his old age her Egyptian handmaiden, Hagar, as his concubine. Hagar bore Abram a son, Ishmael, one who should "dwell in the presence of his brethren" (16:1–3; 16:12; 16:16: 21:10) and the Lord changed Abram's name to Abraham ("father of a multitude") and his wife's name to Sarah (17:5, 15). Then, in her own old age, Sarah bore Abraham a son of their own, whom she called Isaac (21:2–3). At Sarah's command, Abraham now cast out Hagar and their son Ishmael (21:9, 14) but later appears to have taken a second concubine, Keturah, who bore him six sons (I Chronicles 1:32), although a discrepant reference in Genesis 25:1 refers to Keturah as Abraham's second wife (25:5, 6). In either event, Abraham gave "all that he had" to Isaac while to the sons of his concubines he gave only gifts, just as Carothers gives his whole inheritance to his twin sons—named Theophilus (Uncle Buck) and Amodeus (Uncle Buddy), the Greek and Latin twin names for "loved of God"—by his written will while orally instructing that one thousand dollars be delivered to his unacknowledged mulatto son by Tomasina, Tomey's Turl: thus the enslaved black son, dispossessed himself in large measure, remained the ostensible possession of his own half brothers. While technically Abraham's relationships are all sanctioned (as Carothers's clearly are not), he does, at one point, identify Sarah as his sister rather than his wife, claiming she is the daughter of his father but not of his mother (20:12); Lot, however, does have clearly incestuous relationships with his children by both unions (19:30–38). We never know whether Carothers is aware that Eunice's child is his—her suicide may be the result of his denial—but he does clearly recognize his paternity of Tomasina's son.

So far the parallel is so close that we can understand Ike's temptation to employ it: he too was born in Uncle Buck's old age, the first child of Sophonsiba. But he must also employ inversion: it was the biblical Isaac who had twins, Esau and Jacob, rather than being born *of* a twin. And it is Esau, like Ike a cunning hunter and man of the field (25:24–28), who bargains away his inheritance seemingly giving Isaac the subsequent right to bargain away his.

But Ike McCaslin's urgently searching mind combines the sense of relinquishment suggested by Esau with that of sacrifice embodied in the more familiar story of Abraham and Isaac, in which the father is willing to surrender the life of his son—by sacramentally killing him to give witness to his faith and obedience in the Lord (22:1–10). It is only by the strangest and most irrational twistings of his source, then, that Ike McCaslin can claim biblical precedent in sacrificing his own responsibilities for his family's planta-tion and his own responsibility for paternity by both repudiating and relin-quishing his birthright (surely one act should cancel out the other) and by transferring his obligations to a cousin on the distaff side of his family line. Clearly Faulkner's point—if not Ike's—is that Ike's very attempt to rational-ize this selfish bid for release from the past when he confronts Cass in the commissary, the heart of his own soil, is an indication that Ike, like his grandfather and father before him, is attempting to formulate actions which, after he has freed Lucas and Fonsiba with their inheritances, will also pro-vide his liberty. The explicit narrative in which Ike sets *himself* free thus makes of his action a duty and tribute to God; implicitly, he may also have in mind Moses, Abraham's descendant, who was later chosen by God to deliver the oppressed Hebrews out of Egyptian bondage (Exodus 3:2–10). For by Ike's apparent reasoning, his long journey to seek out Fonsiba, his encounter with Lucas, and his search for James Beauchamp, all openly acknowledged to be his cousins, are acts of deliverance for the oppressed black McCaslins. It is in this sense that Molly Beauchamp's final keening wail for a deliverer— " 'Roth Edmonds sold my Benjamin' "; " 'Sold him in Egypt and now he dead' " (pp. 380–381)—becomes a final judgment not only on Roth but, by extension, on Ike, too. Both the last McCaslins and the last white Ed-mondses have had the opportunity to take up the bonds of their inheritance and so free their own kin, yet both have chosen the path of self-interest at the price of freedom for their own blood because of the differing color of their skins. The title *Go Down, Moses* is thus meant to be heavily ironic, and the final judgment one that is as old as the Bible, as fresh as 1940, the time of "Delta Autumn," when both Ike *and* Roth refuse to deliver the same black mother and child by substituting material gifts instead: a hunting horn the child cannot use from Ike and, with greater precedent, an envelope of cash from Roth. " 'That's just money,' " Roth's concubine tells her "Uncle Ike" (p. 358); she knows better than he what has value and what has not. Ike seems even to have forgotten his own admonition to Cass, who had tried to sanction slavery by appealing to the biblical account of the sons of Ham (p. 260). Ike knew then that to presume to mix sacred history with his own personal history was at best specious, at worst damningly delusory.[5]

But "the consciousness that dominates Faulkner's fiction is strongly historical," Minter writes (p. 2), and it is that historical sense, rife with paradox and ambiguity, which secures the irony of Ike's thoughts and actions. Faulkner grew up, as the extended McCaslin family did, in northern Mississippi, a land first settled by Chickasaw and Choctaw Indians with their own advanced history and culture and their own sacred beliefs. The trail that became the Natchez Trace was only one of their economic survivals of some eight thousand years; more recent, and just as visible, are the Indian mounds, large and small, which hold cherished objects, household goods, and sacred burial remains. Theirs was an economy and a culture that was rich, sophisticated, and enduring; yet with the coming of the white man in the late eighteenth and early nineteenth centuries, they became the early victims of a government that chose, almost arbitrarily and surely in substantial ignorance of Indian ways, whether to assimilate them, encourage them to become "white," or expel them. It was the aristocratic Thomas Jefferson, in fact, after whom (through Thomas Jefferson Pettigrew, an intermediary) the county seat of Yoknapatawpha is named, who determined to expel them. But he softened his decision by proposing in a letter to Dupont de Nemours that all Indians removed from the region now known as Mississippi should be relocated in Indian territory in Oklahoma. He "encouraged" their "willingness" to cooperate by reducing their Mississippi lands through cessions, by magnifying their indebtedness at government trading posts, and by agreeing to settle any indebtedness by forcing them to barter their lands. Early government policy required paying set fees for each acre of Indian land; but in 1830 negotiations called for the bulk of the land to be sold at public auction, with the proceeds going to the Chickasaw nation after deducting the whole cost of surveying the land and selling it. While most of these monies were set aside in a fund administered by the government in the name of the Chickasaw nation, the Indians were only given the interest for the first half-century; after fifty years, they were to prove themselves sufficiently competent to handle the principal. While later Jacksonians agreed that the Indians must be divested of their land to make way for white settlement, they urged consistency with moral and statutory law by the extension of their state law over tribal domains. On the surface, this seemed much more humane; in fact, it co-opted Indian governance, loosened tribal solidarity, and effectively hastened migration. The treatment of Indians at the hands of the United States government, then—both the warlike Chickasaws and the peace-loving Choctaws—established a clear pattern for the treatment of blacks in later years. Just as tellingly (and prophetically), early white residents, mostly bachelor traders, married Indian women in order to take possession of their impressive dowries of land; early treaties make frequent references to such exploitation, conscious or not, of Chickasaw custom: with Bernard McLaughlin who married the Chickasaw Katy, for instance, or A. T. Eastman, who married Betsy Colbert. The miscegenation of an Indian chief and a quadroon slave (herself the offspring of a white and black) which produces Sam Fathers as an early inhabitant of Yoknapatawpha, who becomes Ike's childhood mentor and substitute father after Buck dies in Ike's early childhood, embodies the practices of the earliest white settlers of Mississippi and introduces Ike, at an early age, to his own intimacy with the offspring of mixed parentage.

The earliest white settlers in Faulkner's Lafayette County, in the northern hill country of Mississippi, were largely farmers from South Carolina who were driven farther south when erosion and poor conservation practices made continued farming there impracticable. Faulkner's fictional Yoknapatawpha County, loosely based on the history and geography of Lafayette County, is also settled by migrants from the Carolinas, like McCaslin and Edmonds. The rich alluvial soil, supplied by much wider irrigation from the Mississippi River than is true today, allowed Carolina planters to bring with them their experiences of large cotton plantations managed through slavery; not until after the Emancipation Proclamation and the close of the War Between the States did they come to realize the need, both economically and geographically, to diversify their crops. Their inability to operate without cheap labor and their further inability to control the fluctuating price of cotton caused many of them to avoid bankruptcy only by planting corn, wheat, potatoes, and other vegetables, as Cass and Lucas do, or to turn, with more modest means, to truck gardening, as Hamp and Miss Worsham do. Both the increased cultivation of land and the later introduction of the timber industry caused a steady clearing of woodland demonstrating an ignorance of good conservation measures which in time caused more erosion. This historical consideration also contributes to Faulkner's ironic characterization of Ike: in decrying the end of the wilderness, Ike seems concerned only with the loss of hunting, not with the eventual spoliation of the very land itself. Typically, he sees at best only half the picture.

From 1865 until the turn of the century, but especially from 1875 onward, middle-class and lower-class whites and black freedmen swelled the ranks of tenant farmers: in this last quarter century records at the Lafayette County courthouse show more than 25,000 Chattel Deeds (Deeds of Trust on Crop to be Made) and an astounding average of 1,000 loans a year from merchants. It is not surprising, with the vagaries of weather and the need for continual hard labor, that many of these farmers were unable to meet all their notes and over time became entangled in debt—the sort of debt the early Lafayette County planter Washington Price encourages, but that in Yoknapatawpha Cass Edmonds is determined to avoid and about which the arrogant Lucas Beauchamp refuses to concern himself. Oxford historian Walker Coffey has recorded one instance in the case of Wesley Pickens.

On February 20, 1877 he entered into an agreement in which he pledged, "the entire crop of cotton, corn and other produce made by me, my family and tenants during the year 1877 on the plantation of Dr. J. B. McEwen or elsewhere: also one sorrel horse and one bay horse and all other stock of every kind together with one spring wagon. This Trust Deed is an additional security to the ones given November 19th, 1874 and January 13, 1875." The unpaid notes were for $251.80 and interest and an open account of $52.62 with $150.00 to be advanced in supplies during the year 1877. Wesley Pickens could not read or write since he signed the agreement with an X mark.[6]

Pickens's freedman status is hardly distinguishable from bondage, and it is hard to imagine that he did not know despair; his heirs, grown to frustration and resentment, might well become unruly like the Gowries. By the same token, it is easy to see why Lucas Beauchamp, with land of his own and money in the bank, can feel so arrogant. Yet even this does not escape Faulkner's sense of history, and of historic irony: Molly's disgust with Lucas's self-centeredness, and an egoism that easily leads him to believe in a quick fortune, nearly causes their divorce while his lack of caring for others separates them, perhaps irrevocably, during her period of mourning, in Jefferson, for Samuel Beauchamp, the "slain wolf" (p. 382). If, for her, Pharaoh is reincarnated in the white landowners of Yoknapatawpha, there may also be a little of Pharaoh in the comparatively uncaring Lucas. Ike's ignorance is, as ever, even more damaging. Unlike Cass and perhaps also unlike Roth, he seems incapable of realizing that only diversity in industry and commerce, based in part on rail transportation, will aid and perhaps salvage the sagging agricultural economy of Yoknapatawpha. (From 1915 to 1929 the timber industry, while cutting bare hundreds of acres of land, managed more than anything else to bolster the faltering economy of Lafayette County.) Ike's own narrow and jealous desire to maintain the big woods as his own private refuge is, in its pride and arrogance, strikingly analogous to Lucas's narrow and jealous desire to desecrate the sacred Indian mounds in his corrupt and corrupting search for fool's gold; both mistake self-interest and greed for a greater goodness. Faulkner outlived both Ike and Lucas, however, and so saw yet another ironic turn of history: the way in which the denuding of the land gave only a temporary relief to the fortunes of Lafayette County. Ike's position, then, would be partially exonerated, but for different reasons than those he advances. It is the later Priest branch of the McCaslin family that must understand the implications of replacing the farm by the store, and the horse and cow and mule by the automobile, even when it is a dazzling and distracting Winton Flyer. And for all the high spirits that seem to characterize *The Reivers*, there is at the core of Faulkner's last novel an undeniably somber note of racism. The real release for the McCaslin family—the real "expiation for the evil of the past"—rests on Lucius Priest, the last known descendant of Lucius McCaslin, and his recognition that Bobo Beauchamp's plight and Ned McCaslin's obsequiousness are the direct consequences of blacks living in a society controlled still by whites and that this segregation is perhaps the greatest act of what Lucius calls Non-Virtue.

To the very last of his writing and to the very end of his life, then, Faulkner like the McCaslins, Edmondses, Beauchamps, and Priests, seems to have been irrevocably and irretrievably haunted by the idea of slavery, by the multifarious implications of racism, and by the need for deliverance and freedom, to "let my people go," as the black spiritual puts it. Clearly such matters were deeply painful for Faulkner. From his uneasiness in treating the Strother family in *Flags in the Dust/Sartoris* and the Gibson family in *The Sound and the Fury*, the central documents on the Sartoris and Compson families, to his anguished avoidance-and-confrontation with slavery, racism, and miscegenation in *Absalom, Absalom!*—the novel that seems to have caused him the most difficulty and anguish to compose—Faulkner's emergent focus was evolutionary yet unavoidable. In tracing the McCaslin family he concentrates at last openly and fully on those issues which came to epitomize for him as for others the true character, and burden, of Southern history.

Since nearly all of Faulkner's public, nonfictional statements on racism were circumstantial and occasional, there is no reliable index to his deepest thoughts and convictions, especially on matters he took to be so personal. But he was surely aware of the history of the white treatment of blacks, a degradation which, Bernard W. Bell conveniently sums, began far earlier in America than the white settlement of Mississippi.

> By 1638 slaves were introduced into Massachusetts, and in 1641 slavery was given legal sanction in that colony by the "Body of Liberties," statutes prohibiting human bondage "unless it be lawfull Captives taken in just warres, and such strangers as willingly sell themselves or are sold to us." In 1661 Virginia reinforced the system of slavery by legal statute, imposed a fine for interracial fornication in 1662, banned interracial marriages in 1691, defined slaves explicitly as real estate in 1705, and deprived freed blacks of the right to vote in 1723. According to a Maryland law of 1663, "All negroes or other slaves within the province, and all negroes or other slaves to be hereafter imported into the province, shall serve *durante vita;* and all children born of any negro or other slave, shall be slaves as their fathers were for the term of their lives." Because many slaves were fathered by whites, the law was soon changed so that the mother's status determined the children's. Subsequent eighteenth- and nineteenth-century statutes and jurisprudence concerning everything from literacy to politics institutionalized the racist ideology that blacks, bondsmen and freedmen alike, were biologically and culturally inferior, possessing no rights that whites were obliged to recognize.[7]

From all this Mississippi was not exempt: in 1821 the second criminal case officially reported in the state had to argue that it was "as clearly murder to kill a slave as to kill a freeman."[8] Various codes were based on the premise that slaves were personal property, a status so securely fixed by statutory enactment and judicial construction that the writ of *habeus corpus* was considered inapplicable. Color, according to W. W. Magruder, was taken as *prima facie* evidence of liability to servitude (p. 139).[9]

The subordination of blacks extended even to physical violation by whites. Magruder quotes the historian Ulrich B. Phillips, who notes that "The rape of a female slave was not [considered] a crime, but a mere trespass on the master's property" (p. 162). Phillips goes on to show how the legal provisions of the antebellum South were founded on a comparison of slaves with animals. "As with other livestock, the proprietor of the female parent became possessed of her offspring; and as the owner of a horse might use force in breaking him to harness, so the master of a slave might coerce him into subjection, though the law forbade cruel treatment or the destruction of life or limb except when meeting resistance or by mishap in the course of 'moderate correction.' A runaway slave, too, was like a stray horse, to be seized, impounded, advertised, and reclaimed by his owner upon payment for services rendered and expenses incurred" (p. 162).[10] Actual plantation ledgers and letters from antebellum Mississippi bear out this comparison, giving the black a somewhat higher market value. From a plantation in Yalobusha County, adjoining Lafayette County on the south, William Polk writes in 1838 that he had bought three mules for one hundred dollars each; contemporaneously, the New Orleans slave market was getting from $275 to $900 for young men. In 1831 John Wesley Vick, another Mississippi planter, sold twenty-five-year-old Ned for $550, 19-year-old Albert for $525, and, to a second planter, three young men at $625 and a fourth at $900.[11] But even if these were the current rates, Ike's father paid too much for Percival Brownlee—"*Percavil Brownly 26yr Old. cleark @ Bookepper. bought from N.B. Forest at Cold Water 3 Mar 1856 $265. dolars*"—especially when Uncle Buck and Uncle Buddy learn (and record) that Percival can't read, write, plow, or even lead cattle to water (*Go Down, Moses*, p. 264). Other records, such as those to which Faulkner had access in his borrowed copy of *The Southern Plantation Overseer* (1925), excerpted in this volume, recount the frequency of runaways.[12] We can sense even more precisely the impact in Faulkner's historic Lafayette County by turning to the federal census records for this period. The first significant census, in 1840, shows 3,689 whites and 2,842 slaves living there; significantly, however, there was a shortfall in white females as against white males (1,658 to 2,018) but a slight excess of black females to males (1,430 to 1,412). The following decade, from 1840 to 1850, when the first Edmonds came from Carolina to Yoknapatawpha, saw the greatest population boom in Lafayette County history. By 1850 there were 8,346 whites (4,466 male and 3,380 female) and 5,719 blacks, only four of them free. The slave population by 1860 increased by 24%, 7% now listed as mulattoes.[13] The force of such statistics on Faulkner is evident in the history of Yoknapatawpha. Slavery first corrupts the original Indian settlers—there are references to Indians as slaveholders in "Red Leaves," "A Justice," "A Courtship," "The Old People," and *Requiem for a Nun*. But from the beginning slavery is also problematic for them. Three-Basket complains of the changes in Indian life caused by following the white man's practice of black slavery in "Red Leaves,"[14] and he is echoed later in the story by an "old man": " 'We got along fine for years and years, before the white men foisted their Negroes upon us. . . . now what do we do? Even the old wear themselves into the grave taking care of them that like sweating' " (p. 323). Their answer, still aping the whites, is to enter into slave trade, as (later) Ikkemotubbe (named Doom) sells Sam Fathers to Carothers McCaslin. For Faulkner, the Indians' adoption of the white mans's ways with blacks not only corrupted them morally and, in time, economically, but eventually it also alienated them from the land. By contrast, Faulkner's praise often comes for those who refuse to own slaves (Gail Hightower's father, Goodhue Coldfield, the ancestors of Gavin Stevens) or attempt to free them as, too late, Uncle Buck and Uncle Buddy do.

Faulkner is concerned not only with slavery but with slavery's legacy of miscegenation—the "tragic mulatto" in Sterling Brown's useful phrase. The very word "mulatto" mirrors the antebellum association of slaves with animals, for it has a shared etymology with "mule." Lest his readers forget this imposed connection, the early racist novelist Thomas Dixon writes in *The Leopard's Spots* (1906) that "The Negro is the human donkey . . . Mate him with a horse, you lose the horse, and get a larger donkey called a mule, incapable of preserving his species."[15] The McCaslin family history, through the Beauchamps, suggests this is not so for Faulkner; more importantly, it suggests that mixed blood is a "curse," in Ike's word (*Go Down, Moses*, p. 298) from which, Cass says in turn, no McCaslin will ever be free (p. 299). From the first, Faulkner sees the conflict of racial bloods as a fatal battleground, not merely writ historically large in the War Between the States—a central focus of *Flags in the Dust/Sartoris* and *The Unvanquished*—but within the little body of man, as Gavin Stevens describes Joe Christmas in *Light in August*.[16] This conflict of bloods causes Joe to be aggressive and submissive by turn, at last shot by white men as he crouches behind an overturned table just as—equally agonized—Fonsiba crouches behind a table when her own cousin Ike comes to deliver her legacy; but for Faulkner Gavin's too-easy equation of white blood with goodness and salvation, black blood with evil and death, is no more advanced, no more enlightened for all his Heidelberg training, than Thomas Dixon's.

In *From Slavery to Freedom*, John Hope Franklin discusses miscegenation by examining the frequent occasions and various means by which black women were subjected to the whims and desires of white men, noting that "By 1860 there were 411,000 mulatto slaves out of a total slave population of 3,900,000."[17] Slave testimonies collected by John W. Blassingame illustrate Franklin's descriptions. Blassingame cites Robert Small's interview with the American Freedmen's Inquiry Commission in 1863,

> Q. At what age do colored girls begin to have intercourse with white men?
> A. I have known them to as young as twelve years,[18]

and Lewis Clarke's "Leaves from a Slave's Journal of Life," "My grandmother was her master's daughter; and my mother was her master's daughter; and I was my master's son; so you see I han't got but one-eighth of the blood" (p. 152). Blassingame includes a composite report from an interview of a South Carolina slave named Israel in 1861 which has clear resonances in Uncle Hubert Beauchamp as well as Lucius Quintus Carothers McCaslin. Israel tells of James Gerrard who, around 1850,

> wanted to marry a fine lady, but she "kicked him," (Israel's word for rejected,) and, in spite, he took [the black slave] Rose to live with him. He bought her in Savannah, expressly for the purpose. "I went with him for her in de buggy," said Israel, "and 'fore he pay for she, he bring her home and try if she could cook and make pastry. He find she good, stirrin' woman, and he keep her." He added that Garrard had seven children by her—two boys and five girls—the eldest of whom, a girl of about ten years of age, was then living in Savannah. Over a year ago, Garrard died, leaving a will which called for the sale of his entire real estate, slaves, cattle, and other property, excepting Rose and his own children, who were manumitted. Out of the proceeds of the sale of the property, a home was to be purchased for Rose and her young family, and the balance of the funds was to be placed at interest, of which she was to receive one thousand dollars a year for the support of herself and the children, and the remainder was bequeathed to his brother-in-law [brother?], Elliott Garrard, of Savannah. (pp. 361–62)

But this was the exception. More familiar by far was the story John Boggs of Maryland related when he was interviewed in Canada in 1863: "Old William Merrick had children by his slave women and then sold them; and he had as nice a wife as any gentleman need to have anywhere. You couldn't tell the difference between the children he had by his slaves & those he had by his wife, only they were a little brighter. They all favored him. He used to have some Irishmen on the plantation, and he said these children were theirs, but everybody knew they were his. They were as much like him as himself" (p. 423).

In 1880 a new Mississippi code considered miscegenation outside marriage acceptable but inside marriage an act of incest.[19] Faulkner seems aware of this when Carothers McCaslin breeds a son by his own daughter Tomasina (Tomey's Turl) resulting, in time, in Lucas's agony and frustration, an agony and frustration which can know no end: " 'How to God,' he said, 'can a black man ask a white man to please not lay down with his black wife? And even if he could ask it, how to God can the white man promise he won't?' " (*Go Down, Moses*, p. 59). Following Lucas, miscegenation is how Ned McMaslin, called the "family skeleton" because he is mulatto, makes his way in the Priest family, hardened—or driven—to the shame of it, something young Lucius, because of his sense of Ned as a mere schemer, easily overlooks:

> he—Ned—was a McCaslin, born in the McCaslin back yard in 1860. He was our family skeleton; we inherited him in turn, with his legend (which

had no firmer supporter than Ned himself) that his mother had been the natural daughter of old Lucius Quintus Carothers himself and a Negro slave; never did Ned let any of us forget that he, along with Cousin Isaac, was an actual grandson to old time-honored Lancaster where we moiling Edmondses and Priests, even though three of us—you, me and my grandfather—were named for him, were mere diminishing connections and hangers-on.[20]

Although this passage occurs early in *The Reivers*, and so early in the educational escapades of young Lucius, the older Lucius now telling the tale in retrospect also has something yet to learn.

The Reivers is subtitled *A Reminiscence* and many dimensions of Faulkner's last work are drawn from people and places known to him: like Lucius Priest, Faulkner had three younger brothers, a father who ran a livery stable (his name was Murry, not Maury), and a family servant called Aunt Callie; moreover, the Iron Bridge, Ballenbaugh's, and a mudfarm at Hell's Creek Crossing were all on the Oxford-Memphis road in 1910 where his own grandfather's car, a Buick rather than a Winton Flyer, was mired in the Tallahatchie River bottom. In fact, Mammie Callie Barr, to whom *Go Down, Moses* is dedicated, whose frail body and gnarled black hands Faulkner fondly remembered as she sat in her rocking chair before the fireplace at Rowan Oak, his own antebellum home, is clearly the model for Molly Beauchamp, and James Harvey Krefft argues that Faulkner has further memorialized his relationship to Mammie Callie in Roth's relationship to Molly in "The Fire and the Hearth".[21] Others have seen features of Roth in John Faulkner, the author's younger brother, comparing his management of Greenfield Farm eighteen miles east of Oxford to Roth's management of the McCaslin plantation located in roughly the same place on William Faulkner's hand-drawn map of Yoknapatawpha. It is generally agreed that "Uncle Ned" Barnett, originally a slave belonging to Colonel W. C. Falkner (the "Old Colonel"), Faulkner's great-grandfather, was used in drawing the portrait of Lucas Beauchamp, for both were large men with dignified bearing, not a little arrogance, and a certain sartorial splendor; Faulkner's biographer Joseph L. Blotner has noted that Uncle Ned was even known to wear a tie when milking his cow at Greenfield.[22] (A bridge which John Faulkner built in 1938 over Puskus Creek, which flows through Greenfield Farm and swells each winter, is likely to have been the one suggested in part in the opening scene between Chick and Lucas in *Intruder in the Dust*.) There is another possible connection as well: after marrying Kate Redmond, Uncle Ned began living with a woman named Minnie; John Faulkner urged Ned to seek a divorce despite Ned's denial that he had ever married, and their wrangling is suggestive of a dispute between Lucas and Roth in "The Fire and the Hearth."

Faulkner's nephew Jim Faulkner also suggests, in recalling family stories, an incident that may have contributed to "Pantaloon in Black." "Double Dip and Ammonia live in a house out in the back and down the hill from our house, and they have lived on the place and worked for us for years, even before he had to go to Parchman, the state penitentiary, for a few years because he had to kill Dusty in a crap game that time when Dusty tried to pass the smaller part of a torn dollar bill to him."[23] Lewis M. Dabney has even located one possible resource for the creation of Boon Hogganbeck. "He is partly drawn from Buster Callicot, the senior Falkner's stable foreman, with whom Faulkner told of having bought a Texas pony like those in 'Spotted Horses.' Ike recalls the episode when he gives Boon a dollar for a drink in Memphis. John Faulkner says his brother and Buster took the Memphis trip to buy whiskey for Stone's [hunting] camp, and this comic interlude within the hunting scene [of "The Bear"] is autobiographical in feeling."[24] It is not so much that Faulkner wants to memorialize his own associations, or even pay passing tribute to them, for he always works with imaginative and composite reconstructions rather than with one-to-one correspondence, but he does wish to anchor his own chronicle of Yoknapatawpha in the rock-hard actuality of historic time and place. In Faulkner, history can always resonate as metaphor.

Nowhere is this truer than in Faulkner's firm sense of place. As in his other fiction, Jefferson closely resembles Oxford, Mississippi, while Parsham is most likely based on Grand Junction, Tennessee. Faulkner has an accurate sense of architecture, too; the floor plan Uncle Buddy imagines for Warwick follows the traditional H-style of plantation homes, while the log cabin which (variously) is built by Carothers ("The Fire and the Hearth") or Uncle Buck and Uncle Buddy ("The Bear") will become a commonplace four-crib dog-trot in which the dog must run from room to room rather than use a hallway ("Was").[25] But the most fully realized scenes in the McCaslin chronicles are those of the big woods. Faulkner learned to hunt from his father. He gave William an air rifle at the age of eight, a .22-caliber rifle at the age of ten, and a shotgun at the age of twelve; later, Murry Falkner took his sons to the wilderness around the Tallahatchie "Club House" of which he was part owner. Faulkner's stepson Malcolm Franklin recalls when "On one long drive we made together in my jeep, he said, 'This is where "The Bear" took place.' We were passing through the old Stone place, between the Sunflower and Tallahatchie rivers, some seventeen miles southwest of the old river town known as Panola, situated a few miles north of Batesville in Panola County."[26] In Yoknapatawpha, Major DeSpain's hunting camp is built on land acquired from Thomas Sutpen in 1865 by restoring (by 1869) a fishing camp originally built (according to *Absalom, Absalom!*) by Sutpen in 1838 and later, abandoned and rotting, lived in by Wash and Milly Jones. But Faulkner draws heavily on the hunting camp of General Stone, the father of his close friend Phil Stone, where he began going in 1915—first by train to Batesville where a wagon met them to take the hunters and their supplies to Stone's Stop and the lodge and then, later, by truck. Emily Whitehurst Stone, the late Phil Stone's wife, has written that Stone Stop, near where the Stones lived before they moved from the Delta to Oxford, was also near land owned by Phil's great-uncles Theophilus and Amodeus Potts, "whom everybody called Buck and Buddy (and who appeared by name if not in character in many of Faulkner's stories)." She continues,

> the camping trips were elaborate affairs, as was anything connected with General Stone—Major DeSpain in the hunting stories. Days before the hunting parties arrived, Negroes would go by wagon to set up tents, dig barbecue pits, and cut hacks or wide paths through the cane which grew sometimes as thick as a man's wrist and closer than the hairs on a dog's back. . . .
>
> The hacks were cut low enough so that a running horse would not disembowel himself, but high enough to impede a bear. And when the dogs routed one out, he would soon be running down the hacks and would inevitably pass the intersections where the men had taken their stands. . . .
>
> At night everybody, including the help, had some [liquor], and the men sat around the fire, telling their yarns or playing poker or blackjack.

Phil Stone also told her the story of his own vision of a big buck coming to him on a hunt when he was only twelve, an incident Faulkner may have transferred to twelve-year-old Isaac.[27] John B. Cullen, one of Faulkner's more frequent hunting companions, has collected his memories in a volume which tells of possible sources for Old Ben, Lion, Boon, and Uncle Ash,[28] while another hunting partner, Jerrold Brite, recalls that shortly before Faulkner wrote "Delta Autumn," he nearly died while on a hunt and barely reached Dr. Culley in Oxford on time.[29] But death may not have been far from Faulkner's mind either. It was the time of Callie Barr's passing; and a young friend, Dan Brennan, who was visiting Faulkner in 1940, recalls watching him finish typing and then correcting "Go Down, Moses." He told Brennan the story was about "A Negro funeral" and that he had gotten the idea when he " 'was down to the station last week and a coffin came in off the train.' "[30]

Faulkner also displays considerable ingenuity in choosing names. In a local Pontotoc publication on Chickasaws he could have learned that Ishtehotapha was the name of the last Chickasaw king and that the Edmondson family was one of the first white families to settle Indian land.[31] Although records at the Lafayette County courthouse show three ledger pages full of Scots' names similar to McCaslin, Faulkner may have also had in mind the McJunkins, a black family who in the late 1930s were tenant farmers at Greenfield Farm. The given names of Lucius Quintus Carothers McCaslin, however, bear such striking resemblance to the most famous early citizens of Oxford, Lucius Quintus Cincinnatus Lamar, that Faulkner must have meant to play on his power and position. The new name, Carothers, which Blotner suggests was substituted so as not to be "*too* imitative,"[32] may be an attempt at parody, since the two Carothers whom Faulkner surely knew were his grandfather's chauffeur, Chess Carothers, also a model for Ned McCaslin,[33] and Hugh Carothers, who had been a candidate for juror in September 1935 in Oxford during the infamous trial of the black Elwood Higginbotham.[34]

Moreover, Faulkner would have known (as perhaps Sophonsiba did) that Beauchamps were the English owners of the actual Warwick Castle; a different Beauchamp, Hugh Beauchamp, was raised to the baronage by William I after the Norman conquest.[35] But the name was also well known throughout the South for its association with Jereboam O. Beauchamp and his notorious murder of Colonel Solomon P. Sharp, a prominent lawyer in Frankfort, Kentucky, because of Sharp's alleged affair in the 1820s with the well-born Ann Cook whom Beauchamp wished to marry.[36] If Faulkner had Lucas in mind rather than Hubert when choosing the Beauchamp name, then it points ironically to the fact that Lucas fails in his attempt to defend Molly's honor in his duel with Zack Edmonds. But in thus associating Lucas with chivalric honor and with adultery, we are made to realize that Lucas's deep respect for his grandfather McCaslin relies on the white blood that is imparted to him; what he can not realize is that when Carothers impregnated his mother he was also impregnating his own daughter; reversing the story of the white Compsons and Sutpens, what the black Beauchamp can accept is miscegenation; what he cannot accept is incest. In addition to this, Thadious M. Davis has been able to trace suggestively the name of Rider, a tenant of the McCaslin plantation, to various blues songs such as "Yellow Dog Blues" and "Memphis Blues." "In 'Pantaloon [in Black],' Rider's life has the contours of a blues song; he has been a man of the world—a drinker, a gambler, a womanizer, generally a 'bad' man type such as Dupree or Staggolee in blues ballads; he has found a true love, his wife Mannie; and he has lost her. ('Memphis Blues' ends with the lines: 'the Mississippi river's so deep and wide / Gal I love she on the other side.')"[37] Unlike his use of events, places, and names in many other works in the Yoknapatawpha chronicle, though, in the case of the McCaslin fiction, as in the earlier *Light in August* and *Absalom, Absalom!*, Faulkner is always deliberately pointing to (or implying) issues of race, revealing his undeniable desire (or need) to address its attendant problems.

The accuracy and significance of Faulkner's references and allusions to actual moments, locations, and people in history is extended to his account of the Indians in the McCaslin story where they both predate and predict later events. Here he must have supplemented his knowledge of local legend with some research. While Yoknapatawpha County is named for the Yoknapatawpha River (now corrupted to "Yocona") which serves as the southern border of Lafayette County and, by local consent, means "water runs slow through flat land," *A Dictionary of Choctaw Language* published in 1915 gives the following meanings for members of the word:

ik patafo, a., unplowed.

patafa, pp., split open; plowed, furrowed; tilled.

yakni, n. the earth; . . . soil; ground; nation; . . . district . . .

yakni patafa, pp., furrowed land; fallowed land.[38]

The literal meaning of Yoknapatawpha, then, is "plowed or cultivated land, or district," a meaning which Faulkner uses ironically when, in "A Court-ship," he deliberately sets the Indian *Plantation* against the yet-untilled land of the intruding white settlers (*Collected Stories*, p. 361). Subsequent raids by the Indians presaged the theft of the land by the federal government, culminating in the Treaty of Dancing Rabbit Creek on 28 September 1830: dispossessing the Indians allowed planters, ironically, to increase their own possessions of land and slaves. Although the actual removal of Indians to their own territory in Oklahoma took place largely between 1837 and 1847, many of them (especially the peace-loving Choctaws) elected to stay; during Faulkner's childhood there were still 1,344 full-blooded Indians speaking their native Choctaw in northern and central Mississippi.

We may be even more certain that he looked up the means of Indian burial, for the account he apparently follows may be found in a volume of the *Publications of the Mississippi Historical Society* for 1900 near an account of his great-grandfather's work as a novelist (Dabney, p. 37). But Faulkner transferred Choctaw practice to the Chickasaws for Sam Father's death (and, apparently, the earlier death of Jobaker at Sam's hands).[39] While the practical, warlike Chickasaws buried their dead as soon as possible wherever it was convenient, Elmo Howell notes that the Choctaws built a platform.

> Their funeral rite was elaborate, the most curious and most distinctive of all their ceremonies. A body was wrapped in "a bear skin or rough kind of covering" and laid upon "a high scaffold erected near the house of the deceased, that it might be protected from the wild beasts of the woods." It remained exposed until it decayed, during which time the relatives would come to the foot of the platform to wail and mourn. In warm weather, the stench was intolerable, and women sometimes fainted while performing their mourning duties. When the body was decomposed, "the *hattak fullih nipi foni* (bone picker), the principal official in their funeral ceremonies," was called in to pick the flesh from the bones with his long nails, which he let grow for this purpose. The decayed flesh was burned or buried and the clean bones placed in a container or stored.[40]

Awesome and painful, this ceremonial return of Sam Fathers's flesh to the earth is for Isaac far more celebratory than Eunice's desperate suicide which he confronts in the commissary ledgers in the very same year, when he is sixteen.

Sam's importance for our understanding of the McCaslin family, how-ever, is not limited to the alternative life—simple, natural, sacramental—which he offers young Isaac. His own genealogy has dark omens for the McCaslin family history as well. Sam's father Ikkemotubbe, cousin of the fat Moketubbe and later called Doom, gave some white powder he had obtained in New Orleans to a small puppy, killing the animal. Then Sam recalls how

> the next day Mokettube's eight-year-old son died suddenly and that after-noon, in the presence of Moketubbe and most of the others (the People, Sam Fathers called them) Doom produced another puppy from the wine-

hamper and put a pinch of the white powder on its tongue and Moketubbe abdicated and Doom became in fact The Man which his French friend already called him. And how on the day after that, during the ceremony of accession, Doom pronounced a marriage between the pregnant quadroon and one of the slave men which he had just inherited (that was how Sam Fathers got his name, which in Chickasaw had been Had-Two-Fathers) and two years later sold the man and woman and the child who was his own son to his white neighbor, Carothers McCaslin. (*Go Down, Moses*, p. 166)[41]

Although in the McCaslin family there is no murder and no use of opium (the notorious substance of choice associated with New Orleans in the nineteenth and twentieth centuries), the association of Doom with the violation of a woman and the arranged marriage looks forward to Carothers's exploitation of Eunice and Tomasina and his arrangements for Thucydus. In another account of his paternity which Sam delivers to the young Quentin Compson in "A Justice," the meaning at first escapes Quentin, although it can hardly escape us—there is no justice when the exploitation and possession of people are at issue—but the older Quentin's realization of this may contribute to his suicide. In *Go Down, Moses*, Ike realizes that the Indian Sam is alienated from all the others on the McCaslin plantation, but is nevertheless obliged to live among the blacks (pp. 169–70), being exploited and subjected himself, even though "he was still the son of that Chickasaw chief and the negroes knew it" (p. 170). His response makes him similar to Lucas Beauchamp; he "bore himself not only toward his cousin McCaslin and Major de Spain but toward all white men, with gravity and dignity and without servility or recourse to that impenetrable wall of ready and easy mirth which negroes sustain between themselves and white men, bearing himself toward his cousin McCaslin not only as one man to another but as an older man to a younger" (p. 170), and in his account even Isaac makes him a black, not an Indian. In such a context, Sam's plea to Major DeSpain—" 'I want to go,' he said, 'Let me go' " (p. 173)—takes on for us a haunting agony. So, in time, does his singular, lonely life and his death which an older Ike might imagine as in some ways mirroring his: "*And he was glad, he told himself. He was old. He had no children, no people, none of his blood anywhere above earth that he would ever meet again. And even if he were to, he could not have touched it, spoken to it, because for seventy years now he had had to be a negro. It was almost over now and he was glad*" (p. 215). In the slow attenuation of Sam's life, then, from its earliest conception in miscegenation and bondage to its final resignation, we see much of the greater McCaslin-Beauchamp-Edmonds history too. For both Sam and Ike—unlike the unnamed mulatto of "Delta Autumn"—the promise of life also results in doom, in despair; and it is an open question whether, in asking to be set free, they do not also give up, let go.

No specific prototypes were used by Faulkner for Sam Fathers; but in developing his portrait of Lucius Quintus Carothers McCaslin, Faulkner probably had in mind Washington Price, whose large plantation twelve miles east of Oxford near Tula (it was the largest in this area) and whose extensive slaveholdings (he is thought to have arrived in Mississippi with 200 slaves) made him legendary then as now. He was born in October 1803 in Wake County, North Carolina, to Thomas and Rebekah Robertson Price, themselves the owners of a large plantation near Raleigh, which he inherited. He first moved to the area of Jackson, Tennessee, where he married Frances Bushrod Harris in 1836; in 1837 the couple moved to Lafayette County and built their home, Oak Grove, in a stand of oak trees high above the Yocona River. It is a unique home (still standing, it has been moved to Denmark and renamed "7Cs") with a two-story portico that seems rather boldly to enlarge a somewhat smaller and lower house with the usual two symmetrical wings off the central hallway. Lucas's description of Carothers's house, completed by Uncle Buck after his marriage and modified by Cass, now inhabited by Roth, fits Oak Grove almost precisely: "two log wings which Carothers McCaslin had built and which had sufficed old Buck and Buddy, connected by the open hallway which, as his pride's monument and epitaph, old Cass Edmonds had enclosed and superposed with a second storey of white clapboards and faced with a portico" (*Go Down, Moses*, pp. 44–45). Price's operation is summarized in the 1850 census returns housed now in the Department of Archives and History at Jackson, Mississippi: at that time he had 5000 acres of land valued at $6,000 and farm implements worth $4,000; his plantation annually produced 4,000 bushels of corn and 115 bales of cotton.[42]

There is also a large number of entries for Washington Price in the county registry of deeds and wills at Oxford. Of these, a vast majority now extant are indentures for land. Thus in February 1845 he loaned John Frasure $400; in November 1846 he gave Jefrey and Leah Humphrey $200; in the fall of 1847 and the winter of 1848 he forwarded to Tobias Farr $145; in October 1848 John G. and Nancy E. Frazier received eight dollars. A similar indenture was signed with Burgap and Molly Bowles on 10 August 1850; others follow through 1854 with some regularity. In addition, Washington Price bought land from John Wheeler, who defaulted, at a public auction held at 10:00 on the morning of 15 July 1850, at the Oxford courthouse. Other documents are transactions involving slaves. In 1837 M. A. McKerrow signed a promissory note with Washington Price for $500 to purchase "two negro Slaves one a negro Boy named Sal aged about fifteen years the other a negro Girl named Alice about Seven years old." In September 1855 Price loaned W. G. Vaughan a promissory note

> for and in consideration of the sum of five dollars, and the further consideration to be herein after mentioned; have this day bargained, and sold unto H. A. Barr the following ascribed property. to wit. one Negro Woman named Leah, about twenty three years old and her child a girl about five years old named Jane. In trust nevertheless for the following purpose that is to say, I have this day executed my note to Washington Price for Five Hundred and fifty Dollars borrowed money and twelve Months after date,

and it is my object and aspire to secure the payment of said note, which is the further consideration above mentioned.

Now if I fail to pay said note at Maturity then it shall be the duty of Said Barr, if on request of Price, to expose said Negroes to public sale at auction at the court-house room in the Town of Oxford in Said County and sell the same to the highest bidder for cash, and convey therin to the purchaser or purchasers by bill of Sale, after having first given thirty days notice of the time and place of sale by advertisements posted up in three public places in said county, and appropriate the proceeds of the sale first to the expenses of sale, secondly to the payment of said note and interest, and thirdly the overplus if any is to be paid to me. It is expressly understood that I am to retain possession of Said Negroes until demanded by Said Barr for sale under this script. Given under my hand and seal this 5th day of September 1855—W. C. Vaughan

The document is probated by John P. Stockard.

Price invested heavily in Oxford. With Major Paul B. Barringer he built the University Hotel on the square at the site of the present city hall; it was burned by Union forces in Augsut 1864. Washington Price died in October 1855; his wife died six months later—and their seven children—six sons named Huldric, Armead, Bem, Relbue, Manfred, and Ethboll, and a daughter Amma—were returned to the Price plantation in North Carolina where they were reared by their uncle Needham Price. At his death, Washington Price owned 132 slaves valued at $84,615, including fourteen slaves valued at $1,460 who were given jointly to Amma, Bem, and Relbue; their average value was $641. A probate court record of a division of his property shows his children received the following apportionment of his estate: Huldric, twenty slaves valued at $16,000; Armead, twenty-one slaves valued at $16,130; Relbue, twenty-one slaves valued at $16,600; Bem, twenty-four valued at $16,750; Amma, twenty-three valued at $16,675. Slaves not accounted for were apparently too old for further service (Hathorn, pp. 89–90). Late in the 1850s, Huldric returned to Oak Grove to manage the plantation once more with overseers. In 1862 he enlisted in the Lamar Rifles to fight for the Confederacy (like Uncle Buddy) but (unlike Uncle Buddy) he was captured in a battle at Petersburg, Virginia, and spent the rest of the war in federal prison at Fort Delaware. Huldric returned to the plantation after the war where he was joined by Bem. After six years, Bem Price, now married to Delle Bowles, moved to Oxford, buying from Charles Roberts a brick mansion on North (now North Lamar) Street and renaming it Ammadelle in honor of his sister and wife. In 1875 Bem Price and Roberts organized the Southern Bank. Two years later, they dissolved the bank and sold their building on the square to the Bank of Oxford (now United Southern Bank); in 1880 Bem Price joined the Bank of Oxford and was serving as its president when he died in 1903 at the age of 53. Throughout these years he continued to farm a thousand acres of the old Price plantation. In these joint ventures he resembles Cass Edmonds who, according to General Compson, keeps

" 'one foot straddled into a farm and the other foot straddled into a bank' " and even invents them both (*Go Down, Moses*, p. 250).

While today, according to Jack Case Wilson, "More than any other house in Lafayette County, the old home of Washington Price retains the appearance and feel of an 1840s Mississippi plantation," [43] the description of life on the McCaslin plantation, especially the latter-day scenes of farming in "The Fire and the Hearth," draw on activities at Greenfield Farm located, like " 'Carothers Edmonds' farm seventeen miles from Jefferson, Mississippi' " (*Go Down, Moses*, p. 370) just north on a gravel road off Highway 30 eighteen miles east of Oxford. Faulkner bought the farm in 1938 with Hollywood earnings and invited his brother John to live there and manage it for him; but almost at once he built himself a separate wooden cabin in which he would retire for reading and writing in privacy. Michael Millgate has said that the "main importance" of Greenfield Farm was that it gave Faulkner "an opportunity to acquire the kind of knowledge about farming—about the crops, the animals, the seasons, the weather, the land, and, not least, the tenants" that he would require in writing *Go Down, Moses*. [44] But by 1939 Michel Mok noted in the *New York Post* that "he bosses his cotton plantation near Oxford, Miss." [45] James Michael Grimwood adds that

> His impersonation of a cotton baron naturally had extensive racial implications, which are graphically displayed in a photograph that Faulkner commissioned in May 1938, two months after building Greenfield. He had invited about a dozen friends to attend, in costume, a "hunt breakfast" at Rowan Oak; and he asked J. R. Cofield, the Oxford photographer, to preserve the occasion on film. In the center of a group portrait that Cofield snapped on the front steps of the renovated mansion, Faulkner placed himself and the lady of the estate on either side of Uncle Ned Barnett, the black major domo whom he had "inherited" from his parents and for whose welfare he had always assumed responsibility. Faulkner dressed the old man in the formal regalia of a butler, with a heavy gold chain looped across his vest. In his hands Ned held a silver tray, from which the man he habitually addressed as "Master" had apparently just received the glass of bourbon he held. Faulkner had turned out in "shining boots and fawn-colored breeches, huntman's cap, ruffled shirt, . . . velvet jacket, and gray gloves." From a thong about his neck hung a "hunting horn," which he had blown to welcome the guests. To his right stood Estelle, a little Negro girl named after the "Mistress," who lived on the estate and played with Faulkner's daughter Jill. The composite resembled an Anglicized parody of seigneurial splendor before Emancipation: such was the image with which Faulkner chose to commemorate his proprietorship of a Mississippi mule farm. First at Rowan Oak and later at Greenfield Farm, he indulged a fantasy of plantation pomp. At Rowan Oak in 1938, he captured that illusion on film; in *Go Down, Moses*, which he began to write less than two years later, he recorded it—much less directly and much more ambiguously—in print. [46]

The Washington Price Plantation House after the grove of oaks was destroyed in 1903.
Photograph copyright © 1984 Jack C. Wilson, *Faulkners, Fortunes and Flames.*

L. C. W. Lamar, putative model for L. C. Q.
McCaslin at thirty-five. Photograph by the
Cofield Studio.

Ned Barnett, a Faulkner family servant and
probable model for Lucas Beauchamp.
Photograph by the Cofield Studio.

An indenture between Washington Price and Burgap and Molly Bowles filed 6 September 1830. Photograph by Arthur F. Kinney.

Wash. Price deed
By W. G. Vaughan
Filed 5th Sept 1855
Recorded Sept. 6th 1855

Know all men by these presents
that I W. G. Vaughan of the County of
La Fayette County and State of Mississippi:
for and in consideration of the sum
of five dollars, and the further consideration to be herein in after mentioned, have this day
bargained, sold sold unto H. A. Barr the following
described property to wit. One Negro Woman named Leah,
about twenty three years old and her child a girl about
five years old named Jane; In trust nevertheless for
the following purpose that is to say, I have this day
executed my note to Washington Price for Five Hundred
and fifty Dollars borrowed money, due twelve months
after date, and it is my object and desire to secure
the payment of said note, which is the further
consideration above mentioned;

Now if I fail to pay said note at maturity
then it shall be the duty of said Barr, upon request
of Price, to expose said Negroes to public sale at
auction at the Court house door in the Town of Oxford

in said County, and sell the same to the highest
bidder for cash, and convey them to the purchaser
or purchasers by bill of sale, after having first given
thirty days notice of the time and place of sale by
advertisements posted up in three public places
in said county, and appropriate the proceeds of the
sale first to the expenses of sale, secondly to the payment
of said note and interest, and thirdly the overplus
if any is to be paid to me. It is expressly understood
that I am to retain possession of said Negroes
until demanded by said Barr for sale under this
inst. Given under my hand and seal this 5th day
of September 1855

W. G. Vaughan. {Seal}

The State of Mississippi
La Fayette County   Personally appeared before me
John P. Stockard. Judge of the Probate Court of said
County, the within named W. G. Vaughan who

An indenture between Washington Price and W. G. Vaughan concerning the ownership of slaves filed 5 September 1855. Photograph by Arthur F. Kinney.

Callie Barr, Faulkner family servant and probable model for Molly Beauchamp, with Jill Faulkner. Photograph supplied by Eva Miller.

Faulkner's Greenfield Farm, exactly matching the description of Lucas Beauchamp's farm and house. Photograph by Eva Miller.

Callie Barr's grave, noting "Her white children bless her." Photograph by Arthur F. Kinney.

A house similar to that owned by Rider and Mannie. Photograph by Eva Miller.

The commissary at Greenfield Farm, probable setting for part 4 of "The Bear." Photograph by Arthur F. Kinney.

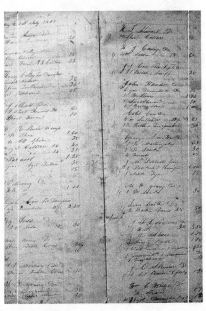

Nineteenth-century plantation ledgers. Photograph by Eva Miller.

The first power-driven sawmill in the area, at Enterprise, Mississippi, and the probable model for "Pantaloon in Black." Photograph by Arthur F. Kinney.

General Stone's hunting lodge and the model for the hunting lodge in "The Bear." The tree may have suggested the burial place of Sam Fathers. Photograph by Arthur F. Kinney.

Winter hunting in the Delta. Photograph by Arthur F. Kinney.

Woman farming, similar to Miss Worsham in "Go Down, Moses." Photograph by Eva Miller.

A country store similar to the one where Lucas is accused of shooting Vincent Gowrie. Photograph by Arthur F. Kinney.

Puss Kuss Creek, near Greenfield Farm, the model for the opening scene of *Intruder in the Dust*. Photograph by Arthur F. Kinney.

The county jail used as a setting in *Intruder in the Dust*. Photograph supplied by Eva Miller.

Woman boiling laundry, as in
Intruder in the Dust.
Photograph by Eva Miller.

30

A country house similar to that
occupied by the Gowrie families.
Photograph by Arthur F. Kinney.

A country graveyard similar to the
one in which Vinson Gowrie
is said to be buried.
Photograph by Arthur F. Kinney.

Putatively the first car in Oxford,
Mississippi, and a probable model
for Boss Priest's Winton Flyer.
Photograph supplied by Eva
Miller.

Faulkner family photograph of Col. Falkner (in white) in mudhole on the road to Memphis. Faulkner had this event in mind for the scene of Hell Creek Bottom in *The Reivers.* Photograph supplied by Eva Miller.

The old lobby of the Gayoso Hotel "to which all of us McCaslins-Edmondses-Priests devoted our allegiance as to a family shrine." Photograph supplied by Eva Miller.

If the pomp and circumstance we associate with Lucas Beauchamp and the sense of dominance which others associate with Carothers McCaslin is present with Faulkner here, there is also, in the presence of his friends, a good degree of self-parody.

While Faulkner did not do much manual labor at Greenfield, he did keep the commissary books for two years, and this exercise may have demonstrated to him just how such ledgers can be crucial documents of plantation life, as they become Ike's chief resource for understanding the McCaslin family line in *Go Down, Moses*. We know that Faulkner borrowed a copy of John Spencer Bassett's *The Southern Plantation Overseer* from W. C. Bryant and took from the overseers' letters to the absentee landlords, the Polks, a style for the McCaslin ledgers; he also had seen, in the general store at Taylor, a ledger with an entry for "Carothers Edmonds."[47] In addition, Joseph Brogunier, following the lead of David H. Stewart, has written that the diary of Dr. Martin W. Philips, a planter from Columbia, South Carolina, who was born in 1806 and who later founded Log Hall plantation twenty miles from Vicksburg, Mississippi, left a diary of events from 1 January 1840 to April 1863 which was later edited by Franklin L. Riley for the *Publications of the Mississippi Historical Society* and which comes even closer to being a probable model for the McCaslin ledgers. What come closest are entries on the personal lives of slaves; perhaps because they represent property, births are recorded, if laconically. But they are indiscriminate with entries on animals. "July 25, 1843—'Amy delivered of a girl this afternoon'; August 4, 1843—'Emily had a calf this morning'; December 11, 1841—'Eliza gave birth to a girl child on the morning of the 11th of December. The smallest Devon cow calved a heifer calf, all red.' "[48] The same inclusiveness is true when he records his wife's inheritance: "Inheritance of Mary Philips from the estate of William Montgomery (Lot No. 4, January 5, 1860); Philip, $1,300; Rosetta, $900; Scott, $650; Spencer, $500; Philip Jr., $300 (all given to Mary Kells); Wyatt, $700; Jerry, $800; 'Fits' Hardy, $25; Montgomery, $1 (gone off and stayed, too); Mule, Topsy, $150; Mule, Mike, $140; carriage horse, $125; Dolly (in 1830), $800; 200 acres (in 1845), $800; Jacob (in 1856), about $750; 2 mules, 1 horse, 2 cows, $320; cash, $500; cash, $500" (p. 549). As with Eunice in the McCaslin accounts, deaths are given slightly more attention. " 'Maria died the morning of the 8th September [1848]. Amy's child, 2 years old.' . . . 'Jane died today, Sunday, half-past 3 P.M.—disease, pneumonia. Since I have been in Mississippi 5 grown negroes and no telling the number of younger ones—well, it is for man to submit.' . . . 'Hannah lost her young one last night. Mule also died last night—never saw a worse case of distemper' (April 18, 1859). . . . 'I had the misfortune to lose Easter's boy on the night of the 21st' (September 21, 1846)" (p. 550). Longer eulogies are supplied for Peyton, a slave who missed fewer than fifteen working days in twenty-one years (p. 550) and a pet dog and cow (p. 551). But Dr. Philips was happy to be rid of one Samuel as Buck and Buddy are to be rid of Percival Brownlee (p. 552). There are also runaway slaves; one is caught with dogs, and another, when caught for a second time, attempts to kill himself with a razor, cutting his throat for some two inches (p. 552). Finally, Brogunier finds covert references to miscegenation in especially oblique references:

> Several entries in the "Diary," often cryptic like those in the [McCaslin] ledgers, suggest similar events. Miscegenation is revealed in the death entry, "Eliza's mulatto child by Elisha Nail died on 27th July [1847]." (Elisha Nail was Dr. Philips' overseer between Januaury 13, 1845, and a date not later than March 14, 1847, when another overseer was employed.) In addition it seems that this same Eliza had attracted the notice of another besides Elisha Nail, for on February 9, 1840, in an entry which suggests miscegenation again, Dr. Philips wrote, "Henry, son of —— (so she says) and Eliza, born A.M. 9th." Like [the McCaslins'] Eunice, Eliza was apparently a house servant, for she is not listed in the year-end ratings of hands. With the other slaves she was given blankets in the fall, but whereas they got a blanket each and sometimes had to share one, two blankets were given to "Eliza and family" (October 26, 1842) and two to "Eliza" (December 22, 1844). Moreover, on February 12, 1841, Dr. Philips wrote, "Eliza sick two days; more lazy and mad than sick," and on July 31, "Eliza sick all week, as I was away." And finally, there is Dr. Philips' April 23, 1846 birth entry for Eliza's child by Elisha Nail: "Eliza delivered of a boy this forenoon, Thursday. *We name him Nail*" (the emphasis is Dr. Philips,' who otherwise used it sparingly). Dr. Philips was thus unusually attentive to and interested in Eliza; and since he was at about this time unhappy in his marriage, one may wonder if Nail was the child, not of Elisha Nail, but instead of Dr. Philips, passed off by him on his employee in an act of repudiation and concealment. (pp. 552–53)

Eunice, in a similar manner, is passed on to Thucydus and, before that, Doom passes Sam's mother on to an unnamed slave.[49]

One final comparative statement—in this instance Faulkner's own—which has its parallel in the McCaslin family history is a clause Faulkner added to his 1940 will. In *Intruder in the Dust*, Zack Edmonds grants land to Lucas Beauchamp. Chick Mallison recalls how Cass Edmonds's father "had deeded to his Negro first cousin and his heirs in perpetuity the house and the ten acres of land it sat on—an oblong of earth set forever in the middle of the two-thousand-acre plantation like a postage stamp in the center of an envelope—the paintless wooden house, the paintless picket fence whose paintless latchless gate the man kneed open still without stopping."[50] In 1940, Faulkner changed his will to incorporate Greenfield Farm, giving his brother John the first option to purchase. Then he attached the condition that until his death Ned Barnett was to be given title to his house and grounds, five acres of rent-free land to cultivate, and the use of such tools and livestock as necessary.[51] Uncle Ned died in 1947 and Faulkner removed this section when he revised his will again on 1 February 1951. But his desire (or need) to play the role of the indulgent plantation owner like Cass or, for example, when he modeled himself on Carothers McCaslin (or his kind) in the 1938 photograph, demonstrates how keenly Faulkner was affected by the issues of plantation and of race that the McCaslin family story addresses and how close he may have felt to the McCaslin family line even as he was creating it.

"*Go Down, Moses* has a great deal more over-all unity than a superficial glance might suggest," Cleanth Brooks writes; "A more useful, though more prosaic title would be *The McCaslins*, for the book has to do with the varying fortunes of that family."[52] The clan's progenitor, Lucius Quintus Carothers McCaslin, evidently of a Scots origin now lost, migrates from Carolina to Mississippi at about the same time that Thomas Sutpen, raised in the Piedmont and Tidewater parts of Virginia, arrives by way of Haiti. But unlike Sutpen, who is also at the center of his family saga and whose influence also stretches well beyond him, we never see or hear Carothers: all we have are memories, reports, and reconstructions of him by his descendants. Yet, his descendants seem to be everywhere; once Dan Brennan reported that in the first draft of "Go Down, Moses" Samuel Worsham Beauchamp was named Carothers Edmonds Beauchamp, joining all the family lines together that had grown apart over the generations,[53] we find that all of them, save for Zack and Isaac, bear Lucius's name. This somehow reincarnates his sense of domination and possessiveness and Carothers's concern with race that characterizes the family line.

The episodes of *Go Down, Moses* are so structured that we are never permitted to forget the entanglement of the various blood lines. "Was" presents all of them at once: Cass Edmonds tells Ike McCaslin about his forebears and their provision for the marriage of Tomey's Terrel and Tennie that will first take the *Beauchamp* name from Sophonsiba and propagate that line. The white Beauchamps, the McCaslin twins, and the two young blacks all understand the racial implications to some degree, but Cass is only dimly aware of them and Ike, upon first hearing the story, is blissfully ignorant. In time no one remains ignorant; the story of the McCaslins is the story of how they come to learn and deal with their blood heritage. Their "family's chronicle" (p. 110) is, as Roth puts it, "the old curse of his fathers, the old haughty ancestral pride based not on any value but on an accident of geography, stemmed not from courage and honor but from wrong and shame, descended to him" (p. 111). Indeed, race becomes so powerful and so self-conscious that the three main branches of the family must in time be treated separately— Ike McCaslin in "The Bear," Roth Edmonds in "Delta Autumn," and Mollie and Samuel Beauchamp in "Go Down, Moses."

The curse of fallen nature that first divides them—when Carothers damns himself and Eunice both—is repeated in the sense of divided races through each succeeding generation with variations on the themes of domination, possession, and violation, as when Roth refuses to sleep with Henry in "The Fire and the Hearth" (pp. 111–12). In time the curse comes to threaten even the " 'communal *anonymity* of brotherhood' " which alone, says Ike, will " 'hold the earth mutual and intact' " (p. 257). Instead, after Carothers's death, Uncle Buck and Uncle Buddy in trying to make repairs only give over the plantation house to "skulking McCaslin slaves" who, "dodging the moon-lit roads and the Patrol-riders to visit other plantations," continue to extend and entangle the McCaslin family (p. 262). Ike's answer is the reverse—to contain the family by paying off their final legacy and remaining childless himself—but in taking cash to Fonsiba, in paying Lucas, and in searching for James, he continues Ikkemotubbe's curse of selling land, Carothers's of buying slaves, and presages Roth's giving an envelope of money to his mistress. Ike's trip to Midnight, Arkansas, to visit Fonsiba especially—what Albert J. Guerard has called "the night journey into the self"[54]—is a foolish hope, a kind of fond dream following his own fantasy of Carothers and Eunice (a kind of replicated incest). Ike comes to realize the attraction and passion of their sin, even for him, when he allows himself in fascination and horror to piece together the meager ledger entries into a full-blown account of the McCaslin past, and the McCaslin primal scene.

> The old frail pages seemed to turn of their own accord even while he thought *His own daughter His own daughter. No No Not even him* back to that one where the white man (not even a widower then) who never went anywhere any more than his sons in their time ever did and who did not need another slave, had gone all the way to New Orleans and bought one. And Tomey's Terrel was still alive when the boy was ten years old and he knew from his own observation and memory that there had already been some white in Tomey's Terrel's blood before his father gave him the rest of it; and looking down at the yellowed page spread beneath the yellow glow of the lantern smoking and stinking in that rank chill midnight room fifty years later, he seemed to see her actually walking into the icy creek on that Christmas day six months before her daughter's and her lover's (*Her first lover's* he thought. *Her first*) child was born, solitary, inflexible, griefless, ceremonial, in formal and succinct repudiation of grief and despair who had already had to repudiate belief and hope. (pp. 271–72)

And then "that was all. He would never need look at the ledgers again nor did he" (p. 271). The resolution which subsequent McCaslin generations attempt—Buck and Buddy through action, Ike through narrative under-standing—is denied not only by the forces unleashed by violation, racism, and incest, but by the very chronology of events as they unfold. Just as Ike needs to unscramble the cryptic entries in the family ledgers, so we have to unscramble the chronology of events which diverge from the order of their presentation. When we do so, we find that Ike's repudiation of his heritage in 1888 is relatively contemporaneous with Lucas's attempt to repudiate his in his attack on Zack (1898). Butch Beauchamp's execution in Chicago the very year that Ike sends James Beauchamp's granddaughter and great-grandchild back to that same city to await racial assimilation (1940) and Lucas's loss of sanity over his feverish search for gold, which nearly de-stroys his marriage, are events that coincide with Rider's madness since he has actually (but inexplicably) lost his wife (1941). These ironic analogies demonstrate that blood will beget blood; they draw an infinite conceptual line that, at the end of the novel, becomes its own circle, its own encircling doom. At the close of "Delta Autumn," Roth (through Ike) offers new cash payment to a new generation of mulattoes—and in doing so both Ike and Roth become Carothers all over again. At the close of "Go Down, Moses," a dead Beauchamp is brought back for burial on the McCaslin plantation now managed by an Edmonds—but there is no communication among the three lines. In the last words of "Go Down, Moses," in fact, Gavin Stevens can only echo the final words (by Cass) of "Was." Despite the cost of understanding and the price of grief, nothing has essentially changed.

Faulkner's own grief can also be measured with some accuracy when we recognize what dimensions of local history most disturbed or attracted him as he wrote the story of the McCaslin family both at Greenfield Farm and in his Oxford antebellum home of Rowan Oak. There was the Price family, for one thing. According to local legend, each generation of the Washington Price family made cash gifts not recorded in their wills submitted to probate to a black family thought possibly to be related to them. One of the existing descendants recalls that either Washington or Bem Price had a girl named Margaret by one of the slaves on the old Price plantation. Taking the name of Boles from a white family that farmed part of the Price land, Margaret went to work at a rooming house in Holly Springs where, at the age of 15, she met and fell in love with a white bachelor merchant from Oxford. The two were privately married in due course and raised a number of children. One of their sons, Robert Boles, Sr., founded a shoe repair shop on the Oxford square in 1893; in the 1940s he was succeeded in the business by a brother, Clifton, and later it was taken over by Robert Boles, Jr., who sold it to one of his fellow workers in 1969. From early on, this Boles family was industrious, enterprising, and highly successful; Robert Boles, Sr., through shrewd investment in stocks, built a small fortune which he shared with the family. The Boles family was extremely light colored—Robert Boles, Jr., had red hair and blue eyes as well—but they chose nevertheless to become leaders of the black community in and around Oxford, even dealing in real estate for blacks. Robert Boles, Jr., was one of Faulkner's good friends; Faulkner had his shoes repaired at the shop (as nearly everyone else in town did), hunted with Rob, and often dropped by the store for a chat. Rob's wife Julia, a talented seamstress, would mend Faulkner's clothes and patch the elbows of his tweed jackets. It is clear that the Boles family was, like Callie Barr and Ned Barnett, important to Faulkner.

These people provided Faulkner with an abiding respect and admiration for blacks, but there was also the matter of lynching. The fundamental forces that initially caused lynching in the South are uncertain: the strongest tradition holds that they were an extension of the old master-slave psychology which continued after emancipation; John Hope Franklin, in *The Militant*

South, 1800–1860 (1956), argues it stemmed from a tradition of active militancy peculiar to the American South; Gunnar Myrdal, in *An American Dilemma* (1944), proposes that whites lynched blacks for fear of losing the status of racial supremacy. According to statistics compiled at Tuskegee University, Mississippi led the nation in recorded lynchings between 1882 and 1968 with the deaths of 539 blacks and 42 whites; but researchers warn that such numbers do not include unidentified bodies that may have been lynched, those who disappeared, and those who fled in fear, nor does it take into account the near-victims of threats, terror, and sadism.[55] Two lynchings in Lafayette County in particular profoundly influenced Faulkner.

The first was that of Nelse Patton, a trusty who was thought drunk when he made advances on the white Mrs. Mattie McMillan around ten o'clock on the morning of 8 September 1908, while delivering to her a message from her husband, then in the Oxford jail. She ordered him to leave and went for a pistol; Patton sprang forward, slashed her throat with a razor and nearly decapitated her, and then fled. He ran across the railroad at Saddler's Crossing and jumped into the vine-choked ditch that ran through town to Toby Tubby Bottom to avoid his pursuers. When he was finally captured, the larger portion of the bloodied razor blade was still in his pocket. According to John B. Cullen, Faulkner's schoolmate, who was 15 at the time,

> The news spread over the county like wildfire, and that night at least two thousand people gathered around the jail. Judge Roan came out on the porch and made a plea to the crowd that they let the law take its course. Then Senator W. V. Sullivan made a fiery speech, telling the mob that they would be weaklings and cowards to let such a vicious beast live until morning. Mr. Hartsfield, the sheriff, had left town with the keys to the jail, because he knew people would take them from him. My father was deputized to guard the jail. Had he had the slightest doubt of Nelse's guilt, he would have talked to the mob. If this had not proved successful, they would have entered the jail over his dead body. After Senator Sullivan's speech, the mob began pitching us boys through the jail windows, and no guard in that jail would have dared shoot one of us. Soon a mob was inside. My brother and I held my father, and the sons of the other guards held theirs. They weren't hard to hold anyway. In this way we took over the lower floor of the jail.
>
> From eight o'clock that night until two in the morning the mob worked to cut through the jail walls into the cells with sledge hammers and crowbars [taken from nearby hardware and blacksmith shops]. In the walls were one-by-eight boards placed on top of one another and bolted together. The walls were brick on the outside and steel-lined on the inside. When the mob finally got through and broke the lock off the murderer's cell, Nelse had armed himself with a heavy iron coal-shovel handle. From a corner near the door, he fought like a tiger, seriously wounding three men. He was then shot to death and thrown out of the jail. Someone (I don't know who) cut his ears off, scalped him, cut his testicles out, tied a rope around his neck, tied him to a car, and dragged his body around the

streets. Then they hanged him to a walnut-tree limb just outside the south entrance to the courthouse. They had torn [all] his clothes off dragging him around, and my father [the next morning] bought a new pair of overalls and put them on him.[56]

Most subsequent accounts note that Patton ripped an iron post off the bed in his cell and swung it at his assailants before crouching in a dark corner where he was shot to death. While the coroner's jury reported simply that "the said Nelse Patton came to his death from gunshot or pistol wounds inflicted by parties to us unknown,"[57] the Patton case has remained the county's most notorious crime. In 1987 Marvel Ramey Sisk, aged 89, told the Oxford *Eagle*, " 'I also remember when they hung some black man in the Courthouse Square for rape and murder. They left him there quite a long time. I was a little girl and I saw that.' "[58] Faulkner first used this event as a basis for *Light in August* (1932), but this did not exorcise the memory of it; the chase, the prisoner's self-defense with an iron railing, and the mob's attitude all resurge centrally and powerfully as part of Rider's story too in *Go Down, Moses*.

Before either novel was written, however, the story of Nelse Patton was reinforced for Faulkner, according to Donald P. Duclos in an unpublished essay, by the effect on him of Eugene O'Neill's *The Emperor Jones* and by a story in the *Clarion-Eagle* that suggested one of Faulkner's most powerful newspaper stories, "Sunset," published in the New Orleans *Times-Picayune* on 24 May 1925. That the treatment of blacks continued to disturb him is clear in a story a few years later, "Dry September," published in *Scribner's* in January 1931. Then, in 1935, Lafayette County witnessed a second lynching, that of Elwood Higginbotham, recorded as the last ritual lynching in the state and closely resembling, in conception and force, the situation of Lucas Beauchamp in *Intruder in the Dust* (1948). The first announcement of the death of Higginbotham, twenty-eight, came for Faulkner in the weekly issue of the *Oxford Eagle* for 23 May 1935, when it was reported that men were "closing in" on him in connection with the death of Glenn Roberts on 21 May. Roberts was a 54-year-old farmer, fox hunter, and fiddler with the Roberts Brothers Fiddlers; Higginbotham was a tenant on his farm ten miles northeast of Oxford in Lafayette County. The two men had some difficulty between them, the story says, although the nature of their argument was not known. Roberts accosted Higginbotham and he responded by shooting Roberts in the face with a shotgun at close range, killing him almost instantly; he then fled. There is no further word until 29 August, when the *Eagle* reported that Higginbotham had been captured in Pontotoc County three months previously and safely held some distance away in the Hinds County jail in Jackson. He was brought to Oxford during the week of 9 September for one day (presumably for arraignment) and then returned to Oxford on Tuesday, 17 September, for trial. The jury retired later that day but, although locally Higginbotham's guilt seems not to have been doubted, jury members were unable to reach a decision, voting 10–2 for conviction. It is not clear how this vote became public—perhaps ít was only known that the jury could not reach agreement—but a crowd began gathering at all four corners of the Oxford square at dusk to carry out its own judgment. There was electricity in the air, one observer remembers, who with a schoolmate was playing on the nearby schoolhouse lawn; another eyewitness recalls that the local police had all been assigned to a portable skating rink that had been set up that day and was also drawing crowds. The action of the gathering mob seems to have been based on foreknowledge and was apparently premeditated, however; telephone wires were cut, the men's faces were partially hidden with dirt, and they moved on the jail as one at precisely 8:30 P.M. Forcing their way past the jailer and three deputies, the group of seventy-five men located the keys, unlocked Higginbotham's cell, and took him by truck to "the three corners," the intersection of Route 30 and Camp Ground Road about five or six miles east of Oxford, then in the heart of a hilly black residential district. There they hanged him from a tree; two white boys who followed them were sworn to secrecy and hastened back to their homes in Oxford.

There are few local records of the Higginbotham trial and lynching extant and locally many details may still be unknown or untested. But the Communist-oriented *Daily Worker* in New York, claiming to have the unimpeachable testimony of a white reporter, wrote a fuller and more inflammatory account entitled "Elwood Higgenbotham—Hero of Sharecroppers—Victim of Lynch Mob" published on 24 September that emphasizes stereotypes pursued by that newspaper.

> On Wednesday, Sept. 18, Elwood Higgenbotham, a 28-year-old Negro sharecropper, was lynched by a mob at Oxford, Mississippi, while a Circuit Court all-white jury was "deliberating" at his trial for the "murder" of Glen Roberts, a white landlord.
>
> The local press reported that "a restless crowd, estimated to number 100 to 150 men, stormed the jail, dragged the prisoner out of his cell and whisked him out to the country where his screaming pleas for mercy were refused and he was hanged to a tree beside a lonely, wooded road."
>
> Official whitewash of the lynchers followed promptly. Circuit Court Judge McElroy, in whose court the "trial" took place, stated that Sheriff S. T. Lyles had told him that none of the mob was recognized either by the sheriff, his deputies or the jailer from whom they had obtained the keys to the prison "by force."
>
> ### Was Leader of Union
>
> "Sheriff Lyles told me the men were masked and could not be identified, so I don't suppose there is anything that can be done right now," Judge McElroy said. He "indicated" that the matter "might be referred" to the County Grand Jury "when it meets several months hence."
>
> Higgenbotham was one of the leaders of the Share Croppers Union in Oxford and had long been singled out by the landlords. The "excuse" for the mob assault and lynching of this heroic worker goes back to another unsuccessful effort to murder him some months ago.

Higgenbotham had a field cultivated through which landlords tried to cut a short road. Higgenbotham fenced off the field to save it from destruction. This move immediately put him into the class of "uppity niggers" in the langauge of the arrogant landlord class.

Soon after this short cut was blocked off, Roberts, a white landlord, organized a lynch mob against Higgenbotham. A native white worker, and Communist Party leader in Oxford, wrote at that time of the events of the succeeding two murderous days and nights, and of the final capture and jailing of Higgenbotham.

Tells of Lynch Attempt

The letter states: "Tuesday night a mob of at least 25 white farmers armed with pistols went to Higgenbotham's house. Higgenbotham, his wife and three children had gone to bed and were awakened by Tom Likkings demanding of him that he open the door and come out. Now, Glen Roberts with pistol in hand forced his way into the house. Higgenbotham who didn't have time to dress ran and when Roberts started after him Higgenbotham shot him down with a Winchester.

"When the mob of white lynchers on the outside heard the shot, they became so frightened that they left the lynch leader to his own fate and sent to town to get the law to come. Now started one of the typical manhunts with bloodhounds and the mob, armed to the teeth rushing through the woods, hills and swamps. Infuriated over the failure to capture Higgenbotham, Oxford's "finest" with the officers of the law leading them on, started to hunt up his family.

Sister Is Beaten

"A brother-in-law was dragged out of bed and lodged in jail without any charges against him, and released only a week after on bond and told to get out of town at once. Higgenbotham's sister was beaten so mercilessly by a mob while officers looked on until her clothes in tatters was mangled in with her flesh and blood [sic]. The mob also hunted his brothers with the intention of burning them in the father's front yard should they fail to find and lynch Higgenbotham. Wherever kinfolk of Higgenbotham's could be found the armed mob fell over them like maddened hyenas, bent on murder.

"The boys in the C.C.C. camps nearby were recruited for the murderous manhunt.

Hunted in Swamp

"The second day after spending most of the day in the swamp in water, sometimes to his very neck, tired and hungry, not having a bite to eat and no clothes, having had to jump out of bed and run for his life, wounded and torn by briars, Higgenbotham was found by officers in an adjoining county unable to get out of the water. The fact that he was caught in another county is the only explanation for Higgenbotham being here yet. He was rushed to Jackson, Miss., for safekeeping. . . ."

This wanton murder of an innocent Negro sharecropper has aroused a tremendous anger among many Southern workers. At the same time the heroic struggle that Higgenbotham put up to save his life stands as another milestone in the blood-covered road to final emancipation.

The Mississippi white worker concludes his letter with the deep pledge of intensified working class loyalty, and of Higgenbotham he writes:

"There runs through this horrible two day man-hunt a thread of glorious and heroic self-defense of one single Negro with no clothes on and nothing to eat for two days and nights defending himself with a rifle against a maddened horde, running into the hundreds of the most lawless characters, armed with the finest high powered rifles to be had. The Negro workers of the South have reason to look with confidence to the coming struggle for power, while the white landlords have just as much reason to think about the same struggle with fear and despair. And we white workers should feel proud of our Negro brothers."

Other reports on file are considerably more reserved. In "Lynched During Trial," the Charlotte, North Carolina, *Observer* reported on 22 September that

AFTER HIS TRIAL in court on a murder charge had gone to the jury and while the jury still was deliberating, Ellwood Higginbotham, negro, was lynched late Tuesday night by a mob estimated by officers at 150 to 200 men, which stormed the jail at Oxford, Miss.

The negro was charged with having slain Glen Roberts, a white planter, in "cold blood," last May.

The mob broke down the jail doors and seized the negro, took him to a lonely side road a few miles from town and almost within sight of the State university, and hanged him.

When Judge Taylor McElroy was officially informed of the lynching, he called the jury into court and dismissed it.

Earlier, on 19 September, the Spartanburg, South Carolina, *Herald* published a story called "Another Lynching."

Mississippi records another lynching. This time it followed the disagreement of a jury and the defendant was taken from jail and hanged after the jury was dismissed by the presiding judge.

The state of Mississippi will come in for justifiable criticism for not making an effort to protect this prisoner. No matter how heinous the crime of which he was charged may have been the defendant was in the hands of the authorities and it seems they made no effort to protect him.

The case is more to be criticized because the negro defendant had been tried by a jury of white men and in the face of infuriated public opinion. Failure to reach a verdict under such circumstances would indicate that there was no excuse for a body of 150 men to raid the jail, and execute the man whom a jury refused to convict. Incidents like this are the cause of agitation for a federal anti-lynching law.

The story did not continue in the Oxford paper, however, nor was there any forthcoming editorial comment. But the fears of Lucas, Gavin, and Miss Habersham in *Intruder in the Dust* have authentic roots; and from the Higginbotham affair Faulkner may also have taken the portrait of a black man whose ways of independence and forthrightness appeared arrogant and "uppity" to his neighboring whites. The diverse and antagonistic sentiments at Higginbotham's house the night it was raided as well as the tension on the square the night of his trial contribute immeasurably to the electricity of Faulkner's own novel, as well as to his grievous understanding of the consequences of a society of whites and blacks sometimes living uneasily with one another.

Because of this, the blacks receive special emphasis in the story of the McCaslin family, although (especially in *Intruder in the Dust*) such a focus can introduce a nervous and awkward obscurity into Faulkner's prose. There is, for instance, an attempt at a graphic description of a race—tense, terrified, and subdued when Lucas is imprisoned. As Gavin and Chick speed through a countryside of black tenant farmers in Yoknapatawpha, Chick sees "the fields geometric with furrows where corn had been planted . . . vacant of any movement and any life." His acculturated perspective further sees "the paintless Negro cabins where on Monday morning in the dust of the grassless treeless yards halfnaked children should have been crawling and scrabbling after broken cultivator wheels and wornout automobile tires and empty snuff-bottles and tin cans and in the back yards smoke-blackened iron pots should have been bubbling over wood fires beside the sagging fences of vegetable patches and chickenruns which by nightfall would be gaudy with drying overalls and aprons and towels and unionsuits" (*Intruder in the Dust* pp. 146–47). Then he observes, perhaps romantically, perhaps sentimentally, one lone black man at the plow, "the face black and gleamed with sweat and passionate with effort, tense concentrated and composed" (p. 148). The description is controlled by a sense of divided races. Earlier his uncle Gavin had been unaware but not surprised, in *Go Down, Moses*, to learn that Hamp Worsham and Mollie Beauchamp were related (p. 371); there is less premium placed on black genealogy by whites. Thus Faulkner persistently is at pains to show what was for him the awful rift and he signals its consequences: Uncle Ash, forced to sleep on the floor at the hunting camp where brotherhood is said to flourish (*Go Down, Moses*, p. 206), or Fonsiba crouching when her own cousin comes to visit her (pp. 277–78), for Yoknapatawpha is part of a larger world where race becomes an abstract slogan for private profiteering by "politicians earning votes and the medicine-shows of pulpiteers earning Chatauqua fees" (p. 284). This is the context in which an older Cass can tell Ike that the man-hunt for Tomey's Terrel is, simply, "the best race he had ever seen" (p. 8) and then add, even more innocently, that Tomey's Turl "had been running off from Uncle Buck for so long that he had even got used to running away like a white man would do it" (p. 9). And this is the context in which the wager for winning (or unloading) Sophonsiba is likened to " 'this nigger business' " (p. 24), or, even among the hunters, Walter Ewell can make a racist slur about Tennie's Jim's superstitiousness (p. 215). Such incidents are metonymic for a more permanent anguish, as Ike begins to learn in the commissary, for there is no way in which one race can free itself from the presence and the burden of the other—" 'No, not now nor ever, we from them nor they from us' " (p. 299)—just as, more comically and so more pathetically, even more sardonically, Uncle Hubert, freed at last from Sophonsiba, cannot free himself from black cooks and mistresses (pp. 302–3). When Faulkner returns to such issues in *Intruder in the Dust*, it has become clear that past rituals that have tried to accommodate matters of race (as when Aleck Sander eats separately from whites or waits for a command before acting or making suggestions) will not do when they are challenged (as when Lucas wears Carothers's gold toothpick or, worse, will not give testimony to a lawyer who is not willing to believe him). Lucas senses, knows, Gavin's intolerant and intolerable attitude which the lawyer later shares with his nephew:

> And as for Lucas Beauchamp, Sambo, he's a homogeneous man too, except that part of him which is trying to escape not even the best of the white race but into the second best—the cheap shoddy dishonest music, the cheap flash baseless overvalued money, the glittering edifice of publicity foundationed on nothing like a cardboard house over an abyss and all the noisy muddle of political activity which used to be our minor national industry and is now our national amateur pastime—all the spurious uproar produced by men deliberately fostering and then getting rich on our national passion for the mediocre. . . . (p. 155)

This attitude is based on examples that have no basis at all in Lucas Beauchamp. Gavin's striking and ignorant irrelevancies here render suspect his final counsel to Chick—" 'Some things you must always be unable to bear. Some things you must never stop refusing to bear. Injustice and outrage and dishonor and shame. No matter how young you are or how old you have got. Not for kudos and not for cash: your picture in the paper nor money in the bank either. Just refuse to bear them' " (p. 206)—as well as, in the last book of the McCaslin trilogy, *The Reivers*, this irresolution passes for an elder's wisdom when Boss Priest tells young Lucius simply to " 'Live with it' " (p. 302).

For the whole point of Carothers's legacy to his black offspring, of Ike's anguish and of Lucas's sullen and overt resistance is, of course, that they cannot just live with it. For these reasons, Lucas succeeds Ike as the central member of the McCaslin family line even though his name remains Beauchamp (and because of that). We first learn in *Go Down, Moses* that Lucas is

> the oldest living person on the Edmonds plantation, the oldest McCaslin descendant even though in the world's eye he descended not from McCaslins but from McCaslin slaves, almost as old as old Isaac McCaslin

who lived in town, supported by what Roth Edmonds chose to give him, who would own the land and all on it if his just rights were only known, if people just knew how old Cass Edmonds, this one's grandfather, had beat him out of his patrimony; almost as old as old Isaac, almost, as old Isaac was, coeval with old Buck and Buddy McCaslin who had been alive when their father, Carothers McCaslin, got the land from the Indians back in the old time when men black and white were men. (pp. 36–37)

Lucas's pride in his heritage causes him—so we are told, or so Ike imagines—to keep and change the badge of his lineage, his very name: "not *Lucius Quintus @c @c @c,* but *Lucas Quintus,* not refusing to be called Lucius, because he simply eliminated that word from the name; not denying, declining the name itself, because he used three quarters of it; but simply taking the name and changing, altering it, making it no longer the white man's but his own, by himself composed, himself selfprogenitive and nominate, by himself ancestored, as, for all the old ledgers recorded to the contrary, old Carothers himself was" (p. 281). Providing and accepting his own name, Lucas can carry old Carothers's gold toothpick and, on Saturdays, wear old Carothers's gun for, as Donald M. Kartiganer has noted, while Ike seeks vainly for values all about him, Lucas needs only the context of his own McCaslin ancestry.[59] Yet such autocracy, while it may be understandable, can also be troublesome or even dangerous. It allows Lucas to be bold, but also to be ruthless and reckless when he invades Zack's bedroom to duel for an honor he can no longer ever guarantee.

> You knowed I wasn't afraid, because you knowed I was a McCaslin too and a man-made one. And you never thought that, because I am a McCaslin too, I wouldn't. You never even thought that, because I am a nigger too, I wouldn't dare. No. You thought that because I am a nigger I wouldn't even mind. I never figured on the razor neither. But I gave you your chance. Maybe I didn't know what I might have done when you walked in my door, but I knowed what I wanted to do, what I believed I was going to do, what Carothers McCaslin would have wanted me to do. But you didn't come. You never even gave me the chance to do what old Carothers would have told me to do. You tried to beat me. And you wont never, not even when I am hanging dead from the limb this time tomorrow with the coal oil still burning, you wont never. (p. 53)

His need for self-assertion and self-identification in order to gain any respect, any self-esteem, leads inextricably to pride, arrogance, and a certain coldness (even toward Molly in his later years) that sets him decisively apart from Tomey's Turl (and his love for Tennie) or even George Wilkins (and his love for Lucas's daughter Nat): an inwardness of concern that bars him from grieving, with Molly and Miss Worsham and Hamp, for Samuel Worsham Beauchamp, the last of his own line.

Yet despite nearly superhuman efforts, Lucas cannot escape being black. When we meet him next, in *Intruder in the Dust,* that is his badge.

When Chick is forced by his near drowning to take refuge in Lucas's home, he approaches a paintless wooden house with a bare front yard defaced in time (or so Chick thinks) with chicken droppings; once inside, Chick "could smell that smell which he had accepted without question all his life as being the smell always of the places where people with any trace of Negro blood live" (p. 9). Here he is provided with the best there is, yet it is only "Lucas' dinner—collard greens, a slice of sidemeat fried in flour, big flat pale heavy half-cooked biscuits, a glass of buttermilk: nigger food" and he muses further about such fare "that out of their long chronicle this was all they had had a chance to learn to like except the ones who ate out of white folks' kitchens but that they had elected this out of all eating because this was their palates and their metabolism" (p. 13); he is truly Uncle Gavin's nephew. It is precisely the understanding and the attitude that allow him to reconstruct the incendiary moment of Lucas's presumed murder of Vinson Gowrie from meager rumor of Lucas's arrogance at a white country store because he thought they treated him more like an Edmonds than a McCaslin (pp. 18–19). Gavin, by turn, is less circumstantial and more to the point. " 'Your friend Beauchamp seems to have done it this time,' " he tells Chick (p. 31) and Chick, properly schooled, agrees: " 'Yes,' he said, 'They're going to make a nigger out of him once in his life anyway' " (p. 32).

But *Intruder in the Dust* is centrally about Lucas's intrusion into the debris of such clichés. Chick is his first student. Despite the ease with which he can visualize Lucas killing Gowrie (p. 37) and how much he may long to put in his place the black who acted as a superior host, Chick finds certain facts cannot bear the weight of his assumptions. There was Lucas's rescue of him, after all—a kind of cold baptism into the facts of race and racism. And there was a paintless house that was as much a home, with its ritual meals, as the Mallison home with its Sunday dinners. Both of these facts are brought into sharp relief for Chick when he sees the cold jail cell in which the whites place Lucas. When Chick learns further that Lucas did not recognize him on the street because he was still grieving over the recent death of his wife— that black men grieve too—he graduates at last to a wider and more humane perspective (p. 25). He is also prepared to learn terror. The lynchings Cass had conceived in the commissary—"barbers and garage mechanics and deputy sheriffs and mill- and gin-hands and power-plant firemen, leading, first in mufti then later in an actual formalised regalia of hooded sheets and passwords and fiery christian symbols, lynching mobs against the race their ancestors had come to save. . . . men armed in sheets and masks rode the silent roads and the bodies of white and black both, vicitms not so much of hate as of desperation and despair, swung from lonely limbs. . . ." (*Go Down, Moses*, pp. 290–91)—Chick now understands Lucas may suffer in "darkness or at least invisibility" with his own "crucifixion" (p. 138) either in flames or as expendable "bait" in the "hunt" for the real murderer (p. 221). Yet *Intruder in the Dust* is so structured that Lucas alone can save himself just as his own behavior first seems to have threatened him. He, too, must learn the consequences of a racism he would deny. "With the appearance of Lucas Beauchamp, most of Faulkner's previous attitudes toward the Negro are transcended," Irving Howe tells us. "Too proud to acquiesce in submission, too self-contained to be either outcast or rebel, Lucas has transformed the stigma of alienation into a mark of dignity and assurance. He is truly a character who has 'made' himself, who has worked through to his own kind of authenticity. The gain is high, so too the price: for Lucas is friendless, and his grandeur is a crotchety grandeur." The black's problem is not only one of self-identity but of necessary accommodation in a divided society. Faulkner addresses this problem too with Lucas in *Intruder in the Dust*. Howe notes that

> Occasionally Faulkner lets him slip into the stubborn old nigger who grumbles and bumbles his way to domination over the delightfully helpless whites. This may be justifiable, for, to an extent difficult to specify, the "stubborn old nigger" is Lucas' social mask—and Faulkner realizes now that in white society Negroes must often use a social mask. Because he is so aware that they can seldom risk spontaneity in the company of whites, Faulkner, like the boy Chick Mallison, circles about Lucas with humor and a shy respect, never daring to come close lest the old Negro growl at him. He feels about Lucas somewhat as Chick and Stevens do, sharing the boy's irritated awe and the man's uneasy admiration. Toward no other character in any of his books does Faulkner show quite the same uncomfortable deference; of none other can it be said that Faulkner looks up to him with so boyish and pleading an air, as if he wishes to gain from the old man a measure of forgiveness or acceptance, perhaps finally even love. (pp. 129–30)

But the love, or at least irrevocable concern, extends to other blacks in the other works of the McCaslin trilogy. In *Go Down, Moses,* a novel about freedom and bondage (am I free? how do I get free? how do I stay free?), Rider's plight is particularly agonizing. He himself comes from no family, but with Mannie he attempts to build one, to simulate a family home, as he too builds a fire on his hearth (p. 138), and, despite the sheriff's deputy who compares him to an animal (p. 154), it is his anguished search for Mannie, his attempt to restore and perpetuate a family that allows him to accost the crooked diceman, allows him to take pride in his very blackness (pp. 153–54). Michael Millgate believes that "Faulkner's refusal to make the few minor changes in names and relationships which would have made Rider a McCaslin has the effect not of isolating the episode in which Rider is the major character but actually of expanding, beyond the limits of the single McCaslin family, the whole scope and relevance of the book" (p. 204).

Faulkner returns to the McCaslin family, however, in the third work, *The Reivers.* In a novel which begins by accounting for three generations of Priests, and ends with the beginning of a new Priest-Hogganbeck line, the real focus is on Ned McCaslin and, behind him, Bobo Beauchamp. Ned is for Lucius " 'Uncle' Ned" (p. 30) and Bobo is "another motherless Beauchamp child whom Aunt Tennie raised" (p. 229). Like Rider and like Lucas, Bobo

" 'got mixed up with a white man,' " Ned tells us, and latter-day racial relations put him into bondage.

> "But why didn't he come to me?" Mr van Tosch said.
> "He did," Ned said. "You told him No." They sat quite still. "You're a white man," Ned said gently. "Bobo was a nigger boy."
> "Then why didn't he come to me," Grandfather said. "Back where he should never have left in the first place, instead of stealing a horse?"
> "What would you a done?" Ned said. "If he had come in already out of breath from Memphis and told you, Dont ask me no questions: just hand me a hundred and a few extra dollars and I'll go back to Memphis and start paying you back the first Saturday I gets around to it?"
> "He could have told me why," Grandfather said, "I'm a McCaslin too."
> "You're a white man too," Ned said. . . .
> "You can't know," Ned said. "You're the wrong color." (pp. 287–91)

"Maybe nothing ever happens once and is finished," Quentin Compson sums in *Absalom, Absalom!*[60]

Melvin Backman contends that "*Go Down, Moses* voices the concern of conscience over the Negro's plight in a white man's world, yet it also voices the grief of conscience over its own helplessness. The South that denies the Negro his manhood," he writes, "denies the white man his right to love."[61] With Faulkner such love always begins and remains grounded in the love of family, the arena that, paradoxically, provides identity and security but may also eliminate privacy and freedom. Yet the family remains for Faulkner the only source of meaningful instruction. As Sam is able to teach Isaac about the dignity of the enslaved, so Lucas teaches Chick and Ned, Lucius; conversely, Cass's formulations restrict Ike, just as Gavin's restrict Chick and Boss Priest's Lucius. Yet the three members of the McCaslin trilogy of works hold important differences too: Sam retains his dignity only by retreating to the woods; Lucas uses miscegenation to achieve an assertive dignity; Ned equivocates. Together they suggest the range of Yoknapatawpha, and of the Lafayette County and the South that remain their foundation: "The strands are all there," Eudora Welty has remarked in another context; "to the memory nothing is lost." And just as family love and understanding hold what hope there is, so its very opposite—fratricide—can be permanently destructive. It is this that the Gowries represent, the dust of man found in the dust of their empty coffins (*Intruder in the Dust*, p. 166) as in the empty tin coffee pot of Hubert Beauchamp (*Go Down, Moses*, pp. 306–8). Yet even these can be overcome with the power of blood, and of bloodlines.

> "Why not?" McCaslin said. "Think of all that has happened here, on this earth. All the blood hot and strong for living, pleasuring, that has soaked back into it. For grieving and suffering too, of course, but still getting something out of it for all that, getting a lot out of it, because after all you don't have to continue to bear what you believe is suffering; you can always

choose to stop that, put an end to that. And even suffering and grieving is better than nothing; there is only one thing worse than not being alive, and that's shame. But you cant be alive forever, and you always wear out life long before you have exhausted the possibilities of living. And all that must be somewhere; all that could not have been invented and created just to be thrown away." (*Go Down, Moses*, p. 186)

And the suggestively named McCaslin Edmonds is, we remember, Ike's cousin, or "rather his brother than cousin and rather his father than either, out of the old time, the old days" (*Go Down, Moses*, p. 4).

The critical reception of William Faulkner is a well-known story, often told. Despite early support from Sherwood Anderson (who helped Faulkner to publish his first two novels, *Soldiers' Pay* and *Mosquitoes*, and advised him to write about Mississippi for his third, *Flags in the Dust*, shortened by his agent Ben Wasson for publication as *Sartoris* in 1929), most of his early recognition came from scattered reviews. These were uneven; Faulkner's work was often thought to be derivative, tangled, obscure, or morbid. *Sanctuary* (1931) was his first successful novel because it was thought sensational, not serious; Faulkner himself called it a "potboiler." Indeed, throughout the 1930s, when Faulkner was publishing much of his finest fiction, he was more admired in Europe than in his own country; Jean-Paul Sartre's acclaim for *Sartoris* is a representative example. In the United States, the first important critical reception came in 1939, and with two essays: Conrad Aiken's "William Faulkner: The Novel as Form" and George Marion O'Donnell's "Faulkner's Mythology." This was also the year of Faulkner's election to the National Institute of Arts and Letters. Yet, he had to wait until 1946, and the publication of *The Portable Faulkner* edited by Malcolm Cowley, before he would gain a growing, serious audience. It was Cowley's anthology—coupled with the 1949 Nobel Prize for Literature (awarded in 1950, the year Faulkner's *Collected Stories* won the National Book Award)—that led directly to his current popularity with readers, students, critics, and scholars. Now Faulkner is the subject of more criticism in English than any other author except Shakespeare. Detailed examinations of the public response to Faulkner's work from his earliest days have been conducted, in differing perspectives, by Frederick J. Hoffman, Robert Penn Warren, John Bassett, O. B. Emerson, and Thomas L. McHaney and need not be summarized here.[62] There are also excellent bibliographies of Faulkner's work and of work on his fiction.[63]

This collection brings together resources that help us to understand Faulkner's creation of the McCaslin-Beauchamp-Edmonds-Priest family and interpretive responses to each of the family lines, many of them published here for the first time. Clement Eaton and Vernon Lane Wharton provide helpful analyses of Southern history and Southern attitudes while John Spencer Bassett, in a book Faulkner saw, and Booker T. Washington, in a famous document Faulkner probably knew, give first-hand accounts of plantation overseers and plantation slaves. "The Sheriff's Children," a well-known story in the South by the respected black writer Charles W. Chesnutt bears striking resemblances to Faulkner's work, especially "Pantaloon in Black." Whether or not Faulkner actually read W. E. B. DuBois' important account of the "double-consciousness" of blacks, he knew it instinctively and used it in nearly all the accounts of black McCaslins. Faulkner was only four when Nelse Patton was lynched, but the incident is so close to events in his fiction that he must have heard the story; the lynching of Elwood Higginbotham occurred when Faulkner was in his thirties and a member of his family was trying other court cases simultaneously. Faulkner's two brothers John and Murry share family information on which Faulkner drew while Willie Morris gives an observer's view of Mississippi during the period of "Go Down, Moses" and *Intruder in the Dust*. William Faulkner's own first fiction on blacks, "Sunset," as well as two pages which Faulkner wished to add to *Intruder in the Dust* but which were never published, are also reproduced here. Yet other resources of substantial value were not included only because space did not permit; but readers may wish to consult later letters collected by Bassett, Frederick Douglass's account of slavery in *My Bondage and My Freedom* (1855), George W. Cable's widely influential essay on "The Freedman's Case in Equity" in *Century* magazine for January 1885; Elizabeth M. Kerr's discussion of caste, class, and family in *Yoknapatawpha: Faulkner's "Little Postage Stamp of Native Soil"* (1969), (especially pp. 105–23, 126, 131–33, 140–43, and 162–69); Nollie Hickman's history of lumbering in *Mississippi Harvest* (1962), the commentaries on Mississippi by James W. Silver (*Mississippi: The Closed Society*, 1964; *Running Scared*, 1984) and James Weldon Johnson's *Autobiography of an Ex-Coloured Man* (1927). Other accounts of incidents in Faulkner's own life besides the splendid biographies of Joseph Blotner and David Minter may be found in John B. Cullen and Floyd C. Watkins, *Old Times in the Faulkner Country* (1961) and *Bitterweeds* by Malcolm Franklin, Faulkner's stepson (1977); in "A Geographical Approach to William Faulkner's 'The Bear'" Charles S. Aiken examines Faulkner's actual settings (*The Geographical Review* for October 1981). Useful fiction includes the folk tales collected by Zora Neale Hurston, especially in *Mules and Men* (1935), pp. 140–42, and other stories by Charles W. Chesnutt. Faulkner's first fiction on blacks—and an important work in its own right—is "Sunset," but there are also useful texts in his *Essays, Speeches, & Public Letters* (1965), particularly "Mississippi," "A Letter to the North," and "If I Were a Negro"; his own remarks about the McCaslin saga are collected in *Faulkner in the University* (1959), *Lion in the Garden* (1968), and *Faulkner at West Point* (1969).

Parts 2 and 3 of this volume are composed of essays which examine the various lines of the McCaslin family, beginning with their forebears, from varying perspectives; but readers may wish to supplement these insights with work not included here. For the Ikkemottube line: Wesley Morris, *Friday's*

Footprint (1979), pp. 12–19; for the McCaslin-Edmonds line: Arthur F. Kinney, who relates family members by fictional strategies in *Faulkner's Narrrative Poetics* (1978), pp. 214–41; Carl E. Rollyson who examines the commissary books as primary historical documents in *The Markham Review* 7 (1978), 31–36; Sandra Delores Milby on Ned McCaslin in *The Development of Black Characters in the Fiction of William Faulkner* (PhD. diss., University of Michigan, 1979); C. Douglas Canfield on "Ike McCaslin's Empty Legacies" and the problem of immortality (*Arizona Quarterly* 36 [1980], 359–83); Richard H. King on the McCaslin family legacy in *A Southern Renaissance* (1980), pp. 131–45; Karl F. Zender on "Reading in 'The Bear,' " in *Faulkner Studies* 1 (1980), 91–99; and David Paul Ragan on Faulkner's development of Roth Edmonds in *Mississippi Quarterly* 38:3 (1985), 295–309; for the Beauchamp line: Walter Taylor on Rider in *American Literature* 44:3 (1972), 430–44; Myra Jehlen on Faulkner's treatment of race in *Class and Character in Faulkner's South* (1976), pp. 97–132; and Darwin T. Turner on "Faulkner and Slavery" in *The South and Faulkner's Yoknapatawpha*, ed. Evans Harrington and Ann J. Abadie (1977), pp. 62–85; for the Priest line: Elizabeth M. Kerr in *Modern Fiction Studies* 13:1 (1967), 96–115.

The Appendix included here reprints material that may be used as reference: Faulkner's early genealogical sketch on the McCaslin family and a later, fuller one prepared by Robert W. Kirk with Marvin Klotz; Harry Runyan's capsule biographies of each member of the various lines of the McCaslin family; Meredith Smith on the tangled chronology of *Go Down, Moses;* and Robert L. Yarup explicating the highly elliptical poker game in "Was." For those who wish to know more of Faulkner's actual composition of the various books in the McCaslin trilogy, the introductions to the new Garland edition of *William Faulkner: Manuscripts* are definitive; see Thomas L. McHaney on the composition of *Go Down, Moses* (16, vii–xvi), Noel Polk on *Intruder in the Dust* (17, vii–xi), and Michael Millgate on *The Reivers* (23, vii–xii). An initial range of responses to these books can be found in early reviews: for *Go Down, Moses*, see especially Horace Gregory in *New York Times*, 10 May 1942, 4; Lionel Trilling in *The Nation*, 30 May 1942, 632; Malcolm Cowley in *The New Republic*, 29 June 1942, 900; and *TLS* (unsigned), 10 October 1942, 497; for *Intruder in the Dust*, Maxwell Geismar, *Saturday Review of Literature*, 25 September 1948, 8–9; Edmund Wilson, *The New Yorker*, 23 October 1948, 106–13; Eudora Welty, *Hudson Review*, 1:4 (1949), 596–98; Charles Glicksberg, *Arizona Quarterly* (Spring 1949), 85–88; Nathan Glick, *Commentary* 7 (May 1949), 502–3; and Walter Allen, *New Statesman and Nation* (London), 15 October 1949, 428–30; for *The Reivers*, George Plimpton in New York Herald Tribune Books 27 May 1962, 3; Hilary Corke in *The New Republic* 16 July 1962, 20–22; and V. S. Pritchett, *New Statesman and Nation* (London), 28 September 1962, 405–6.[64]

The very range and complexity of issues raised by the McCaslin family has made this collection especially difficult and many of its contributions are due in part to the generous counsel and support of others. I wish to thank in particular several colleagues and friends including Mrs. Katherine Andrews; Bernard W. Bell; Mrs. Julia Boles; Frank Childrey, Jr.; Walker Coffey; Martha Cofield; John R. Cooley; A. B. Cullen; Lewis Dabney; Charles Dean; J. M. Faulkner; Evans Harrington; Aston Holley; Will Lewis, Sr.; Eva Miller; Marc A. Nigliazzo; Sharron Eve Sathou and the staff of Archives and Special Collections, John Davis Williams Library, University of Mississippi; David G. Sansing; David Toomey; William Lamar Wilder; and Daniel T. Williams, University Archivist, Tuskegee University.

ARTHUR F. KINNEY

University of Massachusetts, Amherst

Notes

1. Irving Howe, *William Faulkner: A Critical Study*, 3d ed., rev. and exp. (Chicago: University of Chicago Press, 1975), 8–9.

2. *Go Down, Moses* (New York: Vintage Books, 1973), 236. All future citations are to this edition which uses the same pagination and setting as the Modern Library edition.

3. David Minter, *William Faulkner: His Life and Work* (Baltimore: The Johns Hopkins University Press, 1980), 187.

4. A convenient generational chart may be found in Walton Litz, "Genealogy as Symbol in *Go Down, Moses*," *Faulkner Studies* 1, no. 4 (Winter 1952): 52–53.

5. This discussion builds on the account given by Elizabeth Meeks, *A Contextual Approach to the Teaching of Two Novels by William Faulkner at College Level* (DEd. diss., University of Houston, 1965), 107ff.

6. Walker Coffey, "Lafayette County," in *The Heritage of Lafayette County Mississippi* (Oxford, Miss.: Skipwith Genealogical Society, Inc., 1986), 21–22.

7. Bernard W. Bell, *The Afro-American Novel and Its Tradition* (Amherst, Mass.: University of Massachusetts Press, 1987), 7.

8. W. W. Magruder, "The Legal Status of Slaves in Mississippi before the War," *Publications of the Mississippi Historical Society* 4 (Oxford, Miss.: The Mississippi Historical Society, 1901), 138.

9. Cf. Alfred H. Stone, "Early Slave Laws of Mississippi," *Publications of the Mississippi Historical Society* 2 (Oxford, Miss.: The Mississippi Historical Society, 1899), 133 *passim*.

10. A note indicates this resumé was based upon the analysis of William Goodell, *The American Slave Code in Theory and Practice*, and T. R. R. Cobb, *An Inquiry into the Laws of Negro Slavery in the United States*.

11. These facts are recorded by Phillips, 155–56.

12. See Meeks, 86–92.

13. And their ownership was widespread. For statistics, see John Cooper Hathorn, *A Period Study of Lafayette County from 1836 to 1860 with Emphasis on Population Groups* (M. A. thesis, University of Mississippi, 1939), 76–86.

14. William Faulkner, *Collected Stories* (New York: Vintage Books, 1977), 314. All future citations are to this edition.

15. Thomas Dixon, Jr., *The Leopard's Spots: A Romance of the White Man's Burden, 1865–1900* (New York: A Wessels Co., 1906), 464. According to Joseph Blotner in *Faulkner: A*

Biography (New York: Random House, 1974), vol. 1, 498, Sherwood Anderson, in his *Memoirs*, said Faulkner too thought miscegenation resulted in sterility. The chronicle of the McCaslins clearly shows this could not have been so by 1940 and probably never was (see also Blotner's demur, 498–99).

16. *Light in August: The Corrected Text*, ed. Noel Polk (New York: Vintage Books, 1987), 495–96.

17. As quoted in Charles D. Peavy, *Go Slow Now: Faulkner and the Race Question* (Eugene, Ore.: University of Oregon Books, 1971), 34.

18. John W. Blassingame, *Slave Testimony: Two Centuries of Letters, Speeches, Interviews, and Autobiographies*, ed. Blassingame (Baton Rouge, La.: Louisiana State University Press, 1977), 376.

19. Vernon Lee Wharton, *The Negro in Mississippi 1865–1890* (Chapel Hill, N.C.: University of North Carolina Press, 1947), 229.

20. William Faulkner, *The Reivers* (New York: Vintage Books, 1962), 30–31. All future citations are to this edition.

21. James Harvey Krefft, *The Yoknapatawpha Indians: Fact and Fiction* (Ph.D. diss., Tulane University, 1976), 311.

22. Blotner (1974), vol. 1, 53.

23. Jim Faulkner, *Across the Creek: Faulkner Family Stories* (Jackson, Miss.: University Press of Mississippi, 1986), 74.

24. See Lewis M. Dabney, *The Indians of Yoknapatawpha: A Study in Literature and History* (Baton Rouge, La.: Louisiana State University Press, 1974), 147–48.

25. The best discussion of architecture in Faulkner, with some diagrams, is William T. Ruzicka, *Faulkner's Fictive Architecture: Natural and Man-Made Places in the Yoknapatawpha Novels* (Ph.D. diss., University of Dallas, 1970).

26. Malcolm Franklin, *Bitterweeds: Life with William Faulkner at Rowan Oak* (Irving, Tex.: The Society for the Study of Traditional Culture, 1977), 36–37.

27. Emily Whitehurst Stone, "How a Writer Finds His Material," *Harper's* 231, no. 1368 (November 1965): 159–61.

28. John B. Cullen in collaboration with Floyd C. Watkins, *Old Times in the Faulkner Country* (Chapel Hill, N. C.: University of North Carolina Press, 1961).

29. Jerrold Brite, "A True-Blue Hunter" in *William Faulkner of Oxford*, ed. James W. Webb and A. Wigfall Green (Baton Rouge, La.: Louisiana State University Press, 1965), 157.

30. "Interview with Dan Brennan," in *Lion in the Garden: Interviews with William Faulkner 1926–1962*, ed. James B. Meriwether and Michael Millgate (New York: Random House, 1968), 48.

31. E. T. Winston, *Story of Pontotoc*, part 1: *The Chickasaws* (Pontontoc, Miss.: Pontontoc Progress Print, 1931).

32. Letter from Joseph Blotner to Frances Willard Pate on 13 March 1967 and quoted by Pate in *Names of Characters in Faulkner's Mississippi* (Ph.D. diss., Emory University, 1969), p. 192, n. 105.

33. Joseph Blotner, *Faulkner: A Biography*, one-volume ed. (New York: Random House, 1984), 34, 87.

34. Oxford *Eagle*, 29 August 1935, p. 4, col. 5

35. These suggestions are made by Pate, 53.

36. Novels, plays, and dissertations—including Robert Penn Warren's *World Enough and Time*—deal with this affair. A good place to begin is with *The Beauchamp Tragedy*, ed. Jules Zanger (Philadelphia: J. B. Lippincott Co., 1963).

37. Thadious M. Davis, "Faulkner's Development of Black Characterization," in *Faulkner and Race: Faulkner and Yoknapatawpha 1986*, ed. Doreen Fowler and Ann J. Abadie (Jackson, Miss.: University Press of Mississippi, 1987), 89.

38. This citation and the following remarks are taken from A. A. Hill, "Three Examples of Unexpectedly Accurate Indian Lore," in *Texas Studies in Literature and Language* 6, no. 1 (Spring 1964): 82–83.

39. *Go Down, Moses*, 172.

40. Elmo Howell, "William Faulkner and the Chickasaw Funeral," in *American Literature* 36, no. 4 (January 1965): 524.

41. The fullest account of "the most consistent genealogy" of Faulkner's Indians is Marc A. Nigliazzo, *Indians in the Works of William Faulkner* (Ph.D. diss., University of New Mexico, 1973). Some of his observations disagree with Dabney's.

42. These statistics are reprinted in Hathorn, Appendix 1, 187.

43. Jack Case Wilson, *Faulkners, Fortunes and Flames* (Nashville, Tenn.: Annadale Press, 1984), 27.

44. Michael Millgate, *The Achievement of William Faulkner* (London: Constable and Co., 1965), 39.

45. "Interview with Michael Mok," first published in the New York *Post* for 17 October 1939; reprinted in *Lion in the Garden*, 39.

46. James Michael Grimwood, *Pastoral and Parody: The Making of Faulkner's Anthology Novels* (Ph.D. diss., Princeton University, 1976), pp. 305–6. The quotations are from Blotner (1974), 991–93, 998.

47. Blotner (1974), vol. 2, 147n; vol. 1, 433.

48. Joseph Brogunier, "A Source for the Commissary Entries in *Go Down, Moses*," *Texas Studies in Literature and Language* 14, no. 3 (Fall 1972): 549.

49. A quite different source for the McCaslin ledgers may be *Clotel*, a novel by the nineteenth-century black writer William Wells Brown, in which the injustice of miscegenation causes the violated mulatto protagonist to commit suicide by drowning.

50. *Intruder in the Dust* (New York: Vintage Books, 1972), 8. All future citations are to this edition.

51. The text is in Robert W. Hamblin, "Lucas Beauchamp, Ned Barnett, and William Faulkner's 1940 Will," *Studies in Bibliography* 32 (1979): 282.

52. Cleanth Brooks, *William Faulkner: The Yoknapatawpha Country* (New Haven, Conn.: Yale University Press, 1963), 244.

53. Russell Roth makes something of this in "The Brennan Papers: Faulkner in Manuscript," *Perspective* 2, no. 4 (Summer 1949): 223. Brennan's own interview is in *Lion in the Garden*, 42–51.

54. Albert J. Guerard, "Faulkner the Innovator," in *The Maker and the Myth: Faulkner and Yoknapatawpha 1977*, ed. Evans Harrington and Ann J. Abadie (Jackson, Miss.: University Press of Mississippi, 1978), 86.

55. This brief account is drawn from records in the archives of Tuskegee University in Alabama and from *Encyclopedia of Black America*, ed. W. Augustus Low and Virgil A. Clift (New York: McGraw-Hill/De Capo, 1981), 541–42.

56. *Old Times in the Faulkner Country*, 91–92. Later corrections have been incorporated editorially.

57. Blotner (1974), vol. 1, 114.

58. Quoted by Betty Brenkert, "Mrs. Sisk remembers early Oxford events," in the Oxford *Eagle*, 30 June 1987, p. 13B, col. 2.

59. Donald M. Kartiganer, *The Fragile Thread: The Meaning of Form in Faulkner's Novels* (Amherst, Mass.: University of Massachusetts Press, 1979), 132.

60. *Absalom, Absalom!: The Corrected Text*, ed. Noel Polk (New York: Vintage Books, 1987), 326.

61. Melvin Backman, "The Wilderness and the Negro in Faulkner's 'The Bear,' " *PMLA* 76 (1961): 600.

62. Frederick J. Hoffman, "William Faulkner: An Introduction," in *William Faulkner: Two Decades of Criticism*, ed. Hoffman and Olga W. Vickery (East Lansing, Mich.: Michigan State College Press, 1951), 1–31; Hoffman in *William Faulkner: Three Decades of Criticism*, ed. Hoffman and Vickery (East Lansing, Mich.: Michigan State University Press, 1960), 1–50; Robert Penn Warren, "Introduction: Faulkner: Past and Present," in *Faulkner: A Collection of Critical Essays*, ed. Robert Penn Warren (Englewood Cliffs, N.J.: Prentice-Hall, Inc., 1966), 1–22; John Bassett, "Introduction," *William Faulkner: The Critical Heritage* (London: Routledge & Kegan Paul, 1975), 1–46; O. B. Emerson, "William Faulkner's Literary Reputation in America" (diss., Vanderbilt University, 1962); and Thomas L. McHaney, "Watching for the Dixie Limited: Faulkner's Impact upon the Creative Writer," in *Fifty Years of Yoknapatawpha*, ed. Doreen Fowler and Ann J. Abadie (Jackson, Miss.: University Press of Mississippi, 1980), 226–47.

63. John Bassett, *William Faulkner: An Annotated Checklist of Criticism* (New York: David Lewis, 1972) and Thomas M. McHaney, *William Faulkner: A Reference Guide* (Boston: G. K. Hall and Co., 1976; now being updated). (Earlier, and somewhat outdated, is Irene Lynn Sleeth, *William Faulkner: A Bibliography of Criticism* [Denver: Alan Swallow, 1962]).

64. There is still other important material. While "The Bear" episode in *Go Down, Moses* has been a major focal point of Faulkner scholarship and criticism since the beginning—and first conveniently collected in *Bear, Man, and God*, ed. Francis L. Utley, Lynn Z. Bloom, and Arthur F. Kinney (1964; heavily revised, 1971),—all the works dealing with the larger McCaslin family have become increasingly popular. Detailed examinations of Faulkner's composition of each of the books on the family can be found in Joseph Blotner's two biographies of Faulkner, and briefer accounts are included in Michael Millgate, *The Achievement of William Faulkner* (1965), at the beginning of the chapter on each separate work. In addition, readers will want to consult Edward M. Holmes, *Faulkner's Twice-Told Tales: His Re-Use of His Material* (1966) and Joanne V. Creighton, *William Faulkner's Craft of Revision* (1977). More specific studies include Jane Millgate, "Short Story into Novel: Faulkner's Reworking of 'Gold Is Not Always,' " *English Studies* 45, no. 4 (August 1964): 310–17; and Lawrence H. Schwartz, "Publishing William Faulkner: The 1940s," *Southern Quarterly* 22 (1983–84): 70–92. Besides basic general studies on Southern history and society, there are a number of helpful dissertations and theses, including Robert Douglas Bamberg, *Plantation and Frontier: A View of Southern Fiction* (Cornell University, 1961), Joe Carl Buice, *The Rise and Decline of Aristocratic Families in Yoknapatawpha County* (East Texas State University, 1970); Gerald Fred Webb, *Jeffersonian Agrarianism in Faulkner's Yoknapatawpha* (Florida State, 1972); William John McDonald, *The Image of Adolescence in William Faulkner's Yoknapatawpha Fiction* (University of Oregon, 1979); and Edward L. Corridori, *The Quest for Sacred Space: Setting in the Novels of William Faulkner* (Kent State University, 1971).

The most comprehensive studies of Faulkner's Indians are Lewis M. Dabney, *The Indians of Yoknapatawpha: A Study in Literature and History* (1974), and two dissertations, James Harvey Krefft, *The Yoknapatawpha Indians: Fact and Fiction* (Tulane University , 1976) and Marc A. Nigliazzo, *Indians in the Works of William Faulkner* (Albuquerque: University of New Mexico, 1973).

Recommended readings on *Go Down, Moses* include Edmund L. Volpe's chapter in *A Reader's Guide to William Faulkner* (1964); Lawrence Thompson's chapter in *William Faulkner: An Introduction and Interpretation* (1963, 1967); Thomas J. Wertenbaker, Jr., "Faulkner's Point of View and 'The Chronicle of Ike McCaslin' " *College English* 24, no. 3 (December 1962): 169–77; Stanley Tick, "The Unity of *Go Down, Moses*," *Twentieth Century Literature* 8, no. 2 (July

1962): 67–73; Walton Litz, "Genealogy as Symbol in *Go Down, Moses*," *Faulkner Studies* 1, no. 4 (Winter 1952): 49–53; Weldon Thornton, "Structure and Theme in Faulkner's *Go Down, Moses*," *Costerus*, N.S. 3 (1975): 73–112; Mark R. Hochberg, "The Unity of *Go Down, Moses*," *Tennessee Studies in Literature* 21 (1976): 58–65; Ronald Schleifer, "Faulkner's Storied Novel: *Go Down, Moses* and the Translation of Time," *Modern Fiction Studies* 28, no. 1 (Spring 1982), 109–27; chapter 5 of John T. Matthews, *The Play of Faulkner's Language* (1982); Walter F. Taylor, Jr., "Let My People Go: The White Man's Heritage in *Go Down, Moses*," *The South Atlantic Quarterly* 58, no. 1 (Winter 1959): 20–32; Joseph W. Reed, Jr., "Uncertainties: *Go Down, Moses*," in *Faulkner's Narrative* (1973), 185–200; Thomas C. Foster, "History, Private Consciousness, and Narrative Form in *Go Down, Moses*," *The Centennial Review*, 28, no. 1 (Winter 1984); Annette Kolodny, *The Lay of the Land* (1975), 140–45; Lyall H. Powers, *Faulkner's Yoknapatawpha Comedy* (1980), 162–91; James A. Snead, *Figures of Division: William Faulkner's Major Novels* (1986); Stanley Sultan, "Call Me Ishmael: The Hagiography of Isaac McCaslin," *Texas Studies in Literature and Language* 3, no. 1 (Spring 1961): 50–66; and Eugene J. Hall, *William Faulkner: Character as Theme and Structure* (Ph.D. diss., Columbia, 1952), chapter 5.

Included in important studies on individual episodes in *Go Down, Moses* are the following. For "Was": David Walker, "Out of the Old Time: 'Was' and *Go Down, Moses*," *Journal of Narrative Technique* 9, no. 1 (Winter 1979): 1–11; Daniel Hoffman, "Faulkner's 'Was' and Uncle Adam's Cow," in *Faulkner and Humor: Faulkner and Yoknapatawpha 1984*, ed. Doreen Fowler and Ann J. Abadie (1986); and Helen M. Poindexter, "Faulkner, the Mississippi Gambler," *Journal of Modern Literature* 10 (1983): 334–38. For "The Fire and the Hearth": Joanne Vanish Creighton, "Revision and Craftsmanship in Faulkner's 'The Fire and the Hearth,' " *Studies in Short Fiction* 11, no. 2 (Spring 1974): 161–72. For "The Bear": John B. Cullen in collaboration with Floyd C. Watkins, *Old Times in the Faulkner Country* (1961), 4–5, 12–24, 31–41, 46–47; Calvin S. Brown, "Faulkner's Manhunts: Fact into Fiction," *Georgia Review* 20, no. 4 (Winter 1966): 388–95; Thomas L. McHaney, "A Deer Hunt in the Faulkner Country," *Mississippi Quarterly* 23, no. 3 (Summer 1970): 315–20; "Yazoo," "Deer Hunting in the Yazoo Swamp," *Georgia Review* 20, no. 1 (Spring 1966): 104–7; and Floyd C. Watkins, "Delta Hunt," *Southwest Review* 45, no. 3 (Summer 1960): 266–72.—all background material; in addition there are these critical studies of Faulkner's text: Kenneth LaBudde, "Cultural Primitivism in William Faulkner's 'The Bear,' " *American Quarterly* 2, no. 4 (Winter 1950): 322–28; Thomas P. Carpenter, "A Gun for Faulkner's Old Ben," *American Notes and Queries* 5, no. 9 (May 1967): 133–34; Richard P. Adams, "Focus on William Faulkner's 'The Bear': Moses and the Wilderness," in *American Dreams, American Nightmares*, ed. David Madden (1970); John Pikoulis, *The Art of William Faulkner* (1982), chapter 7; Melvin Backman, *Faulkner: The Major Years* (1966), 160–74; Susan V. Donaldson, "Isaac McCaslin and the Possibilities of Vision," *Southern Review* 22, no. 1 (January 1986): 37–50; Herbert A. Perluck, " 'The Heart's Driving Complexity': An Unromantic Reading of Faulkner's 'The Bear,' " in *Accent* 20 (1960): 23–46; and Christine A. Jackson, *Sound and Spirit: Oral Tradition in Selected Short Works by Hawthorne and Faulkner* (Ph.D. diss., State University of New York at Albany, 1982), 106–35. For "Delta Autumn": Carol Clancey Harter, "The Winter of Isaac McCaslin: Revisions and Irony in Faulkner's 'Delta Autumn,' " *Journal of Modern Literature* 1, no. 2 (1970–71), 209–25; and Arthur F. Kinney, "Faulkner and the Possibilities for Heroism," *Southern Review*, N.S., 6 (Autumn 1970): 1110–25.

References of use to other works involving branches of the McCaslin family are the following: For *Intruder in the Dust*: Donna Gerstenberger, "Meaning and Form in *Intruder in the Dust*," *College English* 23, no. 3 (December 1961): 223–25; Aaron Steinberg, " 'Intruder in the Dust': Faulkner as Psychologist of the Southern Psyche," *Literature and Psychology* 15, no. 2 (Spring 1965): 120–24; Lyall H. Powers, *Faulkner's Yoknapatawpha Comedy* (1980), chapter 10; Olga W. Vickery, *The Novels of William Faulkner* (1959), 134–44; Patrick Samway, S. J., "*Intruder in the Dust*: A Re-evaluation," in *Faulkner: the Unappeased Imagination*, ed. Glenn O. Carey (1980), 83–113; and David W. Mascitelli *Faulkner's Characters of Sensibility* (Ph.D. diss., Duke University, 1967), 147–68. For *The Reivers*: Ben W. McClelland, *Not Only to Survive but to Prevail; A*

Study of William Faulkner's Search for a Redeemer of Modern Man, Ph.D. diss., Indiana University, 1972), chapter 4. For *Big Woods:* Glen M. Johnson, *"Big Woods:* Faulkner's Elegy for Wilderness," *Southern Humanities Review* 14, no. 3 (Summer 1980): 249–58.

Faulkner's concern with race has become especially important in recent years. A good place to begin is *Faulkner and Race: Faulkner and Yoknapatawpha 1986*, ed. Doreen Fowler and Ann J. Abadie (1987), but see also Lee Jenkins, *Faulkner and Black-White Relations* (1981), especially 261–79; and Charles D. Peavy, *Go Slow Now: Faulkner and the Race Question* (1971). Also compare Robert Penn Warren, "Faulkner: The South and the Negro," *The Southern Review*, N.S. 1, no. 3 (Summer 1965): 501–29; Irving Howe, "William Faulkner and the Negroes: A Vision of Lost Fraternity," *Commentary* 12, no. 4 (October 1951): 359–68; Erskine Peters, *William Faulkner: The Yoknapatawpha World and Black Being* (1983); Aaron Steinberg, *Faulkner and the Negro* (Ph.D. diss., New York University, 1963); John McMillon Gissendanner, *The "Nether Channel": A Study of Faulkner's Black Characters* (Ph.D. diss., University of California at San Diego, 1982); Sandra Delores Milby, *The Development of the Black Character in the Fiction of William Faulkner* (Ph.D. diss., University of Michigan, 1979); and Fay E. Beauchamp, *William Faulkner's Use of the Tragic Mulatto Myth* (Ph.D. diss., University of Pennsylvania, 1974).

For individual characters in the McCaslin saga, see William J. Sowder, "Lucas Beauchamp as Existential Hero," *College English* 25, no. 2 (November 1963): 115–19; Esther McClard Alexander, *A Critical Analysis of the Roles of Lucas Beauchamp in William Faulkner's "Go Down Moses" and "Intruder in the Dust"* (M.A. thesis, University of North Carolina, Chapel Hill, 1962); Gerald W. Walton, "Tennie's Jim and Lucas Beauchamp," *American Notes and Queries* 8, no. 2 (October 1969): 23–24; Walter Taylor, "The Freedman in *Go Down, Moses:* Historical Fact and Imaginative Failure," *Ball State University Forum* 8, no. 1 (Winter 1967): 3–7; and J. Edward Schamberger, "Renaming Percival Brownlee in Faulkner's 'Bear,' " *College Literature* 4, no. 1 (Winter 1977): 92–94, along with A. J. Lofquist, "More in the Name of Brownlee in Faulkner's *The Bear,*" *College Literature* 5, no. 1 (Winter 1978): 62–64.

Not all useful reference material has been collected in the appendix here, and readers may also wish to consult Michel Gresset, *A Faulkner Chronology* (1985), 60–64; "McCaslin-Edmonds" and "Priest" in Harry Runyan, *A Faulkner Glossary* (1964), 258–66; Gerald W. Walton, "Some Southern Farm Terms in Faulkner's *Go Down, Moses,*" *Publication of the American Dialect Society* no. 27 (April 1967): 23–29; E. O. Hawkins, *A Handbook of Yoknapatawpha* (Ph.D. diss., University of Arkansas, Little Rock, 1961); and Emma Jo Grimes Marshall, *Scenes from Yoknapatawpha: A Study of People and Places in the Real and Imaginary Worlds of William Faulkner* (Ph.D. diss., University of Alabama, 1978), amply illustrated with new and old photographs.

Following are some noteworthy book reviews: Of *Go Down Moses: Saturday Review of Literature* 25, no. 18 (2 May 1942): 16–17; *New Statesman and Nation* 24, no. 610 (31 October 1942): 293; *New Yorker* 18, no. 13 (16 May 1942): 62; *Yale Review* 31, no. 4 (Summer 1942): 31; *Atlantic* 170, no. 3 (September 1942): 136. Of *Intruder in the Dust, College English* 10 (December 1948): 178; *Virginia Quarterly Review* 25, no. 1 (Winter 1949): 132–33; *Newsweek*, 4 October 1948, 91; *New Republic* 119, no. 1768 (18 October 1948): 21–22; *Harper's* 197, no. 1183 (December 1948): 101–10; *New York Times Book Review*, 26 September 1948, 4; *Time*, 4 October 1948, 108–12. For *The Reivers: Nation* 194, no. 23 (9 June 1962): 519–21; *Time*, 8 June 1962, 92; and *Newsweek*, 4 June 1962, 100.

RESOURCES

The Mind of the Old South

The plantation society of the Old South emphasized the family to a much greater degree than was done in the North. Family graveyards were a familiar sight in the landscape of the Old South; the family altar was a part of its religious mores; and the devotion to kin was expressed in the phrase "kissing cousins." Southerners tended to evaluate people not so much as individuals but as belonging to a family, a clan. This characteristic has survived into the twentieth century in many villages of the Deep South, as Harper Lee's recent novel *To Kill a Mockingbird* has demonstrated. Here, far from the industrial world, the villagers judged people within the family context, as displaying hereditary characteristics. They were accustomed to lump all the Ewells together as being no-account for generations; the Cunninghams could always be trusted to pay their debts; "all the Burfords walked like that"; the Penfields had a "flighty streak"; the Crawfords, a "mean streak"; and the Goforths, a "stingy streak." . . .

White Southerners maintained that, having lived intimately with Negroes for generations, they knew the Negro mind. Yet their views of the Negro were distorted by powerful stereotypes, especially concerning a belief in the inherent inferiority of the Negro. The slave studied closely the white man, and seems to have been far more astute in reading the mind of the master than was the latter in penetrating the psychology of the black man. Beverly Nash, a prominent colored leader of the Reconstruction, observed that the Negro "will know more of your character in three days than you [the white man] will of his in three months. It has been his business all his life to find out the ways of the white man—to watch him—what he means." Even highly intelligent masters and mistresses whose interest it was to understand the subject race found the inner thoughts of the slaves veiled and inscrutable, for they were noncommittal and evasive in conversation with the white man. . . .

In the Slave Papers of the Library of Congress is a manuscript autobiography of the slave "Fields," dated at Richmond in 1847; the manuscript gives

*Reprinted with permission from *The Mind of the Old South*, rev. ed. (Baton Rouge, La.: Louisiana State University Press, 1967), 292, 170–71, 194, 172, 195–96.

an example of the stimulus of white contacts upon the Negro. Fields relates that he never knew what "the yoke of oppression" was until he was nearly grown, for "the black and white children all fared alike." He became very attached to the master's son; but when the latter had become a teenager, he asserted his superiority over his dark-skinned playmate and friend, "like a peacock among chickens," and soon the master's son was sent away to school and the slave boy was put in the fields to work. . . .

The Southern Negro's strong sense of social distinctions (which he may have absorbed from the white master class) extended into social relations among the slaves and free Negroes. Horace Fitchett in a Ph.D. dissertation entitled "The Free Negro in Charleston, S.C.," has observed that the mulatto segment of the free Negro population of Charleston emphasized the difference between themselves and darker slaves or free Negroes. They formed an exclusive social and fraternal organization called the Brown Fellowship Society; qualifications for membership were that one be free, light-skinned, economically independent, and "devoted to the basic tenets of the social system." The excluded Negroes of dark color formed a rival society named the "Society of Free Dark Men," headed by Thomas Small, a carpenter who owned eleven slaves. William Tiler Johnson, a mulatto barber of Natchez, Mississippi, seems also to have been strongly influenced by the colored caste system, for he never attended "darkey parties, dances," or other social occasions, and apparently did not mingle socially with the slaves. An elderly planter and doctor of Greenville, South Carolina, told John William De Forest, the Freedmen's Bureau agent stationed there, that he had only once flogged a slave, but the cause for this unique occasion throws a sombre light on "the peculiar institution" and on the Negro caste system. After his slave girl, Julia, had borne a mulatto baby, she defied his command to take a Negro husband, declaring, "Doctor, I've had one white man's child. I'm never going to have no black man's child." Moreover, in referring to each other, the slaves often used the term "Nigger," a designation employed by the lower class whites but not generally by planters of good breeding. . . . The average slave could not overcome the handicaps of human bondage, which warped his mind, and personality into what Ulrich B. Phillips, the eminent student of American Negro slavery, has described as "a standard plantation type." The slave was constantly accommodating himself to the pressures of an authoritarian society. Although the Negro was noted for his loud guffaw, which seemed to indicate an uninhibited sense of humor and a relaxed personality, there was another kind of laugh characteristic of the slave—a nervous laugh of ingratiation when he felt embarrassed in the presence of the white man. After the Civil War the northern journalist Edward King visited a cotton plantation in Louisiana when a delegation of humble field hands came to see the master. "If I looked at them steadily," he wrote, "they burst into uneasy laughter and moved away." So common was this physical manifestation that he called it "the regulation laugh." He found the country Negroes diffident in expressing opinions before the white man. The sense of inferiority and insecurity, induced in part at least by the over-lordship of the white man, seems to have been mainly responsible also for the shuffling gait, the slouching posture, and the downcast look in speaking to white men. Moreover the stuttering that advertisements for runaway slaves often mentioned probably resulted from this same sense of inferiority and insecurity.

Southern slavery, a modern student has observed, had much the same effect on the Negro's personality as confinement for a considerable period in a German concentration camp of World War II had on white prisoners. It tended to produce a Sambo type of personality, reducing its subjects to a child-like behavior—submissive, irresponsible, living from day to day.

[Accounts of a Southern Plantation] John Spencer Bassett*

We must not forget . . . that an important part of the problem [of over-seeing a plantation] was the negro himself. A fundamental part of the slave problem was the negro problem. The African slaves were close to savagery. They were to learn much in the process of forced labor and they learned it very slowly. The finer feelings of advanced peoples were not for them. They had not developed such feelings in Africa—they could not be expected to acquire them in American slavery in one, two, or five generations. For them uplift was a thing that could only come gradually and painfully. The first generations died in order that those who came afterwards might make a slow and meager advance in culture.

Of course there were exceptions among the slaves such as the black-smith Harry. . . . Harry presents himself to our view as a man of great faithfulness. For thirty years and a half, he tells us, he had stood over the anvil. He had hammered out the tools with which his companions in slavery had dug riches out of the soil for the benefit of the master. Eleven children he had given to his owner, he and his wife, all representing wealth and the power to create more wealth. He did not rebel against his lot. To [James Knox] Polk he sent his loyal respect, to his old mistress he sent the cheering words, "Yours till death." Few men could offer a richer tribute. Slavery gave him the opportunity of manifesting an admirable spirit of faithfulness.

On the other hand is Eva, whom the overseers persistently called "Evy." We are not told in any letter who was her husband but it is well

---

*Reprinted, with permission, from *The Southern Plantation Overseer As Revealed in His Letters* (Northampton, Mass.: Smith College, 1925), 264–67, 128–33, 136–37, 139, 190–91, 200, 202, 204–5. Copyright by the Trustees of Smith College. Faulkner owned a copy of this book and may have consulted it when composing the ledger accounts for the McCaslin plantation cited in part 4 of "The Bear" in *Go Down, Moses*. This Mississippi plantation belonged to James Knox Polk.

established that she was a fertile breeder. She was not able to raise her children. The overseer said that she did not have any luck in rearing or in keeping her offspring alive. What they died of we are not told. The statement is quite bare: Evy's child died last week or last night, that is all. But we may judge that a controlling cause was her inefficiency in taking care of them. Perhaps she did not feel much interest in their health. They were not hers, but her Master's. Why should she be interested in taking care of master's negroes? Here was mother love at a low ebb. Here was the inability to realize what was good for the child. Fortunately not all slave women were indifferent on this point.

Another thing about these letters that seems significant is the infrequent mention of deaths among the adult slaves. It has often been asserted that slaves were worked so hard in the Gulf State that they died rapidly, the master consoling himself that it was more profitable to work them hard and replace by purchase. It has also been said that this habit was especially pronounced on plantations under the sole control of overseers. If the assertion were well founded it ought to be supported by occurrences on Polk's Mississippi plantation. So far as the evidence in the letters . . . goes the assertion is erroneous. Deaths of infant slaves were common. In all the letters running from 1835 to 1858 there is mention of very few deaths of adult slaves. In fact, a larger proportion of the overseers died on the plantation than of the slaves.

Two facts should, however, be mentioned as serving to modify the weight of my statement. One is the incompleteness of the series of letters. It is possible that more adult slaves died and that the overseer reported the deaths to the employer in letters not now preserved. On the other hand, the gaps in the correspondence are long, the longest being for the four years of Polk's service as president of the United States. And by the same token there are long periods during which the letters preserved are fairly complete. By the law of probability we may expect that the condition affecting life and death would be the same for the first of these periods as for the second. On that basis it is safe to say that the death rate of adults on the plantation was low.

Another thing bearing on the argument is the fact that the group of men and women taken to the plantation in 1835 was composed of young and healthy slaves, selected for the purpose. Undoubtedly such persons could be expected to have a low death rate. That is what could have been expected and that is what resulted. But the argument against which I am protesting is that the slaves were worked so hard that they broke down and died, and if it were true we might expect that Polk's slaves would have broken down whether young people or not. The argument had it that the work was severe enough to break the strength of young and strong men. As to old or weak workingmen, a large per cent of them continually break down in free labor.

To support the old assertion attention was called to the steady carrying of slaves into the gulf region from the older parts of the South. It was said that they went to replace those whom slavery had killed by hard labor. That there was a constant movement of slaves from the upper to the lower section of the South is undoubted; but it is sufficiently explained by the enlargement of the arable acreage in that region. Occurrences on Polk's plantation amply bear out this assertion. In 1839 the cleared land amounted to 271 acres, in 1842 it was 374 acres and in 1851 it was 566 acres. To cultivate this enlarged area required more slaves than could be supplied by the growing of young slaves into the age for working on the fields. What was happening on Polk's plantation was happening on a great many others.

Moreover, during the period covered by these letters there was in this part of the South a constant enlargement of the cultivated area through the taking up of land from the state. After the Choctaw, Chickasaw, and Creek Indians surrendered their ample lands in 1830, 1832, and 1833 respectively and moved to the region which became known as Indian Territory, the lands they had formerly occupied were put on the market. The best were seized on quickly. The patents for Polk's plantation, which he bought from the patentee, were dated October 31, 1833, and it was only a year and one month later that Polk paid ten dollars an acre for the land. After the first years of enthusiasm in which the best land was taken up there remained a large amount of less fertile ungranted land which came more slowly into private hands. As it was taken up gradually through the next twenty-five years there was an enlarging demand for slaves to work it. Probably it would not be as vigorous a demand as the size of the newly granted acreage would seem to imply; for the poorer land fell to the poorer men who did not use slaves to the same extent as the large planters. But they used a certain number and as they prospered they were sure to buy more slaves.

[LETTERS TO POLK FROM JOHN I. GARNER]

[3 November 1839]

DEAR SIR:

I take my pen in hand to say something of the affares of your plantation in yalabusha county I shold have written to you sooner had it not bin for a hurt that I receive in the wriste from the fawl of a mule. We are enjoying the best of helth at presant bothe my famaly and the negrows are entirely helthey and I think we are getting along verry wel a saving the crop I have seventy fore bales of cotton packed fifty fore of them delivered to Chisholm and Winter and I think a nofe picked out to make something about one hundred foour hundred pound bales, and I think if the weather continues good until chrismos I can have 125 bales of cotton packed and delivered to troy your crop of cotton is turning out fare better than I though when I came here I will ceep your cotton halled off as fast as I pack it I cant say how many bales you will make but I think the wrise of 125 bales I have stoped picking at this time for the purpose of gethering the corne Mr. Tranum and myself thought perhaps it wold make fore hundred Barrels of corne I have gethered a little part of it and think wil hardley gow that mutch I can give you a purty corect noledge in my next letter we also made an estimate of the cuantaty of porke made we estimade it at 4500 lbs. we thought 6000 lbs wold bee little a nuf to serve the plase there is a fine chance of shoats here for the next yeare if they have any attention to them. The Boy charls you sent down last spring run away some fore weeks agow witheout any cause whatever I think he has goun back to tennessee where his wife is I am pestered withe mareners conduct stroling over the contery and corect her she goes to sqr Mcneal for protection with them exceptions we are dwoing wel the negrows you last sent down apere to dwo very wel the boy allen apere to bee weakly at this time he says caused from a mans stabbing him before you bought him. I havent yet put my hogs up to fatten bin weighting for rain to put them up they wold bee in a bed of dust if it donte rain soon I must tri them up as they are to fatten with corn entirely I will conclude by saying your directions shal bee punctialy attended two.

Yours respectfully

[23 November 1839]

DEAR SIR:
      After my respects to you I wil inform you that we are all wel at presant bothe my famaly and the negrows   Phil got his hand caught in the gin a few days after I wrote to you   cut his hand very bad but has got very near wel   I have not yet herd anything of charles   I have cept a lookout for him and wil continue so to dwo   the boy allen has aperently not bin able for hard servis sence he has bin here and I believe caused from the wond which he received in the side before he came here [I got] Mr. Walker to look at him a few days a gow and he thought with myself that it wold not dwo to put him to hard work yet
      I have gethered the crop of corn and agreable to the waggon I hald the corn in there is three hundred and fifty barrels of corn fel shorter than myself and Mr Tranum estimated   I have packed 102 bales of cotton them weighing 41,993 lbs, making 410 lbs. and something over to the bales, and I think there will bee thirty bales more, twenty five at least
      N.B. I think if I have luck I shal make 4500 or 5000 lbs of pork I have forty hogs fatning and a plenty of young hogs for the next year. I have agreed with sqr Mcneel for the next year for this place and I shold like for you to bee at your plantation as soon as convenient after chrismos as I wold like to have your advise on sertin things. your friends here speak if this beeing a sickly place from some cause and speek of its beeing proper to moove the cabins to some other point convenient to the farm I have omited stating how many bales delivered to Troy 84 of them delivered and three days more I wil deliver the others

Yours respectfuly

[24 December 1839]

DEAR SIR:

I received your letter a few days agow dated the 14th of november my famaly was not in a condishun to live to gow to Troy to lern whather or not the inshurence was affected or not Mr. Chisholm and Minter agent in troy informed mee that all cotton is inshured unless a man says not inshured there is open polacy to that affect and they wrote to your comisheon merchant in new Orleans to inshure it as a speticial contract that it should bee inshured certain I intended saying to you in my last letter that myself and sqr Mcneel, had agreed for another yeare it was neglect in mee that I sayd nothing about it I persume you have received a letter from sqr Mcneel before this time to that affect N. B. Charles came in the 5th of December and the ballance of the negros ar well and we have got 130 bales packed and I will get done in some fore or five days more picking I have kiled three thousand nine hundred lbs of pork and have nine hogs to cil yet nothing more at presant

Yors respectifuly

The escape of Charles to the woods had caused James K. Polk much concern, and he wrote to his brother, William H. Polk, to make inquiries for the man around Columbia and in the region where Charles had been born and brought up. William's reply gives us an idea of what migrations had been made by Charles in his brief existence. In connection with other letters in this collection it also has a bearing on the contention so often made by some Southerners that nobody sold his slaves unless they were "bad negroese." While these letters do not show that Polk sold his "good" slaves they do show that he was continually buying slaves, which means that someone else was selling them. The letter of William H. Polk to James K. Polk about Charles was written from Columbia, December 30, 1839, and runs as follows:

DEAR BROTHER:

I have been delayed in answering your Letter, by not being able to see Mr. John L. Smith and obtain, the information which you requested in your letter, relative to your negro Boy *Charles.* I this day, saw Mr. Smith, and he informed me that your Boy, the year you bought him was hired to Mr. Hatch Esq and would refer you to a Mr. Dickerson the son-in-law of Capt. Jones as a person who is well acquainted with the Negro. Also Matthew Rhea and Mr. Fain. That the Mother and family connexion of Charles belong to the family of Cox's near Cornersville. I will in the course of ten days, ride up to that Neighborhood, and endeavour to catch him, if he is there, though Smith is of opinion, that he is still in or about Somerville.

My circumstances are such at this time, that I cannot afford to buy *Reuben* at any price for *cash.* But if it would suit you I am willing to give the *last note* which you owe me, which note amounts to one thousand and eighty three dollars. That is more than your cash price and the interest, which would amount to $1062. If you are willing to accept this proposition, you must let me know in a day or two. Reuben informs me that you give him the privilege, if I do not buy him, of being hired at this place, if he could find anyone who would give a fair price for him. he informed [me] late this evening, that Mr. Fisher the Druggist, was willing to give $130 for him next year. That is a fair price for him according to the rates at which negroes are hiring here. I would like to have Reuben, and I think the price which I offer is a very fair one, though it may not suit your *present necessities.* . . . . . .

These necessities had not been met a year later, and William was again urged to sell one of Polk's slaves to get money. The reply of William, December 4, 1840, in part is as follows:

DEAR SIR:

Having been unable to see Genl. Pillow until today, I could not answer your letter with the required information concerning Herbert at the time you requested. I conversed with him and Mr. Young today, they looked at Herbert, but would make no definite offer, further than that they would give six hundred dollars cash for him. I informed them that you would not under any circumstances take $600. They then informed me that they would probably give $650 cash. I of course refused it—though that is the price now given for likely negro fellows—until I could write to you and ascertain what you would do. For cash I do not think he can be sold for more, there being so few persons who desire to buy negroes. . . . .

[Ed. note: *As a consequence of the panic of 1837, Polk attempted to sell some of his slaves, enlisting the aid of Albert T. McNeal of Coffeeville, Mississippi. His reply of 15 January 1840 runs as follows:*]

DEAR SIR:

I acknowledge the receipt of your favour of the 1st inst. postmarked the 5th and also that of the 5th inst. which came to hand by last night's mail. I wrote to you from Holly Springs early in December, and on my return to Coffeeville from that place learned that Charles had come in. I did not advise you of his return learning that Garner had written about that time, and shortly afterwards I visited Bolivar, Te., and reached Home again on the 8th Inst. I fear I shall not be able to sell Charles. It is a very unfavourable time for a cash sale. Money is extremely scarce and I have never in my life witnessed "such screwing and twisting"[1] to get it. Charles ought to bring $750 or $800, cash. But few men have money, and those who have it, will be disposed to hold on with the expectation of buying negroes low for cash at sheriffs sales before and at the Spring term of the approaching circuit courts. In consequence of low waters the planters have not been able to ship their cotton, nor have they found a merket at Home. I have not the least doubt that you might sell Charles for good Mississippi funds in Fayette Co., Te., at a better price than I can get here, and as it is probable I may fail to sell him here you might in the mean time sell him there to some one who may know the boy with the understanding that it shall be no contract in the event of a sale here, which is not probable. I saw Mr. Garner today. All are well at the plantation, Addison however in the woods. Garner, as instructed, is clearing more land. Your crop of cotton (136 bales) is at Troy, ready for the first rise in the river.

Carroll County lies immediately south of this county and I practice law there. The first time I visit that county I will see Mr. Hamon and get his note with security as desired. Mr. Hamon ought to give you about $400 a year for Harry, possibly I may be able to get more. A boy of his age and such as you describe ought I think to be worth $1200. The time has been when he would have sold for $2000 here. If Harry be the same blacksmith, who worked at the Caldwell place 5 miles from Columbia, then owned by Uncle Sam Polk, I remember him *well* (tall and muscular) though some 18 years have elapsed since I saw him, and my recollection admonishes me that I am fast growing an old bachelor. . . . .

P.S. I will visit the plantation Sunday and probably we may determine to remove the buildings, etc.

[John I. Garner to Polk, 3 May 1840]

DEAR SIR:

After my respects to you I will inform you that we are all wel with the exception of the girl matilda she had child some ten days a gow and is grunting yet, nothing serious her child died after some ten or twelve hours, from what cause I dont now she has not worked more than half her time cence you was here N. B. we are getting along very wel with our crop taking the whether into consideration it has been raining near half the time sence you left but I am in hopes from the presant apearence we wil have some good wether. I believe I have as good a crop of cotton as I ever saw for the time a year. I will git over hit with my hoes in a few days. my fored [forward] corn is indiferent owing to the wrain it being on wet low land. I have to plow when the mules wold mier to the nees in places and of course it cant look wel.

Yours respectifuly

Note

1. The state of the currency in Tennessee at this time is shown in the following memorandum, preserved in the Polk MSS., dated June 5, 1839, and signed by Wm. H. Polk.

"Due Richard B. Moore, one hundred and forty-five dollars, sixty Mobile, Ala., fifty Tuskaloosa, fifteen Decatur, five Montgomery, five Huntsville, and ten Tennessee, for value received.

"Recd. on this note by the hands of James Walker one hundred dollars in huntsville money. July the 2d, 1839."

[A Slave among Slaves]   Booker T. Washington*

I was born in a typical log cabin, about fourteen by sixteen feet square. In this cabin I lived with my mother and a brother and sister till after the Civil War, when we were all declared free.

Of my ancestry I know almost nothing. In the slave quarters, and even later, I heard whispered conversations among the coloured people of the tortures which the slaves, including, no doubt, my ancestors on my mother's side, suffered in the middle passage of the slave ship while being conveyed from Africa to America. I have been unsuccessful in securing any information that would throw any accurate light upon the history of my family beyond my mother. She, I remember, had a half-brother and a half-sister. In the days of slavery not very much attention was given to family history and family records—that is, black family records. My mother, I suppose, attracted the attention of a purchaser who was afterward my owner and hers. Her addition to the slave family attracted about as much attention as the purchase of a new horse or cow. Of my father I know even less than my mother. I do not even know his name. I have heard reports to the effect that he was a white man who lived on one of the near-by plantations. Whoever he was, I never heard of his taking the least interest in me or providing in any way for my rearing. But I do not find especial fault with him. He was simply another unfortunate victim of the institution which the Nation unhappily had engrafted upon it at that time.

The cabin was not only our living-place, but was also used as the kitchen for the plantation. My mother was the plantation cook. The cabin was without glass windows; it had only openings in the side which let in the light, and also the cold, chilly air of winter. There was a door to the cabin—that is, something that was called a door—but the uncertain hinges by which it was hung, and the large cracks in it, to say nothing of the fact that it was too small, made the room a very uncomfortable one. . . . There was no cooking-stove on our plantation, and all the cooking for the whites and slaves my mother had to do over an open fireplace, mostly in pots and "skillets." While the poorly built cabin caused us to suffer with cold in the winter, the heat from the open fireplace in summer was equally trying.

The early years of my life, which were spent in the little cabin, were not very different from those of thousands of other slaves. My mother, of course, had little time in which to give attention to the training of her children during the day. She snatched a few moments for our care in the early morning before her work began, and at night after the day's work was done. One of my earliest recollections is that of my mother cooking a chicken late at night, and awakening her children for the purpose of feeding them. How or where she got it I do not know. I presume, however, it was procured from our owner's farm. Some people may call this theft. If such a thing were to

---

*From *Up from Slavery: An Autobiography* (New York: A. L. Burt, Co., 1900), 1–5, 9, 35.

happen now, I should condemn it as theft myself. But taking place at the time it did, and for the reason that it did, no one could ever make me believe that my mother was guilty of thieving. She was simply a victim of the system of slavery. I cannot remember having slept in a bed until after our family was declared free by the Emancipation Proclamation. Three children—John, my older brother, Amanda, my sister, and myself—had a pallet on the dirt floor, or, to be more correct, we slept in and on a bundle of filthy rags laid upon the dirt floor. . . .

I cannot remember a single instance during my childhood or early boyhood when our entire family sat down to the table together, and God's blessing was asked, and the family ate a meal in a civilized manner. On the plantation in Virginia, and even later, meals were gotten by the children very much as dumb animals get theirs. It was a piece of bread here and a scrap of meat there. It was a cup of milk at one time and some potatoes at another. Sometimes a portion of our family would eat out of the skillet or pot, while some one else would eat from a tin plate held on the knees, and often using nothing but the hands with which to hold the food. When I had grown to sufficient size, I was required to go to the "big house" at meal-times to fan the flies from the table by means of a large set of paper fans operated by a pulley. . . .

More than once I have tried to picture myself in the position of a boy or man with an honoured and distinguished ancestry which I could trace back through a period of hundreds of years, and who had not only inherited a name, but fortune and a proud family homestead; and yet I have sometimes had the feeling that if I had inherited these, and had been a member of a more popular race, I should have been inclined to yield to the temptation of depending upon my ancestry and my colour to do that for me which I should do for myself. Years ago I resolved that because I had no ancestry myself I would leave a record of which my children would be proud, and which might encourage them to still higher effort.

The Negro in Mississippi, 1865–1890
Vernon Lane Wharton*

[LYNCHING]

It is impossible to make any estimate of the number of individual Negroes lynched or murdered by whites during the period. Such matters attracted little or no attention in the press. When reported at all, they were

*Reprinted with permission from *The Negro in Mississippi, 1865–1890* (Chapel Hill, N.C.: University of North Carolina Press, 1947), 224–33.

generally given a line or two in very small type in the "Mississippi Brevities" or "Miscellaneous Items" columns of the papers. In one such column in 1881, the *Clarion* mentioned in passing the unprovoked murder of two Negroes and the lynching of two others.[1] The *Gazette* managed to get five lynchings into one line of type which was almost too small to be read: "Four negroes were lynched at Grenada last week; also one at Oxford."[2] Although there were numerous reports of the murders of Negroes by whites, for causes ranging from insolence to assault, indictment in such cases was almost unknown. There are a few records of jail or prison sentences for such murders, but there seems to have been no single instance throughout the period in which a white man was hanged for killing a Negro.

The first case after the war involving the lynching of a Negro for the rape of a white woman was probably one in Oktibbeha County in the summer of 1865. Upon the receipt of a payment of two hundred dollars, the captain of a troop of Federal soldiers stationed in the county allowed the Negro to be run to death by hounds.[3] There seems to have been an almost universal agreement throughout the period that death by lynching was to be the punishment for either rape or attempted rape. There was a fairly uniform number of such occurrences each year, with a distinct increase in the violent years of 1874 and 1875. There also seems to have been a general understanding that a Negro who murdered a white was to be lynched; to this rule there were few, if any, exceptions. The fact that lynching was considered to be preeminently the punishment for rape and murder did not prevent its use in a wide variety of circumstances. There were reports of Negroes lynched for assault, robbery, being in a woman's room at night, insulting a woman, burning gins, burning barns, stealing hogs, renting land, participating in politics, and robbing a grave to obtain material for a "charm bag."[4] In many cases the crime involved was unknown or not reported.

Not all of the extra-legal executions of the period involved the lynching of Negroes by whites. During 1866, a number of white men in the eastern portion of the state were punished in this fashion for stealing horses.[5] The few occurrences of this type in later years involved rape, attempted rape, or murder.[6] There were also a few cases in which Negroes, usually urged on by whites, lynched members of their own race.[7] Such incidents, however, were so rare as to have little significance. Essentially lynching was recognized as one of the methods of control which were to be used by the dominant race in its relations with the Negroes.

During the greater part of the period, there was little open criticism of lynching as an institution. It was defended, and even applauded, by the press. As late as 1889, the editor of the *Gazette* argued that the people would be justified in lynching insane Negroes, who, kept in county jails because there was no place for them at the asylum, proved to be nuisances and noise makers.[9] The public attitude was most clearly revealed in a case in Jefferson County in 1884. A Negro suspected of attempting the rape of a girl three years old was delivered to the sheriff by the girl's father and finally was carried to the jail in Hinds County for safe-keeping. There was an immediate storm of protest, and citizens gathered in a mass meeting near the scene of the supposed crime. The sheriff, thoroughly alarmed, tried to shift the blame to the public. They had been negligent in allowing the Negro to come into his hands. Even after this occurred, he had given them every possible opportunity to take the man away from him. It was only after four or five days in which they took no action that he, with the approval of the judge, had become convinced that the law and his duty required him to take the Negro out of the county. Public opinion turned even more strongly against the girl's father. Both a neighbor and the sheriff felt that it was necessary to defend him at length. His judgment had been swayed, they declared, by the pleas of a pregnant wife who was sick and extremely nervous.[10] The feeling of the citizens that their community and their county had been disgraced, the anxiety of the sheriff about his political office, and the concern of the father and his friends about his social position were all significant.

Although lynching continued to be upheld by the mass of the white population, some opposition to it was beginning to be heard by the end of the period. Early in 1889, the editor of the *Clarion-Ledger* suggested the mobs were going too far, and that the legislature ought to consider some means of checking them.[11] The editor of the Greenville *Times* agreed.[12] Early in the following year the strength of these convictions was put to the test. A Negro named Anthony Thomas was arrested in Hinds County for the murder of a white woman in Smith. On the order of Governor J. M. Stone, the sheriff in Hinds refused to deliver Thomas to deputies who came to carry him back to the scene of the crime. It was generally known that the deputies intended to allow him to be lynched. The Raymond *Gazette* defended the action of the Governor as intended to protect the good name of the state, but also took the attitude that the action was illegal.[13] The *Clarion-Ledger* joined in the half-hearted defense of the Governor, but printed in full a bitter attack on him taken from the New Orleans *Picayune*. Throughout the state, those papers friendly to the Governor gave him qualified support, while others generally based their attacks on the claim that he had exceeded his power.[14]

Governor Stone finally sent Thomas to Smith County with a company of militia for his protection. A newspaper account carried the statement, "There is not a man in the crowd but would enjoy helping to hang the negro, but at the same time they have a high sense of honor and duty, and will carry out their instructions to the letter."[15] Thomas was tried on May 2, and sentenced to be hanged on May 28. Immediately after the passage of the sentence, he was taken by a mob, but, after an appeal by the judge and other influential leaders, he was returned to the jailer. On the following day a meeting of citizens approved this action, and asked that the law be allowed to take its course.[16] It appears that this was done.

The importance of the Thomas case lay in the fact that it revealed a large number of whites who were opposed to lynching as a matter of principle, and who were willing to make public their attitude in a case where immediate passion had had time to cool. This group continued to grow in numbers and influence, and that growth has resulted in an encouragingly steady decline in the number of cases in which mob law is applied.

MISCEGENATION

Under the ante-bellum plantation system, there was naturally a certain amount of sexual relationship between some of the owners, their sons, and overseers and the female slaves. The situation was seldom openly discussed. With proper discretion, such indulgence apparently did not seriously affect the relations of the white participant with others of his own social group. Among the Negroes, the mistress of the master often occupied a highly respected and coveted position.

In general, the small farmers and poor whites were strongly opposed to the easy-going tolerance displayed by the planting and professional groups toward such relationships. This attitude was another expression of their lack of economic and social security, and of their determination to emphasize the difference between the Negroes and themselves. It was to this feeling that such leaders as A. G. Brown appealed most effectively in their successful efforts to enlist the support of the non-slaveholders in the campaign for secession. Freedom for slaves, they said, would inevitably mean social equality; Negroes would obtain white girls in marriage, and soon all racial distinction would be lost.[17]

These small-farmer and poor-white groups, who held a controlling influence over the legislature of 1865, took heed of their misgivings, and lost no time in writing into law their feelings on the question. A section of the Black Code, adopted in December, 1865, provided:

> ". . . it shall not be lawful for any freedman, free negro or mulatto to intermarry with any white person, nor for any white person to intermarry with any freedman, free negro or mulatto, and any person who shall so intermarry shall be deemed guilty of felony, and on conviction thereof shall be confined in the State penitentiary for life; and those shall be deemed freedman, free negroes and mulattoes who are of pure negro blood, and those descended from a negro to the third generation inclusive though one ancestor in each generation may have been a white person."[18]

Although it appears that a Northern white officer married a Negro woman in Vicksburg in January or February of 1866,[19] the first case under the law did not come up until June of that year. Ben***, a Negro who had been a soldier in the Federal army, married Mollie***, a white girl from Simpson County. A raid by county officers in the early hours of the morning of June 13 was followed by a trial of the couple before the circuit court. Found guilty, each was sentenced to serve six months in the county jail, and to pay a fine of five hundred dollars.[20]

Two months later, a Negro man and a young white woman from Leake

County endeavored to be married in Vicksburg. The girl, who was the daughter of the former owner of the Negro, declared that she desired to marry him because she loved him. Investigation revealed the fact that they had been having relations in defiance of the law, and the judge ordered that they be held for trial in the ensuing term of the criminal court.[21] It appears that the matter must have been hushed up in some fashion, as there is no further public record of the case. With the exception of the arrest in Vicksburg of a woman from Lauderdale County on the charge of cohabitation with a Negro,[22] there seems to have been no further application of the law.

The repeal by the legislature of 1870 of all laws involving racial discrimination was followed almost immediately by a case that attracted wide attention. A. T. Morgan, a cultured and formerly affluent planter from Ohio, who had been a member of the constitutional convention, was at the time a state senator, and later served as sheriff of Yazoo County, married a young octoroon teacher who had come down from New York. The state followed with interest the difficulties of their honeymoon journey, which included ejection from a bus in Louisville, Kentucky, and the printing of vulgar comments by Northern papers.[23] This marriage, the only one during the period which received wide attention, appears to have been happily maintained for many years after the couple left the state in 1876.

Another case which attracted some attention within the state was the marriage of Haskins Smith, mulatto member of the state legislature, to the daughter of the owner of the hotel in which Smith worked in Port Gibson. Although leading citizens of the community held Smith to be a good man and refused to be aroused over the matter, lower classes among the whites created a great deal of disturbance.[24] References to this marriage in a speech by a Negro in Vicksburg helped to bring about the overthrow of the Republican government in that city a little later in the summer.[25]

It is impossible to estimate how many interracial marriages occurred between more obscure people. It seems probable that there were not very many. Evidence that some did occur is offered by such small items as a passage in the diary of a pious Irish contractor in Claiborne County: "*Confirmation at Chadenel* I was discusted to see *Joe O Brian* as god father for Boys, he who has a lot of *Niger* Bastards & is now married to a ½ *Niger* wife What a scandle to me."[26]

The restoration of Democratic control in the state in 1876 was followed by a return of legal prohibition of intermarriage of the races. Such marriages were declared to be "incestuous [sic] and void," and the parties participating were made subject to the penalties for incest. These included a maximum term of ten years in prison. For the purposes of the act, a Negro was any person who had one-fourth or more of Negro blood.[27]

Very few opportunities were found for the application of the law. In 1883, a white man in Rankin County, who had formerly been fined for unlawful cohabitation with a Negro woman, persuaded a Negro preacher to marry them.[28] Although the newspaper report predicted that he would receive a sentence to prison, no further mention of his case is to be found. In 1885, a resident of Hinds County, charged with incest on the grounds of his marriage to a Negro woman, received the maximum sentence of ten years.[29]

The abolition of the possibilities of legal marriage, which in any case would have involved very few individuals, did not do away with concubinage and unlawful cohabitation. The matter received little public attention, but now and then legal complications or violent tragedies revealed its existence.[30] It appears, however, that such relationships became steadily less frequent as time went on. The racial code of the poor white came more and more to be that of the public at large.

JIM CROW LAWS

The determination of the mass of the whites to set up legal differences between the races was further demonstrated in the enactment in 1865 of the first "Jim Crow" law in the South. The few Negroes who traveled on public conveyances before the war had generally been directly in the service of their masters. There was little or no objection to their presence.[31] With the coming of freedom, all this was changed. Large numbers of the freedmen now took advantage of the opportunity to move about from place to place, and there can be no doubt that in the crowded cars the low standards of sanitation observed by most of them added greatly to objections based on racial difference. The better railroads immediately adopted the custom of refusing to Negroes admission to the first-class, or "ladies'" cars.[32] On smaller roads, which did not carry the two classes of cars, the freedmen, although they paid full fare, were relegated to old cars, freight cars, or open platforms.[33] The law approved by the Governor of the state in November, 1865, simply gave legality to a practice which the railroads had already adopted. According to its provisions it became unlawful for an employee of any railroad in the state to allow "any freedman, negro, or mulatto, to ride in any first class passenger cars, set apart, or used by, and for white persons. . . ." The law was not to apply to Negroes traveling with their mistresses in the capacity of nurses.[34] It is to be noticed that under this law those whites who were unable to pay first-class fares, or who did not choose to do so, continued to travel with the Negroes. White men also continued to use the second-class car for smoking, drinking, and impolite conversation. These circumstances not only led to racial difficulties, but also brought discomfort to the small number of cultured Negroes, of both sexes, who were forced to travel in such surroundings.[35] Although the law applied only to railroads, the principle which it recognized was followed on passenger boats, in theaters, and in a number of other places of public entertainment.[36]

With the assembly of the legislature in 1870, a number of the Negro members, especially Senators Robert Gleed and William Gray, set to work to prevent by law any discrimination against those of their race on public conveyances. After several disappointments, they succeeded in gaining enough votes from the reluctant white Republicans to secure the passage of such a law in June,[37] and to retain it in the revised code the following April.[38] The law provided that the right of any citizen to travel on any railroad, steamboat, other water craft, or stage coach was not to be denied or infringed. Any employee who refused that right, or who should "compel, or attempt to compel, any person or persons to occupy any particular seat, or any particular part" of such conveyances on account of race or color was made subject to a fine, a suit for damages by the person injured, and a term in the county jail.[39] In spite of its stringent provisions, the law had almost no effect. The captains of the river boats, the chief means of travel in the black counties, simply disregarded the law. On the trains, practically all of the Negroes, either from choice or economic necessity, continued to ride in the second-class cars.[40] A conductor in 1871 did not hesitate to ask James Lynch, secretary of state, to leave the "ladies' " car. Lynch immediately complied with the request.[41]

The failure of the general railroad act did not prevent efforts of the Negroes to extend its provisions in a civil rights bill in the next session of the legislature. After a great deal of argument, some chicanery, and much discomfort on the part of the white Republicans, this bill finally failed by one vote to gain the approval of the senate.[42] Renewed agitation in the following year finally gained its passage. In essence, it extended the provisions of the railroad act to cover hotels, inns, and theaters and other places of public amusement, and added to the penalties a requirement for the forfeiture of the charter of any corporation that violated the act.[43]

Early in the following year, a decision in a test case in Vicksburg exempted from the provisions of the act all those organizations save those which held a public charter.[44] Although a Supreme Court decision a little later in the year upheld the act in its limited sense,[45] it enjoyed little more success than its predecessors. Here and there a few Negroes braved public wrath by refusing to leave sections set apart for the other race,[46] but such cases were rare. Congressman John R. Lynch, requested to leave a white table in a railroad dining room at Holly Springs, retired without protest.[47]

By 1888, this working arrangement was not satisfactory to the white-line element of the hill counties which was rapidly increasing its influence in the state. The first- and second-class arrangement, with a practical white monopoly of the first-class accommodations, did not sufficiently emphasize racial differences. The result was the passage of "an act to promote the comfort of passengers on railroad trains." This ordered all railroads carrying passengers in the state to provide "equal but separate accommodations" for the races.[48] A few days later, a supplementary act made this regulation applicable to sleeping car companies "so far as practicable," and authorized the railroad commissioners to designate and provide, if deemed proper, separate waiting rooms for the sexes and the races.[49]

Since it was the determination of a large mass of the white population to apply a code of racial distinctions to all possible situations and places in which the races might be thrown together, it is apparent that the matter was not entirely a problem of law. The development of a ritual to be followed by whites and blacks under varying conditions was a slow and tedious process. In the early part of the period, most of the saloons served whites and Negroes at the same bar. Many of the restaurants, using separate tables, served both races in the same room. By 1890, such cases were practically unknown. On May 21, 1879, the Negroes of Jackson, after a parade of their fire company, gave a picnic in Hamilton Park. On the night of May 29, "the ladies of the Episcopal Church" used Hamilton Park for a *fete*.[50] After their picnic, the Negroes went to Angelo's Hall for a dance. The same hall was used for white dances and parties, and was frequently the gathering place of Democratic conventions. By 1890, both the park and the hall were closed to the Negroes. Throughout the state common cemeteries, usually in separate portions, held the graves of both whites and Negroes. In 1890, the city of Jackson, in line with a policy which was being adopted all over the state, established a new cemetery, and ruled that on and after January 1, 1891, all interments of Negroes should take place in it.[51]

Sidewalks, depot platforms, and promenades offered a more difficult problem. The code held that the Negro on a sidewalk must always give way to the white man, especially if the white was accompanied by a woman. "Jostling" sometimes led to beatings, shootings, or lynchings.[52] Negroes were warned to keep their distance and mind their language in public gathering places, or the citizens would "make a striking example of somebody."[53] Negroes at Natchez received instructions that of the promenades along the river, the bluff to the right of Main Street was "for the use of the whites, for ladies and children and nurses,—the central Bluff between Main Street and State for bachelors and the colored population, and the lower promenade for the whites." There was no law on the subject, but the people would see to it that the warning was heeded.[54] The question as to what streets were to be used by white and Negro children in their play also demanded attention.[55]

The Negro must also learn to be careful in his expression of an opinion, and to avoid unfavorable criticism of white people or white enterprises. In 1886, the Tougaloo *Quarterly* carried an article entitled "Life Incidents of One of Our Boys." Some of these incidents were not flattering to the white people from whose state treasury came money for the school. The president escaped censure by promising careful examination of all future material.[56] A "little popinjay didapper of a half coon who [had] learned to spell 'baker' at the expense of the tax-payers" wrote to a Negro paper in New Orleans letters which contained "several mischievous lies on the good people of Woodville and Wilkinson County." The editor of the *Clarion-Ledger* demanded that he be identified, strapped across a log, soundly whipped, and made to leave the county.[57]

Newspapers had their own peculiar problems. The Natchez *Courier* took Negro advertising;[58] the *Clarion* refused to handle it without a distinguishing label.[59] Some newspapers of the state carried formal notices of

Negro weddings, but the editor of the Hinds County *Gazette* would have none of them.[60] The name used for the race varied with circumstances, usually it was "the negroes," or "our laboring population." When a fusion ticket against Greenbackers or Populists was to be promoted, the terms were "the colored population," or "our colored citizens"; in times of bad feelings the expressions "niggers," "coons," "kullud pussons," and "blacks" were used. In normal times throughout a large part of the period, Negroes of prominence were given the title "Hon." or "Mr." by most of the papers of the state. By 1890, however, this usage had almost entirely disappeared.

Thus, within twenty-five years after the end of the war, a new code had come to replace the slave code of 1857. Few of its provisions could be found in the statute books. Its application was at times capricious and unpredictable. But, in general, members of both races understood and observed its content. In almost any conceivable contact with a white man, there were certain forms of behavior which the black man must observe. The Negro, at last, was "in his place."

Notes

1. Jackson *Weekly Clarion*, December 7, 1881.

2. Raymond *Gazette*, July 18, 1885.

3. Fred Z. Browne, *op. cit.*, XIII, 274.

4. Mississippi *Weekly Pilot*, November 19, 1870; Natchez *Daily Courier*, March 15, 1866; Hinds County *Gazette*, January 26, 1876, April 18, July 11, 1877, September 8, 1883, October 27, 1888; J. C. Brown, *op. cit.*, XII, 239, 240; E. F. Puckett, *op. cit.*, XI, 130; Ruth Watkins, "Reconstruction in Newton County," *P.M.H.S.*, XI, 216–217.

5. Natchez *Daily Courier*, February 21, March 15, July 26, 1866; Aberdeen *Examiner*, July 15, 1866.

6. Hinds County *Gazette*, April 27, 1870, June 7, 1884; Mississippi *Weekly Pilot*, August 14, 1875; Raymond *Gazette*, October 24, 1885, April 3, 1886.

7. Hinds County *Gazette*, August 11, 1875, August 24, 1881; Raymond *Gazette*, July 4, August 8, 1885.

8. Hinds County *Gazette*, January 26, February 9, 1876, July 23, 1879; Jackson *Weekly Clarion*, May 24, 1882.

9. Raymond *Gazette*, August 17, 1889.

10. Hinds County *Gazette*, June 7, 21, 1884.

11. Jackson *Clarion-Ledger*, February 28, 1889.

12. *Ibid.*, March 14, 1889, quoting the Greenville *Times*.

13. Raymond *Gazette*, March 22, 1890.

14. Jackson *Clarion-Ledger*, March 6, 13, 1890.

15. *Ibid.*, April 10, 1890.

16. Raymond *Gazette*, May 3, 1890; Port Gibson *Reveille*, May 2, 1890.

17. P. L. Rainwater, *Mississippi, Storm Center of Secession*, pp. 144–149.

18. Mississippi *Session Laws*, regular session, 1865, p. 82.

19. Natchez *Tri-Weekly Democrat*, February 24, 1866.

20. Jackson *Clarion and Standard*, June 14, 1866; Hinds County *Gazette*, June 22, 1866. It is impossible to explain this sentence in terms of the penalty provided by the law.

21. Natchez *Tri-Weekly Democrat*, August 21, 1866, quoting the Vicksburg *Herald*, August 14, 1866.

22. Jackson *Clarion*, August 26, 1866.

23. J. S. McNeily, "War and Reconstruction in Mississippi," *P.M.H.S.C.S.*, II, 403; Hinds County *Gazette*, August 17, 1870; Mississippi *Weekly Pilot*, November 26, 1870; A. T. Morgan, *Yazoo*, pp. 345–351.

24. *Senate Reports*, no. 527, 44th Congress, 1st session, pp. 159, 191–192.

25. *Ibid.*, pp. 1312–1313, 1367; J. S. McNeily, "Climax and Collapse of Reconstruction in Mississippi," *P.M.H.S.*, XII, 297.

26. Patrick Murphy, "Diary," vol. 16, Sunday, April 12, 1885, Patrick Murphy Papers.

27. Mississippi *Code*, 1880, sections 1145–1147. The constitution of 1890, like the law of 1865, classified as a Negro any person having one-eighth or more of Negro blood.

28. Jackson *Weekly Clarion*, January 24, 1883.

29. Raymond *Gazette*, August 1, 1885.

30. Hinds County *Gazette*, May 27, June 3, 24, September 2, 1874, August 25, 1880; Jackson *Weekly Clarion*, August 9, 1882; A. T. Morgan, *op. cit.*, pp. 494–495.

31. Jackson *Clarion*, February 18, 1866.

32. W. Reid, *After the War*, p. 421.

33. *Ibid.*, note, p. 386.

34. Mississippi *Session Laws*, 1865, p. 231.

35. Mississippi *Weekly Pilot*, May 15, 1870, August 31, 1872.

36. J. T. Trowbridge, *The South*, p. 352; Natchez *Tri-Weekly Democrat*, July 9, 1867.

37. Mississippi *Weekly Pilot*, May 15, 28, June 4, 1870; Jackson *Semi-Weekly Clarion*, June 10, 1870.

38. Jackson *Clarion*, April 14, 1871.

39. Mississippi *Revised Code*, 1871, sections 2731–2732.

40. J. S. McNeily, "War and Reconstruction in Mississippi," *P.M.H.S.C.S.*, II, 414–415.

41. Hinds County *Gazette*, January 25, 1871.

42. J. S. McNeily, "War and Reconstruction in Mississippi," *P.M.H.S.C.S.*, II, 431.

43. Mississippi *Session Laws*, 1873, pp. 66–69.

44. Hinds County *Gazette*, March 19, May 7, 1873; Vicksburg *Herald*, May 8, 1873.

45. Vicksburg *Times and Republican*, May 7, 1873; Gilbert Stephenson, *Race Distinctions in American Law*, p. 134.

46. Hinds County *Gazette*, February 11, 1874.

47. *Ibid.*, July 15, 1874.

48. Mississippi *Session Laws*, 1888, p. 48.

49. *Ibid.*, 1888, pp. 45–48.

50. Jackson *Weekly Clarion*, May 21, June 4, 1879.

51. Jackson *Clarion-Ledger*, January 1, 1891.

52. Vicksburg *Herald*, April 9, 1873; Hinds County *Gazette*, August 18, 1888; *Senate Miscellaneous Documents*, no. 166, 50th Congress, 1st session, pp. 88, 99, 170.

53. Hinds County *Gazette*, August 18, 1888.

54. Natchez *Daily Courier*, May 29, 1866.

55. Hinds County *Gazette*, March 8, 1871; Mississippi *Weekly Pilot*, March 23, 1871.

56. Jackson *Weekly Clarion*, June 16, 1886.

57. Jackson *Clarion-Ledger*, October 17, 1889.

58. Natchez *Daily Courier*, May 31, 1866.

59. Meridian *Clarion*, November 18, 1865.

60. Hinds County *Gazette*, March 9, 1866.

The Sheriff's Children   Charles W. Chesnutt*

Branson County, North Carolina, is in a sequestered district of one of the staidest and most conservative States of the Union. Society in Branson County is almost primitive in its simplicity. Most of the white people own the farms they till, and even before the war there were no very wealthy families to force their neighbors, by comparison, into the category of "poor whites."

To Branson County, as to most rural communities in the South, the war is the one historical event that overshadows all others. It is the era from which all local chronicles are dated,—births, deaths, marriages, storms, freshets. No description of the life of any Southern community would be perfect that failed to emphasize the all pervading influence of the great conflict.

Yet the fierce tide of war that had rushed through the cities and along the great highways of the country had comparatively speaking but slightly disturbed the sluggish current of life in this region, remote from railroads and navigable streams. To the north in Virginia, to the west in Tennessee, and all along the seaboard the war had raged; but the thunder of its cannon had not disturbed the echoes of Branson County, where the loudest sounds heard were the crack of some hunter's rifle, the baying of some deep-mouthed hound, or the yodel of some tuneful negro on his way through the pine forest. To the east, Sherman's army had passed on its march to the sea; but no straggling band of "bummers" had penetrated the confines of Branson County. The war, it is true, had robbed the county of the flower of its young manhood; but the burden of taxation, the doubt and uncertainty of the conflict, and the sting of ultimate defeat, had been borne by the people with an apathy that robbed misfortune of half its sharpness.

The nearest approach to town life afforded by Branson County is found in the little village of Troy, the county seat, a hamlet with a population of four or five hundred.

Ten years make little difference in the appearance of these remote Southern towns. If a railroad is built through one of them, it infuses some enterprise; the social corpse is galvanized by the fresh blood of civilization that pulses along the farthest ramifications of our great system of commercial

*Reprinted from *The Wife of His Youth and Other Stories of the Color Line* (Boston: Houghton, Mifflin & Co., 1899), 60–93.

highways. At the period of which I write, no railroad had come to Troy. If a traveler, accustomed to the bustling life of cities, could have ridden through Troy on a summer day, he might easily have fancied himself in a deserted village. Around him he would have seen weather-beaten houses, innocent of paint, the shingled roofs in many instances covered with a rich growth of moss. Here and there he would have met a razor-backed hog lazily rooting his way along the principal thoroughfare; and more than once he would probably have had to disturb the slumbers of some yellow dog, dozing away the hours in the ardent sunshine, and reluctantly yielding up his place in the middle of the dusty road.

On Saturdays the village presented a somewhat livelier appearance, and the shade trees around the court house square and along Front Street served as hitching-posts for a goodly number of horses and mules and stunted oxen, belonging to the farmer-folk who had come in to trade at the two or three local stores.

A murder was a rare event in Branson County. Every well-informed citizen could tell the number of homicides committed in the county for fifty years back, and whether the slayer, in any given instance, had escaped, either by flight or acquittal, or had suffered the penalty of the law. So, when it became known in Troy early one Friday morning in summer, about ten years after the war, that old Captain Walker, who had served in Mexico under Scott, and had left an arm on the field of Gettysburg, had been foully murdered during the night, there was intense excitement in the village. Business was practically suspended, and the citizens gathered in little groups to discuss the murder, and speculate upon the identity of the murderer. It transpired from testimony at the coroner's inquest, held during the morning, that a strange mulatto had been seen going in the direction of Captain Walker's house the night before, and had been met going away from Troy early Friday morning, by a farmer on his way to town. Other circumstances seemed to connect the stranger with the crime. The sheriff organized a posse to search for him, and early in the evening, when most of the citizens of Troy were at supper, the suspected man was brought in and lodged in the county jail.

By the following morning the news of the capture had spread to the farthest limits of the county. A much larger number of people than usual came to town that Saturday,—bearded men in straw hats and blue homespun shirts, and butternut trousers of great amplitude of material and vagueness of outline; women in homespun frocks and slat-bonnets, with faces as expressionless as the dreary sandhills which gave them a meagre sustenance.

The murder was almost the sole topic of conversation. A steady stream of curious observers visited the houses of mourning, and gazed upon the rugged face of the old veteran, now stiff and cold in death; and more than one eye dropped a tear at the remembrance of the cheery smile, and the joke—sometimes superannuated, generally feeble, but always good-natured—with which the captain had been wont to greet his acquaintances. There was a growing sentiment of anger among these stern men, toward the murderer who had thus cut down their friend, and a strong feeling that ordinary justice was too slight a punishment for such a crime.

Toward noon there was an informal gathering of citizens in Dan Tyson's store.

"I hear it 'lowed that Square Kyahtah's too sick ter hol' co'te this evenin'," said one, "an' that the purlim'nary hearin' 'll haf ter go over 'tel nex' week."

A look of disappointment went round the crowd.

"Hit 's the durndes', meanes' murder ever committed in this caounty," said another, with moody emphasis.

"I s'pose the nigger 'lowed the Cap'n had some greenbacks," observed a third speaker.

"The Cap'n," said another, with an air of superior information, "has left two bairls of Confedrit money, which he 'spected 'ud be good some day er nuther."

This statement gave rise to a discussion of the speculative value of Confederate money; but in a little while the conversation returned to the murder.

"Hangin' air too good fer the murderer," said one; "he oughter be burnt, stidier bein' hung."

There was an impressive pause at this point, during which a jug of moonlight whiskey went the round of the crowd.

"Well," said a round-shouldered farmer, who, in spite of his peaceable expression and faded gray eye, was known to have been one of the most daring followers of a rebel guerrilla chieftain, "what air yer gwine ter do about it? Ef you fellers air gwine ter set down an' let a wuthless nigger kill the bes' white man in Branson, an' not say nuthin' ner do nuthin', *I'll* move outen the caounty."

This speech gave tone and direction to the rest of the conversation. Whether the fear of losing the round-shouldered farmer operated to bring about the result or not is immaterial to this narrative; but, at all events, the crowd decided to lynch the negro. They agreed that this was the least that could be done to avenge the death of their murdered friend, and that it was a becoming way in which to honor his memory. They had some vague notions of the majesty of the law and the rights of the citizen, but in the passion of the moment these sunk into oblivion; a white man had been killed by a negro.

"The Cap'n was an ole sodger," said one of his friends solemnly. "He'll sleep better when he knows that a co'te-martial has be'n hilt an' jestice done."

By agreement the lynchers were to meet at Tyson's store at five o'clock in the afternoon, and proceed thence to the jail, which was situated down the Lumberton Dirt Road (as the old turnpike antedating the plank-road was called), about half a mile south of the court-house. When the preliminaries of the lynching had been arranged, and a committee appointed to manage the affair, the crowd dispersed, some to go to their dinners, and some to secure recruits for the lynching party.

It was twenty minutes to five o'clock, when an excited negro, panting and perspiring, rushed up to the back door of Sheriff Campbell's dwelling, which stood a little distance from the jail and somewhat farther from the latter building than from the court-house. A turbaned colored woman came to the door in response to the negro's knock.

"Hoddy, Sis' Nance."

"Hoddy, Brer Sam."

"Is de shurff in," inquired the negro.

"Yas, Brer Sam, he's eatin' his dinner," was the answer.

"Will yer ax 'im ter step ter de do' a minute, Sis' Nance?"

The woman went into the dining-room, and a moment later the sheriff came to the door. He was a tall, muscular man, of a ruddier complexion than is usual among Southerners. A pair of keen, deep-set gray eyes looked out from under bushy eyebrows, and about his mouth was a masterful expression, which a full beard, once sandy in color, but now profusely sprinkled with gray, could not entirely conceal. The day was hot; the sheriff had discarded his coat and vest, and had his white shirt open at the throat.

"What do you want, Sam?" he inquired of the negro, who stood hat in hand, wiping the moisture from his face with a ragged shirt-sleeve.

"Shurff, dey gwine ter hang de pris'ner w'at's lock' up in de jail. Dey're comin' dis a-way now. I wuz layin' down on a sack er corn down at de sto', behine a pile er flour-bairls, w'en I hearn Doc' Cain en Kunnel Wright talkin' erbout it. I slip' outen de back do', en run here as fas' as I could. I hearn you say down ter de sto' once't dat you would n't let nobody take a pris'ner 'way fum you widout walkin' over yo' dead body, en I thought I'd let you know 'fo' dey come, so yer could pertec' de pris'ner."

The sheriff listened calmly, but his face grew firmer, and a determined gleam lit up his gray eyes. His frame grew more erect, and he unconsciously assumed the attitude of a soldier who momentarily expects to meet the enemy face to face.

"Much obliged, Sam," he answered. "I'll protect the prisoner. Who's coming?"

"I dunno who-all *is* comin'," replied the negro. "Dere's Mistah McSwayne, en Doc' Cain, en Maje' McDonal', en Kunnel Wright, en a heap er yuthers. I wuz so skeered I done furgot mo' d'n half un em. I spec' dey mus' be mos' here by dis time, so I'll git outen de way fer I don' want nobody fer ter think I wuz mix' up in dis business." The negro glanced nervously down the road toward the town, and made a movement as if to go away.

"Won't you have some dinner first?" asked the sheriff.

The negro looked longingly in at the open door, and sniffed the appetizing odor of boiled pork and collards.

"I ain't got no time fer ter tarry, Shurff," he said, "but Sis' Nance mought gin me sump'n I could kyar in my han' en eat on de way."

A moment later Nancy brought him a huge sandwich of split corn-pone, with a thick slice of fat bacon inserted between the halves, and a couple of baked yams. The negro hastily replaced his ragged hat on his head, dropped the yams in the pocket of his capacious trousers, and, taking the sandwich in his hand, hurried across the road and disappeared in the woods beyond.

The sheriff reëntered the house, and put on his coat and hat. He then took down a double-barreled shotgun and loaded it with buckshot. Filling the chambers of a revolver with fresh cartridges, he slipped it into the pocket of the sack-coat which he wore.

A comely young woman in a calico dress watched these proceedings with anxious surprise.

"Where are you going, father?" she asked. She had not heard the conversation with the negro.

"I am goin' over to the jail," responded the sheriff. "There's a mob comin' this way to lynch the nigger we've got locked up. But they won't do it," he added, with emphasis.

"Oh, father! don't go!" pleaded the girl, clinging to his arm; "they'll shoot you if you don't give him up."

"You never mind me, Polly," said her father reassuringly, as he gently unclasped her hands from his arm. "I'll take care of myself and the prisoner, too. There ain't a man in Branson County that would shoot me. Besides, I have faced fire too often to be scared away from my duty. You keep close in the house," he continued, "and if anyone disturbs you just use the old horse-pistol in the top bureau drawer. It's a little old-fashioned, but it did good work a few years ago."

The young girl shuddered at this sanguinary allusion, but made no further objection to her father's departure.

The sheriff of Branson was a man far above the average of the community in wealth, education, and social position. His had been one of the few families in the county that before the war had owned large estates and numerous slaves. He had graduated at the State University at Chapel Hill, and had kept up some acquaintance with current literature and advanced thought. He had traveled some in his youth, and was looked up to in the county as an authority on all subjects connected with the outer world. At first an ardent supporter of the Union, he had opposed the secession movement in his native State as long as opposition availed to stem the tide of public opinion. Yielding at last to the force of circumstances, he had entered the Confederate service rather late in the war, and served with distinction through several campaigns, rising in time to the rank of colonel. After the war he had taken the oath of allegiance, and had been chosen by the people as the most available candidate for the office of sheriff, to which he had been elected without opposition. He had filled the office for several terms, and was universally popular with his constituents.

Colonel or Sheriff Campbell, as he was indifferently called, as the military or civil title happened to be most important in the opinion of the person addressing him, had a high sense of the responsibility attaching to his office. He had sworn to do his duty faithfully, and he knew what his duty was, as sheriff, perhaps more clearly than he had apprehended it in other passages of his life. It was, therefore, with no uncertainty in regard to his course that he prepared his weapons and went over to the jail. He had no fears for Polly's safety.

The sheriff had just locked the heavy front door of the jail behind him when a half dozen horsemen, followed by a crowd of men on foot, came round a bend in the road and drew near the jail. They halted in front of the picket fence that surrounded the building, while several of the committee of arrangements rode on a few rods farther to the sheriff's house. One of them dismounted and rapped on the door with his riding-whip.

"Is the sheriff at home?" he inquired.

"No, he has just gone out," replied Polly, who had come to the door.

"We want the jail keys," he continued.

"They are not here," said Polly. "The sheriff has them himself." Then she added, with assumed indifference, "He is at the jail now."

The man turned away, and Polly went into the front room, from which she peered anxiously between the slats of the green blinds of a window that looked toward the jail. Meanwhile the messenger returned to his companions and announced his discovery. It looked as though the sheriff had learned of their design and was preparing to resist it.

One of them stepped forward and rapped on the jail door.

"Well, what is it?" said the sheriff, from within.

"We want to talk to you, Sheriff," replied the spokesman.

There was a little wicket in the door; this the sheriff opened, and answered through it.

"All right boys, talk away. You are all strangers to me, and I don't know what business you can have." The sheriff did not think it necessary to recognize anybody in particular on such an occasion; the question of identity sometimes comes up in the investigation of these extra-judicial executions.

"We're a committee of citizens and we want to get into the jail."

"What for? It ain't much trouble to get into jail. Most people want to keep out."

The mob was in no humor to appreciate a joke, and the sheriff's witticism fell dead upon an unresponsive audience.

"We want to have a talk with the nigger that killed Cap'n Walker."

"You can talk to that nigger in the courthouse, when he's brought out for trial. Court will be in session here next week. I know what you fellows want, but you can't get my prisoner to-day. Do you want to take the bread out of a poor man's mouth? I get seventy-five cents a day for keeping this prisoner, and he's the only one in the jail. I can't have my family suffer just to please you fellows."

One or two young men in the crowd laughed at the idea of Sheriff Campbell's suffering for want of seventy-five cents a day; but they were frowned into silence by those who stood near them.

"Ef yer don't let us in," cried a voice, "we'll bu's' the do' open."

"Bust away," answered the sheriff, raising his voice so that all could hear. "But I give you fair warning. The first man that tries it will be filled with buckshot. I'm sheriff of this county; I know my duty, and I mean to do it."

"What's the use of kicking, Sheriff?" argued one of the leaders of the mob. "The nigger is sure to hang anyhow; he richly deserves it; and we've got to do something to teach the niggers their places, or white people won't be able to live in the county."

"There's no use talking, boys," responded the sheriff, "I'm a white man outside, but in this jail I'm sheriff; and if this nigger's to be hung in this county, I propose to do the hanging. So you fellows might as well right-about-face, and march back to Troy. You've had a pleasant trip, and the exercise will be good for you. You know *me*. I've got powder and ball, and I've faced fire before now, with nothing between me and the enemy, and I don't mean to surrender this jail while I'm able to shoot." Having thus announced his determination, the sheriff closed and fastened the wicket, and looked around for the best position from which to defend the building.

The crowd drew off a little, and the leaders conversed together in low tones.

The Branson County jail was a small, two-story brick building, strongly constructed, with no attempt at architectural ornamentation. Each story was divided into two large cells by a passage running from front to rear. A grated iron door gave entrance from the passage to each of the four cells. The jail seldom had many prisoners in it, and the lower windows had been boarded up. When the sheriff had closed the wicket, he ascended the steep wooden stairs to the upper floor. There was no window at the front of the upper passage, and the most available position from which to watch the movements of the crowd below was the front window of the cell occupied by the solitary prisoner.

The sheriff unlocked the door and entered the cell. The prisoner was crouched in a corner, his yellow face, blanched with terror, looking ghastly in the semi-darkness of the room. A cold perspiration had gathered on his forehead, and his teeth were chattering with affright.

"For God's sake, Sheriff," he murmured hoarsely, "don't let 'em lynch me; I did n't kill the old man."

The sheriff glanced at the cowering wretch with a look of mingled contempt and loathing.

"Get up," he said sharply. "You will probably be hung sooner or later, but it shall not be to-day, if I can help it. I'll unlock your fetters, and if I can't hold the jail, you'll have to make the best fight you can. If I'm shot, I'll consider my responsibility at an end."

There were iron fetters on the prisoner's ankles, and handcuffs on his wrists. These the sheriff unlocked, and they fell clanking to the floor.

"Keep back from the window," said the sheriff. "They might shoot if they saw you."

The sheriff drew toward the window a pine bench which formed a part of the scanty furniture of the cell, and laid his revolver upon it. Then he took his gun in hand, and took his stand at the side of the window where he could with least exposure of himself watch the movements of the crowd below.

The lynchers had not anticipated any determined resistance. Of course they had looked for a formal protest, and perhaps a sufficient show of opposition to excuse the sheriff in the eye of any stickler for legal formalities. They had not however come prepared to fight a battle, and no one of them seemed willing to lead an attack upon the jail. The leaders of the party conferred together with a good deal of animated gesticulation, which was visible to the sheriff from his outlook, though the distance was too great for him to hear what was said. At length one of them broke away from the group, and rode back to the main body of the lynchers, who were restlessly awaiting orders.

"Well, boys," said the messenger, "we'll have to let it go for the present. The sheriff says he'll shoot, and he's got the drop on us this time. There ain't any of us that want to follow Cap'n Walker jest yet. Besides, the sheriff is a good fellow, and we don't want to hurt 'im. But," he added, as if to reassure the crowd, which began to show signs of disappointment, "the nigger might as well say his prayers, for he ain't got long to live."

There was a murmur of dissent from the mob, and several voices insisted that an attack be made on the jail. But pacific counsels finally prevailed, and the mob sullenly withdrew.

The sheriff stood at the window until they had disappeared around the bend in the road. He did not relax his watchfulness when the last one was out of sight. Their withdrawal might be a mere feint, to be followed by a further attempt. So closely, indeed, was his attention drawn to the outside, that he neither saw nor heard the prisoner creep stealthily across the floor, reach out his hand and secure the revolver which lay on the bench behind the sheriff, and creep as noiselessly back to his place in the corner of the room.

A moment after the last of the lynching party had disappeared there was a shot fired from the woods across the road; a bullet whistled by the window and buried itself in the wooden casing a few inches from where the sheriff was standing. Quick as thought, with the instinct born of a semi-guerrilla army experience, he raised his gun and fired twice at the point from which a faint puff of smoke showed the hostile bullet to have been sent. He stood a moment watching, and then rested his gun against the window, and reached behind him mechanically for the other weapon. It was not on the bench. As the sheriff realized this fact, he turned his head and looked into the muzzle of the revolver.

"Stay where you are, Sheriff," said the prisoner, his eyes glistening, his face almost ruddy with excitement.

The sheriff mentally cursed his own carelessness for allowing him to be caught in such a predicament. He had not expected anything of the kind. He had relied on the negro's cowardice and subordination in the presence of an armed white man as a matter of course. The sheriff was a brave man, but realized that the prisoner had him at an immense disadvantage. The two men stood thus for a moment, fighting a harmless duel with their eyes.

"Well, what do you mean to do?" asked the sheriff with apparent calmness.

"To get away, of course," said the prisoner, in a tone which caused the sheriff to look at him more closely, and with an involuntary feeling of apprehension; if the man was not mad, he was in a state of mind akin to madness, and quite as dangerous. The sheriff felt that he must speak the prisoner fair, and watch for a chance to turn the tables on him. The keen-eyed, desperate man before him was a different being altogether from the groveling wretch who had begged so piteously for his life a few minutes before.

At length the sheriff spoke:—

"Is this your gratitude to me for saving your life at the risk of my own? If I had not done so, you would now be swinging from the limb of some neighboring tree."

"True," said the prisoner, "you saved my life, but for how long? When you came in, you said Court would sit next week. When the crowd went away they said I had not long to live. It is merely a choice of two ropes."

"While there's life there's hope," replied the sheriff. He uttered this commonplace mechanically, while his brain was busy in trying to think out some way of escape. "If you are innocent you can prove it."

The mulatto kept his eye upon the sheriff. "I did n't kill the old man," he replied; "but I shall never be able to clear myself. I was at his house at nine o'clock. I stole from it the coat that was on my back when I was taken. I would be convicted, even with a fair trial, unless the real murderer were discovered beforehand."

The sheriff knew this only too well. While he was thinking what argument next to use, the prisoner continued:—

"Throw me the keys—no, unlock the door."

The sheriff stood a moment irresolute. The mulatto's eyes glittered ominously. The sheriff crossed the room and unlocked the door leading into the passage.

"Now go down and unlock the outside door."

The heart of the sheriff leaped within him. Perhaps he might make a dash for liberty, and gain the outside. He descended the narrow stairs, the prisoner keeping close behind him.

The sheriff inserted the huge iron key into the lock. The rusty bolt yielded slowly. It still remained for him to pull the door open.

"Stop!" thundered the mulatto, who seemed to divine the sheriff's purpose. "Move a muscle, and I'll blow your brains out!"

The sheriff obeyed; he realized that his chance had not yet come.

"Now, keep on that side of the passage, and go back upstairs."

Keeping the sheriff under cover of the revolver, the mulatto followed him up the stairs. The sheriff expected the prisoner to lock him into the cell and make his own escape. He had about come to the conclusion that the best thing he could do under the circumstances was to submit quietly, and take his chances of recapturing the prisoner after the alarm had been given. The sheriff had faced death more than once upon the battlefield. A few minutes before, well armed, and with a brick wall between him and them he had dared a hundred men to fight; but he felt instinctively that the desperate man confronting him was not to be trifled with, and he was too prudent a man to risk his life against such heavy odds. He had Polly to look after, and there was a limit beyond which devotion to duty would be quixotic and even foolish.

"I want to get away," said the prisoner, "and I don't want to be captured; for if I am I know I will be hung on the spot. I am afraid," he added somewhat reflectively, "that in order to save myself I shall have to kill you."

"Good God!" exclaimed the sheriff in involuntary terror; "you would not kill the man to whom you owe your own life."

"You speak more truly than you know," replied the mulatto. "I indeed owe my life to you."

The sheriff started. He was capable of surprise, even in that moment of extreme peril. "Who are you?" he asked in amazement.

"Tom, Cicely's son," returned the other. He had closed the door and stood talking to the sheriff through the grated opening. "Don't you remember Cicely—Cicely whom you sold, with her child, to the speculator on his way to Alabama?"

The sheriff did remember. He had been sorry for it many a time since. It had been the old story of debts, mortgages, and bad crops. He had quarreled with the mother. The price offered for her and her child had been unusually large, and he had yielded to the combination of anger and pecuniary stress.

"Good God!" he gasped, "you would not murder your own father?"

"My father?" replied the mulatto. "It were well enough for me to claim the relationship, but it comes with poor grace from you to ask anything by reason of it. What father's duty have you ever performed for me? Did you give me your name, or even your protection? Other white men gave their colored sons freedom and money, and sent them to the free States. *You* sold *me* to the rice swamps."

"I at least gave you the life you cling to," murmured the sheriff.

"Life?" said the prisoner, with a sarcastic laugh. "What kind of a life? You gave me your own blood, your own features,—no man need look at us together twice to see that,—and you gave me a black mother. Poor wretch! She died under the lash, because she had enough womanhood to call her soul her own. You gave me a white man's spirit, and you made me a slave, and crushed it out."

"But you are free now," said the sheriff. He had not doubted, could not doubt, the mulatto's word. He knew whose passions coursed beneath that swarthy skin and burned in the black eyes opposite his own. He saw in this mulatto what he himself might have become had not the safeguards of parental restraint and public opinion been thrown around him.

"Free to do what?" replied the mulatto. "Free in name, but despised and scorned and set aside by the people to whose race I belong far more than to my mother's."

"There are schools," said the sheriff. "You have been to school." He had noticed that the mulatto spoke more eloquently and used better language than most Branson County people.

"I have been to school, and dreamed when I went that it would work some marvelous change in my condition. But what did I learn? I learned to feel that no degree of learning or wisdom will change the color of my skin and that I shall always wear what in my own country is a badge of degradation. When I think about it seriously I do not care particularly for such a life. It is the animal in me, not the man, that flees the gallows. I owe you nothing," he went on, "and expect nothing of you; and it would be no more than justice if I should avenge upon you my mother's wrongs and my own. But still I hate to shoot you; I have never yet taken human life—for I did *not* kill the old captain. Will you promise to give no alarm and make no attempt to capture me until morning, if I do not shoot?"

So absorbed were the two men in their colloquy and their own tumultuous thoughts that neither of them had heard the door below move upon its hinges. Neither of them had heard a light step come stealthily up the stairs, nor seen a slender form creep along the darkening passage toward the mulatto.

The sheriff hesitated. The struggle between his love of life and his sense of duty was a terrific one. It may seem strange that a man who could sell his own child into slavery should hesitate at such a moment, when his life was trembling in the balance. But the baleful influence of human slavery poisoned the very fountains of life, and created new standards of right. The sheriff was conscientious; his conscience had merely been warped by his environment. Let no one ask what his answer would have been; he was spared the necessity of a decision.

"Stop," said the mulatto, "you need not promise. I could not trust you if you did. It is your life for mine; there is but one safe way for me; you must die."

He raised his arm to fire, when there was a flash—a report from the passage behind him. His arm fell heavily at his side, and the pistol dropped at his feet.

The sheriff recovered first from his surprise, and throwing open the door secured the fallen weapon. Then seizing the prisoner he thrust them into the cell and locked the door upon him; after which he turned to Polly, who leaned half-fainting against the wall, her hands clasped over her heart.

"Oh, father, I was just in time!" she cried hysterically, and wildly sobbing, threw herself into her father's arms.

"I watched until they all went away," she said. "I heard the shot from the woods and I saw you shoot. Then when you did not come out I feared something had happened, that perhaps you had been wounded. I got out the other pistol and ran over here. When I found the door open, I knew something was wrong, and when I heard voices I crept upstairs, and reached the top just in time to hear him say he would kill you. Oh, it was a narrow escape!"

When she had grown somewhat calmer, the sheriff left her standing there and went back into the cell. The prisoner's arm was bleeding from a flesh wound. His bravado had given place to a stony apathy. There was no sign in his face of fear or disappointment or feeling of any kind. The sheriff sent Polly to the house for cloth, and bound up the prisoner's wound with a rude skill acquired during his army life.

"I'll have a doctor come and dress the wound in the morning," he said to the prisoner. "It will do very well until then, if you will keep quiet. If the doctor asks you how the wound was caused, you can say that you were struck by the bullet fired from the woods. It would do you no good to have it known that you were shot while attempting to escape."

The prisoner uttered no word of thanks or apology, but sat in sullen silence. When the wounded arm had been bandaged, Polly and her father returned to the house.

The sheriff was in an unusually thoughtful mood that evening. He put salt in his coffee at supper, and poured vinegar over his pancakes. To many of Polly's questions he returned random answers. When he had gone to bed he lay awake for several hours.

In the silent watches of the night, when he was alone with God, there came into his mind a flood of unaccustomed thoughts. An hour or two before, standing face to face with death, he had experienced a sensation similar to that which drowning men are said to feel—a kind of clarifying of the moral faculty, in which the veil of the flesh, with its obscuring passions and prejudices, is pushed aside for a moment, and all the acts of one's life stand out, in the clear light of truth, in their correct proportions and relations,—a state of mind in which one sees himself as God may be supposed to see him. In the reaction following his rescue, this feeling had given place for a time to far different emotions. But now, in the silence of midnight, something of this clearness of spirit returned to the sheriff. He saw that he had owed some duty to this son of his,—that neither law nor custom could destroy a responsibility inherent in the nature of mankind. He could not thus, in the eyes of God at least, shake off the consequences of his sin. Had he never sinned, this wayward spirit would never have come back from the vanished past to haunt him. As these thoughts came, his anger against the mulatto died away, and in its place there sprang up a great pity. The hand of parental authority might have restrained the passions he had seen burning in the prisoner's eyes when the desperate man spoke the words which had seemed to doom his father to death. The sheriff felt that he might have saved this fiery spirit from the slough of slavery; that he might have sent him to the free North, and given him there, or in some other land, an opportunity to turn to usefulness and honorable pursuits the talents that had run to crime, perhaps to madness; he might, still less, have given this son of his the poor simulacrum of liberty which men of his caste could possess in a slave-holding community; or least of all, but still something, he might have kept the boy on the plantation, where the burdens of slavery would have fallen lightly upon him.

The sheriff recalled his own youth. He had inherited an honored name to keep untarnished; he had had a future to make; the picture of a fair young bride had beckoned him on to happiness. The poor wretch now stretched upon a pallet of straw between the brick walls of the jail had had none of these things,—no name, no father, no mother—in the true meaning of motherhood,—and until the past few years no possible future, and then one vague and shadowy in its outline, and dependent for form and substance upon the slow solution of a problem in which there were many unknown quantities.

From what he might have done to what he might yet do was an easy transition for the awakened conscience of the sheriff. It occurred to him, purely as a hypothesis, that he might permit his prisoner to escape; but his oath of office, his duty as sheriff, stood in the way of such a course, and the sheriff dismissed the idea from his mind. He could, however, investigate the circumstances of the murder, and move Heaven and earth to discover the real criminal, for he no longer doubted the prisoner's innocence; he could employ counsel for the accused, and perhaps influence public opinion in his favor. An acquittal once secured, some plan could be devised by which the sheriff might in some degree atone for his crime against this son of his—against society—against God.

When the sheriff had reached this conclusion he fell into an unquiet slumber, from which he awoke late the next morning.

He went over to the jail before breakfast and found the prisoner lying on his pallet, his face turned to the wall; he did not move when the sheriff rattled the door.

"Good-morning," said the latter, in a tone intended to wake the prisoner.

There was no response. The sheriff looked more keenly at the recumbent figure; there was an unnatural rigidity about its attitude.

He hastily unlocked the door and, entering the cell, bent over the prostrate form. There was no sound of breathing; he turned the body over—it was cold and stiff. The prisoner had torn the bandage from his wound and bled to death during the night. He had evidently been dead several hours.

[The Double-Consciousness of Black Folk]

W. E. Burghardt DuBois*

After the Egyptian and Indian, the Greek and Roman, the Teuton and Mongolian, the Negro is a sort of seventh son, born with a veil, and gifted

*Reprinted from *The Souls of Black Folk: Essays and Sketches*, 5th ed. (Chicago: A. C. McClurg & Co., 1904), 3–4, 204–6.

with second-sight in this American world,—a world which yields him no true self-consciousness, but only lets him see himself through the revelation of the other world. It is a peculiar sensation, this double-consciousness, this sense of always looking at one's self through the eyes of others, of measuring one's soul by the tape of a world that looks on in amused contempt and pity. One ever feels his *two-ness*,—an American, a Negro; two souls, two thoughts, two unreconciled strivings; two warring ideals in one dark body, whose dogged strength alone keeps it from being torn asunder.

The history of the American Negro is the history of this strife,—this longing to attain self-conscious manhood, to merge his double self into a better and truer self. In this merging he wishes neither of the older selves to be lost. He would not Africanize America, for America has too much to teach the world and Africa. He would not bleach his Negro soul in a flood of white Americanism, for he knows that Negro blood has a message for the world. He simply wishes to make it possible for a man to be both a Negro and an American, without being cursed and spit upon by his fellows, without having the doors of Opportunity closed roughly in his face. . . .

To-day the young Negro of the South who would succeed cannot be frank and outspoken, honest and self-assertive, but rather he is daily tempted to be silent and wary, politic and sly; he must flatter and be pleasant, endure petty insults with a smile, shut his eyes to wrong; in too many cases he sees positive personal advantage in deception and lying. His real thoughts, his real aspirations, must be guarded in whispers; he must not criticise, he must not complain. Patience, humility, and adroitness must, in these growing black youth, replace impulse, manliness, and courage. With this sacrifice there is an economic opening, and perhaps peace and some prosperity. Without this there is riot, migration, or crime. Nor is this situation peculiar to the Southern United States,—is it not rather the only method by which undeveloped races have gained the right to share modern culture? The price of culture is a Lie.

[The Case of Nelse Patton]   *The Lafayette County Press**

NEGRO BRUTE CUTS WOMAN'S THROAT

Mrs. Mattie McMullen, a White Woman the Victim—Lived but Ten Minutes after the Tragedy. Sheriff Hartsfield and Posse of Citizens Give Chase and Land Negro in Jail

---

*Reprinted from the issue for 9 September 1908; a transcription also appears in *Old Times in the Faulkner Country* by John B. Cullen in collaboration with Floyd C. Watkins (Chapel Hill, N. C.: University of North Carolina Press, 1961), 93–98.

MOB STORMS JAIL AND KILLS DESPERADO

Officers and Guards Overpowered, and Failing to Find the Keys the Orderly Mob Quietly and Deliberately Took Matters in Their Own Hands, Forced Entrance to Cell Where Negro Was Confined Negro Armed with Poker Puts Up Desperate Fight and is Killed.

One of the coldest blooded murders and most brutal crimes known to the criminal calendar was perpetrated one mile north of town yesterday morning about ten o'clock, when a black brute of unsavory reputation by the name of Nelse Patton attacked Mrs. Mattie McMullen, a respected white woman, with a razor, cutting her throat from ear to ear and causing almost instant death. Reports as to the cause of the tragedy vary, but as near as can be learned the particulars are these:

Mrs. McMullen, whose husband was confined at the time in the county jail at this place, was a hard working woman living alone with her 17-year-old daughter and two other very small children. It seems that Mr. McMullen wanted to communicate with his wife, and as was his custom at such occasions, he called the murderer, who was a "trusty" prisoner at the jail, to carry the missive. Arriving at the house, the negro, who was in an intoxicated condition, walked into the house without knocking and took a seat. Seeing the woman apparently alone and without protection, his animal passion was aroused and he made insulting remarks to her. He was ordered from the house and some angry words passed between them, when the woman started toward the bureau drawer to get her pistol. The brute seeing her design made a rush at the woman from behind and drawing the razor cut her throat from ear to ear, almost severing the head from the body. The dying woman rushed out of the house, and the daughter hearing the confusion rushed in, and was instantly grabbed by the negro. Jerking herself from the brute's grasp, she followed her mother who had fallen dead a few yards from the house. The daughter's screams alarmed the neighbors who quickly responded to the call and immediately sent in a hurried telephone message to the Press office to summon officers and a physician, who in less than twenty minutes were on the way to the scene of the murder. The news spread like wild fire and it was but a short while until the sheriff was joined by a posse of citizens all in hot and close pursuit of the brute. After chasing the negro three or four miles over fences, through briars and fields he suddenly ran amuck of Johnny Cullen, the 14-year-old son of Lin Cullen, who was out with a double-barreled shotgun. Seeing the negro coming towards him, he called a halt, but the negro paid no attention to the command and the boy let him have a load of No. 5 shot in the chest, which slackened his speed but did not stop him. The boy gave him another charge in the left arm and side which stopped him. The negro was at once surrounded by his pursuers and gladly gave up. Over a hundred shots were fired from all kinds of weapons but the negro was out of range. Being weak from loss of blood, the brute was put on a horse and hurried to jail.

As soon as the news spread of the capture, hundreds of people began to gather around the jail and in small groups about the street. They were not indulging in idle threats, but from the seriousness of their expression one could see the negro's fate was sealed.

Between nine and ten o'clock the crowd began swelling to large proportions about the jail. Speeches were made advocating letting the law take its course and vice-versa, but patience had fallen far short of being a virtue in a crowd like that. One wild shout went up, with a rush the crowd advanced on the jail, pushing open doors and jumping through windows. Officers and guards were overpowered and disarmed. The keys could not be found, but the hardware stores and blacksmith shops were made to furnish the necessary tools and a set of quiet and determined men plied them. Four and one-half hours of hard and persistent work it took to break through the thick walls of steel and masonry. The hall was at last reached, and a search of the cell occupied by that black fiend incarnate was made. It was at last found and broken into. Crouched and cringing in a dark corner of the cell, with the gleam of murder in his eye, stood the miserable wretch armed with an iron poker awaiting the advance. In one, two, three order the mob entered the cell, and in the same order the iron descended upon their heads, blood flew, the negro having all the advantage in his dark corner, held the crowd at bay and refused to come out. Only one thing was left to do. It was done. 26 pistol shots vibrated throughout the corridors of the solid old jail, and when the smoke cleared away the limp and lifeless body of the brute told the story.

The body was hustled down stairs to terra-firma, the rope was produced, the hangman's noose properly adjusted about the neck, and the drag to the court house yard began.

This morning the passerby saw the lifeless body of a negro suspended from a tree—it told the tale, that the murder of a white woman had been avenged—the public had done their duty. Following is the verdict of the Coroner's Jury:

We the Coroners Jury of inquest impaneled and sworn to investigate the death of Nelse Patton, colored, find after inspecting the body and examining necessary witnesses that to the best of our knowledge and belief, the said Nelse Patton came to his death from gunshot or pistol wounds inflicted by parties to us unknown. That any one of a number of wounds would have been sufficient to cause death. We find further that Sheriff J. C. Hartsfield and his deputies were diligent in their efforts to protect said Nelse Patton from the time of his arrest until they were overpowered by a mob of several hundred men who stormed the jail and dug their way through the walls until they reached the cell in which said Nelse Patton was confined and that said officers never surrendered the keys of jail or cells but that the locks were forced by some party or parties to us unknown and that the said Nelse Patton was shot with pistols or guns while in his cell and while attempting to protect himself with an iron rod. We further find that said Nelse Patton was dead before being brought from the jail and being hung.

Respectfully submitted,

E. O. Davidson

R. S. Adams

P. E. Matthews

B. P. Gray

A. F. Calloway

F. Wood

[Ed. note: *In addition, the Associated Press issued a second story; the text that follows is from the Jackson, Mississippi,* Daily Clarion-Ledger *for Thursday, 10 September 1908.*]

SULLIVAN'S HOT TALK ON OXFORD LYNCHING

FORMER UNITED STATES SENATOR FROM MISSISSIPPI LED THE MOB

(Associated Press Report)

Memphis, Tenn., Sept. 9.—A special from Oxford, Miss., quotes former U. S. Senator W. V. Sullivan as follows, with reference to the lynching of last night:

"I led the mob which lynched Nelse Patton and I am proud of it.

"I directed every movement of the mob, and I did everything I could to see that he was lynched.

"Cut a white woman's throat? and a negro? Of course I wanted him lynched.

"I saw his body dangling from a tree this morning and I am glad of it.

"When I heard of the horrible crime, I started to work immediately to get a mob. I did all I could to raise one. I was at the jail last night and I heard Judge Roane advise against lynching. I got up immediately after and urged the mob to lynch Patton.

"I aroused the mob and directed them to storm the jail.

"I had my revolver, but did not use it. I gave it to a deputy sheriff and told him: 'Shoot Patton and shoot to kill.'

"He used the revolver and shot. I suppose the bullets from my gun were some of those that killed the negro.

"I don't care what investigation is made, or what are the consequences. I am willing to stand them.

"I wouldn't mind standing the consequences any time for lynching a man who cut a white woman's throat. I will lead a mob in such a case any time."

Sunset

William Faulkner*

Black Desperado Slain

The negro who has terrorized this locality for two days, killing three men, two whites and a negro, was killed last night with machine gun fire by a detachment of the -th Regiment, State National Guard. The troopers set up their gun before the copse in which the black man was hiding and when there was no reply to their fire, Captain Wallace entered the place and found the negro dead. No reason has been ascertained for the black's running amuck, though it is believed he was insane. He has not been identified.

———The Clarion-Eagle.

He came part of the way on or in or beneath freight cars, but mostly he walked. It took him two days to come from Carrollton avenue to Canal street, because he was afraid of the traffic; and on Canal street at last, carrying his shotgun and his bundle, he stood frightened and dazed. Pushed and shoved, ridiculed by his own race and cursed by policemen, he did not know what to do save that he must cross the street.

So at last, taking his courage in both hands and shutting his eyes, he dashed blindly across in the middle of the block. Cars were about him, a taxi driver screamed horrid imprecations at him, but, clutching his gun and bundle, he made it. And then a kind white man directed him to the river which he sought.

And here was a boat, all tied up to the bank, waiting for him. In climbing down a pile and leaping six feet of water to get on it, he nearly lost his gun; and then another white man, cursing, drove him from the boat.

"But, cap'n," he protested, "I jest wants to go to Af'ica. I kin pay my way."

"Africa, hell," said the white man. "Get to hell off this boat. If you ever try to get on here again that way I'll shoot you. Get on up yonder and get a ticket, if you want to ride."

"Yes, suh. 'Scuse me, cap'n."

"What?" repeated the ticket seller, in amazement.

"Lemme have a ticket to Af'ica, please um."

"Do you mean Algiers?"

"No'm; Af'ica."

"Do you want a ferry ticket?"

"Yassum, I expec' so: so I kin ride dat boat waitin' yonder."

"Come on, come on, up there," said a voice from the waiting queue behind him, so he took his ticket and was hustled through the gate and was once more on board the ferry.

To his surprise the boat, instead of going down the river, in which

*From *New Orleans Sketches*, ed. Carvel Collins (New York: Random House, Inc., 1958), 76–85. Reprinted with permission of the publisher.

direction he vaguely supposed Africa to be, held straight across the stream, and he was herded ashore like a sheep. Clinging to his gun he stared about him helplessly. At last he diffidently approached a policeman.

"Cap'n, suh, is dis Af'ica?"

"Huh?" said the startled officer.

"Ah'm tryin' to get to Af'ica, please suh. Is dis de right way?"

"Africa, hell," said this white man, just as the steamboat man had done. "Look here, what are you up to?"

"Ah wants to go back home, whar de preacher say us come fum."

"Where do you live, nigger?"

"Back up yonder ways, in de country."

"What town?"

"Ain't no town, suh, 'ceptin' Mist' Bob and de fambly and his niggers."

"Mississippi or Louisiana?"

"Yessuh, I 'speck so."

"Well, lemme tell you something. You go back there on the first train you can catch. This ain't no place for you."

"But, cap'n, I wants to go to Af'ica."

"You forget about Africa, and go buy yourself the longest railroad ticket you can, do you hear?"

"But, cap'n—"

"Beat it, now. Do you want me to take you up?"

At the foot of Canal street again, he looked about him in perplexity. How did one get to Africa? He was hustled and shoved this way and that, and he allowed destiny to carry him along the river front. Here was another boat tied up to the wharf, with niggers carrying things up a plank and dumping them down upon the floor. A coatless white man was evident, loudly.

Niggers pushing trucks rattled and banged, singing, about him. He was still thrust around, leaping from the path of one truck only to find another bearing down upon him. "Look out, black man!"

Suddenly the boss whirled upon him.

"What in hell are you doing? Grab aholt of something there, or get off this job. I don't have no spectators on this job at all. You hear me."

"Yas suh, cap'n," he returned equably; and soon he was throwing sacks onto a truck. His blood warmed with activity, he began to sweat and to sing. This was where he was at home—for the first time in how long? He had forgotten. "Af'ica, where is you?" he said.

Quitting time: the sun hung redly in the west and the long shadows were still and flat, waiting for dark. The spinning golden motes spun slower in the last sunlight; and the other hands gathered up coats and lunch pails and moved away toward the flashing street lights, and supper. He picked up his gun and bundle and went aboard the boat.

Among soft, bulky sacks he lay down to munch the loaf of bread he had bought. Darkness came down completely, the lapping of water against the hull and the pungently sweet smell of the sacked grain soon put him to sleep.

Motion waked him, a smooth lift and fall and a' steady drumming of engines. Light was about him and he lay in a dullness of comfort, not even thinking. Then he found that he was hungry, and wondering mildly where he was, he got up.

As soon as he appeared on deck another mad white man fell upon him.

"Ah wants to go to Af'ica, cap'n," he protested, "when I holp dem niggers loadin' yestiddy Ah thought us was all goin' on dis boat."

The white man bore him down with tides of profanity. "God in heaven, you niggers will drive me crazy. Don't you know where this boat is going? It's going to Natchez."

"Dat suit me all right, jes' so she pass Af'ica. You jes' tell me when we gits dar and if she don't stop I kin jump off and swim to de bank."

The man looked at him for a long minute quite in amazement.

"En don't worry about de fare neither, suh," his passenger hastened to reassure him. "I got money: I kin pay it."

"How much you got?"

"Plenty, cap'n," he replied grandly, digging in his overalls. His outthrust hand held four silver dollars, and some smaller coins. The white man took the four dollars.

"Well, I'll take you as far as Africa for this. And you get on up there and help them niggers shift cargo until we get there."

"Yas suh!" he said with alacrity. He paused again. "But you'll sho' tell me at de right station, won't you, cap'n?"

"Yeh, sure. But beat it now, and help them other boys. G'on, now."

He helped the other boys while they passed under the perfect day from one shimmering reach of the river to another; and again the sun hung redly in the west. Bells rang somewhere and the boat sheered in toward the shore. More bells, the boat lost speed and nosed easily into the mud beneath a row of barrels. The white cap'n, the mad one, leaned down from the front porch above his head.

"All right, Jack," he roared, "here you are. Help put them barrels on board, and Africa is about a mile across them fields yonder."

He stood to watch the boat draw away from the shore, trailing black smoke from its tall funnels across the evening; then he shouldered his gun and struck inland. He had not gone far when he thought of the lions and bears he would probably meet, so he stopped and loaded his gun.

After walking until all the light was gone and the Dipper swung majestically down the west, he knew that he must be well into Africa, and that it was time to eat and sleep again. To eat he could not, so he decided to find a safe place to sleep. Tomorrow he could probably kill a rabbit. He suddenly found a fence beside him; across it loomed something that might be a haystack. He climbed the fence and something rose horribly from almost under his feet.

He knew stark and terrible fear. His gun leaped to his shoulder and roared and flamed in the darkness, and the lion or whatever it was plunged bellowing away into the night. He could feel sweat cold as copper pieces on his face and he ran toward the haystack and clawed madly at it, trying to climb it. His fear grew with his futile efforts, then cooled away, allowing him to mount the slippery thing. Once on top he felt safe, but he was cautious to place the shotgun close to his hand as he lay on his belly staring into the night. The thing he had shot was quiet now, but the night was filled with sound.

A light came twinkling along the ground and soon he could see legs criss-crossing it, and he heard voices in a language he could not understand. Savages, he thought, folks that eat you; and he crouched lower in his straw. The light and the voices passed on in the direction the beast he had shot had taken; soon the light stopped beside a blotched thing that swelled up from the ground, and the voices rose in imprecation.

"Gentlemen!" he breathed. "I mus' a shot dem folks' own private lion."

But a lion was a lion. And so he lay hidden while the light moved on away and was lost at last, and the stars swung over him, and he slept.

He was shaken into wakefulness. He threw an arm across his eyes. That strange language was in his ears again and he opened his eyes to see a small dark-skinned man kneeling over him with a pistol. The language he could not understand, but the language the pistol talked he could.

They are going to eat me! he thought. His leg gathered and sickled, the man toppled backward toward the ground, and as an animal leaps he flung himself bodily earthward. A pistol went off and somthing slapped him dully high in the shoulder. He replied, and a man flopped to the ground. He leaped to his feet and ran, while bullets whined past him. The fence was before him: he turned to follow it, seeking a gate.

His left arm was warm and wet, and there at the turn of the fence was a gate. The shooting behind him continued, he clutched his own gun as he saw a running figure, trying to cut him off at the gate. As they drew together he saw that this one was a member of his own race. "Out de way, nigger," he gasped at the other's waving arms; and he saw the expression of ludicrous amazement on the man's face as his gun crashed again.

His breath came in gulping lungsful. He must stop. Here was a ditch, and a long embankment. Just ahead, where another embankment intersected it, was a small copse. Into this he plunged, concealed, and lay on his back, panting. His heaving lungs at last breathed easier. Then he discovered the wound in his shoulder. He looked at his blood in surprise. "Now when you suppose dat happen?" he thought. "Whew! Dese Af'ikins shoots niggers jes' like white folks does."

He bound it crudely, then took stock of the situation. He had shelter, and that was all. There were still eighteen shells left. And he would need them: there was already one man about two hundred yards away, holding a rifle and watching his thicket. "Don't act like he gwine bother me right soon," he decided. "I'll jes' rest here twell dark, and den I'm gwine back to Mist' Bob. Af'ica sho' ain't no place fer civilized folks—steppin' on lions, and bein' shot, and havin' to shoot folks yo'self. But I guess dese Af'icans is used to it."

His shoulder began to throb dully. He twisted and turned in his mounting fever. How thirsty he was! He had been hungry, but now he was only thirsty, and he thought of the cool brown creek at home, and the cold spring in the wood lot. He raised his sweating face, and saw the watchman had drawn closer in. He raised his gun, aiming the best he could with one hand, and fired. The watchman fell backward, leaped to his feet and ran dodging beyond range. "Jes' to skeer you," he muttered.

Things were beginning to look funny, and his shoulder hurt dreadfully. He dozed a moment and thought he was at home again; he waked to pain and dozed again. Dozing and waking, he passed the long day, crawling at intervals to sip the muddy, stinking water in the ditch. At last he waked to night, and lanterns and fires, and men walking in the firelight and talking.

He had dragged himself down to the bank for water, and as he returned an automobile's lights were suddenly turned full on him. A voice screamed, and bullets whipped about him. He plunged back into his copse and fired blindly at the lights. A man shrieked and bullets ripped and tore at the thicket: the limbs were whipped as by a gale, tortured against the sky. He was seared as with hot irons, and he lowered his head, pressing his face into the muddy earth.

The firing suddenly ceased; the silence literally dragged him from the regions of oblivion. He thrust his gun forward, waiting. At last the darkness detached itself and became two things; and in the flash of his point-blank explosion he saw two men crouching. One of them fired a pistol almost in his face, and fled.

Again it was dawn. The sun rose, became hot, and marched above his head. He was at home, working in the fields; he was asleep, fighting his way from out a nightmare; he was a child again—no, he was a bird, a big one like a buzzard, drawing endless black circles on a blue sky.

Again the sun sank. The west was like blood: it was his own blood painted onto a wall. Supper in the pot, and night where there were no fires and people moving around them, and all stopping as though they were waiting for something to happen.

He raised his face from the mud and looked at the circle of fires about him. It looked as though everybody had gathered at one place, directly in front of him, all watching or waiting for something. Let them wait: tomorrow he'll be at home, with Mr. Bob to curse him in his gentle voice, and regular folks to work and laugh and talk with.

Here was a wind coming up: the branches and bushes about him whipped suddenly to a gale fiercer than any yet; flattened and screamed, and melted away under it. And he, too, was a tree caught in that same wind: he felt the dull blows of it, and the rivening of himself into tattered and broken leaves.

The gale died away, and all broken things were still. His black, kind, dull, once-cheerful face was turned up to the sky and the cold, cold stars. Africa or Louisiana: what care they?

[The Case of Elwood Higginbotham]

Oxford *Eagle**

Jurors Drawn for September Term

Selections Being Notified of Jury Duty for
September Term of Circuit Court Starting 9th

The circuit clerk, sheriff, and chancery clerk have drawn the list of jurors to serve for the first week of September term of the circuit court to get under way September 9 with Judge Taylor H. McElroy presiding.

There are some eight or ten criminal cases and about twice that many civil cases listed for attention of the circuit court and likely several other cases will be docketed before the term starts. The most noted or notorious case is that of Jesse Tatum held on two charges, one for arson and the other for murder.

The grand jury will also consider the plight of Elwood Higginbotham, negro slayer of Glen D. Roberts. The negro has been in the Hinds county jail every [sic] since his capture in Pontotoc county about three months ago.

The following will make up the jury for the September term:

Beat 1—Posey Franklin, Douglas Walker, Ed Dooley, Buster Littlejohn, Hulett Johnson, Jess Anderson, George Young, Jim Blasengame, Elco McClarty, Curt Mize.

Beat 2—Toy Duncan, U. G. Smith, John Jordan, Erle Sparks, B. G. Coffey, J. J. Littlejohn, W. E. Ferrell, Mack Parks, Ed Stone, Menken Sneed.

Beat 3—Jesse Smith, Lon Weaver, L. L. Hargrove, J. R. Sullender, J. A. Lewis, J. A. Wolfe, Frank Smith, W. P. Haley, G. C. Landreth, R. L. Young.

Beat 4—L. V. Gray, C. A. Martin, [p. 4] John A. Cooper, E. H. Byers, Fred Higginbotham, J. H. Cannon, Hugh Carothers, R. X. Williams, P. D. Ayles, Dud S. Foust.

Beat 5—A. S. Cooper, R. R. Sockwell, C. B. Davis, C. P. Hall, W. E. Brown, D. D. Oswalt, R. H. Morrison, Dewey McClarty, J. W. Gault, Lee J. Garrison.

—August 29, 1935, p. 1, col. 2; p. 4, col. 5

---

*Transcribed from the Oxford (Mississippi) *Eagle*, a weekly newspaper, by Frank Childrey, Jr., and Arthur F. Kinney especially for this volume.

JESSE TATUM'S MURDER TRIAL FRIDAY;
HIGGINBOTHAM'S IS SET FOR MONDAY

Elwood Higginbotham, Negro, Brought from
Jackson Jail, Pleads Not Guilty to Murder Charge

Elwood Higginbotham, confessed negro murder [sic] of Glen D. Roberts, pleaded not guilty to the charge of first degree murder Tuesday and will face trial Monday of next week. A special venire of 50 Lafayette county citizens has been drawn for jury duty in the case.

The court appointed L. C. Hutton, local attorney, to represent the negro in the case.

Glen Roberts, well known and popular Lafayette county farmer, was killed on the night of Monday, May 21st. A discharge from a shotgun in the hands of the negro brought almost instant death.

After the killing, the negro eluded posses for two days and night [sic], finally being captured near Pontotoc from whence he was taken to the Hinds county jail at Jackson where he stayed until brought to Oxford the first of the week for trial.

—September 12, 1935, p. 1, cols. 3–4

COURT ENDS AFTER 9 DAYS

Longest Term in Years, Murder Trials Consuming Most of Time;
Several Minor Cases Settled

Circuit court, in session nine days, closed court Wednesday evening. This was the longest term of court held during the past four years. The Tatum and Higginbotham murder trials accounted for the greatest part of the time. . . .

—September 19, 1935, p. 1, col. 3

LIFE IMPRISONMENT FOR TATUM;
MOB LYNCHES HIGGINBOTHAM NEGRO

Career of Negro Who Killed Glen Roberts Terminates
at the End of a Rope Tuesday Night

Mob law walked in Lafayette county Tuesday night.

Judge Lynch passed sentence: "Hanged by the neck until dead" on the person of Elwood Higginbotham, confessed negro murderer of Glen D. Roberts. The black man was hanged by a mob of about 75 men just north of Three-Way, on the old Russell road, about 9 o'clock Tuesday night.

Mr. Roberts was killed by the discharge from a shotgun in the hands of the negro on the night of Monday, May 21st.

The case against the negro for murder went to trial Tuesday morning and was given to the jury that evening. The jury was still out, disagreeing, when the hanging took place.

Rumors that the jury stood 10 for conviction with 2 for acquittal were said to have incited the mob.

Entirely Unexpected

The mob action came as a complete surprise to all the court officials. The negro was in Oxford for one day last week and was brought back for trial Tuesday morning. During that time no demonstration of any kind was made.

A crowd of approximately 75 men, with faces smudged with dirt to prevent identification, converged on the jail about 8:30 o'clock. Jailer Pritchard and three deputies were unable to reason with the determined white men.

The attack was evidently well planned and went off with little noise of any kind. The jail telephone wires were out. The mobsters quickly searched the jail until the keys were found and then broke into the cell block. A messenger was hurriedly sent for Sheriff S. T. Lyles who arrived at the jail just as the mob was leaving with the prisoner. His attempts to stop the man were futile. He was overpowered by the mob members who held him until fellow mobsters carried the negro off to his death.

Prisoners Attempt Escape

As the door to the cell block was unlocked by the mob, two desperate federal prisoners, Claude Lott and Wilton Smith, made an attempt to escape by running down the stairs but were captured and returned to their cells by the mob.

Court was still in session, with court officials present, waiting for the jury to come in when word reached town that there was no need of any further court action in the case of state versus Elwood Higginbotham, negro.

—September 19, 1935, p. 1, col. 7; p. 4, col. 3

AROUND THE COURT HOUSE
SIMPLE AND QUIET

Outside of a few negroes stealing horses and shooting craps, the "simple have been very quiet" this week, said Justice Bennett. It sounded as if the justice meant that only the simple violated the law and were yanked up in his court. However, he probably meant that only the simple get caught.

—October 3, 1935, p. 1, col. 2

[Greenfield Farm]

John Faulkner*

I began living on the farm as soon as we bought it. Bill stayed in town but came back and forth every day. Some days he would take an airplane and fly over the farm to get a better picture of just what we had and how to develop it. He was having the time of his life. . . .

When Bill put me in charge, he left the running of the farm up to me. He told me in a general way what he wanted, then left it up to me to carry out his plans however I thought best. The main thing he wanted was to take good care of his brood mares. We broke all our land with the tractor and only used Negroes and mules to cultivate the crops. That was light plowing and the exercise was good for the stock.

After the first of June, it was hot and close in the bottom where we planted our corn. From eleven in the morning until about three in the afternoon it was too hot there for our mares, especially in belly-high corn. The Negroes did not work too well through that part of the day either. No one could. It was stifling.

So we set up a schedule to take advantage of the coolest parts of the day. We would get up at two-thirty in the morning and I would go out on the front porch and blow a boy scout bugle Chooky, my youngest son, had. It would wake the Negroes and we would all meet at the barn and feed the stock. While the horses were eating, we would return to our houses and get our breakfast. By the time we got back to the barn, the horses would be ready to harness and we'd go to the field and be ready to start plowing as soon as it was light enough to see the rows.

We would knock off at eleven and go in and hole up through the hottest part of the day. Then at three we would go back to the fields and work till it got too dark to see.

We were getting a lot of work done that way and had good crops and it suited Bill. In fact, I sort of think he liked doing different from his neighbors, trying out something new. . . .

We had a Negro blacksmith in town named Gate Boone. He was pretty good with horses, or at least Bill thought he was. Bill took Gate along when he bought the brood mares and the Spanish jack and moved Gate out to the farm to board with one of our Negroes. He wanted Gate there to look after the stock.

The other Negroes didn't think much of Gate's know-how about horses, or of Gate, for the matter of that. They used to laugh at him among themselves, though they never let Bill see them do it. Gate had pulled the wool over Bill's eyes but they didn't want Bill to know they knew it. They figured Bill would find out when the time came and until then it wasn't any of their business. . . .

*Reprinted with permission from *My Brother Bill: An Affectionate Reminiscence* (New York: Trident Press, 1963), 178–83, 200. Courtesy of Yoknapatawpha Press.

Bill had moved Uncle Ned out to the farm from his back yard because he said he wanted to come out there. Uncle Ned was supposed to keep the barn, tend to the feeding and milk the cows, something that would not require too much of him yet make it look like he was working. That didn't suit Uncle Ned. He wanted to take part in everything and boss all of it. He was there with us the day Lightning threw the fit in the field.

"Master," he said, "I used to handle horses for your daddy and I can handle that buckskin. The rest of them just don't know nothing about horses."

"Are you sure you won't get hurt?" Bill asked.

"A horse hurt me, master? I knows all about horses."

Uncle Ned was old. He'd been a slave belonging to my great-grandfather. Dad and Uncle John remembered him from Ripley, when they both used to live over there. When he got along in years and was unable to work steady any more, he came to Oxford looking for them to help him.

Dad looked after him at first and found him what jobs he would take. After Dad died Bill took him over and finally moved him down into his back yard. Then when Uncle Ned wanted to come out to the farm he moved him out, with a Negro woman named Ella whom he called his companion.

Uncle Ned liked to own his own stuff. He had a cow of his own that he had kept at Bill's and he brought her along. Then he wanted a pasture of his own, fenced off from ours, so he could have his own cow in his own pasture. Bill drew the line. He told Uncle Ned we were too busy to stop and build him a pasture of his own; he'd just have to keep his cow in the same pasture with ours. . . .

After about two years on the farm Bill's money ran out and I moved back to town and got a job on the W.P.A. Bill did not seem to have the same interest in the farm after I left it. He did not go out there as often as he had before. He sort of furnished the Negroes from in town and let them run it as they pleased. Some of them are still out there.

Uncle Ned moved back to town soon after I did. Bill had someone else in his servant's house by now so he rented Uncle Ned a cabin in the hollow and continued taking care of him.

The Colonel and His Buick   Murry C. Falkner*

The coming of the automobile brought some changes to Oxford, and not necessarily for the better. It pushed back horizons and made people impatient to get to them. When the first cars came to town, gasoline and oil were

*Reprinted with permission of Louisiana State University Press from The Falkners of Mississippi: a Memoir (Baton Rouge, La.: Louisiana State University Press, 1967), 62–66, 69–72. © 1967 by Louisiana State University Press. Murry Falkner was William Faulkner's (here Bill's) younger brother. The last name of the chauffeur Chess was Carothers.

sold from drums in the hardware stores (we had never heard of a filling station), and since there was but one grade of each, every motorist got the same thing. It was amazing to see the transformation in a man whose trusted horse had a top speed of perhaps eight miles an hour, and who had taken a week or a month to even consider when he was going to travel, let alone where. When this same man acquired his first automobile, he immediately set out to run roughshod over everyone in sight in an effort to get under way within the hour.

Grandfather bought one of the first automobiles in town, notwithstanding the fact that he himself had seen to it that an ordinance was passed the previous year forbidding the operation of one within the town limits. It was a 1909 model Buick touring car, no doors in front, a rubber bulb horn attached to the steering wheel column, brass trimmings all over, right-hand drive, gasoline and spark levers on a quadrant above the steering wheel, completely smooth no-tread tires, carbide lights, big gear shift, and hand brake levers offset on a heavy rod extending out from the right front floor board. The motor could be started by an ingenious device known as a hand crank, but whether it worked at any given time or not depended equally upon the strength and persistence of the cranker and the current temperament of the motor.

The lights were gas burners, fed by a double-section, pure brass, vertical cylinder rigidly attached to the right running board. The lower section held carbide, purchased at the drugstore, while the upper was the water container, to which there was fixed a little regulating valve to determine the amount of water allowed to drip down onto the carbide, which, of course, controlled the size of the small flames in the V-burners in each of the big headlights. It took an intrepid soul to travel by night in a car in those days, but, then, for that matter, it took such a one to buy an automobile in the first place. When a ride by night was contemplated the car was first driven to a wide open space, of which Oxford had plenty in those far-off times. This was advisable (a mild word indeed) because when the valve was turned on the carbide unit, one never knew whether the gas would flow through the brass feed pipes to the headlights with a gentle hiss or whether the whole outfit would blow up in one's face.

Now that the Colonel had his automobile, someone was needed to drive it. He selected Chess, a colored man who worked for the family on and off at the home place or the bank, the latter having been established by Grandfather and some friends in 1910 with himself as its first president. Naturally Chess did not know how to drive an automobile. One might say that this was only a small drawback, seeing that all he had to do was to take a few driving lessons, but it wasn't that easy. To begin with, no one in town had ever driven a car and few had ever been inside one. It was to Chess's eternal credit that he had sufficient native ingenuity, perseverance, and imagination (plus, perhaps, a disinclination to cross the Colonel) that he was able to overcome every obstacle and teach himself to operate a machine he had never seen before, with all its gadgets, knobs, levers, pedals, and switches. In the process, he also taught himself to be an expert mechanic, although this was probably an acquired defense against a machine as perverse as the Buick. Its slick tires lasted not over a few hundred miles, and it took the combined efforts of everyone in the neighborhood to get one on or off a rim; the valves had to be reground and reset, carbon cleaned out, and the entire ignition system worked over completely after about two hundred miles of operation.

Colonel had an old harness house near the barn converted into a garage for the car. It was set up about six feet off the ground, and when it was made into a garage it was necessary to remove the entry ladder and construct a ramp in its place, in order that the car could be driven up and into the building. The barnyard was entered from the back street by driving through a sort of hallway in the barn; then a ninety-degree left turn had to be made to face the ramp, but it was too steep, because the Buick motor, big though it was in size, was too lacking in power to enable the car to climb up the ramp from a standing start at the bottom. This meant that it was necessary to back the car against the south fence, then take a running start and hit the ramp wide open. The garage itself was just barely long and wide enough to contain the car, so getting up and into its narrow confines was truly a ticklish business. One had to get enough speed between the fence and the ramp for the momentum of the car to rocket it up the ramp, then, at the precise instant that the rear wheels cleared the top, full brakes had to be applied instantaneously to keep the hurtling car from flying through the rear wall of the garage.

I found that automobiles held a great fascination for me as a boy, as airplanes did in later life. Colonel let me learn to drive the Buick on instructions grudgingly given by Chess. It naturally followed that I soon became convinced that I too could put the car in the garage. Late one afternoon Colonel and Bill and I went to the barnyard with Chess in the car and again I asked to be allowed to drive it in. Colonel must have become tired of refusing, for this time he told Chess to back the car against the lower fence and let me take over. I must have been about twelve or thirteen—and barely big enough to see over the dashboard.

It took all my strength to depress the clutch and the fullest extent of my reaching to stretch out and shove the gear shift into the low speed notch. By this time the back of my neck was shoved against the seat. As I had seen Chess do many times, I tugged the gasoline lever all the way down on the quadrant. The motor roared, the car shook, and yellow flames spewed out from the open exhaust. I cast a quick glance at the Colonel, Chess, and Bill standing safely away from the boiling, bucking Buick. They were—in order—apprehensive, angry, and delighted. I then peeked over the dashboard for a good look to line up the big radiator snout with the ramp and jerked my foot off the clutch pedal. The Buick shot out across the yard like a suddenly uncaged rabbit. I juggled with the steering wheel, keeping the radiator snout lined up on the center of the ramp, which I had to hit no matter what. I did, with a bang that could have been heard in the next county, but I was too intent with the steering wheel to think of the gasoline lever, much less to stamp down on the brakes. When I thought of them a second later it was too late to avoid disaster. The Buick roared up the ramp at such an angle that the front part kept right on going and for a split second I felt certain that the car was going to hang itself on a rafter. I was frozen into immobility, scared almost out of my wits; the gasoline lever remained wide open and I could not have found the brake pedal with a dozen feet. With scantlings, sheared-off posts, and rusty nails flying about my ears, we tore through the back wall of the building and leaped about twenty feet through the air, then plunked down into the soft and welcome earth of the freshly tilled garden. It was a mess; it was also many a day before the Colonel turned me loose again to put the car in the garage. . . .

I remember one trip we made to Memphis with the Colonel. There were, in addition to Chess and the Colonel, Auntee, Sallie Murry, Bill, and me. All roads were dirt then, and it usually took the better part of a full day to get there, depending on the weather, the car, the Colonel's temper, and how many cattle we encountered on the road. When we hit one, and we hit many, it immediately became the top specimen in the aristocracy of cattledom.

Preparing to go to Memphis in a car then was roughly equivalent to preparing for a trip to Mars today. Before a bag was packed, the Buick had to be stored with extra tires and tubes, tire patches, a big hand pump, several pieces of long rope, chains for all four wheels, a lantern, a hammer, a hatchet, and extra cans of gasoline and oil. One did not specify any particular type of gasoline or oil, since all came in bulk and were different only to the extent that one went into the motor by way of the carburetor and the other through the oil spout.

We prepared to start out literally at the crack of day, and it would be a long day, especially for the Colonel who, on orders from Auntee (since the death of Granny he would accept none from anyone else), would have to forego his "chawing" tobacco for a full day. On rides about Oxford he always sat in the back seat, but on cross-country trips he would usually sit in front beside Chess so he could better see what was going on and be in a position to issue driving instructions when he felt they were needed. No matter how many he gave, Chess always contrived to keep right on driving just as he intended doing in the first place.

Our big basket containing lunch and dinner had been carefully placed on the front seat between the Colonel and Chess; tire chains and what-not had been accounted for; a good portion of the family had gathered in the faint light of early dawn to see us off; the motor had been cranked and our spirits soared with exhilaration and unrestrained anticipation. With an expert and meaningful gesture Chess reached proudly for the big brass gear-shift lever and at that precise instant the heretofore completely sound right front tire blew out with a bang that woke all the neighbors who were not already abroad to see us set out. When the tire exploded the Buick shifted abruptly to starboard and shifted Grandfather onto the dinner basket, and his alpaca-coated right elbow dug into a segment of his favorite apple pie. We had been with him often enough to recognize the symptoms and we knew what to expect now, but this time Auntee was within arm's length. Grandfather's face took on the reddish hue of pre-explosion anger, his linen tourist cap trembled on his head, and he was just about to blow up like the tire, when Auntee reached over, touched him gently on the arm, and said, "Now Pappy, don't."

By now a number of folks were about, silently regarding the tilted Buick and its passengers. Not one evidenced any overwhelming inclination to wrestle with a flat tire at four-thirty in the morning, well knowing, as all did, that once such a finger-cracking, back-breaking job was begun it was certain to defy completion for at least two or three hours, and only an unrestrained fool would set out for Memphis as late as seven or eight o'clock in the morning.

The next day things went better. We actually did get under way at the crack of dawn. Well before sunup we had arrived at the long sand bed near College Hill, a good four miles from town. The ruts were deep, the treadless tires were slick, the sand was fine, and Chess decided to make a run at it, which meant putting the car in second gear, then building up to a good, flying start before hitting the sand, with the hope that the speed of the car on entry would be sufficient to keep up momentum and enable it to plow through the deep sand onto solid ground beyond in one mighty and irresistible surge. It didn't work and I don't suppose any of us really believed that it would. We wound up in the middle of the deepest section of the sand and settled down with a jolt up to the running boards.

We used to wonder how word could get ahead of us so quickly that we had started out for Memphis, were about to, or soon would. At any rate, before Chess could shut off the motor up came two citizens of the community driving two sullen mules to which was attached a relatively new chain just right to fit a 1909 Buick touring car. Under similar circumstances on earlier trips, when Auntee was not present, Colonel had blown his top, and if our tender ears had heard some choice cuss words, we could at least say that they had been uttered by a master. But now Auntee was with us, and no doubt Grandfather realized the futility of telling the two bland and uninspiring drivers to their greedy faces that they had dug the ruts deeper, harnessed their mules, and hid out in the brush just waiting for us to come along. No matter now, one way or the other the Colonel had to pay to get out: they knew it and he knew it. Neither the men nor the mules glanced at us or the car. They came up beside it and one of the men scratched the back of his neck, pushed the other, younger, one toward the car, then, as though addressing the empty woods, the red sand, or even the mules, said, "That'll be three dollars." The last time it had been only two and the Colonel's face began to get red again. But once more Auntee quickly reached over, touched him gently on the arm, and repeated, "Now Pappy, don't."

Five blowouts, three more towouts, and fourteen hours later we arrived in Memphis—but still short of our final destination, the Peabody Hotel, then on Main Street. We could see the hard-surface street ahead as we toiled through the last stretch of the rutted surface over which we had labored the live-long day. Now anticipation of better things to come took hold; surely we would soon be rolling smartly along the fine hard-topped road at twenty-five or maybe even thirty miles an hour. Surely now, we thought, our troubles of the day were behind us and ahead was a speedy, exhilarating ride to Main Street.

[Growing Up in Mississippi]   Willie Morris*

In a small town like this one in the lower South,[1] where the population ran close to half and half, one of the simplest facts of awareness was that Negroes were everywhere: they ambled along the sidewalks in the white neighborhoods, they mowed the grass and clipped the hedges in the broad green lawns, they rode down the streets in their horse-drawn wagons, they were the janitors and cleaning-women in the churches and schools and the laundry-women coming to the back doors for the week's wash. On the main street especially, on Saturdays, the town was filled with them, talking in great animated clusters on the corners, or spilling out of the drugstores and cafés at the far end of the narrow street. Their shouts and gestures, and the loud blare of their music, were so much a part of those Saturdays that if all of them had suddenly disappeared the town would have seemed unbearably ghostly and bereft. The different shades of color were extraordinary, for they ranged from the whitest white to the darkest black, with shades in between as various and distinct as yellows and browns could be. One woman in particular, whom we saw walking through the crowds on Main Street on Saturday nights, could have passed for a member of the women's choir in the white Baptist church. "There's that white nigger again," someone would say. "I wonder what the *others* think of her?" Not until I was fourteen or fifteen did it begin to occur to me to ask myself, "Are we *related?*" And it was about then that I began hearing the story of the two white men who had Thanksgiving and Christmas dinner every year with three Negroes, who were the white men's half-brothers. . . .

One summer morning when I was twelve, I sighted a little Negro boy walking with a girl who must have been his older sister on the sidewalk a block from my house. The little boy could not have been more than three; he straggled along behind the older girl, walking aimlessly on his short black legs from one edge of the sidewalk to the other.

*Reprinted with permission from *North Toward Home* (Boston: Houghton Mifflin Company, 1967), 80–81, 77–79, 87–88, 89, 21–23.

I hid in the shrubbery near the sidewalk in my yard, peering out two or three times to watch their progress and to make sure the street was deserted. The older girl walked by first, and the child came along a few yards behind. Just as he got in front of me, lurking there in the bushes, I jumped out and pounced upon him. I slapped him across the face, kicked him with my knee, and with a shove sent him sprawling on the concrete.

The little boy started crying, and his sister ran back to him and shouted, "What'd he *do* to you?" My heart was beating furiously, in terror and a curious pleasure; I ran into the back of my house and hid in the weeds for a long time, until the crying drifted far away into niggertown. Then I went into the deserted house and sat there alone, listening to every noise and rustle I heard outside, as if I expected some retribution. For a while I was happy with this act, and my head was strangely light and giddy. Then later, the more I thought about it coldly, I could hardly bear my secret shame.

Once before, when I had been a much smaller boy, I had caught a little sparrow trapped on my screen porch, and almost without thinking, acting as if I were another person and not myself, I had fetched a straight pin, stuck it through the bird's head, and opened the door to let him fly away. My hurting the Negro child, like my torturing the bird, was a gratuitous act of childhood cruelty—but I knew later that it was something else, infinitely more subtle and contorted.

For my whole conduct with Negroes as I was growing-up in the 1940s was a relationship of great contrasts. On the one hand there was a kind of unconscious affection, touched with a sense of excitement and sometimes pity. On the other hand there were sudden emotional eruptions—of disdain and utter cruelty. My own alternating affections and cruelties were inexplicable to me, but the main thing is that they were largely *assumed* and only rarely questioned. The broader reality was that the Negroes in the town were *there:* they were ours, to do with as we wished. I grew up with this consciousness of some tangible possession, it was rooted so deeply in me by the whole moral atmosphere of the place that my own ambivalence—which would take mysterious shapes as I grew older—was secondary and of little account.

One fact I took for granted was that Negro adults, even Negro adults I encountered alone and had never seen before, would treat me with generosity and affection. Another was some vague feeling for a mutual sharing of the town's past. (I remember going with one of my friends and her parents to take some food to an old Negro woman who lived alone in a cabin in the woods. The old woman told us about growing up in Yazoo, and of the day she saw the Yankee soldiers coming down the road in a cloud of dust. "I looked out the window," she said, "and there was the War, comin' at me from down the road.") Another assumption was that you could never call a Negro woman a "lady" or address her as "ma'am," or say "sir" to a Negro man. You learned as a matter of course that there were certain negative practices and conditions inherently associated with being a nigger. "Keeping a house like a nigger" was to keep it dirty and unswept. A "nigger car" was an old wreck without brakes and with squirrel tails ón the radio aerial. "Behaving like a nigger" was to stay out at all hours and to have several wives or husbands. A "nigger street" was unpaved and littered with garbage. "Nigger talk" was filled with lies and superstition. A "nigger funeral" meant wailing and shouting and keeping the corpse out of the ground for two weeks. A "white nigger store" was owned by a white man who went after the "nigger trade." There were "good niggers" and "bad niggers," and their categories were so formalized and elaborate that you wondered how they could live together in the same town.

Yet in the midst of all this there was the ineluctable attraction of nigger-town, which enclosed the white town on all sides like some other world, and the strange heart-pounding excitement that Negroes in a group generated for me. I knew all about the sexual act, but not until I was twelve years old did I know that it was performed with white women for pleasure; I had thought that only Negro women engaged in the act of love with white men just for fun, because they were the only ones with the animal desire to submit that way. So that Negro girls and women were a source of constant excitement and sexual feeling for me, and filled my day-dreams with delights and wonders.

A young boy grew up with other things: with the myths, the stories handed down. One of them concerned one of the town's policemen, a gnarled and skinny old man by the time I was growing up, who had shot a Negro on the sidewalk on the lower end of Main Street and stood over him with his pistol to prevent anyone from taking him away while he bled to death. Whether it was apocryphal or not was almost irrelevant, for the terror of that story was quite enough; we saw the policeman almost everyday, making his rounds of the parking meters. "Don't fool with ol' ——," someone would say. "He'd just as soon shoot you as *look* at you," and then recount the legend in gory detail. There was the tale of the white planter, who owned one of the big plantations in the delta. When one of his Negro hands looked too closely at his wife one day, the man got his gun and killed him, and there was no trial.

There were a boy's recurring sense impressions of a hovering violence, isolated acts that remained in my memory long afterward, as senseless and unpatterned later as they had been for me when they happened.

. . . Some white men came to see my father, when I was six or seven years old. I heard them talking at the front door. "We hear the niggers might cause trouble tonight," one of them said. My father went to town to buy some extra shotgun shells, and we locked all our doors and windows when the sun went down.

. . . A Negro shot and killed a white man at the honky-tonk near the town dump. When the time came for him to be executed, they brought the state's portable electric chair in a big truck from Jackson. We drove by and saw it parked in the back yard of the jail. The next day some older boys told me they had stayed up until midnight, with the lights on in their house, to watch all the lights dim when the nigger got killed.

. . . One morning I awoke to hear that a neigbbor had shot a Negro burglar. I ran down to his house, and a large crowd milled around on the porch and in the front room. Inside, the man was telling what had happened. He pointed to a bullet hole in the wall, and another in the leg of a table. He had awakened in the night and saw the nigger in the hallway. He pulled out his automatic and shot twice, and he heard a moan and saw the nigger running away. When he telephoned the police, all they had to do was follow the trail of blood to a house in niggertown. That morning we followed the blood ourselves, little drops and big ones in the dust of the alley and onto the concrete pavement. Then we came back and congratulated our neighbor on his aim. Many people came in to hear the story, and he told them: "If that second shot had been two inches to the left, that woulda been one *good* nigger." . . .

And there were the "redneck" boys—not called redneck by us, and not anything at first except "the boys from Graball Hill." They were as distinct a group as any in the school. They wore faded khakis or rough blue denim and heavy torn shoes; their teeth were bad and their hair was never combed. I would notice them at lunchtime, gathered in a large group near the Confederate Monument. Some of them would go across Main Street to Spell's Grocery to buy a nickel Moonpie[2] or a Baby Ruth bar, and wash their lunch down with water from the cool green fountain by the door; some would not eat any lunch at all. I particularly liked one of these boys, the gentlest one from Graball. His name was Bo. He was the slowest reader in the class, and he wore the same clothes every day. Once, after Christmas, when our teacher polled every child in the room about what he got for Christmas, he said: "I didn' get nuthin'. I ain't studyin' toys."

Almost all of them were rough and open, and you learned early to treat them with a diffident respect; they were bigger and often older, from failing a grade or from having to stay out of school, sometimes for days at a time, during picking season. Their habits ran to violence of a general kind, and they performed unique acts on an instant's whim. Sometimes when there was no teacher around three or four of them, in concert, would piss on the floor of the upstairs hall; one afternoon late, having missed their bus home, they crawled through the window to the principal's office and shit on the rug. Next day the teachers were looking for answers, and appealing to school pride if not school sanitation, but there were no takers.

They suffered from strange maladies, like sleeping sickness and diarrhea, which would keep them home longer than the cotton-picking. One of them almost died from having been bitten by a black-widow spider while sitting on a woodpile. They fought hard and long, especially among themselves. Pity the poor colored child who walked past the schoolhouse when they were outside. There would be cries of "coon" or "nigger baby," followed by a barrage of rocks and dirt clods. When I was a grown man, and saw the deputy sheriffs and the mobs pummeling Negro demonstrators on television, I needed no one to tell me they had been doing the same thing since the age of eight.

Notes

Notes supplied by the volume editor.

1. Yazoo City, about 120 miles southwest of Oxford, on the Choctaw Ridge where the delta meets the hill country.

2. A confectionary of marshmallow candy on a cookie covered in chocolate usually associated with blacks and poor whites.

[A Postpublication Addition to *Intruder in the Dust*]   William Faulkner*

7 Feb. 1949

Dear Bob:[1]
    Here is the insert for INTRUDER re our recent correspondence.
    Page 158 as set down through end of the paragraph. Stevens' speech ending: ". . . hide from one another behind a loud lipservice to a flag."

(INSERT—NEW MATTER)

"But what will happen?" he said. "What will we do and he do, both of us, all of us. What will become of him—Sambo?"

"I just told you," his uncle said. "He will disappear. There are not enough of him to resist, to repel, to hold intact his integrity even if he wished to remain a Negro. In time he would have got equity and justice without even asking for it. But by insisting on social equality, what he is actually demanding is racial extinction. Three hundred years ago he didn't exist in America; five hundred years from now he will have vanished and will be no more. Oh, he will still exist now and then as isolate and insulate phenomena, incorrigible, tieless, anachronic and paradox; archaeological and geological expeditions will stumble on him occasionally by individuals and even intact nests in caves in remote Tennessee and Carolina mountain fastnesses or Mississippi and Alabama and Louisiana swamps or, generations ago lost and unrecorded, in the mapless back areas of Detroit or Los Angeles tenement districts; travellers passing through the rotundras of the Croydon or Le Bourget or La Guardia airports or the supra transfer stations of space ships

*Reprinted with permission from *William Faulkner Manuscripts*, vol. 17 (New York: Garland Publishing, Inc., 1987), 719–20.

will gape at him intact[2] with banjo and hound and screenless mudchinked cabin and naked pickaninnies playing with empty snuff-bottles in the dust, even to the washpot in the backyard and his bandana-turbaned mate bending over it, as the Union Pacific railroad used to establish tepees of authentically costumed Blackfoot and Shoshone Indians in the lobby of the Commodore Hotel. But as a race he will be no more; his blood will exist only in the dusty files of genealogical societies for the members of what will then be the Daughters of the Founding Fathers or the Lost Causes to wrangle and brag over as the Briton does over his mystic trace of Norman, so that in five hundred years or perhaps even less than that, all America can paraphrase the tag line of a book a novel of about twenty years ago by another Mississippian, a mild retiring little man over yonder at Oxford,[3] in which a fictitious Canadian said to a fictitious self-lacerated Mississippian[4] in a dormitory room in a not too authentic Harvard: 'I who regard you will have also sprung from the loins of African kings.' "

(RESUME; P. 156)

"Now they were there and not too long behind the sheriff. For though the car . . ." etc etc CONTINUED[5]

Notes

Notes supplied by the volume editor.

1. Robert Haas, Faulkner's editor at Random House.
2. Page 1 of two pages ends here.
3. One of Faulkner's few self-references.
4. Faulkner later crossed out "Mississippian" and wrote "Southerner" in over it.
5. Haas never published this addition.

FOREBEARS

Sam Fathers's Fathers:
Indians and the Idea of Inheritance

Mick Gidley*

Isaac (Ike) McCaslin, unlike his biblical namesake, the favorite offspring of Abraham and progenitor of all the children of Israel, never fully outgrows his status as a son. As the telling first lines of *Go Down, Moses* (1942) indicate, he becomes "past seventy and nearer eighty than he ever corroborated any more, a widower now and uncle to half a county" and, crucially, "father to no one."[1] In his old age he "owned no property and never desired to since the earth was no man's but all men's, as light and air and weather were" (*Moses*, p.3). The last white male McCaslin, Ike, it is recorded later, gave up his inheritance of the McCaslin plantation to repudiate "the old wrong and shame" of his white family's slaveholding, and did so—"at least in principle, and at least the land itself in fact"—"for his son": "he would at least save and free his son." Yet, as these words of "Delta Autumn" have it, "saving and freeing his son," he "lost him" since he was never conceived (*Moses*, p.351). Ike was to be, in perpetuity, always a son and "father to no one."

In F. Scott Fitzgerald's *Tender is the Night* (1934), Dick Diver, at the loss of his natural father, speaks cryptically of the death of "all my fathers." In Robertson Davies's *The Manticore* (1972), David Staunton, the protagonist, receives pressing advice from a close family friend: "Listen, Davey, you great clamorous baby-detective, there is something you ought to know at your age: every man who amounts to a damn has several fathers, and the man who begat him in lust or drink or for a bet or even in the sweetness of honest love may not be the most important father. The fathers you choose for yourself are the significant ones."[2] These fictions both advert to notions of the father figure as formulated by Carl Jung: Staunton's tale is presented as if told to his Jungian analyst, and Diver, an analyst himself, is a product, among other things, of Fitzgerald's investment in his wife's (and his own) Jungian therapy. If such a context exists for *Go Down, Moses*, it is not overtly declared, yet it has been observed that Ike—whose own natural birth certainly came about as much through "drink" and "a bet" as through "the sweetness of honest

*This essay was written especially for this volume and is published here for the first time by permission of the author.

love"—also possesses more than one father.[3] There is the natural parent, Theophilus (Uncle Buck) McCaslin, twin son of Lucius Quintus Carothers McCaslin, founder of the McCaslin line. There is his father's twin brother, Amodeus (Uncle Buddy) McCaslin. There is Ike's cousin, McCaslin (Cass) Edmonds, "born in 1850 and sixteen years his [Ike's] senior and hence, his own father being near seventy when Isaac, an only child, was born, rather his brother than cousin and rather his father than either" (*Moses*, p.4). And, of course, there is Sam Fathers, "the old man born of a Negro slave and a Chickasaw chief who had been his [Ike's] spirit's father if any had, whom he had revered and harkened to and loved and lost and grieved" (*Moses*, p.326). (The experience of loss, primarily through death, lies at the heart of the novel.)

The blatantly named Sam Fathers has had, in his turn, more than one father: "Ikkemotubbe himself, who had named himself Doom" (*Moses*, p. 165) and an unnamed black slave to whom Ikkemotubbe, the Chickasaw chieftain, had married "the quadroon slave woman" (*Moses*, p.166) he had already impregnated with Sam. According to "The Old People," that "was how Sam Fathers got his name, which in Chickasaw had been Had-Two-Fathers" (*Moses*, p.166). Two years later Ikkemotubbe "sold the man and woman and the child who was his own son to his white neighbor, Carothers McCaslin" (*Moses*, p.166). This L. Q. C. McCaslin, a man equally capable of repudiating his own offspring, thus became to Sam a kind of third unloving father.[4] Significantly, Sam (who is in a sense the last Indian McCaslin), like Ike, produces no natural children.

Go Down, Moses and many of the works textually, thematically, or, most significantly in this context, familially associated with it, such as the hunting stories, the Compson Appendix of 1946, and works chronicling the McCaslin/Priest family, down to *The Reivers* (1962), reverberate—resound, even—with ideas, contentions, and tussles over ancestors, pedigree, and property, whether straightforwardly inherited, bartered, sold, or gambled. Indeed, along with representation of virtually the whole gamut of patriarchal attitudes—a matter which will not be addressed here—these fictions, whether serious, comic, or tragicomic, for the most part actually constitute plots of patrimony.

The Indian stories—"Red Leaves" (1930), "A Justice" (1931), the relevant part of "Mountain Victory" (1932), "Lo!" (1934) and "A Courtship" (1948)—are no exception. The plot of "Red Leaves," the much-praised tale of a proud, unnamed black slave's run for freedom and life, and of his ultimate submission to the inescapability of death, is based on the cultural belief of his Indian owners that the body servant of the chief ("the Man"), like the chief's horse and the chief's dog, must be buried beside him to accompany him on his journey to the other world. It is the inheritance of the Man's son—who will, in turn, become the Man—to hunt down the fleeing slave in order to meet all initial formal requirements of chieftainship. On his elevation as the Man, the son, a grossly fat degenerate called Moketubbe, will legitimately inherit, as a sign of his new position, a pair of French red-heeled slippers he has coveted and worn surreptitiously for years despite their smallness on his oversized feet. Just as mismatched and ill-fitting, and infinitely more significant by any measure of values, is the institution of Negro slavery that these Indians have inherited from Moketubbe's grandfather, Ikkemotubbe. In a series of profoundly ironic exchanges, the Indians incessantly discuss its burdens as if they, the masters, were its victims.

The structural power of "Red Leaves" derives from the manner in which all its actions appear ritualistic, predestined, and inevitable. Thus, right at the opening of the story, as the two Indians seeking the slave walk toward the slave quarters, one says to the other, " 'I know what we will find.' " " 'What we will not find,' " replies his companion, because the slave has already run away.[5] Again and again, the present action follows the pattern of what had happened at the death of the previous Man, when his slave had tried to escape. Also repeated is an air of the given, a stamp of doom: the slave must run and the Indians must catch him; he must " 'not wish to die' " (*Collected Stories*, p.335) or to eat or to take water, but his death, sanctioned so to speak by the poisonous snake which strikes at him, has been ordained; the food will not reach his stomach and, though he puts the drinking gourd to his lips three times and works his throat, the unswallowed water cascades each time down his mud-caked chest.

"A Justice" constitutes the earliest account of Sam Fathers's origins; here he is Choctaw rather than Chickasaw, fathered adulterously on a black slave woman by an Indian named Crawfish-ford or Craw-ford rather than by Ikkemotubbe himself, and sold by Ikkemotubbe not to Carothers McCaslin but to General Compson.[6] The tale is related by the adult Quentin Compson from memories of what Sam Fathers himself told him, Sam Fathers having received it when he "was big enough to hear talk" (*Collected Stories*, p.345) from his father's Indian friend Herman Basket. (Again and again he says, "Herman Basket said . . . ") The story, like so many of those we are considering, is itself an inherited object, a kind of heirloom akin to the material family heirlooms in *Go Down, Moses*, such as Hubert Beauchamp's burlap-wrapped coffee pot or General Compson's hunting horn that Ike ultimately passes to Roth's illegitimate baby.

The events of "A Justice," as its title ironically signposts, concern the far from just or fair struggle over the unnamed black slave woman between Craw-ford and the woman's anonymous black husband, all set in train by Ikkemotubbe's offer to give some of the group of slaves, to which she belongs, to Craw-ford and sustained by Ikkemotubbe's derivation of amusement from their continuing rivalry, the absurd and extraordinary forms of which he manipulates and heightens. It is also, thereby a study of Ikkemotubbe himself, of his murderous ruthlessness, cunning, and malicious inventiveness, but with no explicit moral judgments. Ikkemotubbe's rise—from his usurpation of the chieftainship to his establishment of slavery to his supervision of the epic trek across land with the steamboat—serves as a backdrop to the antics of the contending lovers and fathers. Indeed, by transmitting the story unremarked upon, as it were, either by Sam Fathers or by the mature Quentin, the degree to which anyone, including Ikkemotubbe, may be held responsible, in large things or small, is left in abeyance. (It may even be the case that the reader, especially with regard to Herman Basket's revelations, becomes a kind of unwilling accomplice in the action.)

"Mountain Victory," the tale of a violent episode at the end of the Civil War, features Saucier Weddel, the Choctaw owner of Contalmaison, a huge plantation carved out of the Chocktaws' Mississippi domain. In the course of it Weddel refers briefly to the events of the story "Lo!" in which a delegation of his tribe went to Washington to petition the President himself, supposedly about the murder of a white man but actually in order to secure the incontrovertible right to retain in perpetuity the only river ford in their territory. While these two stories about different generations of Weddels—Choctaw in "Mountain Victory" and Chickasaw in "Lo!"—do not treat the Ikkemotubbe/Fathers/McCaslin family as "Red Leaves" and "A Justice" do, they parallel the others both in details irrelevant to the present study and in their larger concerns.[7] "Lo!" and "A Justice" in particular match one another in their rendition of manipulative chiefly power, in their studied playfulness with—even inversion of—the idea of "justice" and, of course, in their investigations of patrimony.

"A Courtship," composed at the latest in 1942, deals with the earliest moment, historically, in the fortunes of Ikkemotubbe's line.[8] The white man has arrived in the land, at least in the massive form of the steamboat captain David Hogganbeck, ancestor of Boon Hogganbeck, and a treaty has stipulated the extent of Chickasaw land holdings, but the Chickasaws still hunt and farm for their own food and have yet to institute slavery. Ikkemotubbe has not yet usurped or assumed the role of the Man—although, significantly, the story of his later treachery in doing so is told in cameo: "Moketubbe was the Man when Ikkemotubbe returned, named Doom now, with the white friend called the Chevalier Soeur-Blonde de Vitry and the eight new slaves which we did not need either, and his gold-laced hat and cloak and the little gold box of strong salt and the wicker wine hamper containing the four other puppies which were still alive, and within two days Moketubbe's little son was dead and within three Ikkemotubbe whose name was Doom now was himself the Man" (*Collected Stories*, p.363). But, at the time of the events recorded in "A Courtship," Ikkemotubbe "was still just Ikkemotubbe, one of the young men, the best one, who rode the hardest and fastest and danced the longest and got the drunkest and was loved the best, by the young men and the girls and the older women too who should have had other things to think about" (*Collected Stories*, p.363). The story recounts the epic series of contests between this man and the elementally powerful Hogganbeck— riding, drinking, eating, running—in their attempt to win the unnamed sister of Herman Basket, a young woman who "walked in beauty. Or she sat in it, that is, because she did not walk at all unless she had to" (*Collected*

Stories, p.362). In the course of their gargantuan contest, through rivalry and mutual respect, the men are bonded together in a kind of camaraderie which is reinforced by the news that in their absence, their own heroic exertions notwithstanding, Herman Basket's sister had settled for Log-in-the-Creek, an unexceptional young man who simply lay around playing a plaintive and insinuating harmonica. Then, in mutual disappointment, both Ikkemotubbe and Hogganbeck quit the domain by steamboat—an ending which in fact marks a beginning: of Ikkemotubbe's movement into the white world to become Doom. Doom, who begets and sells Sam.

Part 4 of "The Bear" in *Go Down, Moses*, which is explicitly devoted to lineage, its inheritance and its responsibilities, and in which Ike certainly acts the "clamorous baby-detective" of Robertson Davies's phrase, draws together parallels between the McCaslin family history and, grandly, all of these (and more): the regional history of the South, the continential history of the New World (from Columbus onward), and the spiritual history of the world, the Fall of humankind. In the wilderness parts of *Go Down, Moses* similar large connections are established, as in the salutation "Chief, Grandfather," first to the stag, then to the snake (pp. 184, 330)—evocations, crudely speaking, of godhood and satanism as well as Faulknerian versions of the notion of (aptly named) familiar spirits. In that "Grandfather" there are resonances to grandfather L. Q. C. McCaslin and his particular offenses as well as symbolic ones to biblical Abraham and to the original Father Figure Himself. And the pairing of the familial expression "Grandfather" to the word "Chief" takes in the "Indian" family line, the other grandfather, the Chickasaw chief Doom, and his offenses. Also, in this context, "Grandfather," like "Old Man" or "Old One," which are so often used in translations of Native American myths and tales as synonyms for the deity (or, as in the case of the Sioux holy man Black Elk, spiritual force), stresses what James Fenimore Cooper—a figure lying behind so many subsequent representations of Native Americans—liked to call "Indian gifts."[9] There can be no doubt that in all the emphasis on "blood"—white, black, Indian—in *Go Down, Moses*, there are fraught and suitably mystified notions of collective, indeed racial, traits and responsibilities which partly determine individual acts and which are exemplified in those acts.

It is certainly no accident that the frequent play upon the word "fathers" in the book has as much applicability to Indian patrimony as it does to white and black patrimony, including the biblical depiction of the jealous God who would "visit the sins of the fathers upon the children unto the third and fourth generation." Thus Ike knows how to lie in wait for a buck returning to its bed at dawn in the way "the old Chickasaw fathers did" (*Moses*, p.210). And thus he can analyze the land as " 'already accursed even as Ikkemotubbe and Ikkemotubbe's father old Issetibbeha and old Issetibbeha's fathers too held it, already tainted . . . by what Grandfather and his kind, his fathers, had brought into the new land' " (*Moses*, p.258–59). This is why, to him, that land constitutes " 'their ravaged patrimony, the dark and ravaged fatherland' " (*Moses*, p.298). It is not surprising that this vision is linked to the notion that the land actually *belongs* to no one in the sense recorded at the opening of the book or as meditated upon by Ike in "Delta Autumn": "because it belong to no man. It belonged to all; they had only to use it well, humbly and with pride" (*Moses*, p.354)—a conception which is at the base of Ike's relinquishment of the McCaslin plantation and which is analogous, as others have observed, to certain generalized Indian teachings.[10] " 'Sell a country! Why not sell the air, the great sea, as well as the earth?' " remonstrated Tecumseh, the Shawnee leader. " 'Did not the Great Spirit make them all for the use of his children?' " Similarly, a Blackfoot chief refused to sign away land, saying, " 'It was put here for us by the Great Spirit and we cannot sell it because it does not belong to us.' "[11]

A related complex of ideas promulgated by Ike as a result of Sam's tutelage concerns human kinship with the animal kingdom—"there was something running in Sam Fathers' vein which ran in the veins of the buck too" (*Moses*, p.350)—and the ultimate unity of all things. Luther Standing Bear, a Sioux, spoke of his people's "brotherly feeling for the animal and bird world" which was sometimes "so close" that "in true brotherhood" people and animals "spoke a common tongue." And, of course, Native Americans have often inveighed against white stances towards the earth. "The white people never cared for land or deer or bear," declared an elderly Wintu woman. "When the Indians kill meat, we eat it all up. . . . When we burn grass for grasshoppers, we don't ruin things. We shake down acorns and pinenuts. We don't chop down trees. . . . But the White people plow up the ground, pull down the trees, kill everything. . . . How can the spirit of the earth like the White man? Everywhere the White man has touched it, it is sore."[12]

Such views went along with belief in a firm connection between the spirits of the dead and the earth they had inhabited in life. Thus, as early as 1811, Tecumseh could warn the Choctaws and Chickasaws of what was to become Faulkner's actual territory and "apocryphal kingdom" that they should "sleep no longer . . . in false security and delusive hopes," asking rhetorically, "Will not the bones of our dead be plowed up, and their graves turned into plowed fields?" Chief Seattle, in one of the most famous speeches of all, predicted to Governer Isaac Stevens that when his "children's children think themselves alone in the field, the store, the shop, upon the highway, or in the silence of the pathless woods, they will not be alone" because the land "will throng with the returning hosts" of vanished Indians. "The dead," he emphasized, "are not powerless," adding, "Dead, did I say? There is no death, only a change of worlds."[13] Ike, revisiting Sam's grave in the pathless big woods, conjures with the thought that Sam *"probably knew"* he *"was in the woods this morning long before"* his arrival there; and, it is said, the grave itself was "no abode of the dead because," simply, "there was no death, not Lion and not Sam: not held fast in earth but free in earth and not in earth but of earth, myriad yet undiffused of every myriad part" (*Moses*, p.328).

Needless to say, we must be wary of creating a set of straightforward, innocent Indian truths to parallel or weigh against Faulkner's fictions or Faulkner's characters' convictions. It has proven all too easy for the dominant culture to reduce the varieties of Native American cultures across the continent to a monolithic construct, the Indian—"the white man's Indian," in Robert Berkhofer's phrase—as a figure fashioned and then remodeled to suit the prevailing assumptions of the moment.[14] One version of the white man's Indian, as several of the passages quoted here testify, is the Indian as primal ecologist; this is not, of course, to deny Native American concern over such issues, but to emphasize the role of ideology in the representation of others, especially when the others cannot speak for themselves but, at best, must be translated. Their speech—as in Seattle's oratory, for example—follows established conventions of what Indian speech is supposed to sound like. Faulkner, for his part, did appropriate such an "Indian" voice for the telling of "A Courtship" and parts of the other stories. Indeed, he readily declared of his Indians, "I made them up."[15] His practice in representation was certainly complex, and subject to change.

In many essentials, Faulkner's Indians conform to the main contours of "savagism" as adumbrated by Roy Harvey Pearce, Robert Sayre, and others.[16] *They are mostly hunters, rather than farmers.* This seems especially true of "A Courtship," which is set furthest back in time, and in "Red Leaves," when land cultivation is introduced on any scale and must be done not by the Indians themselves, but by black slaves. In *Go Down, Moses* Sam's true Indianness, so to speak, is demonstrated by his desire, after Jobaker's death, to live exclusively as a woodsman. *They prove tradition-bound and not susceptible to "improvement."* In "Red Leaves," despite their glimpsing the absurdities of the situation, the Indians feel obliged by ancestral custom to sacrifice the chief's body servant. In "A Courtship" the competitive feats entered into by the protagonists are vouchsafed by tradition, especially the race to the distant cave, which itself takes the designated route for young men on a vision quest. In "Lo!," but also in other stories, they treat their newly acquired white clothes oddly, for instance, by carrying their pantaloons rolled up in neat bundles rather than wearing them. *They are, moreover, childlike innocents—except, significantly, in their cruelty and cunning—who are readily corrupted by the vices of civilization.* Weddel's Choctaws in "Lo!' do not at first see that the trader who buys their ford has found an ingenious way to make a living. In "Red Leaves" one of the Indians tacitly admits to cannibalism, clearly oblivious to any ethical issues raised. Much of the humor in "A Justice" rests on Craw-ford's willingness to go along with Ikkemotubbe's designs. Indians in these works generally become easy conquests to drinking, deceit, and greed. *That is, mostly because of their superstitious paganism, they often appear immune to the virtues of civilization, such as Christianity, thrift, and technological progress, and are thus doomed to extinction.* Much of our sense of Sam Fathers as the last of his race testifies to this.

Nevertheless, while we may not accept Noel Polk's implicit argument that Faulkner transcends all conventions of representation, presenting his Indians as "just folks," so to speak, his vision of them does appear to counter the broad outlines highlighted above in a number of respects.[17] Saucier Weddel's particular clan of Choctaws, for example, unlike the "pure" clan, has not persisted in a life of hunting but opted for "Europeanization" and now, as he says in "Mountain Victory," " 'we lost the title [of the Man] to the branch which refused to become polluted,' " but " 'we kept the slaves and the land' " (*Collected Stories*, p.759). Indeed, Faulkner's Indians are often far from "tradition"—whether in clothes or, more importantly, customs— although such deviations are almost always presented as at best absurd and decadent (a snuff box worn as an earring, say) and at worst degenerate (Moketubbe's extraordinary fatness). And in this they may well seem not at all childlike. Ikkemotubbe especially, and particularly in "A Justice," appears steeped in a guile so beyond mere savage cunning as to be akin not just to worldiness, but malignancy.

Running tangentially to these infringements of savagist conventions, through the period during which the Indian works were composed, there is also a perceptible modulation toward simplification, elegy, and nostalgia. The final sentence of "A Courtship" has the key words: "That's how it was in the old days" (*Collected Stories*, p.380). Subsequent to the old days all is declension.

Desecration of the earth permeates *Go Down, Moses*. Even the black line of the McCaslin family does not prove guiltless in this regard. Commentators too numerous to mention have pointed to Lucas Beauchamp's crazed digging up of the earth in his barren search for treasure, putting the quest ahead of his farming, his illicit moonshine business and, even, his marriage so long symbolized by "the fire in the hearth" of his cabin. It is especially interesting that since the book's structure is a serial one of discrete multiple perspectives, this episode in Lucas's family fortunes is related to the Indianness of the ecological wilderness themes not only in a broad sense, but also in detail. It has often passed unnoticed, for instance, that a frequent Cherokee "Formula for Obtaining Long Life" includes the prescription "the fire of the hearth will be left burning for me incessantly" and that the place Lucas actually excavates is an Indian mound, one of the most ancient signs of an Indian and human presence in the region.[18] James Snead has observed that the language used of Lucas's first "penetration" of the mound is sexual;[19] since the mound is usually described in terms associated with death, as a burial chamber, this serves to stress the degree to which even the act itself is a violation and a desecration. Thus the last falling clod of earth hitting Lucas's face can be figured as "a sort of final admonitory pat from the spirit of darkness and solitude, the old earth, perhaps the old ancestors themselves" (*Moses*, p.38).

The fact that "Indian names" survive "on the little towns" of the Delta— "Aluschaskuna, Tillatoba, Homochitto, Yazoo" (*Moses*, p.341)—but are unregarded by their inhabitants is further evidence of the modulation toward simplification and elegy. By the time the Compson Appendix was published, even Ikkemotubbe's misdeeds may be invoked without emphasis (or, conceivably, in weighty ambiguous irony). He is overwhelmingly "a dispossessed American king"—and the power of civilization in the form of money from oil taken from the earth is such that "the homeless descendants of the dispossessed would ride supine with drink and splendidly comatose above the dusty allotted harborage of their bones in specially built scarlet-painted hearses and fire engines."[20] By the writing of "Mississippi" in 1954 the image is sharper, and simpler: "except for looking occasionally out from behind the face of a white man or a Negro, the Chickasaws and Choctaws and Natchez and Yazoos were as gone as the predecessors."[21]

If such is the case visually, Indian sounds, words, speech are in Faulkner richly problematic. Jobaker, the last full-blooded Indian, can occasionally converse in the "old tongue" with Sam Fathers (*Moses*, p.172), but no words of that conversation or language reach the reader. Several times Sam uses it, but again almost none is transmitted. Ike in his turn, though he is supposed to have "learned" the old language by "listening to [Sam] and Joe Baker" (*Moses*, p.184) speaks only the one word "Oleh"—in actuality, it seems, either a Faulkner neologism or a bastardized Yoruba expression.[22] This aspect of Faulkner's representation is multifaceted. Looked at from one perspective, it abides by the popular stereotype of the inscrutable savage who utters only "How" or other monosyllabic grunts. From another, it conforms to the ideology of Indians as a vanishing race not only visually, in the manner elaborated by Lewis Dabney, for example,[23] but also aurally, in that they advance toward silence.

From yet another vantage, it constitutes a profound acknowledgment of the orality of Indian cultures—in which Thoreau's dictum that "it takes two to speak the truth, one to speak, the other to hear" must be literally (orally) the case—an orality that is invariably betrayed by the primary and most significant translation of all, that of writing. This is exemplified most graphically in the description in *Requiem for a Nun* (1951) of the largest Chickasaw land cessions, where Mohataha, "the Chickasaw matriarch, Ikkemotubbe's mother"—"she could write her name, or anyway make something with a pen or a pencil which was agreed to be, or at least accepted to be, a valid signature—signed all the conveyances as her son's kingdom passed to the white people."[24] (And, as we have seen in the inscriptions on the Delta towns, when the Indian oral sounds survive into writing, they do so only as appropriations.) Writing here, the stain of it, its ineradicable nature, is as dangerous for the Indians as, for example, the writing and accounts in the McCaslin plantation ledgers—"two threads frail as truth and impalpable as equators yet cable-strong to bind for life them who made the cotton to the land their sweat fell on" (*Moses*, p.256)—is for the blacks. In this writing of Mohataha's, in Faulkner's writing of her act and these tales, the Indian inheritance of the McCaslins and Yoknapatawpha is lost forever and caught forever, both together.

Notes

1. William Faulkner, *Go Down, Moses* (New York: Modern Library, 1942), 3. All subsequent page references appear in the text. A fascinating insight into other aspects of family and sexual relationships in the book is provided by Patrick McGee, "Gender and Generation in Faulkner's 'The Bear,'" *The Faulkner Journal* 1 (Fall 1985): 46–54.

2. F. Scott Fitzgerald, *Tender is the Night* (New York: Scribners, 1934), 205; Robertson Davies, *The Manticore* (Harmondsworth: Penguin, 1976), 289.

3. A slightly different set of fathers from mine is summoned up in Annette Benert, "The Four Fathers of Isaac McCaslin," *Southern Humanities Review* 9 (Fall 1975): 423–33.

4. For an elaboration of the similarities between Ikkemotubbe and L. Q. C. McCaslin, see Dirk Kuyk, Jr., *Threads Cable-strong: William Faulkner's "Go Down, Moses"* (Lewisburg, Pa.: Bucknell University Press, 1983), 89–90.

5. William Faulkner, *Collected Stories of William Faulkner* (New York: Random House, 1950), 313. All subsequent page references to the stories appear in the text.

6. For commentary on changes in Sam's character, see James Early, *The Making of "Go Down, Moses"* (Dallas: Southern Methodist University Press, 1972), 13.

7. For an interesting note on these parallels, among other things, see Walter Taylor, "Yoknapatawpha's Indians: A Novel Faulkner Never Wrote,"in *The Modernists: Studies in a Literary Phenomenon*, ed. Lawrence B. Gamache and Ian S. MacNiven (Rutherford, N.J.: Fairleigh Dickinson University Press, 1987), 202–9.

8. For this dating, see Frank Cantrell, "Faulkner's 'A Courtship,'" *Mississippi Quarterly* 24 (Summer 1971): 289, n.2.

9. For typical usages of these expressions, see such collections as T. C. McLuhan, ed., *Touch the Earth: A Self-Portrait of Indian Existence* (New York: Pocket Books, 1972); and Frederick W. Turner III, ed., *The Portable North American Indian Reader* (New York: Viking, 1974). For Black Elk, see particularly Raymond J. DeMallie, ed., *The Sixth Grandfather: Black Elk's Teachings, Given to John G. Neihardt* (Lincoln and London: University of Nebraska Press, 1984). For interesting general commentary on Faulkner's Indians, including remarks on Cooper's possible influence on Faulkner, see Lewis M. Dabney, *The Indians of Yoknapatawpha: A Study in Literature and History* (Baton Rouge: Louisiana State University Press, 1974).

10. For example, Dabney, 151, who cites Chief Joseph of the Nez Perce.

11. For Tecumseh, see Turner, 246; for the Blackfoot chief, McLuhan, 53.

12. For Standing Bear and the Wintu woman, see McLuhan, 6 and 15, respectively.

13. For Tecumseh and Seattle, see Turner, 247 and 253, respectively.

14. Robert Berkhofer, *The White Man's Indian: Images of the Native American from Columbus to the Present Day* (New York: Knopf, 1978).

15. Quoted by Dabney, 11. It is in the nebulous area of tone of voice rather than in some of the areas instanced by James Krefft that Faulkner may have affinities with Oliver La Farge; see Krefft, "A Possible Source for Faulkner's Indians: Oliver La Farge's *Laughing Boy*," *Tulane Studies in English* 23 (1977): 187–92. Another such comparison worthy of investigation is Frank Waters's novel, *The Man Who Killed The Deer* (New York: Farrar, Rhinehart, 1941).

16. See Roy Harvey Pearce, *Savagism and Civilization: A Study of the Indian and the American Mind* (Baltimore: Johns Hopkins University Press, 1965); and Berkhofer, *passim*; in the following discussion I have relied particularly on the succinct account in Robert F. Sayre, *Thoreau and the Indians* (Princeton, N.J.: Princeton University Press, 1977), 3–27.

17. See Noel Polk, *Faulkner's "Requiem for a Nun": A Critical Study* (Bloomington: Indiana University Press, 1981), 255–56.

18. See A. Grove Day, *The Sky Clears: Poetry of the American Indians* (Lincoln: University of Nebraska Press, 1951), 141.

19. James A. Snead, *Figures of Division: William Faulkner's Major Novels* (New York and London: Methuen, 1986), 184. Snead also writes interestingly about the snake imagery in the text, 189.

20. "The Compsons," in *The Portable Faulkner*, ed. Malcolm Cowley (New York: Viking, 1946), 737, 738.

21. "Mississippi," in *Essays, Speeches and Public Letters by William Faulkner*, ed. James B. Meriwether (New York: Random House, 1965), 12.

22. See Dabney, 40.

23. See Dabney, *passim.*

24. *Requiem for a Nun* (Harmondsworth: Penguin, 1960), 22.

[Sam Fathers and Doom]   John R. Cooley*

Go Down, Moses (1940) and its celebrated story "The Bear" include Faulkner's fullest, most revealing portrait of a black natural. Like so many of Faulkner's characters, Sam Fathers appears in a number of works: *Intruder in the Dust, The Reivers,* and the stories "Red Leaves," "The Old People," "A Justice," "The Bear," and "Delta Autumn." Through these stories Faulkner seems to present a character dilemma: Sam has lived a life of complex circumstances; his teachings suggest a wide understanding of the natural world and of human conduct, yet he reveals little awareness or understanding of the forces that have affected his life.

In Faulkner's story "The Old People" one learns that Sam's father, Doom, is a nephew to the old chief, Ikkemotubbe. When Doom returns from his adventure in New Orleans he brings with him a French companion, the Chevalier Soeur-Blonde de Vitry, and a quantity of arsenic contained in a "gold snuff box." To display his new power gained from the white men, he "took one of the puppies from the hamper and put a pinch of white powder on its tongue and the puppy died before the one holding it could cast it away." The next afternoon the young son of Chief Moketubbe mysteriously dies. Moketubbe abdicates that afternoon and Doom becomes "The Man." Shortly after his accession to power, he introduces slavery to the tribe and then a succession of luxuries and artifacts of white civilization, setting in motion the slow deterioration of the Chickasaws and their gradual alienation from the wilderness.

On the day after his accession, Doom conducts a marriage ceremony between the "pregnant quadroon" who had arrived with him and "one of the slave men which he had just inherited (that was how Sam Fathers got his name, which in Chickasaw had been Had-Two-Fathers)" and two years later

*Reprinted with permission from *Black Portraits by White Writers in Modern American Literature* (Newark: University of Delaware Press, 1982), 113–16.

sells the man and woman and the child, who is his own son, to his white neighbor Carothers McCaslin (p. 166).

By all logic one would expect Sam Fathers, when he is old enough to comprehend it, to reject this corrupt birthright and heritage from Doom, but such is not the case. Even though Sam Fathers has been a slave much of his life, "his face and bearing were still those of the Chickasaw chief" (p. 164). Ike's older cousin, Cass, tells Ike that Sam " 'probably never held it against old Doom for selling him and his mother into slavery' " and that Sam " 'probably believed it is the chief's blood which was "betrayed" through the black blood which his mother gave him' " (p. 168). Most likely Cass's interpretation is correct. Sam shows little interest in his fellow blacks on the McCaslin plantation, having always considered himself above them as the son of an Indian chief.

With the death of Jobaker, the last full-blooded Chickasaw, Sam must feel that the heritage of the wildnerness is at last his, despite the mixture of the three bloods in his veins. The morning after burying Jobaker, Sam demands of Cass Edmonds that he be released to live in the woods in order to take Jobaker's place there. " 'I want to go,' ' he said, " 'Let me go.' " And then " 'I'm going now' " (p. 173), not even waiting for Cass to react. Sam not only replaces Jobaker as high priest and chief of the Chickasaw wilderness, but he also sets himself free. As Cass tells Ike, " 'He was born in a cage and has been in it all his life; he knows nothing else' " (p. 167). Life as a black man has been lifelong imprisonment for Sam.

Now, at last, he can be an Indian, the last chief of the Chickasaws. What Sam does not admit is that his kingdom, the great woods, is already corrupted and doomed. He is at last reestablished as his father's son, yet it was his father who sold Sam and his mother into slavery. It was also his father who doomed the wilderness—by selling it to white men—and doomed the Chickasaws by introducing slavery and "civilizing" his people. The patrimony Sam now assumes for a brief tenure is almost as corrupt as the patrimony Ike inherits and rejects in part 4 of "The Bear." There is, of course, no way of knowing whether he decides to claim the tainted patrimony regardless. One knows only that Sam chooses freedom (" 'Let me go,' " " 'I'm going now' "), the great woods, and his Indian heritage over the race and heritage of his mother. Ironically, it was his mother's line that was more nearly uncorrupted, that had retained its strength and its ability to endure, despite—or perhaps because of—its subjugation.

Even if Sam Fathers, in his old age, has idolized his Chickasaw heritage to the exclusion of his black heritage, his function in "The Bear" is heightened by his "dual" fatherhood. Although he becomes a spiritual father to a fatherless Ike McCaslin, one should remember that his name has been shortened from the original, "Had-Two-Fathers." Cass explains to Ike that Sam is " 'himself his own battleground, the scene of his own vanquishment and the mausoleum of his own defeat' " (p. 168). His black blood has been vanquished and enslaved by the blood of his white and Indian ancestors. In leaving the plantation for the wilderness, Sam imagines that he has set himself free from the warfare within him and from the conflict between civilization and wilderness that has always surrounded him. He believes that he is living, at last, the role for which he was born, forgetting or ignoring the corruption that role represents.

FAMILY

The McCaslin-Beauchamp-Edmonds Family

Crying in the Wilderness: Legal, Racial, and Moral Codes in *Go Down, Moses*

Thadious M. Davis*

In 1937, just a few years before Faulkner was to begin the stories compiling *Go Down, Moses* (1942), Bertram Doyle stated: "Tradition . . . assigns the Negro his place in the South, law defines it, sentiment supports it, custom and habit continue it, and prejudice maintains it in those instances where it seems to be breaking down." His conclusion is a linguistically balanced restatement of common knowledge. During the early 1930s, in preparation for her book *After Freedom: A Cultural Study of the Deep South* (1939), Hortense Powdermaker observed that in Indianola, Mississippi, whites believed that blacks were "innately inferior" and "by nature" fit only for servile employment; correspondingly, blacks understood that all aspects of their lives were affected by "the racial situation and the system with which it is interlocked," so that each black person within the commuity believed "that he must watch his behavior in the company of Whites, lest he give offense and suffer for it." Although Powdermaker spent two years completing field research in Mississippi, she, too, concludes the known: that law and custom confirmed the subservient place of blacks; that a system of swift punishment for real and imagined grievances either under the legal system or the racial codes controlled the lives of blacks and the thinking of whites.

Powdermaker, an anthropologist, and Doyle, a sociologist, reiterate a commonplace: the pervasive separate and lower place of blacks in Mississippi life during the same period in which Faulkner, as he revealed in letters to Robert Haas, had already written "four stories about niggers" and intended to "build onto [them] . . . write some more." By May 1, 1941, Faulkner had written a collection of stories which had become, he said, "a volume, collected short stories, general theme being relationship between white and Negro races here." Faulkner's collection already had the title *Go Down, Moses*, as well as much of the material for inclusion. Yet, it was not until he expanded the stories "A Point of Law" and "Gold is not Always" into "The

*Reprinted with permission from *Mississippi College Law Review* 4, no. 2 (Spring 1984): 299–318.

Fire and the Hearth," and added the fourth section of "The Bear," that he clarified the dominant vision of the work, a vision which differentiates it from just another novel about "race relations," and from even such distinguished novels as those by two other Mississippians, *Night Fire* (1946) by Edward Kimbrough and *The Voice at the Back Door* (1956) by Elizabeth Spencer.

Faulkner chose the interfamilial black-white relationships developed over a spectrum of time, from the pre–Civil War period to the World War II era, extending through three generations of whites and four of blacks. However, at the base of the novel and those relationships is the concept of property as it relates to human rights and to the rights of the individual. In part, Faulkner examines the strong belief in the right to property as a basic right, and his characters, both black and white, define self and others in terms of the right to property and the use of property, but readers define the moral code of the novel according to the characters' attitudes toward property. The ideological context inspiring Faulkner's novel stems mainly from the existence of chattel slavery in the South rather than from philosophical treatises on property. He employs property and the rights which arise from ownership of private property to underscore and to illuminate not only black-white relationships, but also fundamental questions about the value and meaning of the human being.[1] He frames his questions, what does it mean to be human and what are the responsibilities as well as the rights of the human being, from the perspective of the white Southerner in a specified environment, who possesses, owns, inherits, and holds "property," and whose right to dispose of it as he chooses is protected by law.

In this discussion, I assume the primacy of four themes already delineated by other Faulkner critics: freedom, bondage or enslavement, the ritual hunt or search, and love.[2] My main focus of attention is to Faulkner's use of legal, racial, and moral codes in the thematic and structural design of *Go Down, Moses*. According to Faulkner's logic in the novel, these codes are all manifestations of or responses to "property" and its attendant "rights," and they are the cause of the complexities within the society he depicts.

Legal codes, those practices of both custom and statute constituting the authorities, interact with racial codes, those beliefs and attitudes regulating interpersonal conduct between whites and blacks, in defining the place of individuals within the society depicted in the novel. In *Go Down, Moses*, moral codes, those virtues, values, and ideals, often abstract and intuitive, operate on a higher level of awareness and authority with regard to the meaning of the human being and intersect with legal and racial codes to define humanity in individual and societal terms. At the point of convergence, the three codes bring together both past and present experience—words, thoughts, and deeds—to create the ideological core of the work, and essentially its complexity. However, because the three codes also exist in diffusion throughout the text, they function to establish individual priorities within social mandates that form the separate patterns of meaning as well. Legal, racial, and moral codes, then, are all single keys to meaning, to the various motifs and themes, but together they assert a positive capacity to determine and modify thought as well as behavior, and thereby bring about social change. Nevertheless, only personal change occurs within the novel, because the dynamic realignment of values, attitudes, practices, and beliefs necessary for reformation in a static society takes place only as potential within a few isolated experiences.[3]

At the static center is Lucius Quintus Carothers McCaslin, old Carothers, who in the 1780s moved from Carolina with slaves, purchased land from a Chickasaw, and established a plantation. Similar to Thomas Sutpen in Faulkner's *Absalom, Absalom!* (1936), Carothers McCaslin dominates the narrative present though he has been dead for nearly one hundred years. His name is borrowed from Lucius Quintus Cincinnatus Lamar, the Mississippi lawyer, politician, and later justice of the United States Supreme Court, who began his career in 1849 after moving to Faulkner's hometown, Oxford. Much like Mr. Justice Lamar, the fictional L. Q. C. achieves influence and power, but his is primarily over his descendants, two of whom provide the dual lens through which old Carothers assumes substance and meaning. The two are his grandsons, the white Isaac McCaslin and the black Lucas Beauchamp. Although both are entitled to a bequest from their grandfather on their twenty-first birthday, Ike renounces his patrimony, the McCaslin plantation, whereas Lucas asks for his inheritance, a thousand dollars. Their actions reflect their different attitudes toward Carothers, as well as their different degrees of removal from the actual experience of Carothers.

Born in 1874, Lucas has assimilated the experience of his grandfather as accomplishment and assertion of manhood. He shares with McCaslin (Cass) Edmonds, Carothers's nephew, the vision of an ancestor who "saw the opportunity and took it, bought the land, took the land . . . no matter how, held it to bequeath, no matter how, out of the old grant, the first patent, when it was a wilderness of wild beasts and wilder men, and cleared it, translated it into something to bequeath to his children, worthy of bequeathment for his descendants' ease and security and pride and to perpetuate his name and accomplishments."[4] Though his own father was one of the Carothers's slaves, Lucas believes in the ethical right of ownership and in the principle of occupation making the right to property. He sees industry in acquiring land and power in holding it, yet he discounts both need for the land and labor performed on it. The latter, of course, applies most directly to the McCaslin blacks, as viable claims to property and ownership.

On his twenty-first birthday, then, Lucas asks for the money left for his father, Tomey's Turl, old Carothers McCaslin's son by his slave daughter. He declares: " 'I'm a man now. I can do what I want. I want to know that I can go when I decide to.' " The money provides him with the opportunity for choice; he can choose to stay or leave the McCaslin plantation because money establishes his manhood in economic independence. However, his acceptance of the money as a legacy acknowledges old Carothers's right to property and to bequeathal of it. In asking for his inheritance, Lucas also asks that a contractual obligation be met. His understanding of rights is primarily in terms of the plantation as a business derived from acquisition, possession, and dispensation, which are protected by law.

"The Fire and the Hearth," the chapter introducing Lucas, relies upon both legal and business words and phrases, such as "interdict," "reprieve," "justice," "partnership," "recompense," "Law" (with a capital "L"), "revenue," "money," "competitor," and "business," all of which mark Lucas's conception of himself as a man cut from the same cloth as his grandfather. The main idea of the introductory section has to do with Lucas Beauchamp's attempts to entrap his competitor, George Wilkins, his daughter's suitor, just as five years before he had taken care of another competitor in the illegal business of running a still. That former competitor is at the present moment in the state penal farm at Parchman, thanks to Lucas who plots to have George suffer the same fate.

From the beginning, Lucas uses the law for revenge and for the control and elimination of his competition, which he accomplishes with the unwitting assistance of Roth Edmonds, the white owner of the land that Lucas has farmed for forty-five years. Thus, legal terms abound in the narrative introducing Lucas; moreover, much of the section uses the language of contracts law, and several of the main ideas are related to contractual obligations, whether those obligations stem from the authority of "the Law" (again with a capital "L") or from that of the head of the family (Lucas himself), or from that of the plantation system.[5]

Lucas, whose values regarding competition and business and money have been shaped by the organization of the plantation, as well as by the conception of patrimony, operates within an ethics of business. His code of honor and of conduct stems from his belief in the necessity of manhood, the primacy of age, and the legitimacy of acquisition, all of which are partly formed out of the plantation system and partly out of Lucas's response to the place of blacks in the plantation world. For instance, he perceives his rights in terms of competition, as when in his youth he determined that he must kill his kinsman Zack Edmonds, the white man who had appropriated Lucas's wife to care for his motherless infant. Lucas tells Zack, " 'You tried to beat me. And you wont never, not even when I am hanging dead from the limb this time tomorrow with the coal oil still burning, you wont never.' " Lucas knows the immediate meaning of compensatory justice for blacks, but he knows also that if he is to avail himself of justice, he must do so in terms understood and practiced by whites, because only those demand respect. And Zack's response is a confirmation of Lucas's ability to circumvent the codes suppressing blacks and to use them to assert himself: " 'By God . . . I never thought to ever pass my oath to a nigger.' " In the next generation of McCaslin-Edmondses, Zack's son Roth recognizes the source of Lucas's power: *He's more like old Carothers than all the rest of us put together. . . . He is both heir and prototype simultaneously of all the geography and climate and biology which sired old Carothers and all the rest of us and our kind*" (118).

Much like his grandfather, Lucas capitalizes on the law and on social practice for power. When he recognizes that the offending George Wilkins might be useful to his search for gold he believes buried on the plantation, Lucas abandons his plan to send George to prison: "So George Wilkins was reprieved without knowing his . . . danger. . . . [H]e even thought of taking George into partnership on a minor share basis to do the actual digging; indeed, not only to do the actual work but as a sort of justice, balance, libation to Chance and Fortune, since if it had not been for George, he would not have found the single [gold] coin" (39).

Lucas's sense of justice extends mainly to what is fair to himself. In whatever arrangements he makes, and in whichever linguistic pattern he chooses, he reveals his concern for what he himself deserves due to this position as the oldest living McCaslin descendant on the plantation, his wisdom about financial and business matters, and his position as head of the Beauchamp family. Therefore, he dismisses the thought of sharing with George.

> [B]efore it even had time to become an idea. [H]e, Lucas Beauchamp . . .
> who actually remembered Buck and Buddy [Old Carothers's twin sons] in
> the living flesh, older than Zack Edmonds even if Zack were still alive,
> almost as old as old Isaac who in a sense, say what a man would, had turned
> apostate to his name and lineage by weakly relinquishing the land which
> was rightfully his to live in town on the charity of his great-nephew;—he,
> to share one jot, one penny of the money which old Buck and Buddy had
> buried almost a hundred years ago, with an interloper . . . whose very
> name was unknown in the country twenty-five years ago. . . . Never. Let
> George take for his recompense the fact that he would not have to go to the
> penitentiary to which Roth Edmonds would probably have sent him even if
> the Law did not. (39–40)

Although he may exaggerate his ability to turn situations to his best advantage, Lucas sees himself both as a worthy descendant of Old Carothers and as protected by that position despite his race. Within his limited situation, he negotiates power in the manner he associates with his ancestor.

At the same time, however, Lucas is aware that the plantation system represented by his grandfather entraps all blacks and negates his individual manhood. For example, he has to ask before depositing his inheritance: " 'Will the bank keep it for a black man same as for a white?' " And after his confrontation with Zack, he poses an even more significant question, which renders in microcosm the place assigned to blacks and the prerogative assured whites: " 'How to God . . . can a black man ask a white man to please not lay down with his black wife? And if he could ask it, how to God can the white man promise that he wont?' " (59). Lucas understands the restrictions placed upon him by the racial codes of his society. He even admits that the "law" is "rich white lawyers and judges and marshalls talking to one another around their proud cigars, the haughty and powerful of the earth." Nonetheless, he still believes that as "the oldest living McCaslin descendant still living on the heredity land" he can circumvent racial restrictions by evoking his connection to Carothers McCaslin and his power over the land. Despite his belief, he cannot escape the truth of the historical condition and treatment of blacks in Mississippi, and its repercussions in his own life.

Although as early as June 1818, in *Harry and Others v. Decker & Hopkins*, (concerning a Petition for Freedom),[6] the Supreme Court of Mississippi ruled that "slavery is condemned by reason and the laws of nature,"[7] by 1821, the court had accepted the legality of slavery in Mississippi, while maintaining that slaves were "reasonable and accountable beings."[8] The court's decision in *State v. Jones*,[9] the case of a white man accused of murdering a slave not only condemned the murderer to death by hanging on July 27, 1821, but also established the legal rights of the slave in Mississippi;[10] Justice Joshua G. Clark, the first chancellor of the state, wrote the decision:

> Has the slave no rights, because he is deprived of his freedom? He is still a human being, and possesses all those rights, of which he is not deprived by the positive provisions of law, but in vain shall we look for any law passed by the enlightened and philanthropic legislature of this state, giving even to the master, much less to a stranger, power over the life of a slave. Such a statute would be worthy of the age of Draco and Caligula, and would be condemned by the unanimous voice of the people of this state, where, even cruelty to slaves . . . meets with universal reprobation.[11]

The slave, then, a "reasonable and accountable being," was deprived of his freedom, but allowed "all those rights of which he is not deprived by the positive provision of law." Unfortunately, under the "positive provision of law," slaves were increasingly denied rights, because enslavement by its very nature forced them into a sub-category of human beings and made them vulnerable to legal encroachments upon their rights.

By 1860, the year of Lincoln's election and one year after John Brown's raid on Harper's Ferry, some of the laws controlling slaves in Mississippi included prohibitions against marriages,[12] contact with free blacks,[13] defense or testimony against whites,[14] learning to read or write,[15] and leaving a plantation without a pass.[16] These were added to numerous existing communally sanctioned customs as well as state and local laws, such as that forbidding the freeing of slaves by will.[17] While chattel slavery in Mississippi neither existed technically after the January 1, 1863, Emancipation Proclamation nor existed legally after the thirteenth amendment to the Constitution, legislative attempts to deny blacks their freedom continued. The Black Code of 1865,[18] for example, was as intent upon the denial of rights as earlier slave codes, such as those of 1857, had been. Although the 1865 codes granted some rights to blacks, such as the right to sue or be sued,[19] to testify in state courts,[20] to marry legally,[21] and to own personal property,[22] these codes also attempted to restrict the liberties of freed blacks, and to deny them justice under the existing legal system. For example, young black children were subject to "binding out" as unpaid apprentices, with their former masters being allowed to choose them for service; or for example, any blacks without a job or home by January 1, 1866, were fined as vagrants, but the fine could be paid by hiring out, again with the former masters receiving preference for their services.[23] In addition, blacks could not bear arms or own guns,[24] could not rent farm land,[25] and could not perform certain forms of work without a license.[26] Even though the vast majority of the Black Code was repealed in 1870,[27] the lasting result was that blacks were kept in a position of inferiority—socially, economically, and for the most part legally as well.

Despite Mississippi's ratification of the fourteenth and fifteenth amendments in 1870,[28] oppressive conditions continued and essentially prepared for a system of "Jim Crow" laws following the Mississippi Constitution of 1890. These laws defined the rights of blacks as different from those of whites, instituted racial codes which continued to stamp blacks as inferior and justified their exclusion from full access to justice and equality. Specifically after the 1883 United States Supreme Court ruled that the Civil Rights Act of 1875 was unconstitutional,[29] recreational, educational, and public facilities became increasingly segregated by race between the late 1880s and the turn of the century. In 1890, the twenty-fifth anniversary of Appomattox, when 744,749 Mississippians were black and 544,851 white, the state enacted the 1890 Constitution, which stated in article III, section 5: "All political power is vested in, and derived from, the people; all government of right originates with the people, is founded upon their will only, and is instituted solely for the good of the whole."[30] Nevertheless, the Constitution virtually dismissed blacks from any consideration in "the good of the whole" by its article XII, "Franchise." Called the "Mississippi Plan," the article introduced prerequisites for voting: proof of having paid taxes for the two-year period preceding an election;[31] residency requirements for the state and district;[32] a uniform poll tax of two dollars;[33] proof of never having been convicted of certain crimes[34] (e.g., bigamy, perjury, theft, and burglary); and an "understanding clause," which required the reading and interpreting of any designated section of the 1890 Constitution.[35] Moreover, section 245 of article XII provided "Electors in municipal elections shall possess all the qualifications herein prescribed, and such additional qualifications as may be provided by law. . . ."[36] This provision opened the way for further local restrictions against prospective black voters.

Upheld by the Mississippi Supreme Court in *Sproule v. Fredericks,*[37] and by the United States Supreme Court in *Williams v. Mississippi,*[38] two years after the Court made the "separate but equal" ruling in *Plessy v. Ferguson,*[39] the "Mississippi Plan" not only avoided the fifteenth amendment, but also effectively disenfranchised and reestablished white supremacy, just as the *Forest Register,* a Mississippi newspaper, had proclaimed in its masthead for years: "A white man in a white man's place. A black man in a black man's place. Each according to the 'eternal fitness' of things." Although Justice John Marshall Harlan had dissented from the Supreme Court's 1896 *Plessy v. Ferguson* finding by stating: "Our Constitution is color-blind. . . .

The arbitrary separation of citizens on the basis of race is a badge of servitude wholly inconsistent with the civil freedom and the equality before the law established by the Constitution,"[40] his position had little impact in Mississippi or elsewhere in the United States. From the 1890s through the early decades of the twentieth century that Faulkner depicts in *Go Down, Moses* blacks in the state were legally controlled by a caste position rather than slavery, and despite the fourteenth or fifteenth amendment, they existed in racial degradation and economic deprivation. This inferior position is the one from which Lucas Beauchamp would distance himself by claiming the model of his white grandfather's power and authority wrought from ownership.

Lucas is forced, however, to accept a different authority when his wife Molly threatens to divorce him because of his obsession with acquisition, with obtaining buried money from the land. Unlike Lucas, Molly believes that the land belongs to God who has the power of authority over it and that, therefore, it cannot belong to any human being: " 'Because God say, "What's rendered to My earth, it belongs to Me unto I resurrect it. And let him or her touch it and beware" ' " (102). Both in Molly's explanation and in the spiritual "Go Down, Moses" from which Faulkner took his title, there is a sense of God's power to seek retribution for transgressions against His will, His law. Though she speaks about the buried treasure, Molly also reminds Lucas that the land is defiled by human exploitation, and she draws him away from the egocentric and destructive ways of his grandfather. Ironically, however, she also causes him to abandon his hopes for a change in his condition, and to acquiesce to his subordinate place as a black on the McCaslin plantation.

Lucas is not ultimately free; his life has progressed in a certain pre-scribed way in spite of his efforts to make it otherwise, and at sixty-seven, he cannot change it, as he admits: " 'Man has got three score and ten years on this earth. . . . He can want a heap in that time and a heap of what he can want is due to come to him, if he just starts soon enough. I done waited too late to start' " (131). It is not within his power to remake his life and receive his share of the spoils of the earth. He and Molly and Roth will remain tied to one another as social creatures in a particular social world. The burden of their past is stronger than the possibilities for a recorded future. Lucas's acquiescence is finally to his legal union with Molly, to his moral responsibility toward her, and to his inherited place on the McCaslin-Edmonds plantation. His action signals a necessary renunciation of egocentric dreams, but the cost is his hope for a different future.

Lucas's white kinsman Isaac (Ike) McCaslin equates the experience of their grandfather with possession of the land and of slaves. However, Ike's equation is a negative one. He reasons that when old Carothers bought the land, he

> believed [that] he had tamed and ordered it for the reason that the human
> beings he held in bondage and in the power of life and death had removed

the forest from it and in their sweat scratched the surface of it . . . in order to grow something . . . which could be translated back into the money he who believed he had bought it had had to pay to get it and hold it and a reasonable profit too: and for which reason old Carothers McCaslin, knowing better, could raise his children, his descendants and heirs, to believe the land was his to hold and bequeath since the strong and ruthless man has a cynical foreknowledge of his own vanity and pride and strength and a contempt for all his get. . . . (254–55)

Ike envisions his grandfather as a ruthless man who misappropriates the land and abuses human beings because he assumes the right to property, the plantation itself as well as its chattel slaves.

Born in 1867, Ike's personal history coincided with the difficult period of rebuilding and reconstructing the postwar South: "1874 the boy; 1888 the man, repudiated denied and free; 1895 and husband but no father, unwidowed but without a wife, and found long since that no man is ever free and probably could not bear it if he were. . . ." At twenty-one, Ike repudiates the plantation tradition of his grandfather by renouncing his birthright, ownership of the McCaslin land, because he believes that God "created man to be His overseer on the earth and to hold suzerainty over the earth and the animals on it in His name, not to hold for himself and his descendants inviolable title forever, generation after generation, to the oblongs and squares of the earth, but to hold the earth . . . in the communal anonymity of brotherhood, and all the fee He asked was pity and humility and sufferance and endurance and the sweat of his face for bread" (257).

He adopts his terms from the language of plantation life: God as master, man as overseer, earth and animals as dominated or controlled. Nevertheless, Ike acts in philosophical opposition to the ethics of keeping blacks in bondage, and in opposition to "the very race which for two hundred years had held them bondage and from which for another hundred years not even a bloody civil war would have set them completely free." As a result, he rejects ownership of any personal goods in order to free himself from even the smallest accumulation of property, which would be a reminder of his heritage. By divesting himself of ownership, Ike attempts to expiate the sins of his grandfather and the "whole plantation in its mazed and intricate entirety . . . the whole edifice intricate and complex and founded upon injustice and erected by ruthless rapacity and carried on even yet with at times downright savagery not only to human beings but to valuable animals too."

The point that Ike repeatedly considers is that his grandfather acts upon a belief that he has the right to do what he wishes with his property. The key words in "Was," the chapter introducing Ike, are references to this recurrent concern: "bequestor," "inheritor," "title," "patent," "owned," "property," "will," and "land." But these words do not fully signify what old Carothers's proprietary right has encompassed: his begetting of a child upon his own slave daughter; his alloting a thousand dollar cash legacy to his slave son to be paid by his legitimate sons and heirs, the twins, Amodeus (Buddy) and

Theophilus (Buck). Nor do they allow for the moral conclusion that Ike reaches: that Carothers values property, but not human life; that he finds dignity in possession, but not in the human beings possessed.

Issac McCaslin discovers and verifies in reading the plantation ledgers the truth of his grandfather's values and power; he intuits and reasons the actual facts of use and ownership, and with these the superiority and dominance of his white relative over others. The ideal of natural rights in a natural world is not possible once the land has been held by the Chickasaws, occupied by them, and thus giving them possession and the right to assume ownership of it, until finally they sell the land to Carothers McCaslin. The ledgers, records of the plantation commissary, provide Ike with one truth about his grandfather's treatment of his chattel, his incestuous relationship with his daughter, which is a transgression of the natural law Ike espouses.

Perhaps even more significant is that he discovers that the ledgers themselves are not simply a record of purchases, expenditures, debits, and credits for the plantation, but that they are, in effect, an index to the codes of the land and the society: "strong as truth and impervious as evil and longer than life itself and reaching beyond record and patrimony." As an index, the ledgers contain the regulations, the rules, the contracts, and the customs of the plantation owners in regard to their property. Essentially, the evidence Ike needs to understand his heritage is in "that chronicle . . . a whole land in miniature, which multiplied and compounded was the entire South, twenty-three years after surrender and twenty-four from emancipation—that slow trickle of molasses and meal and meat, of shoes and straw hats and overalls, of plowlines and collars and heel-bolts and buckheads and clevises, which returned each fall as cotton—the two threads frail as truth and impalpable as equators yet cable-strong to bind for life them who made the cotton to the land their sweat fell on" (293–94). The phrase "threads frail as truth . . . yet cable-strong," recurrent especially in "The Bear," (256, 293–94) is suggestive of the language in Jeremy Bentham's discussion of law and property in *Principles of the Civil Code* (1802): "That which in the natural state was an almost invisible thread, in the social state becomes a cable. Property and law are born together. Before laws were made there was no property; take away laws and property ceases."[41]

Ike cannot accept the legacy of his grandfather, because he has a different conception of himself as a human being. He will respect the land and its inhabitants, but he will not accept ownership of the land, for unlike old Carothers, Ike acknowledges that harm has been done to others in the securing of his birthright: "[H]e couldn't speak even to McCaslin [his older first-cousin Cass], even to explain his repudiation, that which to him too, even in the act of escaping (and maybe this was the reality and the truth of his need to escape) was heresy: so that in escaping he was taking with him more of that evil and unregenerate old man who could summon, because she was his property, a human being because she was old enough and female, to his widower's house and get a child on her and then dismiss her because she was of an inferior race. . . ." (294). Whereas Carothers neither recognizes the wrong that he does nor admits responsibility for the damages he causes in the lives of his slaves, Ike can only acknowledge by repudiation; he cannot escape.

Though Sam Fathers, the black Indian who was himself sold by his father Ikkemotubbe, sets Ike free by teaching him the positive values of the natural world, Sam Fathers cannot provide a place for Ike in society. Though Cass Edmonds teaches Ike the practical realities of plantation life, Cass cannot join those practicalities to Ike's ideals. Buck and Buddy McCaslin, his father and uncle, show Ike by their example that they object to the treatment of slaves; that is, they quarter their slaves in the "big house," old Carothers's "tremendous abortive edifice scarcely yet out of embryo," and they refuse to secure the slaves at night, or to have slaves build a house for them and perform the household chores. Nevertheless, Buck and Buddy cannot show Ike how to change the plantation system. Ike cannot escape the complexities of ethical and moral conduct in a society whose laws reinforce the ruthless proprietorship of his grandfather and reduce his father's and uncle's circumvention of ownership to humorous eccentricity. The past with its living legacies combines with reason, intuition, and emotion in the present to destroy both innocence and simplicity and to deflate moral action and ideals. The reality is that the land is not, as Ike had supposed, "held and used in common and fed from and on and would continue to use in common without regard to color or titular ownership." The ledgers and Ike's experience, as well as that of his grandfather, deny the image of community and brotherhood without regard to race or ownership.

The land is divided and owned. The owners declare, as one Mississippi legislator did in 1840, that "the institution of domestic slavery . . . [is] not a curse, but a blessing, as the legitimate condition of the African race"; or as the Supreme Court of the United States did in the 1857 case of *Dred Scott v. Sandford*,[42] that it is "fixed and universal in the civilized portion of the white race" that blacks have "no rights which the white man [is] bound to respect";[43] or as another Mississippi legislator did in 1865, that "the negro exists for the special object of raising cotton, rice and sugar for the whites, and that it is illegitimate for him to indulge, like other people, in pursuit of his own happiness in his own way. Although it is admitted that he has ceased to be the property of a master, it is not admitted that he has the right to become his own master."

Against such division and ownership, Ike has only a broad social idealism. He has rejected emotional ties along with his inheritance. Unlike Lucas Beauchamp who loves Molly and accepts his responsibility toward her, Ike fails to respond to individuals. He forgets that even the custodians of the earth have an obligation to assume responsibility for their caretaking, just as in the system of ownership which he opposes and repudiates, owners must assume responsibility for their actions. While he may have followed Fonsiba, the daughter of Tomey's Turl, to Arkansas in order to give her a share of her father's inheritance, or traced Tennie's Jim to Tennessee to give him money as well, Ike does not understand that he can protect blacks neither with idealism alone nor with money alone, given the realities of their subjugation and oppression. Although his intention is to give his black kin their rightful share of the property left to them by their father's failure to accept a monetary legacy from his father, old Carothers, Ike does not recognize that his action replicates his grandfather's leaving a thousand dollars to Tomey's Turl, an act which Ike himself condemned: "*So I reckon that was cheaper than saying My son to a nigger. . . .*" (269) He acts out of a sense of compensatory justice, but the compensation or reparation is, as it was for his grandfather, only money. While Ike indeed feels a moral obligation to compensate for injustice, he does so with money, since property retains meaning for him. So central is his belief in the negative meaning of property that he cannot rid himself of measurement in terms of it. When Lucas goes to claim his inheritance from Ike, his request and his presence force Ike to reflect on his own situation: "*Fifty dollars a month. He knows that's all. That I reneged, cried calf-rope, sold my birthright, betrayed my blood, for what he too calls not peace but obliteration, and a little food*" (108–9). He suspects that despite his high ideals, his action has resulted in "obliteration." In effect, he brings no meaningful change into his environment because he has given up his opportunity to sustain contact with it.

The climax of the novel may be in the chapter "The Bear" with Ike's discovery of the extent of the moral transgression recorded in the plantation ledgers and with his resulting decision to act according to a higher moral law or authority, but the denouement occurs in "Go Down, Moses," the chapter in which the systems of law and the residue of property in the twentieth-century society come openly into play.

The spiritual, "Go Down, Moses," which lends its title directly to the chapter, identifies three levels of authority and sources of laws affecting the lives of human beings. The Lord speaks, "Go down, Moses, / Way down in Egyptland / Tell old Pharaoh / To let my people go." His command to Moses evokes the highest authority, a transcendent spiritual and moral authority. Moses, his servant, is the human agent, a moral representative and a divinely appointed leader. Pharaoh, ruler of the land and representative of the state, is both social law-maker and moral law-breaker.

The spiritual suggests the right of challenging his legal authority on the grounds of divine law and morality. The command of the Lord, which Moses executes, carries with it the weight of power ("Let my people go; / If not I'll smite your first-born dead."), in which God in His wrath shall seek retributive justice and punish the enslavers. The commands bear as well the appeal of God's righteousness ("When Israel was in Egyptland / Oppressed so hard they could not stand / No more shall they in bondage toil / Let them come out with Egypt's spoil. . . ."); through His grace He will share the benefits of society with the enslaved in a form of distributive justice. The spiritual affirms that there is a righteous and just morality displayed in God's justice and power, goodness and love, and that that morality will operate against harsh, unfair legal edicts. Whether it shall prevail is not addressed.

By means of its metaphorical core submerged in the novel, the spiritual reiterates the conflicting codes within Faulkner's work. It places in opposition an ideal standard and a legal standard for evaluating human actions. On the one hand, Moses' attempt to lead the Israelites out of Egypt is right action not merely because it promotes an ideal, freedom rather than bondage as the right of human beings, whereas on the other hand, Pharaoh's attempt to maintain the enslavement may be considered appropriate action because it conforms to a civil law and the ethics of custom. Yet enslavement is morally objectionable. The rightness of the action or the goodness it achieves within the social order is overwhelmed by the harm done to the Israelites and is negated ultimately by the divine command, "Let my people go."

In the final chapter, Gavin Stevens, lawyer and representative of the legal system,[44] must confront the remainder of the old codes, both racial and moral, in his involvement with the burial of the outlaw, Samuel Worsham (Butch) Beauchamp. This burial must be done in accordance with the wishes of two old women who act not in response to the legal codes, but to moral codes, and ironically to one set of racial codes as well. As Miss Worsham says of Mollie, " 'Mollie's . . . parents belonged to my grandfather. Mollie and I were born in the same month. We grew up as sisters.' " Both the white woman and the black woman assume what the role of whites must continue to be in the lives of blacks—that is, paternalistic and, in part, moral response to the legacy of property. This culture, Faulkner concludes by his depiction of Mollie and Miss Worsham, has its limited but best hope in the women who function outside of the dominant male codes of property, position and ownership.

The final alliance in the novel is primarily between these two females, Mollie Worsham Beauchamp and Miss Worsham. As a single older woman, who is also poor and without property, Miss Worsham is dependent upon blacks for her livelihood; she lives off the truck garden of Hamp, Mollie's brother. Her alliance with Mollie does not argue strongly for an alliance between the races that could move toward either social change or the common good, because Miss Worsham as a relic of the past is removed from the present-day social order. Granted that the lawyer, Gavin Stevens, and the editor of the newspaper, as well as some of the townspeople and presumably Roth Edmonds, cooperate in paying for the return of Butch Beauchamp's body from Chicago and for his burial, but in the final analysis, they act out of duty to codes of conduct, primarily respect for the elderly white woman; they act neither out of any faith or belief that attention to blacks is ethical behavior, nor out of a belief that the law has functioned to control and subordinate blacks. They fail to recognize that for blacks the law has not primarily been a means of achieving justice, and that the law is partly to blame for the condition of an "antisocial" black, such as Butch Beauchamp who was not "properly" socialized by the plantation system. In fact, the townspeople are mainly quite content to believe that somehow Butch is merely the bad son of a bad father, but not that the duality of legal, racial, and moral codes followed by their society and which persistently dehumanize blacks or undermine the ability of blacks to be or to do may be equally responsible for what Butch becomes.[45]

By insisting that Roth Edmonds sold her Benjamin (Butch) into slavery, Mollie is only partly aware of the reality which faced a young black man in a society still enmeshed in the old ways. She herself is part of the traditional system as her and her brother Hamp's relationship with Miss Worsham suggests. The very fact that Mollie cannot be "Mrs. Beauchamp" or even "Miz Beauchamp," as her white counterpart is always "Miss Worsham," reinforces the kind of lack of respect for black people that the younger Butch may have been more keenly aware of. Though Faulkner concludes that the North was in the early 1940s no better than the South for a black youth because there Butch falls into crime and is electrocuted, whereas in the South he is given a proper burial, Faulkner does not and perhaps cannot, given the moral vision of the novel, address the lack of opportunity for manhood in the world into which Butch was born.

Unlike Lucas, who can claim direct descent from the anti-hero L. Q. C. McCaslin, old Carothers, who was strong enough to take the land and to hold it, Butch reaches majority at a point in the 1930s when the claim of white blood does not distinguish some blacks from other blacks. It might be argued that Lucas was a better man than his grandson Butch, yet it is apparent that, in the context of the narrative, he is a better man in part because he is McCaslin's grandson, not because of his blackness, which is only allowed the primacy of an older race, but not an equal one. It is improbable that the young man Butch Worsham Beauchamp, living not unlike his ancestors in earlier times on the McCaslin-Edmonds place and working on shares, could be anything other than entrapped and limited. When Butch, a victim of modern bondage to the land, commits crimes against the existing order, he breaks laws that are necessary for the common good. At the same time, his action of stealing from the plantation commissary may also be a form of rebellion against the existing codes and laws that deny him access to property and ownership which define manhood and that relegate him and his kind to their "place." Just as Butch's criminal activity cannot be condoned, neither can the paternal, restricting social order into which he is born be condoned. Importantly, his death not only externalizes what Miss Worsham labels as "our grief," the experience she shares with Mollie and Hamp and from which Gavin Stevens is excluded, but it also produces an opportunity for communal reflection and action which includes the conscious mourners as well as the rest of the society.

Ike, who has had the moral vision and the potential for effecting social change within the modern world of the denouement, is finally an old man truncated by the inflexibility of his society and his own rigidity. Right moral decisions have nonetheless negated his moral impact. He does not even appear as a reference in "Go Down, Moses." " 'There are good men everywhere, at all time,' " he tells his young kinsman Roth Edmonds in "Delta Autumn." " 'Most men are. Some are just unlucky, because most are a little better than their circumstances give them a chance to be.' " But Roth replies, " 'And you've lived almost eighty years. . . . And that's what you've finally learned about the other animals you live among. I suppose the question to ask you is, where have you been all the time you were dead?' " Ike is, in a sense, figuratively dead to his society, a condition which recalls the verse from the spiritual "Go Down, Moses": "Let my people go; / If not I'll smite your first-born dead."

While the major virtues Ike espouses are, as he himself indicates, "pity and love of justice and of liberty," he does not act out of love, out of love of abstractions, which remain abstract even though moral. Thus, when a young black woman, who is a descendant of Tennie's Jim, Lucas's brother and the grandson of Ike's own grandfather, reveals that she is the mistress of Roth Edmonds and the mother of his son, she realizes that Ike cannot respond with love. She poses a crucial question: " 'Old man . . . have you lived so long and forgotten so much that you dont remember anything you ever knew or felt or even heard of love?' " The answer, however, is not that Ike has forgotten, but rather that he has not loved. The major burden of his heritage, its codes and values, is the inability to love. "The way of love may be the only way to justice,"[46] Reinhold Neibuhr states in his 1960 introduction to *Moral Man and Immoral Society* (1932). Without love, Ike cannot attain the purity he seeks for himself, the justice he desires for blacks, or the differentiation he needs from his grandfather. He can forcefully resist evil in society only if he acts; passivity is no solution because it cannot generate a social reformation. And within this novel, love becomes the most viable motivational force allowing individuals, such as Lucas and Mollie and Miss Worsham, to act according to "the dictates of the human heart," as Faulkner put it in his Nobel Prize acceptance speech. To be fully effective in his moral stance against the legal and racial codes enslaving whites as well as blacks, Ike must, like Moses in the spiritual, act and lead others to follow a higher authority in defiance of unjust laws. To renounce Pharaoh's authority but to leave the Israelites in bondage is not enough. Even limited actions such as those of Miss Worsham, Mollie, and Lucas argue for the necessity of the human being to act, and to do so according to a guiding moral authority that is higher than the cultural norm.

Unfortunately, when Ike recognizes that Roth's mistress is, in fact, black, not only does he once again offer money, but he also compounds his offense by advising her to go North and marry a black man: " 'That's the only salvation for you—for a while yet, maybe for a long while yet. We will have to wait' " (363). He concludes in a final admission of his helpless adherence to the racial codes of his time and place: " 'Get out of here! I can do nothing for you! Cant nobody do nothing for you!' " (361) Though he gives the woman a boon of property for her son, Ike does not believe in the equality of the races: " 'You are young, handsome, almost white; you could find a black man who would see in you what it was you saw in him, who would ask nothing of you and expect less and get even still less than that, if it's revenge you want' " (363). Implicit in his statement is the belief that Roth is the woman's superior because he is white and that the woman will be the superior of any black man because she is "almost white," and the even more invidious belief that what she saw in Roth was his whiteness, his race, just as any future black husband will see in her her almost-whiteness, the visible sign of her almost-escape from an inferior race. In one sense, property in the end is the property of blood; the right to humanity is defined once more according to possession. Ike has not been able to translate his strong moral convictions into social action, perhaps because the belief in property and ownership is too ingrained in his community or perhaps because his sense of individual justice, of renunciation and expiation by withdrawal, leaves him unengaged, suspended, and isolated.

"A static being," Melvin Rader observes, "cannot be moral because he is not confronted by choice. It is the temporal and ongoing character of life that poses problems: our existence is charged with concern because we must look before and after."[47] In this last encounter between black and white descendants of L. Q. C. McCaslin, Ike has become as static as his grandfather or his society. His movement is inward and further away from the demands of living in the world: "the territory in which game still existed drawing yearly inwards as his life was drawing inward." He looks backward not only to a time before ownership and possession and property and law, but also to his own finest moment in the wilderness with Sam Fathers and the bear; however, he cannot go back, for Sam and the bear are dead, and the wilderness destroyed by a new generation of Carothers McCaslins. His memories and his models are not enough to foster new disciples; his truth and his experience will die with him and the disappearing wilderness. Ike's crying in the wilderness— not for what has been lost, but for the moment of potential reformation that he has been unable to sustain—will be to no avail. For him and for his generation, there is no ameliorating vision accompanied by action to untangle the knotty complexities of property and its problematical impact on white or black individuals.

Notes

1. Not surprisingly women are largely absent from the novel because they rarely own property in this world, though from a series of legislative acts women in Mississippi had their right to property protected by law.

2. See, for example, Lawrance Thompson, *William Faulkner: An Introduction and Interpretation* (1967), and Olga Vickery, *The Novels of William Faulkner: A Critical Interpretation* (1964).

3. My assumption is that the society in *Go Down, Moses* is *static* rather than *stable*.

4. [Ed. note: *Go Down, Moses* (New York: Vintage Books, 1973), 256. Subsequent references are to this edition and will be marked parenthetically in the text.]

5. Roth Edmonds as the representative of that system runs the business of the plantation and controls the commissary, both of which have contractual authority over the lives of black sharecroppers like Lucas.

6. 1 Miss. (1 Walker) 36 (1818).

7. *Id.* at 42.

8. State v. Jones, 1 Miss (1 Walker) 83, 84 (1820).

9. *Id.* at 83.

10. *Id.* at 86.

11. *Id.* at 84–85.

12. MISS. REV. CODE ch. XI, art. 1 (1857).

13. *Id.* at ch. XXXIII, art. 51.

14. *Id.* at art. 62.

15. *Id.* at art. 51.

16. *Id.* at art. 45.

17. *Id.* at art. 9.

18. There is no Black Code *per se*, but the statutes of 1865 dealing with the recently freed Negroes are known as such.

19. 1865 Miss. Laws. ch. IV, § 1.

20. *Id.* at. § 4.

21. *Id.* at § 3.

22. *Id.* at § 1.

23. *Id.* at ch. v, § 1.

24. *Id.* at ch. XXIII, § 1.

25. *Id.* at ch. IV, § 1.

26. *Id.* at § 5.

27. 1870 Miss. Laws ch. X, § 2.

28. *Id.* at chs. CCXCIV–CCXCV.

29. United States v. Stanley, 109 U.S. 3 (1883).

30. MISS. CONST. art. III, § 5.

31. *Id.* at art. XII, § 241 (1890, amended 1972).

32. *Id.*

33. *Id.*

34. *Id.*

35. *Id.* at art. XII, § 244 (1890, repealed 1975).

36. *Id.* at art. XII, § 245.

37. 69 Miss. 898, 11 So. 472 (1892).

38. 170 U.S. 213 (1898).

39. 163 U.S. 537 (1896).

40. *Id.* at 559, 562 (Harlan J. dissenting).

41. 2 William Tait, *The Works of Jeremy Bentham* 297 (1843) (quoting J. Bentham, *Principles of the Civil Code* (1982)).

42. 60 U.S. (19 How.) 393 (1856).

43. *Id.* at 407.

44. Molly Beauchamp, "Mollie" in this essay, refers to the legal system as "the Law."

45. This is not the subject taken up by Faulkner; it becomes the concern of another major writer from Mississippi, Richard Wright.

46. R. Neibuhr, *Moral Man and Immoral Society: A Study in Ethics and Politics* (1960).

47. M. Rader, *Ethics and Society: An Appraisal of Social Ideals* (1950).

[The True Inheritance of Ike McCaslin]
Eric J. Sundquist*

It is nearly as difficult to imagine *Go Down, Moses* without its bear as it is to imagine *Moby-Dick* without its whale. And Ike discovers, as Ishmael asserts, that the secret of his "paternity" lies in the grave of an unwedded mother—not his own mother, of course, but the slave mother who carries the white McCaslin blood into the black Beauchamp family. But there is this difference among others: it is not immediately clear what relation the ritual of the hunt has to the stories concerned with racial conflict and intimacy in the old and new South. To be sure, there are two explicit points of contact—first, Ike's reading about incest and miscegenation in the family ledgers, which coincides with the deaths of old Ben and Sam Fathers in 1883; and second, Ike's later discovery of Roth Edmonds's contemporary act of miscegenation and incest with a "doe . . . that walks on two legs," which coincides with the stage of degradation the annual hunt has reached in 1941. Beyond that, the metaphor of the ritual hunt appears in all the stories, ranging from simple burlesque in "Was" (where Uncle Buck enters "bear-country" when he unwittingly lies down beside Sophonsiba Beauchamp) to ceremonial violence in "Go Down, Moses" (where the catafalque of the executed Samuel Beauchamp would be "the slain wolf"). In "Pantaloon in Black," Rider is one of "them damn niggers," the deputy says, who "look like a man and . . . walk on their hind legs like a man" but, when it comes to "normal human feelings," might as well be "a damn herd of wild buffaloes"; when Lucas faces down Zack Edmonds in "The Fire and the Hearth," his eyes are "like the eyes of a bayed animal—a bear, a fox."[1] Beyond all of this, of course, Ike's repudiation of his patrimony is linked—by all the desperation of style and extrapolated theme Faulkner can summon—to the rites of initiation that the hunt and the surrogate paternity of Sam Fathers represent. Even so, the connections seem as tenuous as Ike's own repudiation, which is significantly paradoxical and certainly fails to lift the McCaslin curse.

Like virtually all of Faulkner's novels, *Go Down, Moses* proceeds by "a method of implication, working as a metaphor works,"[2] and the implications in this case are vexing to the same degree that they grow out of, and respond

*Reprinted with permission from *Faulkner: The House Divided* (Baltimore: Johns Hopkins University Press, 1983), 133–44, 146–54, 155–57.

to, the precarious form of the novel itself. The metaphors of game, ritual, and pursuit that pervade the stories reveal their related strategies by referring, in almost every instance, to the struggles between hunter and beast or white and black. The proximity of these two contests is never far out of view once it is first defined, in "Was," in the ritual pursuit of Tomey's Turl, "that damn white half-McCaslin," who is bayed, flushed, baited, treed, and run to den every time he escapes to court Tennie Beauchamp. The full century that falls between the hunt of Tomey's Turl, who is the son of Carothers McCaslin and his own mulatto daughter, and the "doe hunting" of Turl's unnamed descendant in "Delta Autumn," who bears the illegitimate son of Roth Edmonds, comprises the contest for freedom that Ike McCaslin thinks he has won by renouncing his patrimony at age twenty-one, but which reappears to him more than fifty years later in all its tragic consequences. When Ike touches the hand of Roth's "nigger" mistress—"the gnarled, bloodless, bonelight, bone-dry old man's fingers touching for a second the smooth young flesh where the strong old blood ran after its long journey back to home"— the terrible futility of that renunciation is realized.[3] Ike's encounter with Roth's lover is indeed, as Michael Millgate remarks, "the point at which all the threads of the novel seem to cross, at which the whole pattern of the book emerges with final and absolute clarity."[4] Ike's gift to her of the hunting horn he has inherited from General Compson accomplishes nothing and seems patently repugnant alongside his advice that she go back North and marry a black man. And yet it is the one symbolic act, the one futile but generous gesture, of which Ike is capable; it continues to define the paradox of revulsion in guilt and generosity in shame that characterizes Ike's life from the moment Sam Fathers sets him free.

Ike's momentary touching of the woman's hand re-creates the charged moments of flesh touching flesh in *Absalom, Absalom!* and, for the moment it lasts, reconnects Ike to the paternal blood that will die with him but live on in the monstrous contagion of the Beauchamp line. The futility of Ike's renunciation has several dimensions, but the one the novel revolves around is his failure, not unlike that of Henry Sutpen, to legitimize the McCaslin blood by passing it on and accepting his patrimony. His own marriage fails when his wife demands that he accept his inheritance, when he refuses, and when she in turn, after this "first and last time he ever saw her naked body," refuses to sleep with him again. In "saving and freeing his son" from the "wrong and shame" that is also his inheritance, Ike loses him.[5] Like the marriages that never happen in *Absalom, Absalom!*, the son that is never born to Ike defines a state of possibility that seems both the best solution and at the same time its horrible contrary. Ike's repudiation depends on this paradox; for while his refusal to assume control of the land and freed slaves that are his due saved neither of them from the continuing curse, it does insure that the white McCaslin blood will descend only through the distaff Edmonds line or through the black Beauchamp line. It is this act that makes possible the slight but powerful ascendancy Lucas Beauchamp has over the

Edmonds men, who are nominally his "masters," and it is that ascendancy, along with Ike's own tortured repudiation, that expresses the South's and Faulkner's lingering obsession with the legitimizing power of paternal "blood."

Ike's argument with Cass in 1888 at first depends on his contention that the land belongs to no one, that on the instance Ikkemotubbe realized he could sell it, the land "ceased even to have been his forever, father to father to father." When that argument goes nowhere, Ike enlarges his strategy by invoking the plan of God, who "saw that only by voiding the land for a time of Ikkemotubbe's blood and substituting for it another blood, could He accomplish His purpose," and therefore chose Carothers McCaslin, "the seed progenitive of the three generations He saw it would take to set at least some of His lowly people free." At length, after the reading of the ledgers, interspersed among a long rehearsal of the war, of Reconstruction, and of events that have not yet taken place, Ike and Cass are simply back where they started, Cass asserting that Ike is the only legitimate heir, even—and especially—if the land is seen to belong to Sam Fathers, and Ike declaring, "Yes. Sam Fathers set me free." Far from clarifying Ike's repudiation, the context of Sam Fathers's surrogate paternity only makes it more elusive. The problem cannot be resolved by any simple opposition between wilderness and civilization (for Ike does not clearly choose one over the other, and the hunt itself quite deliberately entangles them) or between pure and "mongrel" blood (for Sam Fathers embodies strains of black, white, and Indian blood, and is thus "the scene of his own vanquishment and the mausoleum of his defeat").[6] It can only be resolved in any fashion whatsoever by recognizing how thoroughly it depends on an act that occurs throughout the novel in various forms and reaches an agonizing but perilously diffused pitch in the last story—the act of grief.

What Ike discovers in the commissary is the same haunting thing Roth later discovers when, reaching the white maturity that is also his inheritance, he refuses to sleep beside Henry Beauchamp: "He knew it was grief and was ready to admit it was shame also, wanted to admit it only it was too late then, forever and forever too late." The accomplished act, suspended forever in the unchangeable moment of its occurrence, divides the two boys as irrevocably as it has their fathers and families before them. Such grief, the true measure of Faulkner's own sympathy and shame, as it would be of Charles Mallison's in *Intruder in the Dust,* is the one expression that unites the lost innocence of the hunting ritual and the assumed manhood of Ike's repudiation: it is not shame alone that Ike discovers when he reads the ledgers at age sixteen (because he has lived side by side with the children of Tomey's Turl, "he knew what he was going to find before he found it") but grief—his own grief, which grows directly out of the suicide of Eunice, who walked into an icy creek one "Christmas day six months before her daughter's and lover's . . . child was born, solitary, inflexible, griefless, ceremonial, in formal and succinct repudiation of grief and despair who had already had to repudiate belief and hope." It is the very nature of Ike's grief that it has no solution; shame alone could be assuaged by his acceptance of his patrimonial responsi- bility and the generosity toward the Beauchamps it might afford, but grief— like the sin itself and like the deaths of old Ben and Sam Fathers—cannot be undone. Although it is Cass who speaks, it is Ike who remembers, on the day of his repudiation, how seven years earlier Cass had read to him from Keats's "Ode on a Grecian Urn" the lines *"She cannot fade, though thou hast not thy bliss, / Forever wilt thou love, and she be fair."* The "truth" of the bear hunt that Cass insists Keats's poem illuminates at that time seems to Ike *"simpler than somebody talking in a book about a young man and a girl he would never need to grieve over because he could never approach any nearer and would never have to get any further away."*[7] But as he recalls Cass's reading of the poem seven years later, he is recalling the preceding phrase that Cass omits—"yet, do not grieve"[8]—and recalling as well what the text of the ledgers and Carothers McCaslin's legacy must also reveal: *"So I reckon that was cheaper than saying My son to a nigger* he thought. *Even if My son wasn't but just two words. But there still must have been love* he thought. *Some sort of love."*[9] That love—doubtful at best, a mockery at worst, and in any event fruitless beside the agony it entails—defines both the limits and the ramifying contours of Ike's repudiation, the one act in which he can enact the grief that is his true inheritance.

One must simply assert this, for the willful complexity of the fourth section of "The Bear" can express only the tangled acts of memory that are, for Faulkner, Southern history and are for Ike the utterly precarious justification of the repudiation he makes to the baffled Cass. The fourth section is the heart of the novel not simply because it contains Ike's repudiation but also because its fragmented form, visibly enacting Ike's own spiritual disembodiment, as well as the chronological disjunctions that characterize the story his repudia- tion dominates, offers a magnified example of the structural complexities of the entire novel. The tangentially connected stories that surround "The Bear" on all sides and define the shifting burden of Ike's repudiation are focused in the pages that read into and out of the family ledgers; and the ledgers are a concentrated representation, a mysterious and seemingly sacred account, of acts and passions whose symbolic value draws into itself and envelops the interpretations it necessitates. As though converging upon the fourth section of "The Bear" from the perspectives of past and present, the stories drive toward, and fall away from, the revelation of grief in the act of incest and miscegenation that coincides with the sacrificial death of the totem animal. Those two acts have a relationship charged with paradoxical significance, but it is worth noting at the outset that the complexities of style that the enactment of Ike's repudiation involves quite deliberately obscure, in a cloud of loose ends and illogical argument, the meaning of that repudiation.

The fourth section's collapse of narrative and chronological distinctions accords in every respect with the potential collapse of racial distinctions, and therefore of the cultural hierarchy, that the ledgers record. To judge the power of the simultaneous collapse and preservation of those distinctions, we need to borrow a phrase from one of the novel's most dramatic and important scenes. Immediately preceding the flashback in "The Fire and the Hearth" to the ritual combat between Lucas and Zack, Faulkner speaks of Lucas and Cass as "coevals in more than spirit even, the analogy only the closer for the paradox."[10] The analogy is blood, and the paradox is that, though Cass's McCaslin blood is distaff and Lucas's McCaslin blood is paternal, this fact is legally voided by the caste of race. The figures of analogy and paradox culminate here in the recollected struggle of Lucas and Zack, which we must return to, but they serve as well to define the peculiarities of Ike's repudiation. For the analogy between the ritual hunt and Ike's refusal of his patrimony, linked as they are by the fragile lines from Keats's ode, can only be described as a full flowering of paradox, one in which forms of opposition are intimately merged in proportion to their necessary separation and near contradiction.

Keats's ode describes this paradoxical intimacy as an event that never *can* but always *will* take place; as it continually eventuates in imagination, the poem's act of love is generated in conjoined nostalgia and anticipation, existing both in the timeless world of art and the projected world of unfulfilled fantasy. Just as the "wild ecstasy" here defined as perpetual pursuit is, paradoxically, one that never takes place at all but at the same time takes place in every imagined reading of the poem, the event itself, and the analogy between poem and event, are themselves closer for the paradox. Likewise, Ike's creation of an act of "love" out of the cryptic lines of the ledger, although it can hardly be said to be exactly analogous to the Keats ode, also depends on the powers of paradox: first, it must have existed even though there is every reason to doubt it; second, even as he asserts the necessity of love, Ike's repudiation seems to deny all possibility of honoring that love; and third, even though the figures of immortality that define the ritual hunting of deer and bear may be seen to correspond to the sexual pursuit of Keats's "unravish'd bride," they define the corresponding relationship between master and slave only by a more agonizing paradox: the ravishment has taken place, and the whole history of Ike's family is its evidence. The incest and miscegenation of Carothers McCaslin is not, like Rosa's in *Absalom, Absalom!*, an "unravished nuptial," but an accomplished fact. To this extent, it *is* like the ritual hunt: it has happened, it is past, it cannot be undone but can only be made the subject of grief. Whatever love it once entailed, and whatever love the contemporary mixing of the races could now provide, are left suspended at a point of imminence that, it seems, will never be capable of realization.

Faulkner had invoked Keats's ode in *Sartoris* and *Light in August*, but in those instances it served to express an ideal of feminine beauty or artistic excellence, and had never been subject (except by the most extreme implication in the case of Lena Grove) to the pressures of racial conflict. Here, however, the "mad pursuit," the "struggle to escape" Keats speaks of is forced to bear a heavy burden, for the pastoral "sacrifice" that Keats's urn and poem render immortally unfulfilled form the very burden of Ike's tormented conscience. The concluding lines from which Cass draws his observations on the "truth" that "covers all things which touch the heart—honor and pride and pity and justice and courage and love"—are preceded by ones that more appropriately characterize Ike's dilemma: "When old age shall this generation waste, / Thou shalt remain, in the midst of other woe / Than ours . . ." What remains in this instance is the immortal moment of the death of old Ben—his "loverlike" embrace of Lion and his ritual death dance with Boon, in which they momentarily resemble "a piece of statuary"[11]—and an irrevocable act of human blood violation in which Ike insists there must have been "some sort of love." Both moments hang suspended in memory, forced by the exertions of Faulkner's hazardous analogy to encompass a timeless truth in which, it seems, the agony and the suffering of consequent generations is overborne by the beauty of the sacrifice.

The timelessness of the sacrifice is very much to the point, however, for what Ike's repudiation most reveals is that it is incapable of translating into a realm of timelessness events that have everywhere the temporally visible and tragic actuality that the text of the ledgers codifies: "all there, not only the general and condoned injustice and its slow amortization but the specific tragedy which had not been condoned and could never be amortized." Both the renunciation of his patrimony and the timeless beauty of the remembered wilderness sacrifice fail to arrest the long agony of racial conflict and, when it occurs once again more than a century later, the horror of miscegenation. It is well to emphasize this, for the moments of greatest achievement in *Go Down, Moses* depend on the tensions of this paradox—depend, that is, on Faulkner's attempts to translate into terms of ritual remembrance and celebration acts that resist the translation at every point, as well they might. That resistance is abundantly evident in "Delta Autumn," where Ike and the wilderness are "coevals," "two spans running out together, not toward oblivion, nothingness, but into a dimension free of both time and space," but where Ike's vision of "wild strong immortal game [running] forever . . . falling and rising phoenix-like to the soundless guns," is abruptly shattered by the appearance of Roth's "white" doe: "*Maybe in a thousand years or two thousand years in America*, he thought. *But not now! Not now!* He cried, not loud, in a voice of amazement, pity, and outrage: 'You're a nigger!' "[12]

In *Light In August* Faulkner brought his work conspicuously into an American tradition by joining the tragedy of race with the Calvinistic rhetoric of damnation; in *Absalom, Absalom!* he set his story in the middle of the nation's most traumatic internal conflict and joined the violence of race hatred to the terror of incest; in *Go Down, Moses* those themes are joined to a third American theme, the sacrifice of the totem animal. That conjunction itself proves paradoxical, but it depends initially on a psychological development that is everywhere evident in the history and literature of American racial violence from its beginnings in slavery to its most recent manifestations in the tragedy of Jim Crow. It depends, in short, on the continued insistence of commentators both more and less "racist" in their points of view that the Negro is a "beast"—physiologically, emotionally, socially, or in every conceivable way. That such assumptions and assertions often, perhaps always, reveal more about whites than blacks is something Faulkner saw with as much penetrating engagement as anyone; what he also saw more clearly than many is that this hardly makes the force and consequences of those perceptions any less real. . . .

The racist fiction and sociological literature of the late nineteenth and early twentieth centuries understandably reflected the current vogue of scientific naturalism; but its arguments for the "bestiality" of blacks were in many ways secular versions of theories that in earlier years had derived either from the biblical curse of the sons of Ham or from the transposition of that curse into a rationalistic chain of being that situated alien and mixed races at levels below the pure and "white."[13] Those arguments were often superimposed in the Southern mind, so that the purported plans of God and Nature circularly supported each other—though not without contradiction; mulattoes, for instance, were often held to be the most degenerate of the black "species" at the same time they were, because of their white blood, seen to be most capable of social and intellectual development. The war made such contradiction inevitable, however, for the destruction of Southern slavery entailed the replacement of failed theories of providential design with physiological theories that would keep blacks in their social and economic place, and defend against the threat of racial mixing that, in a shocking reversal, now came from the freed slaves rather than their masters. This reversal, with all the rhetorical power of repression such a psychic apocalypse could produce, made the Negro more than ever a "beast" and made the mulatto more than ever an emblem of the return and revenge of the repressed. It made "the Negro," as person and particularly as self-projected white image, something always to be feared and kept at bay, often to be hunted down and killed, at times to be made the object of ritual public sacrifice.

We have already noted how the metaphors of ritual hunting radiate out of "The Bear" into all the stories of Go Down, Moses but that, even so, there seems no obvious justification for this aside from Faulkner's desire to give his collection the appearance of thematic continuity. This is certainly the case, yet it is also the case that such continuity rests upon assumptions of thorough intimacy and dependence between master and slave, white and black, or—in this further case—between hunter and beast. The analogous relationship of hunter and beast clarifies the process of inversion that is potential or actual in the other relationships, for the hunt, as it approaches its most vitalized configurations and particularly as it reaches its culminating act, entails a form of ritual intimacy in which the ascendancy of slayer and slain fluctuates, equalizing the respect for, and power over, the other that each has and prolonging the moment of resolution to a degree that defines both the purpose and the success of the hunt. In its perfected form, the hunt, like the "wild ectasy" of ravishing elaborated on Keats's urn, would last forever. It does not last forever, of course, and the pressure of that realization is what Ike McCaslin feels after he kills his first buck and, in "loving the life he spills," ceases "forever to be the child he was yesterday." What he remembers is not the shot, the kill, but the ritual initiation, "the touch" of Sam Fathers's hands that, with "the hot smoking blood" of the buck, "consecrated him to that which . . . he had already accepted," joining the two of them in the ever-suspended moment in which "still out of his instant of immortality the buck sprang, forever immortal."[14]

As it does throughout *Go Down, Moses* in larger and more significant ways, the fluid narrative chronology of "The Old People," mixing act and memory, anticipation and grief, perfectly complements the immortal moment of the hunt and acts out the paradox it depends on: the immortality of the buck in its moment of death depends completely on that death; it has no meaning apart from it and, in fact, reveals that the entire purpose of the hunt is to preserve the moment it necessarily destroys. This act of transfiguring violence signifies the reality of the hunt and expresses its requisite chronological inversion, for as Ortega points out, "one does not hunt in order to kill; on the contrary, one kills in order to have hunted."[15] The context of Keats's ode in which Faulkner places such a moment asks us to recall that its paradox is not unlike that of Caddy Compson's virginity, which as Quentin discovers must be destroyed to have existed at all. The explicit sexual overtones of Ike's hunting of both deer and bear support this analogy, just as the blood consecration, which links Ike to animal mother and surrogate father alike, represents in its own right the paradoxical violence in which the act of love may be expressed. There is, moreover, no other way to account for Ike's assertion that there must have been "some sort of love" between Carothers McCaslin and the daughter whose child he fathers than to see it as desperately attached to the ritual of the hunt: that love, particularly that love, must for Ike have been destroyed in order to have existed at all.

The celibate marriage of hunter and beast in "The Bear," as in Cooper's *The Deerslayer* or in *Moby-Dick*, for example, collapses the sexual identities of each in order to express an androgynous, self-generating and self-consuming union in which either may be lover or mistress, father or mother, in which the hunter, like Ike, loses his "innocence" by taking Nature as "his mistress and his wife," and the animal, like old Ben, is both "the man" and the hunter's "alma mater." The touch, the consummation of the kill brings into actuality "the existence of love and passion" that Ike, as though prematurely entering "the bedroom of a woman who has loved and been loved by many men," recognizes at this point prior to Ben's death "is his heritage but not yet his patrimony."[16] The charged passion of hunter and beast in their act of celibate eroticism resembles, then, the ungenerative "pure and perfect incest" that Quentin's father speaks of in *The Sound and the Fury* and again in *Absalom, Absalom!* But in the same way that the act of incest is there overwhelmed and, indeed, denied its intimate meaning by the act of miscegenation it threatens to become, the two substitutions of blood that Ike's repudiation depends on here (the first, in the ritual consecration that weds him to beast and mentor; the second, in what Ike sees as God's exchange of Indian blood for white and white blood for black) are simply contradictory. The ritual hunt sublimates sexuality and isolates the act of love as immortal, forever unconsummated and still possible; yet unlike the fantasized incest of Quentin or Henry Sutpen, the act of miscegenation on which Ike's repudiation turns does no such thing, despite his rhetorical efforts to the contrary, but continues to reveal its sexual violation as obstinately real, irrevocable, and—it seems—unredeemable.

The difference is not difficult to locate. In the one case the blood substitution is purely figurative (though its symbolic enactment is real), while in the other it is very real (though its symbolic manifestations are, if monstrously so, figurative). No forays into biblical prophecy or romantic imagination can undo it; they can only, as "The Bear" attests, make it more prominent. This does not mean, however, that the mediating function of the hunt has no relevance to Ike's repudiation of his patrimony—far from it. It makes the analogy, once more, all the closer for the paradox. Here again, Ortega's observations are to the point. The essential resemblance between hunter and beast, and the mirroring postures and actions they engage in as the hunt progresses toward its moment of visionary transfiguration, culminate in the violent "spilling of blood." It is in this act that "the essential 'within' comes outside," Ortega remarks, "as if the most radical absurdity had been committed: that which is purely internal made external."[17] The violation of the kill, like the sexual violation it strives to transcend by imitating, exposes the very secret of existence, which can only be made manifest by violence against it. There may be every reason to find that violence repelling, even to consider it a pointless exercise of mastery. By the same token, what act could be more paradoxical, could more proceed out of physical and emotional violence that makes a mockery of love, than miscegenation, or especially incest *and* miscegenation? What "spilling of blood" could more imitate love but reveal in its excess of sexual violence a further ritual of mastery in which identities are collapsed only to be asserted more brutally than ever?

That act is nothing but—to borrow Ortega's phrase—a "radical absurdity," one in which sexual and familial identities are strained into distored shape and in which the essential "within" is made blasphemously external. There is no way, and no reason, to draw an exact parallel between the ritual kill and miscegenation, and Ike's repudiation, precisely because it links them, proves the futility of doing so. As I have already suggested, however, there is a further way to approach the problem, one that clarifies the figurative significance of miscegenation as both the South's original sin and its more contemporary horror as they are exemplified, respectively, in *Alsalom, Absalom!* and *Light in August*.

Because the hallucinating fear of the Negro as "beast" that characterized many theoretical justifications of American slavery and became particularly fierce in postbellum racial hysteria undeniably grew in part out of repressed guilt over the visible actualities of slaveholding miscegenation, the language in which such fears were expressed, both before and after the war, reveals a psychological instability that makes the analogy between repressed white lust and projected black threat acute by frantically denying it, closer for the paradox. In the apt words of Winthrop Jordan, white men attempted "to destroy the living image of primitive aggressions which they said was the Negro but was really their own." The threat comes not from *within* but from *without:* "We are not great black bucks of the fields. But a buck *is* loose, his great horns menacing to gore into us with life and destruction. Chain him, either chain him or expel his black shape from our midst, before we realize that he is ourselves."[18]

When Faulkner later spoke of the "hunting" of Tomey's Turl in the context of Uncle Buck's and Uncle Buddy's strange manumission arrangement, he struck the point rather exactly. Because Buck and Buddy knew by instinct that slavery was wrong but did not know quite what to do about it, Faulkner said, Turl "became quarry . . . that received the same respect that the bear or the deer would." The pursuit of Turl, himself the very product of Carothers McCaslin's incestuous miscegenation, is mostly comic, in "Was," though, as Faulkner noted, this hunt is "of a deadlier purpose than simple pleasure."[19] Even though the full significance of the ritual hunt assumes it, that deadlier purpose is largely hidden from view in Go Down, Moses. Largely, but not entirely, for the story that seems most out of place in the collection, "Pantaloon in Black," has virutally none of the comedy its title implies and stands at an important turning point in the novel. The murder Rider commits in the wake of his profound grief and his consequent lynching, far from being irrelevant to the McCaslin saga, function as a transition between the restrained ritual violence of "The Fire and the Hearth" and the ritual hunting of the beast by Ike McCaslin in the next three stories. Divided between the thoroughly passionate depiction of Rider as he moves toward the act of murder and the white deputy's baffled account of Rider's motives and his lynching, the story expresses utterly contradictory understandings of grief. Although it does not depend on the stock accusation of black sexual violence, Rider's lynching results, in the deputy's account, from an irrational madness that appears to have nothing to do with grief. Of course it has everything to do with it; and like Lucas's ritual challenge of Zack and like Ike's repudiation, it has everything to do with love. Although one of the Beauchamps may have been a better transitional figure, the story of Rider exposes the painful gulf between black and white emotions that is displayed in all the stories and that Ike—or perhaps we should say Faulkner—strives paradoxically to bridge in the grief-stricken repudiation of his patrimony.

Both the hunt and the hysteria of racial fears displace the lust and violence of the subject onto the object of sacrifice. Jordan's observations and the deliberate inversion of sexual desires Faulkner depicts explicitly in Light in August and implicitly in *Absalom, Absalom!* support such a theory of displacement, but we may find further confirmation in the strangest of testimonies, one that is all the more strange for accepting and overriding the very paradox it exposes. The plot of Thomas Dixon's *The Sins of the Father* (1912) suggests a development in his romances of race that is not unlike Faulkner's. Daniel Norton's gubernatorial aspirations and his reputation as a leading white supremacist are vexed when his illegitimate mulatto daughter, through the vengeful plotting of her "white" mother, Norton's maid, returns home and, unbeknownst to all, secretly marries Norton's white son. When the truth is revealed, Norton and his son form a murder and suicide pact; Norton shoots his son and then himself, and though Norton dies, the son lives to discover that the girl is not his sister. The plot is slightly more interesting than this, but the point worth noting here is Dixon's characterization of the affair between the stalwart Norton and the seductive Cleo that sets it in motion. The threat originates with her, a "young leopardess from an African jungle" concealed within "the lithe, graceful form of a Southern woman." The more obvious her advances, the more he weakens. However, once Norton proves to be "defenseless against the silent and deadly purpose that had already shaped itself in the soul of this sleek, sensuous young animal," Dixon shifts the ground in a significant way. Norton struggles not simply against the relentless lust of the mulatto, but also against the Beast within himself—"the Beast with a thousand heads and a thousand legs; the Beast that had bred in the bone and sinew of generations of ancestors, wilful, cruel, courageous conquerers of the world." Carrying "in his blood the inheritance of hundreds of years of lawless passion," Norton exemplifies the sins of the fathers he is doomed to repeat.[20]

Although its final message is not essentially different, *The Sins of the Father* is more penetrating than *The Leopard's Spots* or *The Clansman* because Dixon's central metaphor—the Negro as "beast"—is here revealed, at least provisionally, as the frantic psychological projection that it is. Since Cleo's own lust presumably results from both her physiological "degeneration" and her warped expectations of "equality," the beast within Norton meets itself without as though in a mirror image. It is the more than tacit recognition on Norton's part that the beast is within, however, that makes urgent, in the postbellum South, its renewed mastery—the mastery now of the *self* it is and the *other* it has created. Norton's obsessive campaign theme is sexual segregation of the races, a theme that in all the splendid power of its development between the Civil War and Faulkner's own century marks the ambiguous status of the freed slaves. White lust can no longer be released with impunity, for such an act now adds not to the value of one's property but to the visible threat against it. The "beast" has indeed been loosed, set free; the internal has by a radical act been made external.

It is important to take note of this transition, for Norton's inherited lust, and the language of the new naturalism in which he expresses it, magnifies at a particular level the South's general inheritance of guilt, whose continuing expression throughout Faulkner's life and in his work is a suffocating nostalgia, an innocence frantically remembered and maintained, and one whose manifestation in forms of social proscription and regulation reflect in every instance the psychological division within the white mind. Ike McCaslin seeks to resolve this dilemma by refusing to participate in it, choosing to dwell, as he knows he cannot, in "those old times" that are perpetually present, "not only as if they had happened yesterday but as if they were still happening," as if "none of his race nor the other subject race which his people had brought with them into the land had come here yet." By repudiating his patrimony, Ike removes himself as mediating term and leaves the families of Edmonds and Beauchamp utterly divided, descending in a parallel as neatly separated but intimately dependent as the accounts of the ledger, "two threads frail as truth and impalpable as equators yet cable-strong to bind for life them who made the cotton to the land their sweat fell on." If *Go Down, Moses* is evidence, it would seem that manumission and abolition, far from vitiating the intimate dependence of masters and slaves, on the contrary served to increase it in more comprehensive, more ambiguous forms. Certainly, the South and the nation were no longer half slave, half free, but Lincoln's prophetic phrase, for reasons he himself had feared and partially foreseen, had taken on new meanings that could have been anticipated, but could not be fully controlled, by anyone. . . .

Echoing Jefferson's, and prefiguring Lincoln's, concerns over miscegenation, [Jonathan] Edwards told the Connecticut Abolition Society that white Americans confronting their Negro slaves had two choices: either "raising their color to a partial whiteness" or "leaving to them all their real estates." If slaveholders wish to "balance their accounts with their Negro slaves at the cheapest possible rate, they will doubtless judge it prudent to leave the country, with all their houses, lands and improvements, to their quiet possession and dominion; as otherwise Providence will compel them to much dearer settlement, and one attended with a circumstance inconceivably more mortifying than the loss of their real estates, I mean the mixture of their blood with that of the Negroes into one common posterity."[21] Such a choice between miscegenation and patrimonial repudiation would appear zealously schematic if it did not correspond so closely to Ike McCaslin's dilemma and predict in more complex configurations the history of black emancipation from the Civil War through Faulkner's life. With an irony one can only consider vengeful, it anticipates the fear that would lead Lincoln and others to their utopian plans for colonization and lead the South and the nation to perilous contemporary justifications of the flawed designs of Thomas Sutpen and Carothers McCaslin for decades to come.[22]

Ike, of course, does not turn over his inheritance to the Beauchamps, who have already been raised to a "partial whiteness," but his act of repudiation comes as unthinkably (though paradoxically) close to doing so as anyone, South or North, might imagine. He sees, as Edwards did, that the choice is not between innocence and sin; he sees, rather, that it is too late, forever too late, that the choice is between the abandonment of a myth and the sacrifice of the integrity of the white psyche. The stories of the hunt in *Go Down, Moses* preserve the myth of lost innocence even as the argument between Ike and Cass exposes its endless regression, reaching probably back beyond the sons of Ham, beyond Canaan and Eden itself, and certainly back beyond the sons and fathers of Carothers McCaslin to the "old world's currupt and worthless twilight [carried to America] as though in the sailfuls of the old world's tainted wind which drove the ships."[23] The hunting stories preserve, at the irrevocable moment of its mythical fall, that innocence which must be destroyed to have existed at all and which therefore was doomed and damned to begin with. This, though, is also the history of the South, for whom that moment appeared with startling suddenness in 1865; by superimposing the central myth of the South upon the central myth of America, Faulkner extends one of its essential features, the narcissistic relationship between man and Nature, hunter and beast—or, in this case, between master and slave—to a further level that is capable of expressing, in figures of real and often physical intimacy, the entanglement between projected fantasy and repressed violence such myths require. Ortega's remark that "the past is a voluptuous siren,"[24] as it characterizes the nostalgic lure in hunting of a simpler pastoral life, also describes the lure in the South of a lost world of Confederate grandeur and innocence. Insofar as Faulkner both penetrated that myth with excruciating irony and, with further irony, revealed himself the victim of all its powerful charms, he might have taken his example not from Keats's ode but from Allen Tate's "Ode to the Confederate Dead," which speaks not of urns but of tombstones, not of wild ectasy but of "the patient curse / That stones the eyes, or like the jaguar leaps / For his own image in the jungle pool, his victim."[25]

In the context of *Go Down, Moses* the hunting stories bridge the incipient and actualized violence between black and white in "The Fire and the Hearth" and "Pantaloon in Black" on the one hand, and "Go Down, Moses" on the other, with necessarily marginal success. In this respect they have a therapeutic value not unlike Nick Adams's fishing in "Big Two-Hearted River," for to the extent that the wilderness stories of Faulkner and Hemingway alike are autobiographical projections,[26] they reveal with greater power the psychological collapse they preserve at the brink of actuality. In Faulkner's case, because the resonant dimensions of that collapse are so much larger, the risk is more pointed; and Ike's repudiation, as it appears to be a veiled projection of Faulkner's own, only preserves honor and virtue at a terrible cost. Even as he asserts that there was "some sort of love" in Carothers McCaslin's incest and miscegenation, Ike's repudiation of his patrimony denies the contemporary significance of that love. The translation from myth to actuality is the one that Ike, despite Faulkner's heroic insistence that it be possible, does not make. Like that of Henry Sutpen, Ike's repudiation becomes fratricidal by asserting that racial distinctions cannot be overcome, that the responsibility for them can only be renounced; like that of Quentin Compson, its argument devours itself by assuming responsibility for a grief that is ultimately as abstract and irrevocable as time itself. *Go Down, Moses* writhes and strains under the moral agony of connecting the spilt blood of the hunt to the spilt blood—and, moreover, the violently disseminated blood—of slavery. While it surpasses Sutpen's resolute innocence, the virtue Ike acquires by losing his innocence is ever more paradoxical as it expresses the tormenting forms, the extremities of spiritual wasting such virtue may entail.

"We must resist the North," Gavin Stevens contends in *Intruder in the Dust* (1948), "not just to preserve ourselves nor even the two of us as one to remain one nation because that will be the inescapable by-product of what we will preserve . . . the postulate that Sambo is a human being living in a free country and hence must be free." The six-year lapse between *Go Down, Moses* and *Intruder in the Dust* corresponds more or less to the remainder of Ike McCaslin's life as it is projected in *Go Down, Moses.* Although the identification should not be understood to be in any way complete, Stevens has rightly been seen to articulate a number of Faulkner's own beliefs, ones that Ike begins to express in "Delta Autumn" and that Faulkner's own public statements on race and desegregation in the 1950s amply bear out. The good intentions of Faulkner and Stevens cannot be doubted, but there is no ignoring the moral strain they also express. "That's what we are really defending," Stevens continues, "the privilege of setting [Sambo] free ourselves."[27] But as Twain had brutally put it in *Huckleberry Finn* (whose publication in 1885, by interesting coincidence, corresponds closely to Ike's act of repudiation), Tom Sawyer "gone and took all that trouble to set a free nigger free!"[28] . . .

Although it is generally a ludicrous novel and a depressing social document, *Intruder in the Dust* reveals how close *Go Down, Moses* had come to a similar collapse of moral sensibility. The claustrophobic entanglement of plot and chronology that characterizes most of the earlier novel when it is viewed as a continuous family saga is one reflection of the intimate involvements of white and black, master and slave that converge in, and radiate out of, the family ledgers, "as one by one the slaves which Carothers McCaslin had inherited and purchased" and their descendants take "substance and even a sort of shadowy life" on the pages we read.[29] . . .

The title story of the volume is in this way perfectly expressive of Faulkner's ambivalence. Its relationship to the rest of the stories is enormously distended, almost to the point of breaking; its function as an index of social estrangement is nearly overwhelmed by its leaving unexplained and unexplored the life of Samuel Beauchamp. The impassioned family grief that Gavin Stevens can in no way share, but can only mechanically respond to by arranging for Beauchamp's funeral, is left side by side, for reasons precariously elusive, with Aunt Mollie's confused version of the slave spiritual from which the book and story take their title: "Roth Edmonds sold my Benjamin. Sold him in Egypt. Pharoah got him—."[30] Faulkner, once again, has come face to face with the mask of "Negro" that cannot be penetrated; and though Gavin

Stevens is in this instance the perfect reflector of the alienation of Mollie Beauchamp, and though it is evident here, as it was in *Light in August*, that Faulkner's attitude toward Stevens is one of jaded irony, his continued fascination with him in *Intruder in the Dust* (and later in *Requiem for a Nun*, *The Town* and *The Mansion*) is difficult to fathom. Like the change of the murderer's name from Carothers Edmonds Beauchamp to Samuel Beauchamp, the shifting of the white burden of grief from the Edmonds and McCaslin families to the Worshams and Gavin Stevens seems not to actualize the ironies the story's title offers but to reflect Faulkner's own hasty flight from a tragedy that, as Ike discovers and as *Intruder in the Dust* makes embarrassingly obvious, would admit of no actual or dramatic resolution. . . .

Both "Go Down, Moses" and *Intruder in the Dust* show Faulkner at the limits of his tragic imagination. Their problems are his, and they derive in part from his own increasing recalcitrance on contemporary questions of racial inequality and in part from his difficulty in translating past passions into present vision. When he makes those difficulties one and the same, as in the characters of Quentin and Ike McCaslin, they are nothing but the heart of his fictional representation of the South's long trauma. What the stories dominated by Gavin Stevens reveal, however, is that the brilliant success of that expression seems to depend—has perhaps depended all along—on a further form of enslavement, one that is also Faulkner's necessary burden and that James Weldon Johnson had recognized thirty years earlier: "The Negro is in much the position of a great comedian who gives up the lighter roles to play tragedy. No matter how well he may portray the deeper passions, the public is loathe to give him up in his old character; they even conspire to make him a failure in serious work, in order to force him back into comedy."[31] . . .

By appearing to polarize these tendencies, which are elsewhere merged in all their impassioned fever, *Go Down, Moses* may be Faulkner's most honest and personally revealing novel, even though it is clearly not his best. If one were interested in personal revelation alone, however, one would have to draw the line of descent from Quentin Compson (or Shreve) to Ike McCaslin to Gavin Stevens, each of them partially ironic characterizations to be sure, but each revealing as well the developing trauma that Faulkner's public record on segregation in the 1950s would make visible. Such an interpretation may be important and may, as we noted earlier, prove that an author's chosen materials or themes are never entirely within his control; but we are perhaps equally likely to find meaningful not what an author says in his fiction or in public, but what he does not or can no longer say. *Go Down, Moses* illustrates this in two powerful and telling instances—in Ike McCaslin and Lucas Beauchamp, the two characters on whom Faulkner seems to spend his best powers as they dwindle into two different, but intimately related visions. Ike's relinquishing of his patrimony resembles, in authorial terms, Faulkner's own, for never again does his power to imagine the burden of that inheritance, transcending and entwining historically sequestered events, reappear with such expressive dignity. And never again does Faulkner—aside from the restless, mismanaged attempt in the case of Nancy Mannigoe in *Requiem for a Nun*—approach the tragic dignity of a "black" character he momentarily discovered in Lucas Beauchamp.

The extraordinary power of "The Fire and the Hearth" hold in taut juxtaposition the Sambo comedy of Lucas's hunt for buried treasure with his divining machine (an "object symbolical and sanctified for a ceremony, a ritual") and the explosive tragedy of his ritual combat with Zack Edmonds forty years earlier. That contest between a black man and a white man who "could have been brothers, almost twins too" is Faulkner's most exacting dramatization of the reciprocal powers and impending violence that miscegenation could produce. Having risked his own life to save Zack's son at childbirth, Lucas must endure, first, the humiliation of having his own wife set up for six months as Zack's housekeeper, wet nurse, and possible mistress; and second, the further humiliation of waiting for Zack to claim his own son once Mollie returns home to nurse both the black Henry and the white Roth. As Faulkner imagines it, however, the contest between Lucas and Zack has less to do with contemporary events and the potential act of adultery than with the rivalry between two strains of Carothers McCaslin's blood, as each of its heirs tries to bluff the other into violating the honor that descends with it. When the two men lock and embrace, "kneeling, their hands gripped, facing across the bed and the pistol," the strains of McCaslin blood meet in all the restrained violence that the original act of passion has set in motion. The momentary dispersal of tension that ensues in Lucas's argument (made more to himself than to Zack) that Zack has used old Carothers to beat him, just as Cass had used him "to make Isaac give up the land that was his because Cass Edmonds was the woman-made McCaslin, the woman-branch," affords an even greater ascendancy to Lucas; for his initial answer to that strategy is not to kill Zack (or both Zack and himself), but to kill only himself and thus "beat [Zack] and old Carothers both." We cannot be sure whether or not this is also a bluff, for at that moment Zack springs, "hurling himself across the bed, grasping at the pistol and the hand which held it. Lucas sprang too; they met over the center of the bed where Lucas clasped the other with his left arm almost like an embrace and jammed the pistol against the white man's side and pulled the trigger and flung the white man from him all in one motion, hearing as he did so the light, dry, incredibly loud click of the missfire."[32] . . . When he later examines the misfired cartridge—"the dull little brass cylinder less long than a match, not much larger than a pencil, not much heavier, yet large enough to contain two lives"—Lucas muses: "Have contained, that is. *Because I wouldn't have used the second one*, he thought. *I would have paid. I would have waited for the rope, even the coal oil. I would have paid. So I reckon I ain't got old Carothers' blood for nothing, after all. Old Carothers*, he thought. *I needed him and he come and spoke for me.*" In retrospect, Lucas's threat does indeed seem to have been a bluff, one intended to force into more agonized configuration his suicidal act, but one that strangely enough derives its power, in Lucas's eyes, from the very contamination of blood it is meant to repudiate. One might well contend that Faulkner has destroyed the powerful tensions that the ritual combat brought to culmination by leaving Lucas in the end, like Joe Christmas, the victim of the myth he acts out even as he acts violently against it. But what greater tragedy could there be than that myth, what more potent realization—here again like Joe Christmas and even Charles Bon—that the one irrevocable act of love contaminates all others that devolve from it? "How to God," Lucas asks at the conclusion of the scene that lives with him for life and continues to determine the small power he has as a black man who is and is not a "Negro," "can a black man ask a white man to please not lay down with his black wife? And even if he could ask it, how to God can the white man promise he won't?"[33]

Against the background of this powerful scene, the contemporary contest between Lucas and Roth over the divining machine seems pale and powerless, even if we take seriously Roth's recognition in Lucas's "absolutely blank, impenetrable" face of the composite stalemate of two bloods, the one that was "*pure ten thousand years when my own anonymous beginnings became mixed enough to produce me*," the other that "had heired and now produced with absolute and shocking fidelity the old ancestor's entire generation and thought." The second is the face Lucas shows Ike on the day he appears to collect his legacy, now not the face of Carothers McCaslin alone, but "the tintype face of ten thousand undefeated Confederate soldiers almost indistinguishably caricatured, composed, cold, colder than his, more ruthless than his." Or as Roth sees it again, forty-five years later, "a composite of a whole generation of fierce and undefeated young Confederate soldiers, embalmed and slightly mummified," the heir of everyone "*countless, faceless, even nameless now except himself who fathered himself, intact and complete, contemptuous, as old Carothers must have been, of all blood black white yellow or red, including his own.*"[34] To the degree that these passages impinge upon utter contradiction and grow out of Faulkner's attempt to wrest tragic significance from scenes that otherwise hardly bear close scrutiny, they are bound to appear confusing at best, and at worst to drift toward the pompous theory about Joe Christmas's contest of bloods offered by Gavin Stevens. Such confusion is to the point, however, for it expresses the increasing complication of projected and self-projected masking images that define the reciprocal entanglements between master and slave. . . .

The reciprocal threats and surmises, and the accompanying reversals of power, between Lucas and Zack as they twice struggle over the pistol enforce their identity as brothers or twins; and their mirroring posture, in its intimate antagonism, resembles that of Henry Sutpen and Charles Bon as they approach the crisis of fratricide that will violently reassert racial distinctions that have threatened to collapse. The violent confrontation between Lucas and Zack depends on a similar paradox; for the sexual intimacy over which they fight repeats the original violation of racial distinctions and family honor that has made them mirroring images to begin with. This further resemblance between generations is enhanced by the fact that Lucas combats the contemporary outrage by endorsing the first, by drawing on the marginal patrimony that Charles Bon is denied. Like Ike, he asserts that there was—there must have been—"some sort of love" in the miscegenation of old Carothers and his daughter; and in the contest with Zack, it is the totem father, old Carothers, whose blood and attributes he has internalized, who gives Lucas his courage and "speaks" for him. To suggest that Carothers McCaslin "sets Lucas free" would be misleading in every conceivable way but one: he frees him, as Sam Fathers does Ike, from the caste he belongs to; and though that freedom is ambiguous, even a mocking betrayal, it observes a ritual allegiance to the past that in each case converts an act of violence into an act of love. The psychological pressures of such conversion are themselves analogous but inverted, closer for the paradox, leading Ike to repudiate the patrimony that is undeniably his and allowing Lucas—even as he asserts that Ike has been cheated out of his inheritance by Cass—to exercise the marginal patrimonial power over the Edmonds family that belongs to him only by virtue of Ike's repudiation. Ike and Lucas, separated as they are in the stories they dominate, are in this respect fraternally united by the paternal blood that one denies (though he has every legal right to it) and the other embraces (though he has no legal right to it at all).

Ike's repudiation and Lucas's moral ascendancy, like the ritual hunt they both refer to, are charged with the reciprocal ambiguities that define for Faulkner the paradoxical contest between freedom and mixing of blood; and the ritual of freedom that the combative struggle is meant to play out issues in each case in a moral power whose most conspicuous feature is its enslavement to the past. Even though that enslavement appears to be in one case freely elected and in the other involuntary, they move toward each other, without merging, in such a way as to suggest proximity and dependence. Born Lucius Quintus Carothers McCaslin Beauchamp, grandson of Carothers McCaslin and son of Tomey's Turl, Lucas simply changes his name, "taking the name and changing, altering it, making it no longer the white man's but his own . . . himself selfprogenitive and nominate, by himself ancestored," repudiating what he can repudiate no more or less than Ike: "1874 the boy; 1888 the man, repudiated denied and free; 1895 and husband but no father, unwidowered but without a wife, and found long since that no man is ever free and probably could not bear it if he were."[35] Respectively "freed" from the ancestor and the patrimony they repudiate but can never escape, Lucas and Ike stand poised against each other, as incapable of dramatic involvement as Faulkner leaves them, divided forever by the act of the grandfather they share, the very act that made their respective repudiations necessary. Although they both live into old age, they are barely brought together in the book—except, perhaps, through the transitional grief and violence of "Pantaloon in Black"—and at last, they simply disappear from it, Ike dying some years later with no heirs but the half a county to which he is "uncle," and Lucas completely omitted from the story of his mysterious grandson's execution and funeral.

Notes

1. *Go Down, Moses* (New York: Modern Library, 1955), pp. 337, 22, 282, 154, 55.

2. Karl E. Zink, "William Faulkner: Form as Experience," *South Atlantic Quarterly* 53 (July 1954): 387.

3. *Go Down, Moses*, pp. 6, 388, 361–62.

4. Michael Millgate, *The Achievement of William Faulkner* (1966; reprint ed., Lincoln: University of Nebraska Press, 1978), p. 211.

5. *Go Down, Moses*, p. 351; cf. p. 315.

6. Ibid., pp. 257, 259, 300, 168.

7. Ibid., pp. 112, 268, 271, 297.

8. Here and following the quotations from "Ode on a Grecian Urn" refer to Keats, *Selected Poems and Letters*, ed. Douglas Bush (Boston: Houghton, Mifflin, 1959), pp. 207–8.

9. *Go Down, Moses*, pp. 269–70.

10. Ibid., p. 44.

11. Ibid., pp. 297, 240–41.

12. Ibid., pp. 266, 354, 361.

13. On the figure and status of the Negro during the prehistory and early history of America, see Winthrop Jordan, *White over Black: American Attitudes Toward the Negro, 1550–1812* (1968; reprint ed., New York: W. W. Norton, 1977), especially pp. 136–265, 482–582; and David Brion Davis, *The Problem of Slavery in Western Culture* (Ithaca: Cornell University Press, 1966), especially pp. 165–96, 262–88, 446–82. The curse of the sons of Ham—reputedly the African races—derived from Gen. 9:18–27, where Ham, the father of Canaan, looks upon the nakedness of Noah, his father: "Cursed be Canaan; a servant of servants shall he be unto his brethren."

14. *Go Down, Moses*, pp. 181, 164–65, 178.

15. José Ortega y Gasset, *Meditations on Hunting*, trans. Howard B. Wescott (New York: Scribners, 1972), pp. 110–11. See also Ortega's relevant remarks about the mediating function of dogs (p. 92), the mirroring actions of hunter and beast (pp. 59, 111), and the mystical union of their points of view: "The pursuer cannot pursue if he does not integrate his vision with that of the pursued. That is to say, *hunting is an imitation of the animal*" (p. 142).

16. *Go Down, Moses*, pp. 326, 198, 210, 204.

17. Ortega, *Meditations on Hunting*, p. 105.

18. Jordan, *White over Black*, p. 579.

19. Frederick L. Gwynn and Joseph L. Blotner, eds., *Faulkner in the University: Class Conferences at the University of Virginia, 1957–1958* (1959; reprint ed., New York: Vintage-Random, 1965), pp. 39–40.

20. Thomas Dixon, *The Sins of the Father: A Romance of the South* (New York: Grosset & Dunlap, 1912), pp. 25, 37, 43, 137. A further point, which bears on *Absalom, Absalom!* as well as *Go Down, Moses*, is made by Norton's mother-in-law when she explains to her daughter the cursed passions of Southern gentlemen: "And this is one of the reasons, my child, why slavery was doomed. The war was a wicked and awful tragedy. The white motherhood of the South would have crushed slavery. Before the war began we had six hundred thousand mulattoes—six hundred thousand reasons why slavery had to die" (p. 136).

21. Jonathan Edwards, *The Injustice and Impolicy of the Slave-Trade and of the Slavery of the Africans*, quoted in Jordan, *White over Black*, pp. 543–44. As Jordan remarks, "a blackened posterity would mean that the basest of energies had guided the direction of the American experiment and that civilized man had turned beast in the forest" and betrayed the very purpose and sanction of his errand into the New World. "Here was the brutally real dilemma: the sin of slavery required the wholesale abandonment of America or loss of original identity; either way it was a failure of mission. Edwards's intense Puritan conception of this mission led him to pose superficially ridiculous alternatives which were actually in the very long run probably the only ones possible."

22. Such sentiments have reappeared generation after generation. During Faulkner's lifetime they were embodied in Theodore Bilbo, longtime United States senator and governor of Mississippi, and staunch advocate of African colonization for American blacks, who insisted that he "would rather see his race and civilization blotted out with the atomic bomb than to see it slowly but surely destroyed in the maelstrom of miscegenation, interbreeding, and mongrelization." The day was coming, Bilbo prophesied, when there would no longer be any chance for redemption. "Once the [white] blood is corrupted, there is no power on earth, neither armed might, nor wealth, nor science, nor religion itself, that can restore its purity. Then there will be no Negro problems because the blood of that race will be commingled with the blood of the white race, and a mongrel America would have no reason to worry over the race issue. . . . Shall our generation possess the vision, foresight, and courage to solve forever the race problem so that ours will be the heritage of all the generations of Americans yet unborn? Or shall we pass the problem on and on to grow in magnitude with the passing years until our posterity sinks into the mire of mongrelism?" See *Take Your Choice: Separation or Mongrelization* (Poplarville, Miss.: Dream House Publishing Co., 1947), pp. ii, 10. The "Dream House" was Bilbo's private mansion; the volume also contains a copy of his colonization bill, the "Greater Liberia Act," introduced in the United States Senate in 1939.

23. *Go Down, Moses*, p. 259.

24. Ortega, *Meditations on Hunting*, p. 131.

25. William Pratt, ed., *The Fugitive Poets* (New York: E. P. Dutton, 1965), p. 98.

26. See, for example, Malcolm Cowley, *Faulkner-Cowley File*, p. 98, for Faulkner's 1946 letter: "I missed a beautiful stag last fall. . . . He broke out of a thicket at full speed; I just heard a stick crack and looked around and there he was, running flat like a horse, not jumping at all, about 30 mph, about 100 yards away. He ran in full sight for 50 yards. I think perhaps the first bullet (it was a .270) hit a twig and blew up. But the second shot I missed him clean. He was running too fast for me. He was a beautiful sight. Now it's done, I'm glad his head is still in the woods instead of on a plank on the wall." (In the same letter Faulkner went on to say that he had "become the slave of [a] vast and growing mass of inanimate junk, possessions" that he could not escape.) On the same day, apparently, Faulkner repeated the story of his hunt in a letter to Robert Haas but concluded, "I'm glad now he got away from me though I would have liked his head." See *Selected Letters*, p. 244.

27. *Intruder in the Dust* (New York: Vintage-Random, 1972), p. 154.

28. Mark Twain, *Adventures of Huckleberry Finn* (New York: W. W. Norton, 1977), p. 227.

29. *Go Down, Moses*, pp. 263–65.

30. *Go Down, Moses*, p. 371.

31. James Weldon Johnson, *The Autobiography of an Ex-Coloured Man* (New York: Alfred A. Knopf, 1928), p. 168.

32. *Go Down, Moses*, pp. 87, 47, 55–57.

33. Ibid., pp. 58–59.

34. Ibid., pp. 71, 118, 108, 118.

35. Ibid., p. 281.

Race, Blood, and McCaslins:
The Abstraction Grasped as
a Fine Dead Sound   Panthea Reid Broughton*

Epistemology tells us that the mind can deal only in models of itself and should be under no delusion about fully comprehending and containing actuality. Most of Faulkner's characters, however, make the mistake of insisting that their models or categories are reality. They tend to forget that concepts are only tools for comprehending and ordering experiential reality. These characters manage only to be in touch with the shape of their own conceptual models rather than with what Faulkner calls "the living and fluid world of [their] time" (*The Wild Palms*, p. 25). They mold their convenient beliefs into an elaborate conceptual framework which so obscures the workings of the universe that it seems a shield against actuality or an agent for rendering it known and malleable. Such traditions are founded upon pride which is "based not on any value" (*Go Down, Moses*, p. 111) but on an irrelevant abstraction. The staleness of these concepts typifies what Henry Adams calls "thought-inertia"[1] or what old Doc Peabody in *As I Lay Dying* means when he says " 'When I was young I believed death to be a phenomenon of the body. Now I know it to be merely a function of the mind' " (p. 42).

Faulkner's fiction establishes just how insidious mental deadness or thought-inertia may be. The results are terrifying when man may be irrevocably judged and irreparably placed by a few ready linguistic handles such as *white, nigger, quality, trash, lady, whore, South, North, American, Jew,* or *foreigner*, but the most horrendous example of the power of a label is the word *nigger*. That word attempts to fix a person's behavior and to dictate interests, feelings, and even aspirations. As Olga Vickery explains: "What starts as a verbal pattern of classification thus becomes a social order not to be challenged or changed. And what starts as a category becomes a myth, for certainly the word 'Negro' is a compressed myth just as the stock response to that word is a compressed ritual."[2] In *Go Down, Moses*, for example, the pattern of "what niggers do" is considered set and established. The assumption is that " 'Them damn niggers . . . aint human' " (*Go Down, Moses*, p. 154). Thus, Tomey's Turl is known to be a "damn white half-McCaslin" (p. 6), but because he bears the public label of "nigger," Buck McCaslin hunts him like an animal. The point of view of the young Cass is disturbingly callous; he "closed in too fast; maybe he was afraid he wouldn't be there in time to see [Turl] when he treed" (p. 8). Cass attempts to explain Turl's behavior: "being a nigger, Tomey's Turl should have jumped down and run for it afoot as soon as he saw them. But he didn't; maybe Tomey's Turl had been running off from Uncle Buck for so long that he had even got used to running away like a

---

*This essay was adapted by the author especially for this volume from *William Faulkner: The Abstract and the Actual* (Baton Rouge, La.: Louisiana State University Press, 1974).

white man would do it" (p. 9). The ironic inappropriateness of such racial assumptions is heightened by the exposure in "The Bear" that more McCaslin blood flows in Turl's veins than in Cass's.

When Isaac reads the old commissary ledger in "The Bear," he realizes that his father and uncle, however aware of the wrongs of slavery, could not imagine a black woman's grieving enough to commit suicide; Buck McCaslin wrote in the ledger, *"Who in hell ever heard of a niger [sic] drownding him self"* (p. 267). At twenty-one, Isaac realized why his grandfather left a legacy of $1,000 to Tomey's Turl: *"So I reckon that was cheaper than saying My son to a nigger"* (p. 269). Throughout his fiction Faulkner exposes the dehumanizing power of such abstractions. For example, in "That Evening Sun," when Nancy Mannigoe tries to commit suicide, the jailer theorizes that "no nigger would try to commit suicide unless he was full of cocaine, because a nigger full of cocaine wasn't a nigger any longer" (*Collected Stories*, p. 291). But the results of such labeling are most explicitly examined in *Go Down, Moses* where Lucas Beauchamp protests, " 'I'm a nigger. . . . But I'm a man too' " (p. 47).

As Bergson explains in *Time and Free Will*, "The beliefs to which we most strongly adhere are those of which we should find it most difficult to give an account, and the reasons by which we justify them are seldom those which have led us to adopt them. In a certain sense we have adopted them without any reason, for what makes them valuable in our eyes is that they match the colour of all our other ideas and that from the very first we have seen in them something of ourselves."[3] In *Go Down, Moses* the idea that most insistently matches the color of all the other ideas in the communal mind is the shibboleth of white superiority. Such racial presumption brought old Carothers McCaslin to summon to his bed with impunity both the slave girl Eunice and his own daughter (by Eunice). Isaac thinks *"His own daughter His own daughter,"* and protests *"No No Not even him"* (p. 270), but when he considers the evidence he realizes that his grandfather felt free to commit incest with *"His own daughter"* precisely because to him she was only a "nigger."

Much of *Go Down, Moses* exposes the arbitrariness of the assumption of white superiority. The close foster brother relationships of first Lucas and Zack and then Henry and Roth dissolve when the white "brothers" (actually they are cousins) suddenly recognize racial difference and order their cousins (classified as "niggers") to sleep on pallets rather than beds. Faulkner describes Roth's recognition of racial difference as "the old curse of his fathers, the old haughty ancestral pride based not on any value but on an accident of geography, stemmed not from courage and honor but from wrong and shame" (p. 111). Bergson says that people try to "reconstruct reality—which is tendency and consequently mobility—with precepts and concepts whose function it is to make it stationary."[4] Here the precepts "white" and "black" restructure the "reality" that all four boys are McCaslins.

In *Go Down, Moses*, the specious notion of white superiority is compounded with another specious concept, that of "blood." Lucas Beauchamp feels that the concept "blood" somehow erases the stigmata "nigger." He sees himself as "the oldest McCaslin descendant [on the plantation] even though in the world's eye he descended not from McCaslins but from McCaslin slaves" (p. 36). Lucas has utter contempt for George Wilkins, an "interloper without forbears" (p. 40), and almost equal contempt for the white sheriff who has no ancestry (p. 43). Although Lucas considers himself *contemptuous, as old Carothers must have been, of all blood black white yellow or red, including his own*" (p. 118), he actually defines his existence by the precept of blood: " 'what Carothers McCaslin would have wanted me to do' " (p. 53). Thus he stays in Mississippi, not because he has either material or moral shackles binding him there (p. 105), but because as " 'a McCaslin too and a man-made one' " (p. 53) his specious consciousness of ancestry demands that he stay on the plantation where, despite his status as a Negro, his McCaslin blood is at least acknowledged. Old Carothers's blood does bestow genetically upon Lucas a number of McCaslin characteristics. In *The Reivers* Lucius Priest remembers that his great-grandmother had said Lucas "looked (and behaved: just as arrogant, just as iron-headed, just as intolerant) exactly like [old Carothers] except for color" (p. 229). Lucas did indeed inherit his looks from old Carothers, but he did not inherit arrogance. He acquired arrogance and intolerance through deference to the abstract concept of blood.

When Isaac McCaslin discovers that his grandfather's sins include adultery and incest, he recognizes these sins as the legacy of slavery. Later he determines to eradicate evil in, he assumes, something of the manner of John Brown who "was crude enough to act" (*Go Down, Moses*, p. 284). But Isaac's "action" is chiefly one of dissociation from the evils of the past. And there is some sense in which, by ignoring the past, he grants to it a peculiar potency; for, regardless of humanity's efforts to deny it, the past persists, and it must be acknowledged. All of *Go Down, Moses* asserts that point. We find there that generations repeat themselves (p. 110), that Sam Fathers will live on in Isaac (p. 165), and that, indeed, all time may be "crammed and crowded into one instant of time" (p. 140). Isaac's boyhood novitiate in the wilderness should insure that "those old times would cease to be old times and would become a part of the boy's present" (p. 171). Isaac's mistake, however, is to attempt both to freeze the old wilderness times and to dismiss the plantation past altogether. Repudiating his literal inheritance, Isaac believes he may escape its moral legacy.

There is a curious passage in *Go Down, Moses* in which Faulkner says Isaac McCaslin was "taking with him" something of his "evil and unregenerate" grandfather (p. 294). What Isaac takes with him, apparently, is his grandfather's habit of confronting not the man but the abstraction. When he relinquishes the land, Isaac imagines that his might be a divinely ordained deed intended " 'to set at least some of His lowly people free' " (p. 259). Freeing the lowly is to Isaac, however, largely a matter of committing the "heresy" of saying that the Negroes are " 'better than we are' " (p. 294), as if, to expiate for centuries of treating Negroes as inferiors, all Isaac McCaslin has to do is call them superiors. When Faulkner writes that "even in escaping he was taking with him more of that evil and unregenerate old man . . . than even he had feared" (p. 294), he implies that both Isaac, who can say " 'They are better,' " and the old man his grandfather, who never questioned the Negro's inferiority, are dealing only with the abstraction "Negro."

With his pristine ideal of freedom for the Negroes Isaac makes little show of brotherhood. There is something of compulsion in the manner in which he dispenses the thousand dollars to each of his Negro cousins: to Lucas who banks it as symbol of his station and to Fonsiba who can only assert, " 'I'm free' " (p. 280), even though she is also desperate, impoverished, and hungry. Isaac regrets that Tennie's Jim escapes on his twenty-first birthday before the thousand dollars can be passsed on to him. His regret seems somehow more selfish than not, as if he too wanted to make a payment, discharge a duty, and thereby be freed of an obligation. Isaac tries to free himself from what Faulkner calls the necessarily "slow amortization" (p. 266) of injustice. Isaac's ultimate failure results from his encountering a "specific tragedy which had not been condoned and could never be amortized" (p. 266). Isaac, however, expects to write off the tragedy with a few words, a few dollars, and with one grand sacrifice: the relinquishment of the property which bears the curse.

Isaac makes his sacrifice in the name of freedom. Cass Edmonds has told him freedom will come " 'not now nor ever, we from them nor they from us' " (p. 299), and authorial comment insists that "no man is ever free" (p. 281), but Isaac nevertheless seeks for himself and the Negroes an impossible state idealized as "freedom." For himself, Isaac sees freedom in Sam's terms, which are those of isolation and dedication to a way of life which is no longer a viable choice in the twentieth century. But "adaptability in Faulkner," to quote Arthur F. Kinney, "presages the only meaningful liberty." Isaac, however, is reluctant to adapt to motion and change. Kinney explains: "Ike is able to accommodate new meaning given the wilderness only until the death of Old Ben; at that point his definition is fixed: Ike freezes his picture of the woods in memory willed kinetic; he simultaneously turns a solitary moment of wilderness existence into an external refuge, a personal and private sanctuary."[5]

Indeed, Isaac's life has been "drawing inward" (p. 335) ever since his sixteenth year. The inwardness of his life is signified by his childlessness. Isaac's attempt has been to repudiate "that same wrong and shame [his grandfather's] from whose regret and grief he would at least save and free his son and, saving and freeing his son, lost him" (p. 351). But there is a sense in which Isaac has, in fact, repeated the sin of old Carothers McCaslin, who with a "contempt for all his get" (p. 255) disdained obligation for his descendants. Isaac has no son, and, though he may be "uncle to half a county" (p. 3), he seems to have been unable to pass on any of his code of honor even to his kinsman Roth Edmonds. In "Delta Autumn" he is seen as an old man who has done little since his sixteenth year: he seems only to have " 'lived so long and forgotten so much that [he doesn't] remember anything [he] ever knew or felt or even heard about love' " (p. 363). Isaac, as an old man, even ceases to care that the wilderness is vanishing since there is "just exactly enough" to last his lifetime (p. 354). Freedom, to Isaac, is not what it was to the slave Thucydus who insisted on working out his freedom (p. 266), or to Old Ben, the bear whom humans admire precisely because he puts his freedom in jeopardy (p. 295). It is more like the freedom applauded in "warm and air-proof" (p. 284) legislative halls, a freedom assumed to have been accomplished by the Emancipation Proclamation. In other words, Isaac looks upon freedom as a state of being, accomplished by proclamation or thousand-dollar payment or by relinquishment. For him, the concept becomes another refuge from the living and fluid world.

Ike then is hardly different from Fonsiba and her husband who also grant magical status to the mere concept of freedom. Fonsibia keeps repeating, " 'I'm free,' " as if in her situation freedom makes any difference. It does not. Her "freedom" avails little when on her Arkansas farm there are no crops, no stock, and only a meager and insufficient pension and when her husband only repeats the empty politicians' words about an era dedicated to freedom rather than work. Ike sees all this as the "rank stink of baseless and imbecile delusion," meaning only freedom from work, but still Fonsiba asserts, " 'I'm free' " (p. 280). Just afterwards Faulkner juxtaposes Ike's assertion that he himself is "repudiated denied and free" (p. 281). The irresponsibility, the empty words, the inertia of the Arkansas Negro are to be compared with Ike's escape under the guise of the word *freedom*. As Ike continues to insist " 'I am free' " (p. 299) and " 'Sam Fathers set me free' " (p. 300), it becomes apparent that Isaac, like Fonsiba and her husband, has also endowed the concept itself with magical power.

Isaac knows what Lucas thinks of him: *"That I reneged, cried calf-rope, sold my birthright, betrayed my blood"* (p. 109) and, in fact, that was just what he wished to do. He acknowledges that he is "repudiating and even hoping to escape" from "old Carothers' doomed and fatal blood" (p. 293). Intending to escape it, Isaac confers the status of reality and hence power upon the concept of "old Carothers' doomed and fatal blood." The failure of his attempt to rid his own blood of the legacy of the man who refused to say *"My son to a nigger"* (p. 269) is revealed in his response to Roth's mistress in whom "the strong old blood ran after its long lost journey back to home" (p. 362). Old Ike cries out "in a voice of amazement, pity, and outrage: 'You're a nigger!' " (p. 361).

Notes

1. Henry Adams, *The Education of Henry Adams* (1918; rpt. Boston: Houghton Mifflin, 1961), 484.

2. Olga Vickery, *The Novels of William Faulkner* (Baton Rouge: Louisiana State University Press, 1964), 69.

3. Henri Bergson, *Time and Free Will: As Essay on the Immediate Data of Consciousness*, trans. F. L. Pogson (London: George Allen and Unwin, 1950), 135.

4. Henri Bergson, *An Introduction to Metaphysics*, trans. T. E. Hulme (Indianapolis: Bobbs-Merrill, 1955), 51.

5. Arthur F. Kinney, "Faulkner and the Possibilities for Heroism," *Southern Review*, N.S., 6 (Autumn 1970): 1119, 1118.

The McCaslin-Edmonds Line

The Four Fathers
of Isaac McCaslin

Annette Bernert*

Despite a critical deluge of ink and anxiety, Isaac McCaslin remains a somehow puzzling figure to Faulkner readers. Neither the causes nor the extent of his failure to live out his ideals has been very clearly established. It seems to me that one insufficiently studied clue to his character is, as for his spiritual kin Gail Hightower, the influence of history on his development, a process less obvious than for other Faulkner protagonists because Ike conceived his central act as a repudiation of his past. Our common American yearnings for a lost impossible Eden perhaps make us vulnerable in varying degrees to Ike's mythology. And then the narrator of "The Fire and the Hearth" tells us that Ike in his old age "had acquired something of a young boy's high and selfless innocence."[1] But after "Delta Autumn" we must ask what moral significance such an "innocence" can have, and at what cost it was obtained.

Throughout *Go Down, Moses*, Faulkner carefully provides several levels of juxtaposition, that of Ike to other characters, that of the three Ike sections to the other four, and that of Ike's ideas to his actions. This arrangement demonstrates the essential futility of Isaac's life, and the obsession with the McCaslin and Southern past which accounts for it. Even more significantly, Faulkner dramatizes that history through the active influence of four men, Ike's natural father Theophilus "Buck" McCaslin, his spiritual father the half-caste Sam Fathers, his older cousin McCaslin "Cass" Edmonds, and his grandfather Lucius Quintus Carothers McCaslin. I shall first discuss what each man represented to Isaac, and then how each affected his life.

The incarnation of the evils of the plantation is for Ike, of course, his grandfather, old Carothers McCaslin, the original purchaser of the family land and slaves. The plantation itself saw Ike as "that whole edifice intricate and complex and founded upon injustice and erected by ruthless rapacity and carried on even yet with at times downright savagery" (p. 298). The primal injustice was the ownership of land, in violation of man's God-given

*Reprinted with permission from *Southern Humanities Review* 9, no. 4 (Fall 1975): 423–33. © *Southern Humanities Review*, Auburn University, Auburn, AL 36849.

trusteeship "to hold the earth mutual and intact in the communal anonymity of brotherhood" (p. 257). From it derives the greater horror of the ownership of people, which can lead to that final secret of the commissary ledgers, old Carothers's begetting, without acknowledging, a son upon his own mulatto daughter. Because of this double crime, toward land and toward people, "the whole South is cursed," and while "descendants alone can—not resist it, not combat it—maybe just endure and outlast it until the curse is lifted" (p. 278).

Even as Ike inherited from his grandfather a legacy of guilt and shame, he derived from his father and uncle "a little at least of its amelioration and restitution" (p. 261). Old Carothers's cynical bequest of one thousand dollars to his mulatto son Terrel (which the latter refused), to be paid by his white sons, was increased by the latter to one thousand dollars apiece for Terrel's children. But the major venture of the twin sons was, on the day of their father's death, to free the family slaves, and to move out of the big, unfinished house, leaving it to the Negroes, and into a log cabin the brothers built themselves (pp. 6, 105, 262, 273).

Through the seductive veneer of horseplay in "Was," the flaws in this humanitarianism are visible—in Buck's wild hunt, with dogs, after his own half-brother, and in the placing as stakes in a poker game the marriage of one player's sister (later Ike's mother), and the ownership of the other player's brother (pp. 23–29). As Neal Woodruff notes, neither Buck nor Buddy had "an interest in forwarding the McCaslin dynasty" or "the plantation system."[2] But their positive morality, Faulkner seems to be suggesting, is suitable only for low comedy. Furthermore, after the marriage, "they moved back into the big house," clearing "the remaining negroes out of it" (p. 301). And those legacies are either refused or unused by Terrel's three children.

Important though his ideas may have been, Buck never functions dramatically as a father to Ike; we never even see them together in Go Down, Moses. Ike's active fathers are Sam Fathers and Cass Edmonds, both linked for Ike with the wilderness. Though Sam's "face and bearing were still those of the Chickasaw chief who had been his father" (p. 164)—a chief, however, who had sold mother and son into slavery—sometimes Sam's eyes showed "the mark . . . of bondage" (p. 167). The "warriors' and chiefs' blood in him" had been "betrayed through the black blood which his mother gave him" (p. 168). Though Sam did "white man's work" (p. 169), and bore himself toward Cass "as an older man to a younger" (p. 170), after the death of the other local Indian he went off to live in the woods (p. 175). The only way Sam could devise not to "be a negro," to resolve the racial tensions figured both in his body and perhaps also his surname "Fathers," was to live as a hermit-priest where his father was once chief. That he does not exactly fit this role is hinted by his appearance, "not tall, squat rather, almost sedentary, flabby-looking" (p. 166), by his never actually hunting in the stories, and, I think, by his preparation of Lion as an instrument for the destruction of Old Ben, an image of the wilderness itself.

In any case, it is Sam who taught Ike "the woods, to hunt" (p. 170), who initiated Ike with "the first worthy blood" (p. 165) into the wilderness, who "consecrated and absolved him from weakness and regret too" (p. 182), who, Ike says, " 'set me free' " (p. 300). As Neal Woodruff acutely perceives, Sam is not the "natural man and noble savage" many critics see but "a deeply sophisticated and completely disciplined man."[3] Like his Biblical avatar, Sam is both "lent to the Lord" (1 Samuel 1:28) and given by his father into an alien way of life; further, the Old Testament Samuel anoints the first Israelite king, Saul, later rejected for disobedience ("to obey is better than sacrifice," [I Samuel 15:22]), dying in battle with all his sons—a dim but possible parallel to Ike.

But even as the prophet Samuel was an agent in a national loss of innocence, in providing the king who was a rejection of direct divine rule (I Samuel 8:7), even so did Sam Fathers initiate Ike into a wilderness both potentially destructive and imminently doomed, like the bear which is its living symbol. Those one hundred swampers are not just enacting myths; they have fed the animal enough over the years to " 'have a sheer in him' " (p. 248). The bear left a "corridor of wreckage and destruction" through which he "sped, not fast but rather with the ruthless and irresistible delibera-tion of a locomotive [an image repeated pp. 211, 238] . . . an anachronism indomitable and invincible out of an old dead time" (p. 193). At best, as Otis B. Wheeler notes, Ike is "the last priest of a dying cult,"[4] or as John Lewis Longley observes, his is a "morality . . . highly specialized."[5]

In a sense, Ike's whole future lies in part five of "The Bear," in which he thought of the wilderness as that "within which he would be able to hide himself from it [the train] once more anyway" (p. 318). A rattlesnake, "the old one, the ancient and accursed about the earth, fatal and solitary," its smell "evocative of all knowledge and an old weariness and of pariah-hood and of death" (p. 329), commanded the same courageous ritual as did the bear, and the same salutation as did the mythical deer in "The Old People." The old snake seems to be all that is left worth saluting in the vanishing woods, even as the squirrels are all that is left worth shooting. By the time of "Delta Autumn" all Ike seems practically to have gained is the trust of horses, "possessing no affinity for them as creatures, beasts, but being merely insu-lated by his years and time from the corruption of steel and oiled moving parts which tainted the others" (p. 342), a trust because of what he lacks, not what he has. Ike in his seventies suddenly realized that the reason "he had never wanted to own any of it" was that "there was justly exactly enough of it. He seemed to see the two of them—himself and the wilderness—as co-evals . . . the two spans running out together . . . into a dimension free of both time and space" (p. 354).

Which brings us of course to that idealist Cass Edmonds, Isaac's fourth "father." Cass is referred to twice as "rather his brother than cousin and rather his father than either" (pp. 4, 350), and "Sam always referred to the boy's cousin as his father" (p. 174). Ike himself declared in the commissary, " 'I knew a long time ago that I would never have to miss my father' " (p.

288). But as a father, even as a man, Cass is more complex than any of the other three.

Though Lucas Beauchamp believed Cass took Ike's inheritance from him "simply because he wanted it and knew he could use it better" (p. 44), we witness, at excruciating length, Ike "and his cousin juxtaposed not against the wilderness but against the tamed land . . . not in pursuit and lust but in relinquishment" (pp. 254, 255). He is not the crass materialist many have found him to be, but, if anything, a man over-civilized into cynicism; his presence alone makes Joseph Gold err in declaring that "Ike was the first, and as far as we know, the only member of his family with moral awareness."[6]

It is Cass who spoke of " 'the tedious and shabby chronicle of His chosen sprung from Abraham,' " until " 'men snarled over the gnawed bones of the old world's worthless evening' " (p. 258). It is also Cass who knew that Keats " '*was talking about truth. Truth is one. It doesn't change. It covers all things which touch the heart—honor and pride and pity and justice and courage and love*' " (p. 297).

It was his cousin who brought Ike "for the first time to the camp, the big woods" (p. 192), who bought him his gun, and who in his own youth, and under Sam's sponsorship, had also seen the phantom buck (pp. 187, 289). Ike's vision that "the buck sprang, forever immortal" (p. 178) is essentially Cass's, or at least shared with him. Later, Cass tried to explain to Ike that neither Ike nor Sam would shoot Old Ben when he had the chance because he saw the hunt as an immortal ritual, a dramatic Keatsian urn. Ike's re-peated dreams (pp. 181, 211) and his insistence to Sam that " 'it must be one of us . . . when even he dont want it to last any longer' " (p. 212) mean the same thing, that the bear hunt exists for itself, not to kill the bear. Likewise, though "he should have hated and feared Lion" (pp. 209, 212, 226) as the agent designed for the bear's death, he saw him "like the last act on a set stage" (p. 226). The day before the final hunt, Ike "felt the old lift of the heart, as pristine as ever, as on the first day; he would never lose it" (p. 233). In the woods "death did not even exist" (p. 327), for both a gutted log (p. 205) and funerary offerings in a tin can could "heal . . . into the wilderness" (p. 328). In the climactic death scene, the bear "caught the dog in both arms, almost loverlike" (p. 240), and "for an instant they almost resembled a piece of statuary: the clinging dog, the bear, the man astride its back" (p. 241).

Of the Civil War we are told that Cass "had actually seen it, and the boy even at almost eighty would never be able to distinguish certainly between what he had seen and what had been told him" (p. 291). Cass is, in short, a man "born too late into the old time and too soon for the new" (p. 297). For him, as for the older hunters, as Daniel Hoffman points out, the hunt like "their service in the Confederate Army, another Quest," is "another romantic lost cause."[7]

Though Cass has given Lucas and Molly a house and land, he also holds the ends of "the two threads frail as truth and impalpable as equators yet cablestrong to bind for life them who made the cotton to the land their sweat fell on" (pp. 293–94). To Ike's declaration about being free, Cass responds, " 'No, not now nor ever, we from [the Negroes] nor they from us. . . . I will always be what I was born and have always been" (pp. 299–300). What that is seems to me to be, like Sam but in different ways, a man divided against himself, a socially responsible individual whose idealism and analytical intelligence have driven him, unwillingly, into cynicism.

None of the men, of course, is the proper age for a father. Old Carothers died thirty years before Ike was born, as did Buck and Sam during his adolescence, and they are, chronologically, grandfathers. Cass is but sixteen years older, almost a peer. There is a sense, then, in which Ike really has been fatherless all his life (p. 283). More important, the spiritual legacy from each man, though promising fair (even the grandfather offered at least an opportunity for counteraction) like Uncle Hubert's silver and gold, proved as debased as the tin coffee pot full of coppers and IOU's Hubert actually left. Old Carothers left guilt without freedom from its causes, Buck a chivalric meliorism both inadequate and rather comic, Sam a sacramentalism functionally only metaphorical and for a world in any case which has disappeared, and Cass an aestheticism which is a veneer for a sense of futility approaching nihilism. Ike lacked a father even as he lacks peers and shall lack sons; he is a loner; a hearth fire, that "ancient symbol of human coherence and solidarity" (p. 380), is simply missing from his life.

With all their inadequacies, however, those men are what Ike has, and what makes him what he becomes. The coffee pot enshrined on his mantel (pp. 300,308) is emblematic of his attitude toward all the other "legacies": he is bound by them, staked down, as it were, from four directions.

Ike made the decision, then, to refuse his inheritance, relinquishing to his cousin Cass all but "the trusteeship of the legacy" (p. 106) of his grandfather's black descendants. He became a carpenter "because if the Nazarene had found carpentering good for the life and ends He had assumed and elected to serve, it would be all right too for Isaac McCaslin even though Isaac McCaslin's ends, although simple enough in their apparent motivation, were and would always be incomprehensible to him" (p. 309). Believing he is viewing life *sub specie aeternitatis*, he has polarized his experience into visions of good and evil, projecting each upon specialized environments, without seeing either their temporal relativity or their true moral significance. His practical decision is too unconsciously motivated for him to be able to give account of himself. Inevitably, then, what he actually accomplishes becomes quite other than what he seems to have intended. His life becomes the negative drama of what was essentially a negative act, motivated by the accepted influence of those four fathers. We must now ask what he did, specifically, with each inheritance.

First, though he saw his disinheritance as a repudiation of the sins of his grandfather, he does not overcome the attitudes which made those sins possible. By "Delta Autumn," as Longley observes, "the pattern of shame and wrong has come full circle."[8] His reaction to the fact that Roth's part-

Negro mistress was his own kin is to give her the hunting horn as a kind of heirloom, and then to tell her to " 'Go back North. Marry: a man in your own race' " (p. 363), meaning, despite her white skin, a black man. His denial of family relationship is different only in degree from his grandfather's offense.

Second, what he did accept of the McCaslin inheritance, the legacy left by Buck and Buddy to Terrel's children, clearly establishes its futility. He followed his father's pattern of giving money (or a half-finished house) to his Negro kinfolk, in lieu of establishing any real relationship with them. In "Delta Autumn" the act is repeated as Ike forces Roth's money upon his wronged kinswoman. To his lack of self-awareness it is "as if he had never performed such an action before" (p. 357), though at eighteen he had gone to Tennessee to attempt to deliver the family conscience-money to her grandfather (p. 273), " 'Tennie's Jim, though he had a name' " (p. 361), the rightful name being of course James Beauchamp. Isaac could not understand why all three of old Carothers's Negro grandchildren refused their legacy (there is no evidence that Lucas ever used much of his) with more finality than he himself did, why Fonsiba would say, " 'I'm free' " (p. 280).

Ike's refusal of his patrimony derives from the same pattern of thought. As Robert Penn Warren observes, "Ike tried to buy out of responsibility by refusing his inheritance."[9] In theological terms, Ike sought to counteract the guilt of his ancestry by acts of propitiation, by bribing the gods to overlook the sin, when what was needed was expiation, an act of real purification which virtually erases that sin by nullifying its effects. This of course is what Charles Mallison learns in *Intruder in the Dust*, that he can stand right with Lucas not by gifts reinforcing Lucas's low-caste status, but by an act requiring, yes, all those Nobel Prize speech qualities of "love and honor and pity and pride and compassion and sacrifice." Ike enacted the ancient sin of simony, the purchase of spiritual benefit with material goods.

Third, although the positive motivation for his relinquishment stems from Sam's notions of the natural laws governing land, à la Henry George, Ike's action makes stewardship of either land or people impossible. In reality he gives the McCaslin plantation to whoever happens to be the Edmonds heir. That heir in "The Fire and the Hearth" and "Delta Autumn" is Roth, whose emblematic name is repeatedly emphasized; he is always "wroth" at somebody (pp. 59, 64, 65, 66, 70, 84, 85, 86, 97, 104, 112), usually of course his relative Lucas Beauchamp. "The old curse of his fathers," stemming "not from courage and honor but from wrong and shame, descended" (p. 111) upon Roth at the precocious age of seven, when he lost his sense of companionship with his cousin Henry Beauchamp. In "Delta Autumn" Roth declared that " 'women and children are one thing there's never any scarcity of' " (p. 339), and gave to his part-Negro mistress and infant son "just money" (p. 358), without even the courage to do it in person. Ike has "spoiled" Roth, as his mistress claims, by leaving him property and power he did not know how to manage; and he has "spoiled" that property by leaving it to one unfit to manage it.

Roth thereby reenters the cycle of old Carothers, demonstrating that it was not only not defused by Ike's act but that it was not even short-circuited. We learn in "Go Down, Moses" that it was Roth "who had actually sent the boy [Samuel Beauchamp] to Jefferson in the first place" (p. 373); hence his grandmother Mollie's plaint, " 'Roth Edmonds sold my Benjamin. Sold him in Egypt. Pharaoh got him' " (p. 371). In that story, Roth's act is implicitly contrasted to the efforts of Gavin Stevens to bring the boy's body home again. Further, as Michael Millgate observes, Ike "has failed to pass on to younger men even the practical training he received from Sam Fathers."[10] That is, the last we see of Ike in *Go Down, Moses* is his recognition that Roth has killed a doe (p. 365). What Ike conceived as an act motivated by his "wilderness" ideals has actually led toward mismanagement of the McCaslin plantation and further destruction of the woods. It is an act of irresponsibility, a "cop-out," as the accusations of Cass and Lucas make clear.

Cass protested in several ways that Ike's act is only an " 'escape' " (p. 283), even as Major de Spain said " 'It looks like you just quit' " (p. 309), a phrase used earlier by Sam's doctor (p. 248). Rather than deny, Ike mythicized himself as "an Isaac born into a later life than Abraham's and repudiating immolation" (p. 283). As he faltered over declaring Negroes "better" and "stronger," he recognized "that even in escaping he was taking with him more of the evil and unregenerate old man . . . than even he had feared" (p. 294). It is not, therefore, even a good escape. And Cass pursued, that "it took Him a bear and an old man and four years just for you . . . and you are just one. How long then? How long?' " (p. 299). In Cass's view, Ike's act has meaning only for himself and at that a dubious one; it is an evasion of involvement in the very problems he claims motivate his act; he is an Isaac who violates his own covenant.

Ike's other major critic in the novel is Lucas Beauchamp, his part-Negro first cousin. What Lucas thinks of "old Isaac" is that he "had turned apostate to his name and lineage by weakly relinquishing the land which was rightfully his to live in town on the charity of his great-nephew" (pp. 39–40). And Ike acknowledged of Lucas that *"he knows that's all. That I reneged, cried calf-rope, sold my birthright, betrayed my blood, for what he too calls not peace but obliteration, and a little food"* (p. 108–9). He is thus also an Esau, his Biblical avatar's own son, not only escaping responsibilities, but doing so in order to purchase an economic and moral security which is a kind of death-in-life.[11] Roth once asks him " 'Where have you been all the time you were dead?' " (p. 345).

Fourth, Ike inherited from Cass the ability to transform events into immortal images of beauty and truth. What Keats did with what after all was a Grecian urn, Ike attempted to do with his life—to define it by one exalted act, forever and immortal like the leaping buck or rising bear. As Olga Vickery points out, he "confuses the ritual with the life it orders."[12] What such an act does, of course, is to impose a ceiling on experience, so that, as Arthur F. Kinney observes, "at one moment in life he stopped growing."[18]

Though Ike declared to Cass " 'I am free' " (p. 299)—and we have seen that his act was itself anything but free—his very deed forever limits his freedom, his possibilities. Even at twenty-one he knew that during Reconstruction the blacks had misused freedom "as human beings always misuse freedom, so that he thought *Apparently there is wisdom beyond even that learned through suffering necessary for a man to distinguish between liberty and license*" (pp. 289–90). The implication is, clearly, that he cannot himself so distinguish, that his is an act of license itself enslaving, comparable to that of Fonsiba's shiftless husband, at which Ike shrieked, " 'Freedom from what? From work?' " (p. 279).

But however much one might argue a kind of fatality in Ike's life, his heritage seems to me to be a force not only which he by an act of will accepted but in which he acquiesced. The best case for determinism could be made from the conjunction of traumatic events during Ike's adolescence: that his father died when he was twelve, the year he killed his first deer and became initiated into the wilderness, and that his mentor (not to mention the bear and the wilderness itself) died when he was sixteen, the year he unravelled the secret of the commissary books. Though the conjunctions may be unusual and are certainly symbolically appropriate, in that they heavily underscore the obsolescence of all the inherited patterns, the events themselves are at least common enough for Cass to have shared them, and he became quite a different man. Ike is aware of being the spiritual grandson of old "Doom" (p. 300), but his life is a doom to which he has relinquished himself.

In summary, Ike is dominated by his past because he comes to terms neither with his repugnance at old Carothers's crimes, nor with his attraction to Buck's propitiatory chivalry, nor with his immersion into Sam's wilderness, nor with his fascination with Cass's romantic idealism. He repudiates a plantation system from which he continues to receive support and with which he continues to share certain tainted attitudes. He identifies totally with a wilderness which vanishes, with all its inhabitants, before his eyes. He is, at age twenty-one and for the rest of his life, driven to—even committed to—stalemate by a desire for Eden and a loathing for Egypt, an Eden which is elusive, an Egypt which is inescapable. And Desire and Loathing, as Joseph Campbell reminds us, are the two angels with flaming swords barring man's way to paradise. Like the biblical Moses, he sought to free his people (i.e., to free the McCaslins from guilt toward land and people) and, after passing judgment on one of them, fled into the wilderness; unlike the wilderness of Moses, his wilderness was an illusion from which he never in fact returned.

But in all fairness to what is after all a fascinating and sympathetically treated character, whose limitations must seem, if nothing else, familiar, I shall permit Isaac McCaslin to have the last word: "That was neither the first nor the last time he had seen men rationalise from and even act upon their misconceptions" (p. 215).

Notes

1. William Faulkner, *Go Down, Moses* (New York: Modern Library, 1955), p. 106. All further references will be made parenthetically in the text.

2. " 'The Bear' and Faulkner's Moral Vision," *Studies in Faulkner* (Pittsburgh: Carnegie Institute Press, 1961), p. 51.

3. *Ibid.*, p. 54.

4. "Faulkner's Wilderness," *American Literature*, 39 (1959): 134.

5. *The Tragic Mask: A Study of Faulkner's Heroes* (Chapel Hill: University of North Carolina Press, 1963), p. 81.

6. *William Faulkner: A Study in Humanism from Metaphor to Discourse* (Norman: University of Oklahoma Press, 1966), p. 70.

7. "William Faulkner: 'The Bear,' " in Hennig Cohen, ed., *Landmarks of American Writing* (New York: Basic Books, 1969), p. 350.

8. *The Tragic Mask*, p. 101.

9. "Faulkner: The South, the Negro, and Time," *Southern Review* 1 (1965), rpt. in Robert Penn Warren, ed., *Faulkner: A Collection of Critical Essays* (Englewood Cliffs, N.J.: Prentice-Hall, 1966), p. 265.

10. *The Achievement of William Faulkner* (New York: Random House, 1965), p. 211.

11. Walter Brylowski, *Faulkner's Olympian Laugh: Myth in the Novels* (Detroit: Wayne State University Press, 1968), p. 164, suggests that "this Isaac tendered up the land as a substitute and has only deceived himself."

12. *The Novels of William Faulkner* (Baton Rouge: Louisiana State University Press, 1964), p. 133.

13. "Faulkner and the Possibilities for Heroism," *Southern Review*, 6 (1970), 1123.

History, Sexuality, and the Wilderness in the McCaslin Family Chronicle

Albert J. Devlin*

Almost without exception, the black characters in *Go Down, Moses* share intimate relationships that affirm their engagement with life itself. In this cycle of stories, Faulkner turns invariably to blacks for expressions of emotional commitment and solidarity—to Rider's deep, transforming love for Mannie ("Pantaloon in Black"), to Lucas's early relationship with Molly as marked by the ever-present fire on the hearth ("The Fire and the Hearth"), to Turl's relentless pursuit of Tennie and their fruitful marriage ("Was"), and finally, and most complexly, to the sensuality of Roth's abandoned mistress in "Delta Autumn." The white members of the McCaslin-Edmonds family, by contrast, give no evidence of such engagement. There is instead, as Lionel

*This essay was written especially for this volume and is published here for the first time by permission of the author.

Trilling has remarked, a singular absence of white male-female relationships in *Go Down, Moses*.[1]

Roth, the last of the legitimate Edmondses, is at forty-three still a bachelor. His treatment of James Beauchamp's granddaughter, although marked by southern racial bias, reveals only a halting capacity to experience mature sexual relations. A similar failure is suggested by earlier generations of the McCaslin-Edmonds family. The wives of Carothers and his descendants are typically unnamed, inconsequential to the action, and they die prematurely, leaving their husbands permanent widowers and their children motherless. The white woman's status as adjunct, as mere biologic vessel, is perhaps clearest in the case of Zack's wife, who dies in childbirth in 1898. The rigidity of Molly's installation in the big house makes it appear to her husband Lucas "as though the white woman had not only never quitted the house, she had never existed—the object which they buried in the orchard two days later . . . a thing of no moment, unsanctified, nothing."[2] The arrangement of stories in *Go Down, Moses* implicitly contrasts this disregard for the white woman with the poignant grief of Rider. The death of his wife, in "Pantaloon in Black," makes life intolerable for the young millhand. "Pantaloon in Black" affirms the depth of the black sensibility and comments at the same time upon the corresponding shallowness of the white. It is no accident of design that "Pantaloon in Black" immediately follows the story in which Zack and his wife appear, "The Fire and the Hearth."

In "Was" (the first story in *Go Down, Moses*) Faulkner introduces this contrapuntal design by juxtaposing Turl's pursuit of Tennie with the "courtship" of Isaac McCaslin's future parents, Buck McCaslin and Miss Sophonsiba Beauchamp. At least twice a year, Tomey's Turl, the son of old Carothers McCaslin and the slave girl Tomasina, escapes the McCaslin plantation to visit Tennie who lives at Warwick. This visitation is unsettling for Buck, for if Turl should reach the Beauchamp plantation, Hubert will personally return him with his sister Sophonsiba in attendance. The ideal solution is to intercept Turl before he reaches Warwick. In this way contact with Sophonsiba can be avoided and Buck can still enjoy the excitement of the hunt. Turl, however, is a determined suitor, and in the present instance he does reach Warwick. A wary Buck McCaslin must leave the safety of his neighborhood where "a man could ride for days . . . without having to dodge a single" woman and enter " 'bear-country' " (pp. 7,22). Although Buck's fear of Sophonsiba occasions memorable farce in *Go Down, Moses*, Faulkner's humor points as well to an underlying seriousness: the "love-stricken" Turl actively pursues Tennie, the white Buck McCaslin fears women.

Faulkner's portrait of Sophonsiba is a humorous thrust at antebellum pretension, but it too reveals the seriousness of his design. Sophonsiba, her preposterous appearance aside, is a cunning woman who avidly pursues the wary Buck McCaslin. Once he has reached Warwick, she lays an ingenious trap that nearly claims the sixty-year-old bachelor for marriage. After searching for Turl, Buck and his young nephew Cass return to the Beauchamp

plantation late at night. Buck speculates that Sophonsiba's room will probably " 'be at the back . . . where she can holler down to the kitchen without
having to get up. Besides, an unmarried lady will sholy have her door locked
with strangers in the house' " (p. 20). Buck is wrong on both counts, and
when he innocently climbs into Sophonsiba's bed, she protests in mock
violation and horror. Hubert, who relishes his impending freedom, neatly
sums up Buck's predicament. " 'She's got you . . . and you know it' " (p. 23).
Sophonsiba's marital ambitions are momentarily thwarted by a poker game of
surprising complexity. To the dismay of Hubert and the elation of Turl, Buck
"loses" Sophonsiba while "winning" the slave girl Tennie. Turl, of course,
deals the hand that insures his marriage and issue and, significantly, the brief
freedom of Buck McCaslin. The elaborate gamble was well known to Faulkner as an admirer of the old Southwestern humorists, but his use of this
convention in "Was" is far more subtle in both its thematic and structural
reach. It deftly measures the emotional maturity of the black and white
branches of the McCaslin-Edmonds family, and in so doing creates a psychological perspective from which Isaac's later life can be viewed.

Isaac's relationship with his father is obscured by confusion surrounding
the date of Buck's death. (The circumstances and date of his marriage to
Sophonsiba, I should note, are not revealed by Faulkner.) It is clear that he
was born in 1799 because in 1859, the present time of "Was," "Uncle Buck
didn't mount a horse like he was any sixty years old" (p. 7). It is clear too that
in 1867, the year of Isaac's birth, Buck was approximately sixty-eight: in "The
Old People," the narrator notes that "the boy's father had been nearing
seventy when he was born" (p. 164). Confusion develops, however, when the
same narrator notes, again in "The Old People," that Isaac "would live to be
eighty, as his father and his father's twin brother and their father in his turn
had lived to be" (p. 163). If Buck lived to be eighty, then one must hold that
he died in 1879, Isaac's twelfth year. This is precisely Edmond L. Volpe's
conclusion.[3] As such, Volpe's dating explains how Lucas Beauchamp who was
born in 1874 could have "actually remembered old Buck and Buddy in the
living flesh" (p. 39), but it overlooks a contradictory statement in part 4 of
"The Bear." In 1869 Uncle Buck records the birth of "Fonsiba" Beauchamp,
the only surviving daughter of Turl and Tennie. The narrator explains that
this is the last time Buck writes in the plantation ledger, "for the boy [Isaac]
himself was a year old, and when Lucas was born six years later [17 March
1874], his father and uncle had been dead inside the same twelve-months
almost five years" (p. 274). This dating establishes that Lucas could not have
seen "old Buck and Buddy in the living flesh." Buck died either in late 1869
or early 1870, during Isaac's second year. There is, however, still more
confusion surrounding the date of Buck McCaslin's death. Evidence drawn
from part 4 of "The Bear" indicates that a third date is possible, in 1873,
when Isaac would be nearly six years old.[4]

Faulkner's apparent inattention to detail, exacerbated, one suspects, by
the prolonged composition and revision of *Go Down, Moses*, obscures the

nature and degree of Buck McCaslin's impact upon his only son. If Buck died in 1869, then there is virtually no relationship or fatherly influence to measure. Buck's later "deaths" in 1873 or 1879 would provide, at least hypothetically, firmer bases for speculation. Still, Faulkner's puzzling chronology is revealing: Buck's shadowy demise may point to the essential passivity of his character. This is seen during the abortive courtship when Sophonsiba assumes the dominant role; and it is seen later in their marriage when Sophonsiba insists that she and Buck move into the old plantation house built by the slaves of Carothers McCaslin. Earlier, well before the Civil War, Buck and his brother Buddy had moved out of the big house to repudiate its historic symbolism. Buck's emotional and ethical passivity seem to be modulated by Faulkner into a corresponding distance from his son Isaac. There is neither scene nor passage in *Go Down, Moses* in which Buck directs, informs, or otherwise interacts with his son: they are simply never seen in association with one another. At least on the face of it, Sophonsiba's influence may be the more pronounced. Discovering "how much it takes to compound a man" (p. 308) can begin with consideration of a neglected scene in part 4 of "The Bear," in which Sophonsiba and Isaac are sharply etched.

After Isaac's birth in 1867, Sophonsiba resumes travel between Warwick and the McCaslin plantation. Ostensibly, she returns to pay duty visits and to claim an occasional piece of furniture, but her deeper purpose is to supervise her unmarried brother Hubert. On one such visit, Sophonsiba discovers that this "roaring childlike man" (p. 300) has acquired a voluptuous mulatto who nominally serves as cook and housekeeper. While Hubert desperately explains that " 'I had to have a cook, didn't I?' " (p. 303), Sophonsiba rants magnificently, drives her brother to the front gallery, and there castigates him for his flight from maternalism. " 'My mother's house! Defiled! Defiled!' " (p. 303). Sophonsiba quickly routs the frightened woman, who is last seen by Isaac "hurrying down the lane at a stumbling trot," still wearing one of Sophonsiba's dresses as though it were a "silken banner captured inside the very citadel of respectability" (p. 303).

Faulkner has carefully located the most striking effects of this encounter within the awareness of a very young Isaac McCaslin. In the "same aghast flash" (p. 303), Isaac both hears his mother's sharp soprano voice— " 'Even my dress!' "—and sees, in a closing door, "a glimpse of the silk gown and the flick and glint of an ear-ring." It is "an apparition rapid and tawdry and illicit yet somehow even to the child, the infant still almost, breathless and exciting and evocative" (pp. 302–3). Isaac and Hubert are subtly fused by this "hybrid female flesh," Isaac's childish perspective attaining "perfect rapport and contact" with Hubert's "inviolable and immortal adolescence" (p. 303). Even her hasty retreat fails to dispel Isaac's vision, for the "compounder of his uncle's uxory" remains "exciting and evocative . . . and unforgettable" (p. 303). Faulkner's diction conveys the intensity of Isaac's perception, but his more daring assertion involves the "perfect rapport" of Isaac and Hubert, a fusion pointing to Isaac's imaginative participation in the scene, both as an enchanted admirer of Hubert's mistress and as a receptor of his mother's insistent maternalism. Because Sophonsiba threatens to become their common antagonist, Isaac's intense absorption and apparent assimilation of the scene's sexual tenor should not be divorced from her explosive reaction. Her violent dismissal of Hubert's mistress not only identifies the mulatto as a racially proscribed lover, but may also create for Isaac a more extensive system of association whereby sexuality is tinged with danger, violence, and fear of maternal disapproval.

Perhaps Faulkner has dramatized one source of that implacable, renunciatory conscience which, for many commentators, separates Isaac from the rhythms of actual life. We may see here the incorporation of parental authority in its most prohibiting and punitive function, the crucial stage in a complex process whereby Isaac identifies with his mother, sharing her values and attitudes. The severity of Sophonsiba's impact, if not the forcefulness of her personality, is implied by the passive tenor of Isaac's later experience, especially his acceptance of a sexless marriage, and by his pervasive feelings of guilt which lead him to a life of atonement. Isaac has described this life more affirmatively, but he fails to persuade his cousin, Cass Edmonds, in their discussion in part 4 of "The Bear," or, for that matter, the majority of his current readers. Isaac would argue that his more decisive identification is with his biological father, Buck McCaslin, and with his spiritual guide, Sam Fathers. Buck's moral idealism is reflected in his quasi-abolitionist politics and in his refusal to inhabit the old plantation house built by the slaves of Carothers. Sam Fathers more sharply rejects the concept of ownership to seek in the wilderness an elusive unity of being. Together they define an ethical tradition in which Isaac locates his own repudiation of the land, but upon careful examination, this tradition tends to confirm at every point—social, economic, sexual—the fearful quietism of Isaac McCaslin.

In *Go Down, Moses* Sam Fathers teaches Isaac the rules of hunting and the lore of the woods. Sam begins his instruction when Isaac is still quite young—eight and nine—and responsive to his guardianship. "He taught the boy the woods, to hunt, when to shoot and when not to shoot, when to kill and when not to kill, and better, what to do with it afterward" (p. 170). Gradually these lessons in woodcraft evolve into spiritual principles that Isaac will observe in his advancing age. First, Sam Fathers sensitizes Isaac to the cruel and arbitrary nature of the caste system. He does not accomplish this didactically but merely by an expression in his eyes that bespeaks entrapment: "not the heritage of Ham, not the mark of servitude but of bondage; the knowledge that . . . part of his blood had been the blood of slaves." The melancholic effect of this taint is not lost upon Isaac. At one point he demands that Cass release Sam from his cage. " 'Then let him go!' the boy cried. 'Let him go!' " Cass's reply to his young kinsman is only partially true. " 'His cage aint McCaslins' " (p. 167).

Sam Fathers also directs Isaac in his mastery of fear. The problem is stated by Sam as he mends a tattered dog that tried to keep Old Ben at bay.

" 'Just like a man,' Sam said. 'Just like folks. Put off as long as she could having to be brave, knowing all the time that sooner or later she would have to be brave once so she could keep on calling herself a dog, and knowing beforehand what was going to happen when she done it' " (p.199). Soon after this reflection, Isaac takes up a new stand in the woods and senses an eerie presence. "He . . . heard the drumming of the woodpecker stop short off, and knew that the bear was looking at him. He never saw it. He did not know whether it was facing him from the cane or behind him." Isaac does, however, realize the fate of his selection by Old Ben. "*So I will have to see him. . . . I will have to look at him*" (pp. 203–4). In June of the next year, Isaac returns to the woods and begins to track the legendary bear. Sam tells Isaac that he must leave his gun behind, and later the boy also discards his watch and compass as he enters the deepest woods. Words of Sam Fathers are now recalled: " 'Be scared. You cant help that. But dont be afraid. Aint nothing in the woods going to hurt you if you dont corner it or it dont smell that you are afraid. A bear or a deer has got to be scared of a coward the same as a brave man has got to be' " (p. 207). As Isaac emerges into "a little glade," he is granted a vision of the "dimensionless" bear, who acknowledges the boy's mastery of fear. "It did not emerge, appear: it was just there, immobile, fixed in the green and windless noon's hot dappling" (p. 209).

Sam Fathers's instruction culminates in Isaac's twelfth year when the boy kills his first buck and is "marked . . . forever one with the wilderness." From this "instant of immortality" springs the essence of manhood for father and son. "So the instant came. He pulled trigger and Sam Fathers marked his face with the hot blood which he had spilled and he ceased to be a child and became a hunter and a man" (pp. 177–78). The perfection of this "instant" does not survive the progress of the hunt, but its effect is lodged deeply in Isaac McCaslin, who "humbly and joyfully" (p. 165) accepts "that for which Sam had been training him all his life" (p. 173). Along with "his spirit's father," Isaac McCaslin is absorbed into a mythic past that each succeeding hunt will salute from a still greater remove. Isaac's dedication to the wilderness no doubt permitted Faulkner to explore his own resistance to an encroaching modernity—a world seemingly composed, in Faulkner's words, of "changing red-and-green lights and savage and peremptory bells."[5] But Sam Fathers's instruction is not without troubling prospect, especially when viewed in relation to the circumstances of his own birth, and his pervasive effect upon the impressionable Isaac McCaslin.

The circumstances of Sam Fathers's birth require only brief description. He is the son of a quadroon slave woman and a powerful Chickasaw chief—Doom—who decrees a marriage between the already-pregnant woman and a slave he has acquired. Two years later Doom sells man, woman, and child to Carothers McCaslin for "an underbred trotting gelding" (p. 263). Unlike Lucas Beauchamp who becomes "the composite of the two races which made him" (p .104), Sam Fathers does not adjust to his own mixed blood. He is instead "the scene of his own vanquishment and the mausoleum of his defeat" (p. 168). Although he lives with the other McCaslin blacks, Sam Fathers is not a member of their community. He is always "the son of that Chickasaw chief and the negroes knew it" (p. 170). Wifeless, childless, kinless, Sam makes his isolation nearly complete when, during Isaac's ninth year, he begins to live year-round in the big woods. His anguish and frustration find consummate expression in part 2 of "The Bear": "*And he was glad, he told himself. He was old. He had no children, no people, none of his blood anywhere above earth that he would ever meet again. And even if he were to, he could not have touched it, spoken to it, because for seventy years now he had had to be a negro. It was almost over now and he was glad*" (p. 215). Thus Sam Fathers contemplates his "cage," an apt metaphor of the betrayal which his black blood represents. In commenting upon this traumatic personal history, Cass Edmonds explains to Isaac that Sam was " 'not wilfully betrayed by his mother, but [was] betrayed by her all the same' " (p. 168). As Sam Fathers's later life reveals, his mixed blood and birth into slavery are irremediable wounds that only the wilderness—asexual, unhistoried, and apparently immortal—can assuage. In following this course, Sam Fathers is suggestively related to the womanless tradition of the white McCaslins—a heritage that obsessively interprets the woman as a threatening agent.

Sam Fathers's effect upon Isaac is both pervasive and troubling. Sam gives Isaac an inordinate sense of the past. As he talks about the old times and the old people, Isaac gradually loses all distinction between past and present: ". . . to the boy those old times would cease to be old times and would become a part of the boy's present, not only as if they had happened yesterday but as if they were still happening, the men who walked through them actually walking in breath and air and casting an actual shadow on the earth they had not quitted" (p. 171). The effect of Sam Fathers's reminiscence becomes acute when Isaac thinks that "he himself had not come into existence yet" (p. 171). Ultimately Isaac's identity is diffused into a mythic past that militates against time and sexuality. Wounded himself, Sam Fathers may perpetuate his wounds in Isaac McCaslin. Both reject the passional life to embrace a wilderness whose fantasy of unrestricted movement in time and space can hardly be resisted. Isaac's marriage in approximately 1890 implicitly ratifies this fantasy by confronting the young man with the inevitable impurity of sexual motives.

Some six or seven years after Sam Fathers's death, Isaac marries a woman "with dark eyes and a passionate heart-shaped face" (p. 311). Although the marriage lasts for more than twenty-five years, ending formally with the unnamed wife's death in the 1920s, the relationship is frustrating and sterile. Isaac's wife covets the social position and financial security that ownership of the family plantation would bring, but when it becomes clear to her—by 1895, for example—that Isaac will not claim his patrimony, she reacts bitterly and renounces the marriage. Isaac, who is by turns amazed, terrified, and resigned, becomes "uncle to half a county and father to no one" (p. 3).

Before their marriage, Isaac's wife had apparently accepted her husband's repudiation of his inheritance, agreeing that " 'I dont suppose it matters' " (p. 311); but it does weigh heavily upon her social ambitions and leads to the critical scene of the marriage. The seduction scene, which occurs in a "rented cubicle" (p. 312) soon after their marriage, is too long to discuss in detail or even to summarize, but several observations are warranted. Isaac's wife is the active force. She initiates lovemaking and abruptly signals its completion, demanding throughout the scene that the farm be claimed. Isaac is threatened by her aggression and expertise. At one point he thinks his wife a "composite of all woman-flesh" (p. 314), at another that "*She already knows more than I with all the man-listening in camps . . . ever even heard of.*" The scene dissolves into hysterical laughter and ends bitterly when Isaac's wife forbids further intimacy. " 'If this dont get you that son you talk about, it wont be mine' " (pp. 314–15).

The conjunction of economic and sexual motives is a determinative element in the McCaslin-Edmonds family chronicle. It links the founding generation of old Carothers with the present moment, and it anticipates as well Roth Edmonds's betrayal of his black mistress in "Delta Autumn." By the time of his marriage, Isaac sadly acknowledges the apparent regularity of this pattern, but his grief is subsumed by his dedication to the wilderness. In part 4 of "The Bear," an eighteen-year-old Isaac meditates upon his future: ". . . and he would marry someday and they too would own for their brief while that brief unsubstanced glory which inherently of itself cannot last and hence why glory: and they would, might, carry even the remembrance of it into the time when flesh no longer talks to flesh because memory at least does last: but still the woods would be his mistress and his wife" (p. 326). The sexual tenor of Isaac's relationship with the wilderness is maintained throughout *Go Down, Moses*. The wilderness gives birth to Isaac—when he first entered the big woods as a young child, "it seemed to him that . . . he was witnessing his own birth" (p. 195)—and, loverlike, it permits entry and withdrawal—entering by "the widening inlet" (p. 195), leaving through "the very tiny orifice" (p. 177). A desexualized wife and mistress, the wilderness becomes for Isaac a means of preserving his innocence. ". . . and [he] became steadily younger and younger until, past seventy himself and at least that many years nearer eighty than he ever admitted any more, he had acquired something of a young boy's high and selfless innocence" (p. 106). In the metaphoric terms of *Go Down, Moses*, the failure of Isaac's marriage—his extraordinarily brief possession, if at all, of "glory"—is akin to the betrayal of time, history, and sexuality. Put in slightly different terms, it is the reconstituted essence of the McCaslin-Edmonds family history, an advancing design that Isaac would repudiate through innocence and retreat.

Readers of *Go Down, Moses* have long sensed a kind of classical retribution stemming from Carothers's violation of his black daughter Tomasina. By the early 1940s, the white branches of the McCaslin-Edmonds family are without heir, or the likelihood of one, presumably the sum of a multigenerational failure to sustain mature sexual relationships. More dismaying to Isaac than such lack of offspring is the periodic repetition of the original violation—one that Faulkner presents in many different registers, from the farcical banishment of Hubert's housekeeper in "The Bear" to the more poignant dismissal of Roth's mistress in "Delta Autumn." Through it all, Isaac makes overt ethical response to the promptings of his conscience, but he is drawn into passivity and retreat by an entity no less abstract than the family destiny. The wilderness, mediated by Sam Fathers, absorbs the guilt and fear occasioned by the McCaslin family history and thereby releases Isaac from moral action. Only the receding line of the woods, which is nearly complete by the time of "Delta Autumn," begins to reveal to Isaac the illusory nature of his dreams. Roth's question is put bluntly to his aged kinsman, but it finds the hollowness of Isaac's dedication to the wilderness. " 'Where have you been all the time you were dead?' " (p. 345).

Notes

1. Lionel Trilling, review of *Go Down, Moses, Nation*, 30 May, 1942: 632.

2. William Faulkner, *Go Down, Moses*, 46. All page citations of *Go Down, Moses* follow the Modern Library edition (1955) of the original text (New York, 1942). They are noted parenthetically in the text.

3. Edmond L. Volpe, *A Reader's Guide to William Faulkner* (New York: Noonday, 1964), 231.

4. On 19 January 1873, Hubert Beauchamp takes twenty-five gold pieces from the silver cup which was to have been his nephew Isaac's legacy. Prior to 19 January 1873, and beginning with 27 November 1867, Hubert had taken (piecemeal) another eighteen coins from the total of fifty. His practice of replacing the heavier and more authentic sounding gold with coppers would make it obvious that some dramatic change in the cup's contents had taken place after 19 January 1873. It is, I think, this dramatic change which explains Hubert's unwillingness at one point to let anyone else, even Isaac, touch the burlap parcel containing the silver cup. Sometime during the period of this innocent peculation, Buck becomes enraged and demands that Hubert be fetched from Warwick, where he still lives. ". . . and his father, at last and after almost seventy-five years in bed after the sun rose, said: 'Go get that damn cup. Bring that damn Hub Beauchamp too if you have to' " (304). Perhaps the cup's dramatic change in January 1873 has angered Buck, but such a conclusion, although very likely, would be arbitrary. It is not, however, arbitrary to conclude that Buck would be alive in 1873. Born in 1799, he would be "almost seventy-five years" old when Hubert makes his largest "loan." The above passage strongly implies that Buck is bedridden in 1873; one wonders, then, if he lives until 1879, as Volpe suggests, or if the text also supports a third death date, one between 1869–70 and 1879.

It is important to notice that Buck dies before Warwick burns and Hubert comes to live with Sophonsiba at the McCaslin plantation. ". . . and, his father and Uncle Buddy both gone now, one day . . . the almost completely empty house in which his uncle and Tennie's ancient and quarrelsome great-grandfather . . . lived, cooked and slept in one single room, burst into peaceful conflagration . . . and out of the last of evening, the last one of the twenty-two miles, on the old white mare which was the last of that stable which McCaslin remembered, the two old men riding double up to the sister's door, the one wearing his fox-horn on its braided deerhide thong and the other carrying the burlap parcel wrapped in a shirt. . . . (304–5).

It is after Hubert arrives at McCaslin that he makes his final "loan": for the silver cup he substitutes a tin coffeepot. He includes an IOU—*"One silver cup. Hubert Beauchamp"* (308)—

which the narrator says was "dated after he came to live in the house with them" (307). The burlap parcel, then, undergoes a distinct change in size: "almost three times its original height and a good half less than its original thickness" (305). In 1888, when Isaac is twenty-one and about to unseal his legacy, the "burlap lump" is described as one "which fifteen years ago had changed its shape completely overnight" (306). The silver cup had to be replaced sometime during 1873. Since Buck dies before Hubert comes to live at McCaslin, and Hubert makes the substitution after he arrives there, it is clear that one of Buck's "deaths" occurred in 1873, when Isaac is approximately six.

See Meredith Smith, "A Chronology of *Go Down, Moses*" (in an appendix in this volume) for a thorough discussion of Faulkner's dating practices in this collection of family stories.

5. From Faulkner, "An Introduction [1933] to *The Sound and the Fury*," *Mississippi Quarterly* 26 (Summer 1973): 410–15.

The Distaff Side:
The Women of *Go Down, Moses*   Elisabeth Muhlenfeld*

Go Down, Moses is a novel of the game, the con, the hunt, the quest. It is, in other words, a masculine novel. Its world is a man's world; its voices, male voices. Although it explores the experiences of a family extending through seven generations, the tale has no central female characters. Indeed, across the generations, this is primarily a family of sons, often only sons. The novel mentions one white female McCaslin descendant (old Carothers McCaslin's daughter, grandmother of Cass), and four black women with McCaslin blood: Carothers's illegitimate daughter, the slave girl Tomasina, whom we know only from the ledgers; Fonsiba Beauchamp, Lucas's sister; Nat, his daughter; and Roth's mistress. Lucas and Molly presumably have another daughter, mother of Samuel Worsham Beauchamp, but we never see her and her name is unrecorded. To the McCaslin-Beauchamp-Edmonds men, women are on the whole unimportant; an astonishing number remained unnamed. Their role is simplicity itself: to give birth and carry on the line. Many die in childbirth or soon after.

A pattern thus develops within the novel which denies traditional female roles to women. Caretakers are, for the most part, male; indeed, the novel abounds with fathers. The passing of family history and tradition is performed by males. Even the role of giver-of-food is, in *Go Down, Moses*, largely a male preserve, exemplified by Uncle Buddy's chaotic kitchen and symbolized by the commissary and the hunting camp. This pattern extends to the animal kingdom, where Old Ben stands as patriarch of the wilderness, and where the acknowledgment made by Sam Fathers (and then by Isaac) to the ancient power and mystery of the wilderness is to no female deity, but to "Chief," "Grandfather."[1]

*This essay was written especially for this volume and is published here for the first time by permission of the author.

So apparently insignificant are the women in *Go Down, Moses* that critics who have discussed Faulkner's women at any length have virtually ignored them—an ironic fact inasmuch as each character is largely ignored in the novel itself by the male characters whose voices dominate the narrative.[2] Phillip Weinstein, one of the few scholars to examine the women in the novel, begins his brief discussion by noting that "There is no Caddy nor Lena nor Rosa in *Go Down, Moses*, and what women there are . . . have little to say."[3] He goes on to observe that within the novel the women characters are denied any narrative importance. Weinstein is right, of course, but as we shall see, the women in *Go Down, Moses* carry great artistic weight. The novel cannot be fully understood without a careful exploration of their role within it.

The significance, for good or ill, of the female is clearly signaled by the importance attached by the men in the novel to blood lines. From the opening words, in "Was," it is clear that identity is first defined by one's progenitors and one's progeny:

> Isaac McCaslin, 'Uncle Ike' . . . uncle to half a county and father to no one
>
> this was not something participated in or even seen by himself, but his elder cousin, McCaslin Edmonds, grandson of Isaac's father's sister and so descended by the distaff, yet notwithstanding the inheritor, and in his time the bequestor (p. 3).

The clause is hopelessly tangled, like the lines of descent it describes, and yet it is clear that to be descended "by the distaff" is to be forever suspect, somehow tainted: glorified by the blood of old Carothers McCaslin, yet shamed that the descent is through the female line. Men—both white and black—in the McCaslin-Beauchamp-Edmonds family view the distaff side as a weakening agent.[4] As Lucas approaches the commissary to tell Roth about the still in "The Fire and the Hearth," he muses on the "old time," remembering himself and old Cass as "coevals in more than spirit even, the analogy only the closer for its paradox:—old Cass a McCaslin only on his mother's side and so bearing his father's name . . . Lucas a McCaslin on his father's side though bearing his mother's name" (p. 44). In the ensuing flashback, when Lucas confronts Cass's son Zack over the white man's bed, he accords his opponent both equality and scorn: " 'Because you are a McCaslin too,' he said. 'Even if you was woman-made to it. . . . Maybe that's why you done it: because what you and your pa got from old Carothers had to come to you through a woman—a critter not responsible like men are responsible, not to be held like men are held' " (p. 52).

Years later, Roth, furious over his inability to best Lucas in the matter of the still, looks at the black man's "impenetrable face with its definite strain of white blood, the same blood which ran in his own veins, which had not only come to the negro through male descent while it had come to him from a woman, but had reached the negro a generation sooner" (p. 70). Two generations earlier, Cass, in his long debate with Isaac in part 4 of "The Bear," begins his attempt to persuade Isaac to accept his legacy by reference to blood: " 'You, the direct male descendant of him who saw the opportunity and took it. . . . Not only the male descendant but the only and last descendant in the male line and in the third generation, while I am not only four generations from old Carothers, I drived through a woman and the very McCaslin in my name is mine only by sufferance and courtesy . . .' "(p. 256). Thus the men in *Go Down, Moses* share not only a belief in the primacy of the male, but also a fear that the female shames or diminishes them. Because of this fear, they ignore the women in their lives, use them, reject them, escape them. It would be a mistake, however, to assume that their view of the distaff is shared by the author who created them. The women in *Go Down, Moses* inhabit a world so masculine that, from the point of view of the narrative, they barely exist. Yet a careful look at the way women function in the novel suggests that Faulkner has created among them characters of immense strength whose actions serve to clarify the work's themes.

Our first view of a woman in the novel is of Sophonsiba Beauchamp, described in "Was" in grotesquely comic terms. As Weinstein has noted, Sophonsiba is "singled out for uniquely distortive narrative rendering."[5] She is introduced as "a hand . . . waving a handkerchief or something white through the broken place in an upstairs shutter" and makes her entrance "jangling and swishing" in an aura of perfume (p. 10). "Handkerchief, perfume, cap, ribbon, fan, roan tooth," writes Weinstein, "these component things establish Sophonsiba as a composite thing, a creature of surfaces and effects."[6] Regarded as a major threat to male freedoms, she is a ridiculous figure, pretentiously insisting that the decaying farmhouse she shares with her brother is "Warwick," a baronial estate, and that she herself is a coquette engaged in a charming flirtation with a noble suitor: "Then Miss Sophonsiba said something about a bumblebee . . . the earrings and beads clashing and jingling like little trace chains on a toy mule trotting and the perfume stronger too, like the earrings and beads sprayed it out each time they moved and he [Cass] watched the roan-colored tooth flick and glint between her lips; something about Uncle Buck was a bee sipping from flower to flower and not staying long anywhere and all that stored sweetness to be wasted on Uncle Buddy's desert air" (p. 11). The reader's response to Sophonsiba is carefully orchestrated by the narrative voice; we find her hilarious, absurd, distasteful, perhaps even disgusting.

This response is problematic, however. There is something profoundly disturbing in Sophonsiba's presentation. Granted, her picture is painted from memory by Cass Edmonds, who was nine at the time of the episode. Granted that Cass at nine had had very little experience with women (he has been raised by his grandmother following his mother's death, and has apparently spent most of his time with his uncles, both confirmed bachelors). Nevertheless, the fact remains that Cass tells this tale of long ago to Isaac McCaslin about Isaac's mother. Thus, Cass (guided by Buck, Buddy, and

Hubert Beauchamp) effectively directs that Isaac should regard his mother, as did all the men important to Isaac who knew her, as a figure of fun, something to be dismissed, to be a little bit ashamed of. The very narrative stance of the story, then, renders Sophonsiba less than human, distorts Isaac's view of women, and essentially bars the reader from discovering her true meaning.

However ridiculous she may appear to be, Sophonsiba is actually engaged in a valiant but doomed struggle to extract from her life some small measure of dignity and worth. Apparently in her early thirties at the time of the story, she lives a life of thoroughgoing isolation in a country where, according to Uncle Buck, "ladies were so damn seldom thank God that a man could ride for days in a straight line without having to dodge a single one" (p. 7). Her only companion is her older brother Hubert, a ne'er-do-well who sits cooling his heels in the water of the springhouse and drinking toddies before the midday meal, although broken shutters and rotted floorboards wait year after year to be fixed. Their neighbors, the McCaslins, live a half-day's drive away.

Sophonsiba is no longer young; we assume (despite Cass's recollection that his grandmother said she had been a "fine-looking woman once") that she has never been attractive. Hubert so longs to get rid of her that he periodically takes her to the McCaslins to visit in an effort to sell her to Buck by loudly discussing the dowry he intends to bestow on her, often in Sophonsiba's presence. A year before the events of "Was," on one such visit, Hubert attempted to force the issue by sneaking away in the night, only to have Buck and Buddy get Sophonsiba up and dressed, pack her in the wagon, and overtake her brother before dawn. Sophonsiba is desperate to marry, to escape the boredom and humiliation of living with Hubert, to have children, to give her life some meaning. Inasmuch as Buck is the only available bachelor—albeit far from ideal—it is not surprising that she sets her sights on him. Nor is it surprising that she adopts the language and values of romantic literature, the medieval pageantry of the novels of Sir Walter Scott, to mask the dreariness of her life.

Sophonsiba's all-out assault on the bastion of bachelorhood is at once extremely funny and deadly serious. Because she does not possess the sexual charms sufficient to procure a husband, she tries to use the rules of chivalry, and she is willing to take an enormous risk to her most precious possession, her reputation. Luring the unsuspecting Buck into her virgin bed, she screams to announce the invasion of a woman's sanctity. But again, even in her "violation," Sophonsiba herself is ignored, turned by her brother and Buck into a booby prize in a bizarre game. As Hubert puts it to Buck:

> "You come into bear-country of your own free will and accord. All right; you were a grown man and you knew it was bear-country and you knew the way back out like you knew the way in and you had your chance to take it. But no. You had to crawl into the den and lay down by the bear. . . . After

all, I'd like a little peace and quiet and freedom myself, now I got a chance
for it. Yes, sir. She's got you, 'Filus, and you know it. You run a hard race
and you run a good one, but you skun the hen-house one time too many."
(pp. 22–23)

For Buck and Hubert, Sophonsiba's pursuit is a contest between man and
she-bear or fox and hen, a contest which Buck wins on this occasion, with the
help of Buddy's prodigious skill at poker. For Sophonsiba, however, the
stakes are real.

Sophonsiba's determination to marry Buck stems from basic human
instincts, societal needs and cultural imperatives. To marry and produce
children is to secure some hedge against the future and to preserve her own
heritage through her offspring. To marry Buck McCaslin is to insure for him
the extension of the McCaslin family name into the next generation—a goal
he dares not seek for himself. Admirably, she succeeds, although we are
never told how. (In the world of *Go Down, Moses*, the escape from capture is
worthy of being passed down in the form of family tales; the capture itself is
suppressed.) When Buck returns from the Civil War, the two wed, and
Sophonsiba, now almost certainly near forty, gives birth to Isaac. Within
three years, she is a widow and lives only a few years beyond her husband,
dying before her son's tenth birthday.

The narrative voices of *Go Down, Moses* hardly mention Sophonsiba
beyond the first chapter of the novel.[7] In other words, once she has served as
entertainment, as a case in point of the degree to which women are troublesome creatures, threats, and trials to men, she has no further reality. In fact,
though, her dogged determination to take her appropriate place in society
constitutes the first instance of a pattern which recurs throughout the novel.

The most striking repetition of this pattern is that of Isaac's own wife.
Often dismissed by critics as deceptive and nymphomaniacal, Ike's wife
deserves close attention. We know very little about her. A farmer's daughter,
she is "an only child . . . with dark eyes and a passionate heart-shaped face"
(p. 311). She meets Ike when he is twenty-one, working as a carpenter on her
father's barn. Ike has already repudiated his birthright, but he does not tell
her so:

'That farm is really yours, isn't it?' and he
    'And McCaslin's:' and she
    'Was there a will leaving half of it to him?' and he
    'There didn't need to be a will. His grandmother was my father's
sister. We were the same as brothers;' and she
    'You are the same as second cousins and that's all you ever will be.
But I dont suppose it matters:' and they were married. (p. 311).

Ike's new bride, in other words, marries him believing that her destiny will
be as wife of the rightful owner of the McCaslin farm and mother to its
heirs—for Isaac talks about a son. Brought up in the country herself, she
equates the ownership of land with home and security. Evidence in the novel

suggests that the newlyweds love one another deeply. Indeed, the early marriage, at least from Isaac's point of view, is idyllic: "for that little while at least, one: indivisible . . . living in a rented room still but for just a little while and that room wall-less and topless and floorless in glory for him to leave each morning and return to at night" (pp. 311–12). Passionate and yet sexually modest, Isaac's new bride refuses to allow her husband to see her naked, putting her nightgown on over her dress at night, and reversing the process each morning.

The bride waits in the rented room for the day that she and her husband can move to " 'The farm. Our farm. Your farm' " (p. 312). But Isaac, who has rejected his legacy, secretly builds her a bungalow in town. Her discovery precipitates one of the most striking scenes in the novel—a scene not of sexual revenge but depicting the utter intensity of the death of hope: "the two of them sitting on the bed's edge, not even touching yet, her face strained and terrible, her voice a passionate and expiring whisper of immeasurable promise: 'I love you. You know I love you. When are we going to move?' " (p. 312). Isaac's answer, " 'Who told you—' " confirms her worst fears, and at first she will not let him speak, crushing her hand over his mouth. To her, Isaac's refusal to take up his proper place constitutes the ultimate betrayal, wiping out with one stroke her dreams of the future. In her unbearable need to persuade him to recant, she offers the only thing she knows he wants: her nakedness. Her action does not come easily; she cannot undress until he turns his back, and Isaac's perception of her with "her head still turned away, looking at nothing, thinking of nothing, waiting for nothing, not even him" (p. 313) suggests the depth of her despair.

The sexual encounter which follows is the most passionate in all of Faulkner's fiction—and the most tragic. For Isaac, it "was like nothing he had ever dreamed, let alone heard in mere man-talking until after a no-time he returned and lay spent on the insatiate immemorial beach"; for his wife, it marks the end of their marriage and concludes in bitter hysteria: " 'And that's all. That's all from me. If this dont get you that son you talk about, it wont be mine:' lying on her side, her back to the empty rented room, laughing and laughing" (p. 315). In later years Isaac remembers this moment tenderly, as "that one long-ago instant at least out of the long and shabby stretch of their human lives, even though they knew at the time it wouldn't and couldn't last, they had touched and become as God when they voluntarily and in advance forgave one another for all that each knew the other could never be" (pp. 107–8). But for his wife, the moment is not a moving and romantic memory but a bleak one of ultimate risk and total loss (marriage, modesty, pride) to a man who chose his romantic ideals over her very human needs. She speaks thereafter with a "tense bitter indomitable voice" (p. 107). At her death, she once again tries to give something of herself by leaving Isaac all she has—the bungalow—but this too he only pretends to accept (p. 4), thereby denying in his own mind her right to claim connectedness to him.

Isaac's wife and his mother are the only two white women in the novel to have any narrative reality, and both are blurred and distorted by the men through whose eyes we see them. They fare little better than Zack's wife who dies in childbirth leaving no mark, "as though . . . she had never existed— the object which they [Lucas and Zack] buried in the orchard two days later . . . a thing of no moment, unsanctified, nothing" (p. 46). But most of the black women in the novel fare no better.

Mother, grandmother, and progenitor of the McCaslin (Beauchamp) line in *Go Down, Moses* is Eunice, a slave woman about whose life we know almost nothing and yet whose legacy of shame and despair shapes the life of nearly every character who follows her. Eunice is hidden in the narrative so thoroughly that the characters in the novel (and the reader) must struggle even to perceive her presence. In a real sense, she exists only *between* the cryptic lines of the nineteenth century ledger entries by Buck and Buddy— entries recorded in a kind of shorthand by illiterate men unwilling to commit to paper the tragic truth of her life as they come to understand it. Only on a second or third reading of part 4 of "The Bear" does the reader fully comprehend Eunice's story, but not until that story has been absorbed do myriad events in the novel fall into place. This narrative technique, the most extended instance in Faulkner's fiction of the hidden key to be teased out by the reader, dictates that the meaning of Eunice is not in the sparse facts of her life, but in the painful, slow revelation of that life through Buck, Buddy, Cass, and Isaac to the reader.

These facts, embedded in journal entries, are simple:

> *Eunice Bought by Father in New Orleans 1807 $650. dolars. Marrid to Thucydus 1809 Drownd in Crick Cristmas Day 1832* [Buck's entry]
>
> *June 21th 1833 Drownd herself* [Buddy's entry]
>
> *23 Jun 1833 Who in hell ever heard of a niger drownding him self* [Buck]
>
> *Aug 13th 1833 Drownd herself* [Buddy]
>
> *Tomasina called Tomy Daughter of Thucydus @ Eunice Born 1810 dide in Child bed June 1833 and Burd. Yr stars fell*
>
> *Turl Son of Thucydus @ Eunice Tomy born Jun 1833 yr stars fell Fathers will* (pp. 267, 269)

As sixteen-year-old Isaac struggles with the ledger entries, piecing them together, making some sense of them, he comes to realize that Carothers McCaslin ("who did not need another slave" and yet "had gone all the way to New Orleans and bought one" [p.270]) had himself fathered Tomasina and then dictated the marriage of Eunice and Thucydus, and that he had, when Tomasina grew into womanhood, fathered a child on his own daughter. When Tomasina's pregnancy became evident, her mother waited for a holy day, a day celebrating birth and hope, and quietly committed suicide. Isaac

> seemed to see her actually walking into the icy creek on that Christmas day six months before her daughter's and her lover's (*Her first lover's* he thought. *Her first*) child was born, solitary, inflexible, griefless, ceremo-

nial, in formal and succinct repudiation of grief and despair who had already had to repudiate belief and hope
    that was all (p. 271).

That was, of course, not all. Eunice's suicide has profound ramifications. Almost certainly, it contributed to her daughter's death in childbirth (a death unremarkable on the surface, yet surely marked by shame and grief) and therefore indirectly to the motherless upbringing of Tomey's Turl, three-quarters McCaslin, both slave and half-brother to Buck and Buddy. Isaac believes that Eunice's death was followed by at least tacit recognition of Turl's kinship by old Carothers McCaslin in his will, "that evil and unregenerate old man who could summon, because she was his property, a human being because she was old enough and female, to his widower's house and get a child on her and then dismiss her because she was of an inferior race, and then bequeath a thousand dollars to the infant because he would be dead then and wouldn't have to pay it" (p. 294). And as the ledger entries suggest, the sorry facts of their father's sexual encounters led directly to Buck's and Buddy's bachelorhood and to their eccentric approach to their role as slaveowners, and by extension to Isaac's repudiation of the land. Eunice, then, powerless to protect herself or her daughter in her own lifetime, powerless even to emerge from the text as a flesh-and-blood character, by her death not only shames the race who so wronged and dehumanized her but also empowers her descendants through the generations.

Eunice's death announces the clear human demand for recognition and acknowledgment, a demand reiterated by the actions of generations of black women who follow her. Tennie Beauchamp, who married Tomey's Turl, is similarly vouchsafed no narrative voice of her own. Even the ledger entry which records her entrance into the McCaslin slave family relegates her to the status of mere detail in the more dramatic story, the poker game played to determine the fate of her mistress, Sophonsiba Beauchamp: *"Tennie Beauchamp 21 yrs Won by Amodeus McCaslin from Hubert Beauchamp Esqre Possible Strait against three Treys in sigt Not called 1859 Marrid to Tomys Turl 1859"* (p. 271). Maid and companion to Sophonsiba, nurse to Isaac, foster mother to Zack and mother of six, Tennie is accorded no speech, no scene, no identity. The male voices in the novel acknowledge her only through the naming of her children, and yet by that device alone she teaches their heritage and demands their recognition: *"Amodeus McCaslin Beauchamp . . . 1859 dide 1859"* (p. 271), named for the poker player who had, in saving his brother from Sophonsiba, made possible Tennie's marriage to Tomey's Turl and thus bestowed legitimacy on the child for the brief period of his life; then *"Dauter . . . 1862"* named for Buck and Buddy's sister; then, again in the bleak days of the war, *"Child . . . 1863"*; and a year later, *"James Thucydus Beauchamp Son of Tomes Turl and Tenny Beauchamp Born 29th december 1864 and both Well"* (p. 272), an honor to the man who raised Turl's mother Tomey. Thucydus, after his wife's suicide and Tomasina's degradation, had proudly refused old Carothers's "gifts" of freedom and ten acres of land, insisting instead that he would pay for both by his labor. Of James's naming, Uncle Buddy records, "*Wanted to call him Theophilus but Tride Amodeus McCaslin and Callina McCaslin and both dide so Disswaded Them*" (p. 272).[8] In 1869, a daughter is named "*Miss sophonsiba*" (p. 273), bequeathing to this child perhaps Sophonsiba's weakness for studied elegance, and tying her closely to the McCaslin family. The final child is named for the progenitor himself, Lucius Quintus Carothers McCaslin, leaving no doubt of his heritage. This child calls himself Lucas, "not refusing to be called Lucius . . . not denying, declining the name itself, because he used three quarters of it; but simply taking the name and changing, altering it, making it no longer the white man's but his own" (p. 281).

Tennie lives well into the 1880s, and yet the reader never sees or hears her. Her burial beneath the narrative is perhaps reflected in her own daughter Fonsiba who, like Isaac's wife, marries a man enthralled by ideas and oblivious to the real-world needs of his family. Fonsiba is pictured by Isaac, who tries to help her, as lifeless and blurred:

> she did not even seem to breathe or to be alive except her eyes watching him . . . the tremendous fathomless ink-colored eyes in the narrow, thin, too thin coffee-colored face watching him without alarm, without recognition, without hope. 'Fonsiba,' he said. 'Fonsiba. Are you all right?'
> 'I'm free,' she said (p. 280).

Fonsiba is "free" by virtue of allowing herself to be buried alive (an ironic and self-defeating repetition of Eunice's suicide). Hers is an uncharacteristic choice within the novel, however. Far more characteristic are the choices made by her sister-in-law, Molly Beauchamp, wife of Lucas and perhaps the most admirable female in *Go Down, Moses*. Molly, modeled on Faulkner's own nurse, Mammy Caroline Barr, is accorded more narrative reality than any other woman character; she alone is readily accessible to the reader. Nevertheless, she is most frequently pictured as silent, small, light, ancient—in other words, not fully vigorous and alive. Descriptions of Molly mark her as distorted, something strange and foreign, a primitive shrine which Roth Edmonds visits monthly as a "libation to his luck . . . to his ancestors" (p. 99). Her face is a "shrunken and tragic mask" (p. 119). Molly is "tiny," and appears far older than her chronological age. She moves "slowly and painfully, as the very old move" (p. 99); her gnarled hands are like clumps "of dried and blackened roots" (p. 101). As does every other female in the novel, she enters the narrative without a past. (Not until the last chapter are we given any hint of her upbringing, her brother Hank, and her white "sister" Belle Worsham.) The narrative details of Molly's physical appearance, however, belie the strength of her sheer presence.

That strength is represented by the fire in Molly and Lucas's hearth, lighted on their wedding day, to burn until neither of them remains alive to tend it. Not a blaze, but rather the deep glow of coals, the fire is a powerful

symbol of the simple love by which Molly lives, a symbol repeated in miniature in the bowl of the clay pipe she smokes in moments of repose. Although
we see her caring for her garden and sweeping the yard into intricate designs
in an instinctive cultivation of beauty, or as the stereotypical wife, nagging
Lucas to get to work, her principal reality is maternal. To protect her "children," Molly time and again willingly risks everything she has.

On Molly, then, rests the thematic weight of all the women in the novel,
for she alone is portrayed as actively fulfilling the traditional female roles of
giver of food, warmth, and comfort, and of moral teacher. Roth Edmonds
describes her thus: "the woman who had been the only mother he . . . ever
knew, who had raised him, fed him from her own breast as she was actually
doing her own child, who had surrounded him always with care for his
physical body and for his spirit too, teaching him his manners, behavior—to
be gentle with his inferiors, honorable with his equals, generous to the weak
and considerate of the aged . . . who had given him, the motherless, without
stint or expectation of reward that constant and abiding devotion and love
which existed nowhere else in this world for him" (p.117).[9] For Roth, Molly
represents unquestioning acceptance and approval; in her presence he can
recapture the security of early childhood innocence, a time before a sense of
guilt and separation comes to him with knowledge of his role as a white man,
a plantation owner.

The reader experiences Molly not only through the eyes of Roth, but
through Lucas, who sees her both as subject and object. As a young husband,
Lucas's inarticulate fury at Molly's departure to the white man's house stems
from both sexual love and the need for sexual dominance; from his longing
for her companionship and his conviction that she, his possession, has been
taken from him; and from not only his grief at what he fears is her infidelity
but also his hurt pride.

In the events following Molly's return, Lucas's thoughts are on his
emotional struggle with Zack Edmonds, not on Molly, and thus the reader is
not cued to examine the situation from her point of view. And yet her actions
speak for themselves; she simply has responded to the most urgent needs of
others: the labor, death, and burial of Zack's wife; the motherless newborn
and her own infant; and the grieving young Edmonds. Lucas in his pride says
nothing, makes no attempt to see her or their son, and so she stays on—
waiting, perhaps nursing her own pride, for a sign of his need for her. When
he demands her return, she brings the white baby to her home too: " 'I
couldn't leave him! You know I couldn't!' " (p. 50). It does not occur to her
that Lucas suspects she has become Zack's mistress, and when she compre-
hends his jealousy, she cries, " 'You fool!' " " 'Oh God. . . . Oh God.' " Thereafter, she moves from household to household, caring for both babies, "impervious, tranquil, somehow serene," declining any assistance: " 'I been
taking care of both of them a good while now without no man-help' " (p. 59).

We know almost nothing about the forty-plus years of Molly's marriage;
there have been other children. The last one, Nat, child of her mother's old

age, is seventeen at the time of the events of "The Fire and the Hearth." Like all of the women in the novel, Nat is diminished by the very language which describes her; we see her first as an animal, "crash[ing] into flight" as she spies on her father, "the quarry fleeing like a deer across a field" (pp. 40–41). Lucas recognizes her footprint "as he would have known those of his mare or his dog" (p. 41). And yet Nat has inherited the strength of her mother and the cunning and stubbornness of her father. In "The Fire and the Hearth," she risks her father's wrath and even his arrest to force him to agree to her marriage to George Wilkins and she parlays her demands into a promise of a new porch, well, and stove. The husband she was chosen for herself is weak, and Lucas believes she is "too young to be married and face all the troubles which married people had to get through in order to become old and find out for themselves the taste and savor of peace" (p. 73). We see Nat only at the beginning of her life, but it is clear that she, the woman, will be the preserver of her own family—symbolized by "the grassless and sunglared yard" of the newlyweds, "the light dust swept into the intricate and curving patterns" (p. 76) which her mother had taught her.

It is for Nat's sake that Molly takes her greatest risk. Convinced that Lucas's metal detector is a corrupting influence, Molly fears that the corruption will spread to George, Nat's husband, who shares Lucas's hunger for buried gold. Molly refuses to live with Lucas and watch him bring on his own damnation, but she is more frightened that Nat's George will be similarly damned by the sinful obsession. Thus she takes the astonishing step in her day and time, and at her age, of asking Roth's help in obtaining a divorce. Roth believes the solution is simple: Lucas must get rid of the machine, but Molly knows that Lucas would simply give it to George: " 'No!' she cried. . . . 'Cant you see? Not that he would keep on using it just the same as if he had kept it, but he would fotch onto Nat, my last one and least one, the curse of God that's gonter destroy him or her that touches what's done been rendered back to Him? I wants him to keep it! That's why I got to go, so he can keep it and not have to even think about giving it to George!' " (p. 122). Afraid that in the end Roth will not help her, Molly takes matters into her own hands; as Roth has jokingly suggested, she determines to "cure" Lucas of the gold fever with psychological warfare, by using the divining machine while Lucas is asleep. Too feeble to carry out her mission, she nearly dies in the attempt. She is found a day later "lying on her face in the mud, the once immaculate apron and the clean faded skirts stained and torn, one hand still grasping the handle of the divining-machine" (p. 125).

The gambit fails to cure Lucas, but it convinces Roth to help Molly get a divorce. Lucas allows the legal proceedings to move almost to the point of a final decree, but when he realizes that Molly will not yield in her determination to carry through with her "voce," he folds, sealing his capitulation with a nickel bag of candy and instructions to Roth to get rid of the offending machine. Comic in tone, the divining-machine/divorce sequences in "The Fire and the Hearth" present Molly's outrage as essentially humorous, thus obscuring its serious content. Molly has willingly risked her place, her security and her very life to preserve the eternal soul of her husband, and the marriage of her daughter.

The same unwavering conviction that right must be done emerges again in the novel's final chapter when Molly's instinctive certainty that her grandson, Samuel Worsham Beauchamp, needs help drives her to make her way to Jefferson, where she presents herself to county attorney Gavin Stevens. Her message is again simple: " 'It was Roth Edmonds sold him. Sold him in Egypt. I dont know whar he is. I just knows Pharaoh got him. And you the Law. I wants to find my boy' " (p. 371). To Stevens, she looks as though she has "no more of weight and solidity than the intact ash of a scrap of burned paper" (p. 371), but her demand leaves no room for dismissal. Stevens remembers the grandson as having "something in him . . . not only violent but dangerous and bad" (p. 372); indeed, within the hour, he will discover that the youth's execution for murder is scheduled for that very night. But to Molly, what her "boy" has done is unimportant. He has been wronged by heredity, banished by Roth, hurt by "Pharaoh," her name for a foreign and hostile world. He is family and he is in need.

Stevens arranges to bring the body home and, with the help of the local editor and others, provides for a dignified funeral. He believes that he has given Molly what she wanted: *that casket and those flowers and the hearse and . . . to ride through town behind it in a car* (p. 383). But he is wrong. Although her desires are dismissed by Stevens, they are very clear: " 'I wants hit all in de paper. All of hit' " (p. 383). Molly wants the life and death of her grandson to be recorded; she wants her tragedy published for all to read even though she cannot read it herself. Hers is not a plea but a demand for recognition, acknowledgment, understanding—not for herself, but for the "last and least" of her people.

Finally, it is this very human demand for recognition and acknowledgment that characterizes all the women in *Go Down, Moses* that recurs most dramatically in "Delta Autumn" with the appearance of the young woman who has borne Roth's son—the sixth generation of old Carothers McCaslin's descendants in both the McCaslin-Edmonds and McCaslin-Beauchamp lines. The infant's mother presents herself to Isaac, the last of the McCaslin line itself, now in his seventies. Isaac has unwillingly accepted Roth's "furious and cold" commission to give the woman money and then deny her— " 'Tell her No!' " (p. 356). The old man sits on a cot, his "soiled undergarment bagging about him and the twisted blankets huddled about his hips" (p. 357). In stark contrast, the woman is "young and incredibly and even ineradicably alive" (p. 360); she wears "a man's hat and a man's slicker," and regards him through "queerly colorless" eyes, with "that immersed contemplation, that bottomless and intent candor, of a child" (p. 357). Holding her baby, she rejects the offered money, searching the envelope instead for some note, some message.

The woman knows she has come in vain. She has not been promised marriage, and she has not asked it: " 'I knew what I was doing' " (p. 358). Roth has told her that any future relationship is impossible. " 'And I believed it . . . because he was gone then as we had agreed and he didn't write as we had agreed, just the money came to the bank in Vicksburg in my name but coming from nobody as we had agreed. . . . I even wrote him last month to make sure again and the letter came back unopened and I was sure' " (p. 359). Nevertheless, the woman loves the father of her child, treasuring the memory of the brief affair—a week in the fall, six weeks in New Mexico in the winter, " 'where I could at least sleep in the same apartment where I cooked for him and looked after his clothes——' " (p. 358). Courageous and independent, the woman believes that she and the child could make Roth's life whole. " 'I would have made a man of him' " she tells Isaac. " 'He's not a man yet. You spoiled him. . . . When you gave to his grandfather that land which didn't belong to him, not even half of it by will or even law' " (p. 360).

The young woman understands full well, although Roth does not, the kinship between them, and she shocks Isaac by revealing the depth of her knowledge of family history: " 'Your cousin McCaslin was there that day when your father and Uncle Buddy won Tennie from Mr Beauchamp for the one that had no name but Terrel so you called him Tomey's Terrel, to marry' " (p. 359). When Isaac, the pathetic old man who had righteously repudiated his birthright in shame for his forebears' treatment of blacks, realizes that she is black, he cries " 'You're a nigger!' " But she responds with dignity, " 'James Beauchamp—you called him Tennie's Jim though he had a name—was my grandfather. I said you were Uncle Isaac' " (p. 361).

Ironically, the narrative voice of "Delta Autumn" does not name this woman, despite the fact that names, correct identities, are of the utmost importance to her. College educated and northern bred, the woman faces her situation with complete honesty and pride, but Isaac speaks to her as if she were damned and doomed, as if he has no connection to her, as if her love of Roth is simply the desire of a social climber: " 'Marry: a man in your own race. That's the only salvation for you. . . . You are young, handsome, almost white; you could find a black man who would see in you what it was you saw in him, who would ask nothing of you and expect less and get even still less than that, if it's revenge you want. Then you will forget all this, forget it ever happened, that he ever existed' " (p. 363). To this outburst, utterly uncomprehending of her need, the woman quietly replies, " 'Old man, have you lived so long and forgotten so much that you dont remember anything you ever knew or felt or even heard above love?' " (p. 363).

In the world of Go Down, Moses, Faulkner invests his female characters with great strength, not the mythic strength of Eula Varner in The Hamlet, or the destructive strength of Narcissa Benbow in Sanctuary, but a life-affirming strength firmly rooted in reality. Each woman is a taker of risks, willing to sacrifice things as precious as reputation, wealth, life itself, to preserve the integrity of the family and the value of human life. In this novel so profoundly concerned with honor, these women uphold the "old verities" at the personal level far more successfully than do many of the central male characters, and they do so, in the main, without verbal protest, prolonged debate, or loud agonizing. They simply act, and teach by their example. Their actions flow from a very clear order of priorities which is not opposed to man's code of honor or indifferent to it, but rather essential to the periodic clarification of that code.

In ancient times, the "distaff" was a cleft staff pressed under the left arm, used in spinning. Contrasted with the staff or spear used in the hunt, symbolic of man's sphere, the distaff held wool or flax from which fibers were fed into a spindle and painstakingly transformed into thread. In *Go Down, Moses*, the women of the novel, "the distaff side," are, like the ancient spinners of old, relegated to the background. Their work is hardly noticeable on the surface of the masculine fabric of the novel, but perhaps it is not too fanciful to suggest that, in large part, they have insured the lasting strength of that fabric.

Notes

1. William Faulkner, *Go Down, Moses* (New York: Vintage, 1973), 184. References to the text will hereinafter be cited parenthetically.

2. To my knowledge, there is not a single article on any of the women in the book. The most comprehensive look at the subject of women in Faulkner's fiction, Sally R. Page's *Faulkner's Women: Characterization and Meaning* (Deland, Florida: Everett Edwards, 1972), concludes its analysis with *The Hamlet*, making reference to *The Town* and *The Mansion*, but accords nothing more than mention to female characters in *Go Down, Moses*. David Williams's *Faulkner's Women: The Myth and the Muse* (Montreal: McGill-Queens University Press, 1977), stops with *Light in August*. Sergei Chakovsky's essay in *Faulkner and Women: Faulkner and Yoknapatawpha, 1985*, ed. Doreen Fowler and Ann J. Abadie (Jackson, Miss.: University Press of Mississippi, 1986), 58–80, ends his exploration with *The Wild Palms*.

3. Phillip Weinstein, "Meditations on the Other: Faulkner's Rendering of Women," in *Faulkner and Women: Faulkner and Yoknapatawpha, 1985*, 93.

4. This extends beyond the McCaslin men. Cass believes Sam Fathers was "betrayed" by his mother, "who had bequeathed him not only the blood of slaves but even a little of the very blood which had enslaved it; himself his own battleground, the scene of his own vanquishment and the mausoleum of his defeat" (168).

5. Weinstein, 94.

6. Ibid.

7. Except for a brief tale involving Hubert Beauchamp's silver cup in "The Bear," she is referred to only occasionally, as Isaac's mother.

8. Stanley Sultan in "Call Me Ishmael: The Hagiography of Isaac McCaslin," *Texas Studies in Literature and Language*, 3 (Spring 1961): 65, was the first to notice that this entry suggests conclusively a name for Old Carothers McCaslin's daughter, whom most critics have continued to assume is unnamed in the text. Tennie and James have named earlier children Amodeus and Carolina, and at first wish to call their fourth child Theophilus. Inasmuch as Amodeus and Theophilus are the children of Carothers McCaslin, it is reasonable to assume that the twins' sister (Cass's grandmother) was Carolina. I am indebted to James Hinkle for telling me about the Sultan reference.

9. See the dedication of *Go Down, Moses*, "To Mammy / Caroline Barr / Mississippi / [1840–1940] / Who was born in slavery and who gave to my family a fidelity without stint or calculation of recompense and to my childhood an immeasurable devotion and love"

[The McCaslins' Grievous Legacy]   Kiyoyuki Ono*

The problem of viewpoint in "Was," in *Go Down, Moses*, is to determine how such an apparently lighthearted tale can achieve such a tragic effect. The tale passes through Cass's consciousness, then Ike's, probably first when he is only nine years old, later when he is being trained as a hunter in the woods, and finally when at sixteen he reads his family history in the ledgers and recognizes the deep and complicated meaning of his kinship to Tomey's Turl. The process of his gradual awareness may be comparable to the way in which the records that once seemed to be so far away—"what the old books contained would be after all these years fixed immutably, finished, unalterable, harmless" (*Go Down, Moses*, p. 268)[1]—are altered irrevocably with a great shock: "the yellowed pages in their fading and implacable succession were as much a part of his consciousness and would remain so forever, as the fact of his own nativity" (p. 271). Just as the records become assimilated into his consciousness, so the simple tale of what "was" is integrated with what "is." The story now is at the same level in his consciousness as his perception of the primitive wilderness, which again merges with his recognition of the history and present reality of the South.

What Ike finds in the ledgers is not that Tomey's Turl has a blood relationship with him, because "he already knew this" (p. 268), but how that relationship came about through Old Carrothers's exploitation of Eunice to satisfy his sensual appetites, his sinful incest with her daughter and neglect of her, and Eunice's resulting suicide; Tomey's death in childbed; Carothers's haughty refusal to call Tomey's Turl "my son"; his throwing to him the legacy of one thousand dollars to show he might have had "*Some sort of love*" (p. 270); and Tomey's Turl there before Ike's mind's eye as one born an orphan without parents or relatives, because Tomey's Turl cannot call the twin brothers "brother," since he is a black slave. Knowledge of these facts brings Ike "astonishment, shock, outrage." There reappear before his eyes the running figure of Tomey's Turl, tinted with ineffable sorrows, and the pursuing dogs, as if he were a fox pursued by his own half-brothers. He becomes at once a tangible figure and a symbol of the sin and evil of slavery. For Ike the events in "Was" are neither comic nor tragicomic but deeply tragic, all the more stunning because they first appeared, in their first telling, to be comical. In

*Reprinted with the permission of the University of Georgia Press, and with changes by the author for this volume, from *Faulkner Studies in Japan*, comp. Kenzaburo Ohashi and Kiyoyuki Ono, ed. Thomas L. McHaney (Athens: University of Georgia Press, 1985), 162–73.

one moment, among the tumult of his furious realization of it, he may have taken in all that the tale means—the corruption of the hunting ritual in the slave chase, the cursed land, the tainted history, the extinction of the receding wilderness symbolized in the death of the old bear, the cultivated land as a symbol of invading civilization, a vision of all of human history in decline and man piling up his evil deeds against God's will, as Ike later tells Cass. But because of the intensely personal and individual nature of Ike's perception, Ike's argument on each matter ends incomplete and never by itself explains the reason for his resolution to relinquish the tainted land fully.[2]

It seems that Faulkner wished us to share the impact of Ike's recognition. The structure of this composite novel is such that we, like Ike himself, are not given further information about Tomey's Turl after our first encounter with him in "Was." Even though in "Was" we understand Turl as "that damn white half-McCaslin," obviously a mixed-blood child begotten by a slave woman and a McCaslin ancestor, we do not know his position in the genealogy until Ike reads the record in section 4 of "The Bear." At this moment "Was" becomes an old tale in our consciousness too, because Tomey's Turl's name appears entirely unexpectedly among many other names in the ledgers. At that moment, we come to share at least in part the impact on Ike. We become involved in the intuitive understanding of what he might have read and felt and perceived, he who " 'could comprehend truth only through the complexity of passion and lust and hate and fear which drives the heart' " (p. 160) and who has been taught that " 'there is only one truth and it covers all things that touch the heart' " (p. 260). We come to understand through this involvement that the impact of this recognition is the source of his driving impulse to relinquish the cursed land.

Of course, Faulkner does not show Ike's inexpressible shock only by using such an elaborate and somewhat ambiguous device. He renders it in a more lucid yet allusive way in section 1 of "Was." Here it is suggested in the facts concerning Ike's way of life after his relinquishment of his inheritance, related as if they were irrelevant to the story, that his deep shock drives him to relinquishment and thus to his "freedom" from the plantation. The casual mention of Ike's way of living shows clearly, in advance of the story, how serious an impact the tale has made on his mind and his life: he becomes a childless bachelor living a monkish existence in town. The style in section I of "Was" is strikingly similar to that of section 4 of "The Bear." The pseudo–stream-of-consciousness style in both sections indicates their interconnection and Ike's inextricable consciousness in which *was* becomes *is*. Only by taking into account his behavior after relinquishment can we realize the extent of Ike's shock and understand that it is impossible for him to explain the reason for the relinquishment to Cass, a fellow southerner and heir to the plantation. How could he explain reasonably all of his experiences of both the wilderness and the plantation, his perception of oneness with nature and of nature's immortality together with the contradictory fact of the gradual extinction of the wilderness? When articulated, these notions must fall into a series of dry, abstract, and even absurd ideas " 'something which I have got to do which I dont quite understand myself, not in justification of it but to explain it if I can' " (p. 288). In other words, we understand his " 'heart's driving complexity,' " which has become too personal and individual for abstract generalization, and incommunicable, especially by such generalizations as he uses to explain to Cass—his belief that throughout human history, from the Old World to the New World, human evils and sins continue to increase against God's intention, and both the land of the South and the whites in it are contaminated with a curse revealed in the events of the Civil War.

So it is only the fierceness of Ike's received awareness that can explain his later deeds fully. When he is not yet twenty-one but only nineteen, not qualified as an heir to the McCaslin plantation, he travels in vain to Tennessee to look for James, Turl's eldest son, who has run away from the plantation, for the purpose of handing him his share of the legacy which Old Carothers has bequeathed to him. And in the winter of the same year, he has to travel again as far as Arkansas to search out Turl's daughter, Fonsiba, who has married an intelligent but impotent black preacher and moved far from the plantation. Thinking "*I will have to find her this time*" (p. 277), he rests or stops at "roadside taverns," "the cabins of strangers" or "the hay of lonely barns," on "the slow interminable empty muddy" winter nights. It is the sense of guilt and responsibility which came through the impact of his discoveries that compels him to these painful deeds.

This impact also makes understandable the bitter connotation in his utterance, "Sam Fathers set me free" (p. 300). He means by the word *free* that he has leaped into both time and space a long distance and attained a wide perspective, released from the present situation in which he is living. In space, he moves from the plantation to the wilderness, and in time, from the present to the far past. Under Sam's direction in the woods he learns oneness with nature and the primitive code of human behavior and virtue which is disappearing from southern society. With this new perspective, he can penetrate the reality of society as reflected in the hidden evil of his family history and the sinfulness of slavery, which might be impossible if he were confined like Cass to the plantation society.

Now he is "free" from his surrounding circumstances: hence he becomes personal and individual, that is, free in the proper sense of the word, and his resolution of relinquishment is his own free choice. But his freedom is self-contradictory from the start because no one can be free from the reality of time and space. In spite of Ike's temporal and spiritual leap, both the past and present surrounding reality continue to lie before him, for his memory of the family history has become a part of his consciousness and will remain so forever; and, in spite of his relinquishment of the plantation, slavery, under the changed name of sharecropping after the war, is "not only still intact but enlarged, increased" (p. 298). The conspicuous gap between Ike's free decision and the continuing overwhelming reality makes him appear a total failure, as critics have pointed out, especially as is shown clearly in the last scene of section 4 of "The Bear" and in "Delta Autumn," in which he seems lost in severe ambivalence or acts as an impotent old hermit in the receding wilderness. Critics have also asserted that he should have more insight into his real circumstance and take a more positive attitude than merely to relinquish "weakly" his inheritance to improve the grim southern situation. But we cannot overlook the severe reality of the South in the midst of the fierce counterreaction against the Reconstruction era, and if Ike had taken a more positive attitude, it may have turned out to be a fabulous one, like the corporal's heroic act in *A Fable*. Under the overconservative situation of the South from the 1870s to the 1940s, Faulkner may have recognized this risk, so Ike did his best to change even a little the severe reality of the South, when a decisive alteration of it was utterly impossible.

Ike's relinquishment of the plantation is a meaningful gesture saying the social situation was wrong and a preface to his later assertion recorded in *Big Woods:* " 'You can belong to the farming and hunting business and you can learn the difference between what's right and what's wrong, and do right. And that used to be enough—just to do right. But not now. You got to know why it's right and why it's wrong, and be able to tell the folks that never had no chance to learn it; teach them how to do what's right, not just because they know it's right, but because they know now why it's right because you just showed them, told them, taught them why' " (p. 196). The impact Ike received leads a man to an intuitive understanding of what seem complicated and obscure realities and drives him to a seemingly reckless and even too idealistic but otherwise unattainable deep understanding and resolution.

In emphasizing the impact Ike has received, I mean to show that the reality of the South Faulkner tries to render is beyond an easy, generalized analysis. It must be rendered as something grasped through intuition. Further, I want to suggest that Faulkner's characters do not act upon abstract ideas or theories alone but more often move by an impetus rising from the bottomless unconsciousness of the heart; as a result they feel, hear, smell, and act with the fluidity of tangible human beings. This is perhaps the outstanding quality that makes his major works such as *The Sound and the Fury, As I Lay Dying, Sanctuary, Light in August,* and *Absalom, Absalom!,* and of course, *Go Down, Moses,* the great masterpieces that they are.

But there is another side of this impact. Even before Ike comes to realize or grasp his black uncle's tangible figure through imagination, Tomey's Turl has already existed, and whether or not Ike recognizes it, the reality of the South and its history have continued to exist visibly. Just as Tomey's Turl does not have a chance to express what he feels and thinks about that reality, so also Ike cannot persuade Cass to share his own vision of it. In this way, all the southerners are isolated from one another. They hold, as sediment at the bottom of their consciousness, the heavy and ineffable realities that float densely like miasma around them, which, as a result, they cannot articulate but must keep to themselves, cannot articulate except through gestures of "astonishment, shock, outrage," or bitter silence or resignation.

For example, when Ike, in the winter of 1886, finds Fonsiba's house, after a long, distressing journey to Arkansas—a house, "which seemed in process of being flattened by the rain to a nameless and valueless rubble of dissolution" (*Moses*, p. 277)—she seems to have seen this approaching figure already. At the instant "he shoved open the crazy kitchen door in its awry frame," he sees, "crouched into the wall's angle behind a crude table, the coffee-colored face which he had known all his life but knew no more, the body which had been born within a hundred yards of the room that he was born in and in which some of his own blood ran but which was now completely inheritor of generation after generation to whom an unannounced white man on a horse was a white man's hired Patroller wearing a pistol sometimes and a blacksnake whip always" (pp. 277–78). Fonsiba was born in 1869, after the Civil War, and now it is 1886, when even if the situation of the post–Reconstruction era has not improved for the blacks but has gotten worse because of the black code, the blacks are now freedmen, not slaves. Fonsiba's reaction is extraordinary because the act of hiding behind the table at the sight of an approaching white is exactly what her ancestors must have done and now she is doing the same unawares, not as a wife of a black sharecropper but as an "inheritor of generation after generation" of the slaves' way of reaction, in spite of having had no experience of being a slave or memory of witnessing any slave. This fact clearly shows that, like Ike, she has already taken in, instinctively and intuitively, the miasma of the ineffable traditional atmosphere of the South: the unconscious spiritual legacy of slavery. Hence like Ike, too, she is in an ironical situation in which she cannot attain freedom, in the proper sense of the word, unless she is free from the unconscious burden of time in the South. But because it concerns the realm of the human unconsciousness, it is difficult if not impossible for both Ike and Fonsiba to be free from the southern spiritual legacy, despite their both claiming and openly declaring their freedom or Fonsiba's possible ability to establish her economic independence, owing to her share of the physical legacy of three thousand dollars. Time flies, moves, and changes, but man cannot be free from the chained legacy of time.

This is not only true of Ike and Fonsiba. At the time when Cass's son Zack appears to Tomey's Turl's son Lucas to carry his white man's privilege too far and to treat Lucas's wife as his own mistress, Lucas challenges him, asserting his equality as a man, as a descendant of Old Carothers, yet Lucas does not pour out even one one-hundredth of his anguish and tormenting conflicts, which he may be supposed to hold to himself while Molly, his wife, is taken away from his home. At the close of his sighing words of resignation following the challenge he had made at the risk of a lynching, " 'How to God,' he said, 'can a black man ask a white man to please not lay down with his black wife? And even if he could ask it, how to God can the white man promise he wont?' " (p. 59). In the apparent discrepancy between his coura-

geous demand of his human rights and equality and his resignation, he holds
to himself all the bitter, conflicting, desperate, and ineffable feelings of his
race and heritage. Another example is the mute suffering of Roth, Zack's son.
In his boyhood, at the age of seven, in 1905, Roth suddenly rejects Henry
(his friend and foster brother and Lucas's son), because his companion is a
black, and afterward he agonizes for his deed "in a rigid fury of the grief he
could not explain, the shame he would not admit" (p. 112). How can he grasp
what drives him to do such an incongruous deed, incongruous at least to
himself? Similarly, Rider, a black laborer physically unrelated to the McCaslins but with a spiritual relation to the exemplary marriage of Lucas and
Molly, cannot communicate his grief over a lost wife to anyone else in an
understandable way. On the contrary, each of his anguish-bitten gestures
incurs severe criticism from a white sheriff: " 'Because they aint human . . .
when it comes to the normal human feelings and sentiments of human
beings, they might just as well be a damn herd of wild buffaloes' " (p. 154).
How deeply complicated is that southern white response toward blacks,
which Rider is forced to be involved in whether he likes it or not, without
any tangible recognition of that prejudice, like Lucas in *Intruder in the Dust*.
When Roth has to reject his lover, Tennie's Jim's granddaughter, even after
he has had a baby by her, he does not say a word of his anguish, but what
bitter and gnawing feelings come and go in his mind? Mollie, to express her
sorrow over the death of her grandson and the dark fate of all the blacks in
the South, has no other way but to utter lamentations, incommunicable to all
the whites except Miss Worsham.

Viewed in this way, as anguished humans, all the characters, both white
and black, suppress their feelings in their private selves, their "heart's driving complexity," unable to communicate with one another, moaning in agony
sometimes without a sound. So I think that what Faulkner renders in *Go
Down, Moses* as the reality of the South is the heavy, incommunicable consciousness in which all southerners have had a share of their own hearts'
sorrows and complexities. Faulkner's masterly rendering of Ike's complex
process of repression and recognition of the guilt and shame in his family
history makes his case a paradigm for the same, if less explicit, process in the
novel's other characters as they relate in many ways to their southern circumstances during the gradual change of its history. This novel is not a story of
Ike alone, as is often misunderstood, but is the composite of various con-
sciousnesses illumined by Ike's life. Furthermore, the realities of the South
cannot be grasped by such abstract generalizations as the blood's curse,
human sin, or a synthesis of time and space in the South. It is a reality that
even Ike has proved unable to persuade Cass to accept, although they share
the same blood and heritage. It is a reality that is made visible for the first
time by Faulkner's creative act, itself a result of his deep insight into that
part of human consciousness which defies analysis. His genius was to render
that insight through the device of composite structure, which allows him to
suggest the incommunicable by juxtaposition of the myriad levels of individ-

ual and social consciousness. "Was," as we see, has set the stage for and announced the terms of that revelation.

Notes

1. All quotations are from William Faulkner, *Go Down, Moses* (New York: Vintage Books, 1973).

2. The 1860 census reported 518,000 persons of mixed blood. This represented one-seventh of the Negro population. See Francis Butler Simkins and Charles Pierce Roland, *A History of the South*, 4th ed. (New York: Alfred A. Knopf, 1972), p. 145. Even though most of the fathers of the mixed-blood slaves were their masters, "that 'the father of a slave is unknown to our law' was the universal understanding of Southern jurists" (Elkins, *Slavery*, p. 55). Thus we should understand that it is a human response for Ike to feel fierce outrage against his grandfather's deed.

The Beauchamp Line

[Lucas McCaslin]

Lee Jenkins*

Go Down, Moses is a culmination of the themes fundamental to Faulkner's work which he gives explicit treatment within the confines of the McCaslin family. Carothers McCaslin's descendants, black and white, live under the constant shadow of his mythic apotheosis. To do so is a difficult task, and men like Ike McCaslin and Roth Edmonds do not emerge victorious. Within the confines of the story, however, Lucas Beauchamp—grandson of Carothers by a slave woman—does. Through his point of view Faulkner presents the decay of the tradition, which is brought into strong relief through the force of Lucas's personality acting against it. His is the consciousness through which the present is to be assessed and viewed; he is the bearer of the McCaslin heritage.

Lucas, in contrast to Isaac, is vigorous, tougher, more rigorously self-regarding, like Carothers himself. Lucas shares attributes with Carothers that are the basis, not merely of their psychological identification, but of their shared exemplification of the masculine self-assertive principle. Lucas is like Carothers because he imitates him; yet, at the same time, he imitates him—or he acts like him—because he possesses the same inner substance that was expressed in Carothers. This inner quality, so expressed, takes on its appearance in the hard and uncompromising masculine will to power and dominance. Faulkner reveals it as a raceless and timeless concept, mythic in its power of evocation of the masculine function and its possibilities. The irony here is that this enactment of masculine self-assertiveness, normally taken as an exclusive attribute of the whites, is now most potently expressed in a black.

In conjunction with this, it is interesting to consider the particular way in which Lucas becomes a "McCaslin." Since Carothers, Lucas's grandfather, was also his great-grandfather, having sired Lucas from the slave girl who was also his daughter, Lucas is therefore an inheritor, as it were, of a double dose of the McCaslin substance, and each time from the original source. But

*Reprinted with permission from *Faulkner and Black-White Relations: A Psychoanalytic Approach* (New York: Columbia University Press, 1981), 252–60. © 1981 Columbia University Press.

Lucas's possession of the assertive masculine possibilities also implies that Lucas's actions be delimited or qualified in some way by the constraining effects of his heritage as a black. Lucas has an opposing moral sense and acceptance of the limitations of life which finally prevent him from causing harm to others or from destroying himself, in contrast to the white protagonists. And, in any case, all of Lucas's actions are executed within the confines of the McCaslin family heritage into which he is received with ambivalent tolerance and an understanding not found in the society at large. Roth Edmonds looks at Lucas, at

> the face which was not at all a replica even in caricature of his grandfather McCaslin's but which had heired and now reproduced with absolute and shocking fidelity the old ancestor's entire generation and thought—the face which . . . was a composite of a whole generation of fierce and undefeated young Confederate soldiers, embalmed and slightly mummified— and he thought with amazement and something very like horror: *He's more like old Carothers than all the rest of us put together, including old Carothers. He is both heir and prototype simultaneously of all the geography and climate and biology which sired old Carothers and all the rest of us and our kind, myriad, countless, faceless, even nameless now except himself who fathered himself, intact and complete, contemptuous, as old Carothers must have been, of all blood black white yellow or red, including his own.*[1]

The action of "The Fire and the Hearth" opens with Lucas's involvement in the running of an illicit distillery. [He must engage in deceit with Edmonds as a result and] with George Wilkins, a shiftless and incompetent black who is also involved in the operation of a [rival] distillery who also has the presumption to court Lucas's daughter. Lucas is contemptuous of George, and Faulkner's presentation is such that the psychological distance between Lucas and George is as great as that imagined between George and a white man. At the outset these machinations concerning the operation of a distillery could be thought of as typical "nigger" behavior. This, combined with Lucas's subsequent mania to find hidden gold that drives his aging wife to seek a divorce, has a surface stereotyped verisimilitude. But Lucas is not a social being; he is one of the original McCaslin-made individualists. He is to have vices and weaknesses, but he will always assume responsibility for his actions. Faulkner therefore wishes to show that the things Lucas does wrong, the excesses he indulges in, are not peculiar to blacks and not an indication that blacks are different from white people in this respect. Faulkner wishes to show Lucas as an individual in the sense that he is not a "nigger." Faulkner catalogues event after event, showing Lucas always in a stance of self-affirmation.

As Lucas approaches Edmonds's house, he compares the changed conditions under which his landlord lives with the way things were in the past, and he thinks of events in the past that reflect the history of the region, the traditions and the actions which have created him and the people around him. Faulkner makes use of flashbacks and stream-of-consciousness mono-

logues. Recessed into the texture of the story, as it reflects the necessary
workings of Faulkner's narrative technique, this merging of past and present
is simply another application of Faulkner's concept of time as one simultaneous temporal sequence. Lucas sees the mark of modern technology upon
Edmonds's life and sees this as a weakening of will, disparagingly comparing
Roth to their vital and energetic forebears. Edmonds, moreover, is a
McCaslin descendant through the female line and this fact has forever been
the signature of his inferiority. It is certainly a testimony to Faulkner's self-
evident sense of the superiority of patriarchy that Roth's father Zack, when
questioned by the young Roth, accepts his putative inferiority as a matter of
course, as a result of being a descendant of the female McCaslin. It is a
psychological as well as a physical sex-linked inheritance that is being referred to here; it is the fact of possessing the masculine "blood" that counts.
This naturally reflects Lucas's sense of what it means to be a McCaslin. For
example, Lucas, in his commitment to the heroic ideal, has never understood nor sympathized with Isaac's principles or his actions in repudiating his
heritage. For Lucas, Isaac's giving up the land would be the equivalent of his
giving up the mythic mandates of his possession of McCaslin blood.

Lucas knocks on Edmonds's window pane preparing to set his scheme
into operation, and when Edmonds comes out, his appearance and the
charged nature of the scene remind Lucas of the time when he confronted
Edmonds's father Zack forty-three years ago, the night Roth was born. That
night he swam the flooded river to get the doctor and returned to find the
white woman dead and his own wife Molly already established in the white
man's house. It ought to be mentioned here that the aristocratic woman had
such a decided proclivity for dying off early, for not enduring, that the white
man had a necessary practical need for the black women, among other
needs. Their dying off must be metaphysical in some way, because no similar
mention is made of the black women dying off. Their vulnerability, in fact,
must surely have been greater than that of the white women, and their birth
rate, certainly, was as great if not greater.

Edmonds has kept Lucas's wife for six months without thinking to return her, until Lucas, realizing his outrage, goes to demand her back. Edmonds, in keeping her, was merely arrogating to himself the traditional
privileges allowed him by the racial conventions. It is the exercise of this
right against Lucas which incenses him, although Faulkner seems to wish to
specify that, apart from being guilty of this offense, Edmonds, as a man of
honor, was telling the truth when he denies having had sexual relations with
Molly. This is a matter that can never be known to Lucas, though in regard to
rectifying his honor, it could have made little difference if it were known. But
the implication that Faulkner seems to be making is that there is a difference
in the white man's mind between his using Molly as an object to serve his
household needs and his holding her in concubinage. When he asks Lucas
what kind of man did Lucas take him to be, Lucas's answer can only be that
he takes him to be the kind of man he appears to be, one who takes black

women into his house and uses them as he pleases. Lucas, looking at his wife
the night she has returned, thinks in incredulous rage, "*Why she aint even
knowed unto right now that I ever even suspected*" (p. 49). This seems to
refer to the sexual implications of her staying with Edmonds. It is significant
that Molly remains silent and, it seems, even a little resentful of Lucas's
probing into her affairs, as if she remained still in a kind of secret league with
Edmonds.

However, the complicated nature of the confrontation with Edmonds is
yet to unfold in all its ramifications. Molly has brought Edmonds's infant with
her and the sight of the white infant nestling against the brown of her breast
incenses Lucas. He springs toward Molly and the child she is suckling in her
arms before the hearth, and she catches his wrist, restraining him: " 'Whar's
ourn?' he cried. 'Whar's mine?' " (p. 50). She points vehemently to their son
sleeping peacefully on the bed, declaring that it was not Edmonds who made
her bring the child. She did so of her own volition because she could not bear
to leave it. Her objection is that in the broadest humane sense it would be
inconceivable to leave it, irrespective of her personal feelings for it—though
she does not attempt to deny her own personal affection for it. Molly behaves
according to Faulkner's prescription concerning the maternal function and
the loving nature of blacks. Her love for the child and defense of her actions
in taking and caring for it supersede her sharing in the outrage of her husband at the insult against the integrity of their marital union. The sense of
honor that inflames Lucas does not seem to apply to her, nor is the situation
conceived by her as involving a consideration of her own personal integrity.
When, after a series of fortuitous events, Lucas has returned safely from his
second visit to Edmonds with the intent of killing him, he and Molly afterward establish a normal pattern for their daily life together—tenderly, banter-
ingly, with an edge to their humor. Somewhat gruffly he inquires about an
activity of the day: "She went on, neither answering nor looking back, impervious, tranquil, somehow serene. Nor was he any longer watching her. He
breathed slow and quiet. *Women*, he thought. *Women. I wont never know. I
dont want to. I ruther never to know than to find out later I have been
fooled*" (p. 59).

It should be pointed out here that Lucas's dilemma with regard to his
wife is only one particular instance of the conflict of attitudes between men
and women in Faulkner. From such a perspective we are to understand that
Molly's necessary desire to minister to the needs of the child, and to do so
regardless of the circumstances involved, constitutes in and of itself her
recognition and acceptance of an ethic of behavior that is binding upon her in
its importance before all other considerations. Such a conception ideally
expresses the virtues of Faulkner's women, who stabilize civilization and are
the source of its endurance. From this point of view, Molly cannot be thought
to have betrayed herself with reference to the loyalty she owes to Lucas and
the values he espouses. She is rendered as satisfying her allegiance to values
greater than those of Lucas, and values also which emphasize the selfless and

sacrificial rather than the self-serving action. One can see how Faulkner's general conception of woman's function, applied here to black women, incorporates the effects of the history of victimization of black women, projecting upon them as natural traits what may more serviceably be thought of as the consequence of their degraded exploitation. The legacy of such exploitation is obviously at work in Edmonds's handing of Molly, and so is the conception of her which allows her to view her cohabitation with him without qualm and as no violation of her marital commitment to Lucas. But woman's refusal to adopt masculine notions of honor is also something of which Faulkner's white men find occasion to accuse their women.

When Edmonds does not come to get his son, which would have signaled his adherence to the code of reciprocal relations between equal human beings, Lucas proposes to go and kill him. Assuming full responsibility for his act—because he expects either to die or be lynched afterwards, since it is not his way to run away—he prepares himself. He puts into the sleeping Molly's shoes, which had belonged to the dead white woman, a kerchief knotted with coins which he had been saving since he was ten years old. Had Edmonds come for the child Lucas would have forgiven him. It is the thing that, as he believes, old Carothers would have wanted him to do. But Edmonds had tried to demoralize him. He had tried to beat him, " 'And you wont never,' " says Lucas, " 'not even when I am hanging dead from the limb this time tomorrow with the coal oil still burning, you wont never.' " He continues: " 'Because all you got to beat is me,' " Lucas tells him. " 'I got to beat old Carothers. Get your pistol' " (pp. 53–54). Lucas has to "beat" Carothers by proving that the masculine imperative is no less potent in him, a black, than it was in Carothers, a white. For Lucas this means an honorable acquitting of and accounting for the self in all situations.

The psychological power and physical prowess of the black man are in contrast to the quietly diminished, though dignified, appearance of the white man. When Lucas flings away his razor and demands that Edmonds get the pistol, it is then that Edmonds makes the reply that causes them to fight: " 'Come on then. Do you think I'm any less a McCaslin just because I was what you call woman-made to it? Or maybe you aint even a woman-made McCaslin but just a nigger that's got out of hand?' " (p. 55). Lucas has been attempting to act by the code and Edmonds has again tried to undermine him. It is not so much a statement of self-defense as a denial of Lucas's right as a black man to represent the ideals he articulates, and, therefore, in this context, the statement is tantamount to a denial of his humanity: "Then he cried, and not to the white man and the white man knew it; he saw the whites of the negro's eyes rush suddenly with red like the eyes of a bayed animal—a bear, a fox: 'I tell you! Dont ask too much of me!' [Lucas says]. *I was wrong*, the white man thought. *I have gone too far.* But it was too late" (p. 55). They fight and Lucas overpowers Edmonds, striking and flinging him away, obtaining the pistol. It misfires, however, as in the decisive moment Lucas pulls the trigger.

It is here that Lucas's stream-of-consciousness shifts away from the earlier time to the present and the reader is not given the details of the resolution of the struggle. Afterwards, we find him in the fields, musing upon the unspent cartridge: "*Because I wouldn't have used the second one*, he thought. *I would have paid. I would have waited for the rope, even the coal oil. I would have paid. So I reckon I aint got old Carothers' blood for nothing, after all. Old Carothers*, he thought. *I needed him and he come and spoke for me*" (p. 58). But what really "spoke for" him was his own innate capacity for honor and integrity, as a human being, as a black person, which in this context, unfortunately, is inextricable from the McCaslin heritage. Faulkner can only allow for Lucas's integrity as it reflects his McCaslin heritage. Similarly, Lucas's real capacity for the demonstration of integrity is in complete contradiction to the inhumanity and moral callousness of the real Carothers as he existed in the flesh. Lucas actualizes not merely the bravery and daring, which did exist, but also the honorable possibilities of the mythic inheritance that were not in fact observed by the original progenitor; yet Lucas, in doing so, confers upon them a reality that they did not have until he brought them into being. Curiously enough, what Lucas does is similar to what Isaac does, although the particular context, and motivations for their actions, are worlds apart from each other. Yet each of them performs an act of honor and integrity which is *of* the tradition but has never before really been performed *within* it.

Note

1. William Faulkner, *Go Down, Moses* (New York: Modern Library reprint, 1955), p. 118. All subsequent quotations are from this edition and will be noted in the text.

William Faulkner's "Shining Star": Lucas Beauchamp as a Marginal Man

Bernard W. Bell*

As concept and character "the Negro" in the minds and texts of such classic nineteenth-century American white artists as Twain, Thoreau, Melville, Whitman, and Harriet Beecher Stowe symbolized, as Ralph Ellison has noted, "the darker, unknown potential side of his personality, that underground side, turgid with possibility, which might, if given a chance, toss a fistful of mud into the sky and create a 'shining star.' "[1] As with Mark Twain's "Nigger" Jim in *Adventures of Huckleberry Finn*, "the Negro" as literary sign

*This essay was written especially for this volume and is published here for the first time with the permission of the author.

is central to William Faulkner's narrative vision and achievement. Born the year after the custom of racial segregation and the popular minstrel image of blacks as Jim Crow were encoded in the legal texts as "separate but equal" (*Plessy v. Ferguson*, 1896), Faulkner, a native son of Mississippi, was torn psychologically between the curse and blessing of his Southern heritage. He felt compelled in his quest for personal wholeness and a unified artistic vision to come to terms with "the Negro" in the Southern white psyche as, in Ellison's words, "a malignant stereotype (the bad nigger) on the one hand and a benign stereotype (the good nigger) on the other" (p. 58).

In his novels Faulkner's characters range from the stereotypical Sambo and tragic mulatto to the rebellious marginal man when treating miscegenation and the struggle of "the Negro" to affirm a biracial, bicultural identity—the complex sociopsychological state that W. E. B. DuBois called "double consciousness"—as an Afro-American. The fear and courage, guilt and innocence, shame and pride, of mixed blood and interracial marriage, as *Absalom, Absalom!* and *Light in August* illustrate, involve the social and cultural issues of heritage as well as the sociopsychological myths of white supremacy and Negro inferiority. When, as in the case of Lucas Beauchamp, the individual of mixed blood rejects one social group or culture without achieving a satisfactory adjustment to the other, he "finds himself," as sociologist Everett V. Stonequist explains, "on the margin of each but a member of neither."[2] He becomes a marginal man.

After the American Revolution, miscegenation statutes began to define "the Negro" by two criteria: African ancestry or descent and percentage of Negro blood.[3] Unlike the three racial categories of white, colored (Creole or mulatto), and black that characterized the social structure of the Caribbean, Jim Crow codes in the United States arbitrarily reduced the categories to white and Negro. Despite the unscientific nature of racial classifications, Mississippi law in 1890 defined as Negro any person having one-eighth or more Negro blood. Prior to 1890 miscegenation laws had been repealed in many northeastern and midwestern states, but by 1931 the only states with large Negro populations that had no such laws were Illinois, New York, and Ohio. That all such state laws were not nullified until the 1967 Supreme Court decision of *Loving v. Virginia* reveals the tenacity of the myth of white supremacy, of Jim Crow codes, and of the rituals of miscegenation that inform the theme, style, and structure of Faulkner's important novels.

Etymologically, "negro" is derived from the Latin *niger* and the Spanish *negro*, both signifying the color black. The term was first used around 1441 by the Spanish and Portuguese to designate African slaves from below the Sahara, thus tying color to race and blackness to slavery and degradation.[4] Although such eighteenth-century organizations as the Free African Society and the African Methodist Episcopal Church rejected the term in naming themselves, "negro" was still the preferred racial classification at the turn of the twentieth century. In response to a campaign by the NAACP in 1930, the *New York Times* and other media began to capitalize the term, which in the 1960s was displaced by Black, African, African American, and Afro-American. The concept and sign of "the Negro," "nigger," or "Sambo" in American racial discourse and in Faulkner's novels, though, obscure, devalue, or mythicize the humanity and individuality of Afro-Americans, imaginatively reconstructing or deconstructing them as stereotype, type, or archetype: an oversimplified, reductive popular mental image or judgment of a group; a representative character that embodies a substantial number of significant elements of a group; and "a character type that occurs frequently in literature, myth, religion, or folklore, and is, therefore, believed to evoke profound emotions because it touches the unconscious memory and thus calls into play illogical but strong responses."[5]

In *Go Down, Moses* (1942)—seven stories about the paradoxical bondage and freedom of white and black descendants of Lucius Quintus Carothers McCaslin—Faulkner's compulsion as a Mississippi artist to understand "the Negro" drove him to create a world in which the rituals of miscegenation paradoxically reinforce and undermine the myth of white supremacy as well as the conventions of Jim Crow. This is particularly evident in the instance of Lucas Beauchamp—the product of miscegenation, incest, and probable rape—who functions as "the Negro," as a metonym for the Southern experience and a metaphor for modern man.

Introduced as a narrator-participant in *Go Down, Moses* and as a major character in *Intruder in the Dust*, Lucas is not merely the son of the slaves Tennie and Tomey's Turl, but also a grandson and great-grandson of old Carothers McCaslin, one of the founding white patriarchs of Yoknapatawpha County. Unlike the tragic deaths of Joe Christmas, whose racial mixture is fatally ambiguous in *Light in August* (1932), and of Charles Bon, whose mixed ancestry is seen as a more fratricidal character flaw in *Absalom, Absalom!* (1936), Lucas moves beyond the stereotypical fate of the tragic mulatto and succeeds realistically in asserting his individuality as a black McCaslin. More importantly, he also triumphs metonymically as the archetypal marginal man, the person of mixed blood who straddles two cultures, and metaphorically as the sign of unrealized spiritual brotherhood fundamental to our modern paradoxical sense of human bondage and freedom.

Lucius Quintus Carothers McCaslin Beauchamp, who renamed himself Lucas, is first introduced as a major character in "The Fire and the Hearth"; he appears briefly in "The Bear," and is mentioned in "Pantaloon in Black," "Delta Autumn," and "Go Down, Moses." Initially, "The Fire and the Hearth" presents two melodramatic plots with stereotypical characters who make bootleg whiskey and hunt for gold. On a deeper level, the narrative introduces us through temporal and spatial shifts of memory, reverie, and flashback to Lucas Beauchamp's quest for independence, power, and integrity as a man. The marginal man, we are told, is, at sixty-seven years of age in 1941, "not only the oldest man but the oldest living person on the Edmonds plantation, the oldest McCaslin descendant even though in the world's eye he descended not from McCaslins but from McCaslin slaves."[6]

As his great-grandson and grandson both, Lucas's relationship to old Carothers McCaslin is an ironic affirmation of the myth of the plantation as a harmonious, benevolent socioeconomic system. But it is also the major source of Lucas's personal independence, power, and integrity. He displays his self-confidence in opposing George Wilkins, the young black "interloper without forbears" who sets up a rival still and plans to marry Lucas's seventeen-year-old daughter, Nat. "If George had just stuck to farming the land which Edmonds had allotted him," Lucas reflects, "he would just as soon Nat married George as anyone else" (*Go Down, Moses,* p. 34). But he will brook no competition from George. Then Lucas discovers gold. Reinforcing the demeaning image of minstrelsy, Faulkner depicts Lucas's discovery of a gold coin while he is burying his own whiskey still before informing authorities of George's still. Lucas's discovery is a melodramatic complication of both his plot to have the sheriff get rid of George and his quest to affirm his own manhood.

Already financially independent with more than three thousand dollars of inherited McCaslin money in the bank—money tripled and deposited not by old Carothers but by his twin sons Amodeus (Buck) and Theophilus (Buddy) for their half-brother and Lucas's father, Terrel (Turl) Beauchamp—Lucas experiences a profoundly significant flashback of forty-three years as he pursues his resolve to expose George. The flashback to the 1890s—the period of the rise of Jim Crow, white terrorism, and the industrial New South—occurs when Lucas approaches Roth Edmonds's plantation house and the memory of both Zack Edmonds, Roth's father and Lucas's boyhood companion, and Cass McCaslin, and "the old days, the old time, and better men than these" (p. 44) give dramatic immediacy to the rituals of ancestral miscegenation and spiritual kinship. Pride, honor, and ruthlessness were the values that old Cass, Zack, and Lucas shared. Cass, a maternal grandson, took "the land from the true heir simply because he wanted it and knew he could use it better and was strong enough, ruthless enough, old Carothers McCaslin enough" (p. 44). In the extended flashback, Lucas manifests these values too in his effort to kill Zack Edmonds, with whom he had grown up almost as a brother. He presumed Zack to be guilty of sexually exploiting Molly, Lucas's wife, thereby violating Lucas's authority to maintain the integrity of his family and home, archetypically signified by the "fire in the hearth." During the night of a raging flood, Zack not only summoned the young, nursing Molly to deliver his child, but also sent Lucas across a dangerous river for a doctor. With the death of his wife in childbirth, Zack, faithful to the ethics of Jim Crow and the rituals of miscegenation, keeps Molly in his house as a nursemaid and homemaker: "It was as though the white woman had not only never quitted the house, she had never existed . . . his own wife, the black woman, now living alone in the house which old Cass had built for them when they married, keeping alive on the hearth the fire he had lit there on their wedding day and which had burned ever since though there was little enough cooking done on it now" (p. 46). After nearly six months, however, of "himself alone keeping alive the fire which was to burn on the hearth until neither he nor Molly were left to feed it," (p. 47) Lucas boldly confronts Zack and demands the return of his wife. " 'I'm a nigger,' " Lucas tells his cousin. " 'But I'm a man too. I'm more than just a man. The same thing made my pappy that made your grandpaw. I'm going to take her back' " (p. 47). Lucas asserts his manhood by invoking his white paternity, thus revealing his ambivalence and marginality.

When Molly returns home and continues nursing the Edmonds baby while apparently neglecting her own, Lucas's pride and shame, a legacy of his marginality, cry out for vindication. Standing over Zack in his bedroom, Lucas distinguishes between his responsibility as a man and Molly's, or the woman-born Zack, describing a woman as " 'a critter not responsible like men are responsible, not to be held like men are held' " (p. 52). Consequently, he will kill Zack and accept death by lynching rather than accept dishonor. At first he pulls out a razor but then throws it away and struggles with Zack for his pistol. But when Lucas pulls the trigger, it misfires in Zack's side.

In reverie a year or so later, Lucas thinks of the irony of the misfired cartridge he has kept as large enough to have contained two lives: *"Because I wouldn't have used the second one. . . . I would have paid. I would have waited for the rope, even the coal oil. I would have paid. So I reckon I aint got old Carothers' blood for nothing, after all. Old Carothers . . . I needed him and he come and spoke for me"* (p. 58). As a young mulatto male coping with the myth of white supremacy, Lucas knew that Molly "would leave [his supper] on the hearth for him when she went back to the big house with the children" (p. 58). Amplifying his dilemma to an archetypal level, he asks: " 'How to God . . . can a black man ask a white man to please not lay down with his black wife? And even if he could ask it, how to God can the white man promise he wont?' " (p. 59).

Metonymically, Lucas bears the sociopsychological burden of a marginal man, a person of mixed blood who struggles to reconcile the double consciousness of his dual identity. Lucas explicitly subscribes to the traditional values of males, but this is made ambivalent by the idea of the myth of white supremacy and the corollary myth of black inferiority. Still he struggles to remain, foremost, a man. When much later Molly seeks a divorce with Roth's assistance because Lucas's obsession with hunting for gold results in his neglect of his family, home, and God, Lucas responds tersely and proudly to Roth's inquiry: " 'I'm a man.' Lucas said. 'I'm the man here. I'm the one to say in my house, like you and your paw and his paw were the ones to say in his' " (p. 120). Significantly, Lucas's role models are white patriarchs, not black.

The youngest of three children (his sister Fonsiba was born in 1869 and left the plantation in 1876 after marrying a Northern black; his brother James was born in 1864 and fled north in 1885) and the father of three (Henry, born in 1898; an unnamed daughter who died in childbirth in 1915; and Nathalie, born in 1924), Lucas remained on the Mississippi plantation, yet defied the ethics of Jim Crow and the stereotypical role of "the Negro." He bore the curse and blessing of the legacy of old Carothers McCaslin's blood: handmade beaver hat, gold watch chain, gold toothpick, three thousand dollars, rent-free house and land, altered Christian name, faintly Syriac features, courage, independence, and ruthless individualism. Lucas refused to address whites, especially Zack, as mister; to trust whites financially or morally, including his cousin Isaac McCaslin, the trustee of his money; and to use a razor on Zack for dishonoring his rights and responsibilities as husband and father, for violating his fire and hearth. Most importantly, as we learn in "The Bear," he changed his name from Lucius to Lucas, "making it no longer the white man's but his own, by himself composed, himself selfprogenitive and nominate, by himself ancestored" (p. 281).

In other words, for the omniscient narrator and Roth Edmonds, who was midwifed, nursed, and raised as a foster son by Molly much in the manner as Faulkner was nurtured by "Mammy" Caroline Barr, Lucas was archetypically impervious to time. *"He's more like old Carothers than all the rest of us put together, including old Carothers,"* Roth thinks. *"He is both heir and prototype simultaneously of all the geography and climate and biology which sired old Carothers and all the rest of us and our kind, myriad, countless, faceless, even nameless now except himself who fathered himself, intact and complete, contemptuous, as old Carothers must have been, of all blood black white yellow or red, including his own"* (p. 118).

Although a practical, dominating, selfish man, Lucas, in giving up his obsessive search for gold, transcends his most negative traits and manifests the paradoxical interdependency and independence of modern man. At the end of "The Fire and the Hearth," he tells Roth to sell the divining machine that he used nightly in his search for gold because, he says with biblical resignation, " 'I am near to the end of my three score and ten, and I reckon to find that money aint for me' " (p. 131). Actually, he does so primarily to save his forty-five-year marriage to Molly, to protect his fire and hearth, which is dramatically illustrated by his sentimental gift of candy to his wife with the brusque remark: " 'Here. . . . You aint got no teeth left but you can still gum it' " (p. 130). Lucas, like most of Faulkner's major characters, is "haunted, obsessed, driven forward by some inner necessity," as Malcolm Cowley describes it.[7] Basically, the racial, economic, cultural, and moral complexities of this "inner necessity" for Lucas are to be respected as a man and to affirm the common bond of modern humanity.

Although the five parts of "The Bear" are primarily concerned with young Isaac McCaslin's discovery through the ritual of the hunt of the spiritual and moral bond of man, nature, and God, part 4 reveals Lucas's story and the rituals of miscegenation through Isaac's interior monologue and his dramatic dialogue with his cousin Cass.[8] As Isaac reads the history of the McCaslins, black and white, in the commissary ledgers, he morally and emotionally reconstructs the troubling, complex truth of how " 'God created and man himself cursed and tainted' " the earth that was entrusted to him " 'to hold . . . mutual and intact in the communal anonymity of brotherhood' " (pp. 257, 261). Awed by Faulkner's creation of a complex mosaic of myth, legend, and history through the use of reverie and flashbacks, we, as readers, sympathize psychologically and morally with Isaac's efforts to atone for the sins of his forefathers by repudiating the legacy of the McCaslin possession of the land and slaves, while not repudiating his spiritual kinship to both. We bear witness with him and the omniscient narrator to their common moral freedom and bondage in the divine covenantal order of things. An obsessive, overbearing racial pride in whiteness and the lust for absolute power over the land and the lives of non-whites are egregious violations of this moral order, transgressions for which each generation, as Faulkner challenges us to acknowledge, is socially and personally responsible.

We also bear witness to the fear of whites, derived both from the historical violation of the bodies and souls of black folk and the valuing of property over people, that blacks, especially marginal men like Lucas, are better and stronger than whites. " 'Their vices,' " Isaac argues with his cousin Cass, " 'are vices aped from white men or that white men and bondage have taught them.' " And their virtues are " 'Endurance . . . and pity and tolerance and forbearance and fidelity and love of children . . . what they got not only not from white people but not even despite white people because they had it already from the old free fathers a longer time free than us because we have never been free' " (pp. 294–95).

The enigmatic ledger entries implying a relationship between Eunice's suicide by drowning in 1832 and her daughter Tomasina's death during childbirth six months later explain old Carothers's legacy of a thousand dollars to Tomey's Turl, the product of Carothers's incest and probable rape of his slave daughter. Isaac struggles to understand the psychology and morality of these acts of miscegenation, especially the perversion of love into lust, the abdication of parental responsibility, and the effort to expiate sin with money: *"So I reckon that was cheaper than saying My son to a nigger* he thought. *Even if My son wasn't but just two words. But there must have been love* he thought. *Some sort of love. Even what he would have called love: not just an afternoon's or a night's spittoon"* (pp. 269–70).

By demanding and receiving on his twenty-first birthday the only social acknowledgment of his patrimony that he was to receive, Lucas comes of age. He attains the authority and autonomy of manhood. He also simultaneously and paradoxically affirms his freedom and bondage as a marginal man, for, as Isaac repeatedly reveals, he is " 'the last save himself of old Carothers' doomed and fatal blood which in the male derivation seemed to destroy all it touched.' " Like Isaac, Lucas, as his changing of his Christian name and his ritual wearing of the material symbols of miscegenation dramatize, is ambivalent in " 'repudiating and at least hoping to escape it' " (p. 293). Ironically, while the ritual wearing of the handmade beaver hat, gold watch chain, and gold toothpick establishes order and continuity in Lucas's personal life, it does not create order in the lives of other blacks and whites. As a marginal man, Lucas thus undermines rather than reinforces the myth of white supremacy and suggests the possibilities and limitations of a new moral order of brotherhood based on racial and class, but not sexual, equality. As the rituals of the hunt and miscegenation illustrate, Faulkner's literary vision valorizes the traditional power of men.

This power of men as well as the complex kinship ties of the white and black descendants of old Carothers are further illustrated in the other stories in *Go Down, Moses*. Narrated from the third-person limited omniscience of first the black protagonist and then a white deputy sheriff, "Pantaloon in Black," the story that follows "The Fire and the Hearth," contrasts the stereotypical white image of "the Negro" with the dramatized marital tragedy of Rider, whose quest for wholeness, autonomy, and authority is the antithesis of his racial and spiritual kinsman, Lucas Beauchamp. Overwhelmed by profound grief at the death of his wife of six months, Rider resolves to continue their union in death by a political and racial, as well as a personal, act of solidarity. After a few drinks, the tall, strong young head of a timber gang cuts the throat of the white nightwatchman who had with impunity been cheating him and other black workers at dice for years. He knows that his violent resistance to white exploitation will result in his lynching by whites, who see blacks in subhuman categories as either a "bad nigger" or a "good nigger." Faulkner dramatizes this in the deputy sheriff's emotionally and psychologically distorted report of Rider's lynching.

Metaphorically, Rider's complex humanity beneath the mask of "the Negro" is contrasted with that of Lucas. The marital bond between Rider and Mannie, for example, is contrasted with that of Lucas and Molly through the archetypal sign of the fire and the hearth. After Rider's marriage to Mannie, "he rented the cabin from Carothers Edmonds and built a fire on the hearth on their wedding night as the tale told how Uncle Lucas Beauchamp, Edmonds' oldest tenant, had done on his forty-five years ago and which had burned ever since" (p. 138). The day after Mannie's funeral, the fire falls "to a dry, light soilure of dead ashes" (p. 140), and her spirit appears only briefly in the kitchen door to remind Rider of the sense of wholeness and authority he experienced in intimacy with her. As we discover in "The Fire and the Hearth" and *Intruder in the Dust*, Lucas does not share this type of intimacy with either Molly or the black community. Nor does Lucas value bonding with the black community over his own personal authority and autonomy.

In "Delta Autumn," the nameless granddaughter of Lucas's older brother James, Tennie's Jim, has an illegitimate child by the last white descendant of the McCaslin family line, Roth Edmonds. When Roth fails to meet with her during the hunt, she confronts old Isaac McCaslin with an indictment: " 'I would have made a man of him. He's not a man yet. You spoiled him. You, and Uncle Lucas and Aunt Mollie. But mostly you. . . . When you gave to his grandfather that land which didn't belong to him, not even half of it by will or even law' " (p. 360). Like his great-great-grandfather, Roth seeks to expiate his guilt for miscegenation and evade public acknowledgment of his racially mixed son by leaving money with Isaac for both the mother and child.

After insisting harshly that Lucas's grandniece play her subordinate role by taking Roth's money and General Compson's hunting horn, Isaac, revealing his unregenerate racism despite his repudiation of the McCaslin land, concludes paternalistically, " 'That's right. Go back North. Marry: a man of your own race. That's the only salvation for you—for a while yet, maybe a long while yet. We will have to wait. Marry a black man. You are young, handsome, almost white; you could find a black man who would see in you what you saw in him, who would ask nothing of you and expect less and get even still less than that, if it's revenge you want. Then you will forget all this, forget it ever happened, that he ever existed—' " (p. 363). The last black descendant of the McCaslin family line complies, but not without moral indignation for her blood kin: " 'Old man,' she said, 'have you lived so long and forgotten so much that you dont remember anything you ever knew or felt or even heard about love?' " (p. 363). This invocation of the transcending power of the heart and memory to validate the complex ties of blood and spirit between white and black Americans is characteristic of Faulkner's ambivalent and ambiguous appeal to the collective unconsciousness of modern readers.

In "Go Down, Moses," the paradigmatic final story that ironically rewrites the mythic biblical story and black spiritual of the same title, Roth Edmonds is accused by old Mollie Worsham Beauchamp, Lucas's wife, of selling her young grandson Benjamin (Samuel Worsham Beauchamp) into bondage. Pleading for attorney Gavin Stevens's help, she chants: " 'It was Roth Edmonds sold him. . . . Sold him in Egypt. I dont know whar he is. I just knows Pharaoh got him. And you the Law. I wants to find my boy' " (p. 371). In Mollie's unreconstructed belief in the myth of the plantation tradition, bondage is identified with life in town and in the North. In his metaphorical role as Moses, Gavin Stevens, whose moral ambivalence and rhetorical excess are similar to Faulkner's own, demonstrates the social interdependency of Southern whites and blacks, the system of paternalism and noblesse oblige that was in reality more parasitic than symbiotic, by assuming most of the expense for burying Mollie's grandson, electrocuted in Chicago for killing a policeman. " 'Mr Edmonds will want to help, I know,' " he tells Miss Belle Worsham, the last white descendant of the family that had owned Mollie. " 'And I understand that old Luke Beauchamp has some money in the bank' " (p. 377).

Because he values his autonomy over social ties, however, Lucas does not contribute to his grandson's funeral. Nor is he present when Miss Worsham and Gavin hear Mollie and her brother Hamp chant an improvisation of "Go Down, Moses" in the mourning "circle about the brick hearth on which the ancient symbol of human coherence and solidarity smoldered" (p. 380). Because he is a living repudiation of the Southern stereotype of "the Negro," Lucas is thus socially outside of and symbolically beyond the circle of black solidarity that constituted the traditional ties of human bondage in the United States. Archetypically, Lucas is a marginal man, a product of the pride and shame of his mixed blood that socially and culturally provokes his ambivalence about both whites and blacks and that paradoxically affirms the complex multiracial, multicultural web of kinship ties of modern Americans.

Faulkner's consummate use of myth, ritual, metaphor, and metonymy in *Go Down, Moses* thus gives mythopoeic force to his vision of Lucas Quintus Carothers McCaslin Beauchamp and "the Negro." In his quest for autonomy, authority, and integrity as a man of mixed blood and culture, Lucas represents the promise and limitations of a modern social and moral order which challenges the ideology of white racism while perpetuating traditional ideologies of partiarchy and Christian humanism. For Faulkner, modern man, like Lucas and "the Negro," must personally bear the burden, the moral responsibility, of his humanity. As a marginal man, Lucas Beauchamp is, in other words, Faulkner's "shining star."

Notes

1. *Shadow and Act* (New York: Signet, 1964), 49. Subsequent references to this book will appear in the text.

2. *The Marginal Man* (New York: Charles Scribner's Sons, 1937), 2–3.

3. James Hugo Johnston, *Race Relations in Virginia and Miscegenation in the South, 1776–1860* (Amherst, Mass.: University of Massachusetts Press, 1970), 192–93.

4. Richard Moore, *The Name "Negro": Its Origin and Evil Use* (New York: Afro-American Publishers, 1960), 24.

5. C. Hugh Holman and William Harmon, *A Handbook to Literature*, 5th ed. (New York: Macmillan Publishing Co., 1986), 36, 54, 481.

6. William Faulkner, *Go Down, Moses and Other Stories* (New York: Vintage, 1973), 36. Subsequent references to this book will appear in the text.

7. Malcolm Cowley, ed., *The Portable Faulkner* (New York: Viking Press, 1961), 16–17.

8. For an excellent collection of essays on "The Bear," see *Bear, Man and God; Seven Approaches to William Faulkner's "The Bear,"* ed. Francis Lee Utley, Lynn Z. Bloom, and Arthur F. Kinney (New York: Random House, 1964).

Lucas Beauchamp and William Faulkner: Blood Brothers

Richard H. King*

When a novelist creates a character in one novel only to return to him or her in a later one, we have a sure sign that something important is at stake. Faulkner did this twice—with Quentin Compson and Lucas Beauchamp.

*This essay was written especially for this volume and is published here for the first time with the permission of the author.

But while the Quentin of *Absalom, Absalom!* is as compelling, if not more so, than the Quentin in *The Sound and the Fury*, the Lucas of *Go Down, Moses* is more fully explored and developed than Lucas in *Intruder in the Dust*. Indeed, where Lucas's supporting role in *Go Down, Moses* almost upstages the leading parts played by Sam Fathers and Ike McCaslin, Gavin Stevens and Chick Mallison all but submerge Lucas in *Intruder in the Dust*.

Another way to approach this phenomenon is to ask what happened to Faulkner between 1942 and 1948? No one can pinpoint the reasons or causes for the loss of creative momentum in a writer. Some might speculate that Faulkner wasted too much time and energy in Hollywood. But such a claim would leave unanswered how quantitative expenditure can be turned into qualitative decline. Another answer might be that with *Go Down, Moses* Faulkner had worked through the personal and artistic problems he set himself in the late 1920s. His essential story having been told, the rest tended toward stale repetition rather than powerful representation. Yet another answer would point to Faulkner's growing sense after the war that crucial public problems—particularly the South's racial dilemmas and the threat of nuclear destruction—needed addressing, and that fiction and public issues are scarcely compatible; thus Faulkner's fiction suffered the inevitable state of politically oriented art.[1]

The move I have just made from an initial claim about Lucas's fictional stature to one about Faulkner's fictional achievement is appropriate since one measure of Faulkner's grip on his artistic powers is the way he handles Lucas, the bridging character between *Go Down, Moses* and *Intruder in the Dust*. Further, if we agree that Lucas is perhaps the one black character created by Faulkner who escapes traditional stereotyping, the question becomes this: Was Faulkner's turn to Lucas a cause or a symptom of the decline in his fiction? Did the presence of fictional black "blood" corrupt Faulkner's fictional design in the way Bon had marred Sutpen's? Or, did Faulkner return to Lucas because he (Faulkner) had nothing left of compelling interest to say about his original themes?

Again, these questions allow no sure answer. In what follows I want to explore them and make the following separate but interlocking claims. First, Faulkner's creation of Lucas was artistically and morally daring for a white writer, Southern or not. Ultimately, however, Faulkner couldn't quite "bring it off" because even he lacked the experience of literary resources to do justice to the complexities of the black Southern experience. Second, Faulkner was limited by the inability of the Southern political culture to imagine what being political or acting politically meant, much less approve of an insurgent black politics. The problem with Gavin Stevens's ideas in *Intruder in the Dust* is less that they are a farrago of special pleading and paternalism (which they are) than that they are not put into dialogue with the right audience. They are about, rather than addressed to, black people and they are put forth with no expectation of an answer from any black character. Finally, however, the materials do exist in *Go Down, Moses* and *Intruder in the Dust* to comprise an "answer" to Stevens's polemics, but Faulkner failed to explore to a sufficient degree the political implications of those materials. Thus, *Intruder in the Dust* does not fail because it is a political novel, or a novel of ideas, or because those ideas are somehow "wrong." Rather, *Intruder in the Dust* is not political enough and its ideas are not sufficiently explored to set them or the novel into motion.

FAULKNER AND LUCAS BEAUCHAMP

Although it is difficult to make the various views Faulkner expressed about blacks cohere, two general claims might be made. First, Faulkner did not think that blacks were equal with whites.[2] Whether Faulkner used the term "blood" as a kind of master trope to refer to the assemblage of differences between the races or whether he employed it in a straightforward biological sense, he and his characters, including Lucas, apply the term quite often. Indeed, the difference in Lucas's mind between himself and the Edmonds's side of the McCaslin family comes down to Lucas's genetically dubious but culturally conventional claim to be superior to the Edmondses since they are descendants of the distaff side of the family. Thus "blood" signifies not only racial but also gender differences in Faulkner's world. White and male are privileged over black and female.

On the other hand, Faulkner grew increasingly aware during the 1930s and 1940s of the psychological and physical oppression suffered by black Southerners. His moral achievement as a white man lay in his effort to imagine himself into the state of being black and his achievement as white writer lay in his creation of black characters who undermined, though never completely, conventional fictional representation. With Joe Christmas and Sutpen's black progeny, Faulkner delineated figures plagued by and acting from the internal psychological divisions and wrenching social implications of possessing black blood. Specifically, Faulkner arrived at the view that black people were the psychological and moral creations of whites, projections of denied white fears and anxieties, imaginary "others," who then suffered from the white attempts to act out or to deny those fantasized projections.[3] Even in their roles as moral judges of the foolishness of white folks, Faulkner's black characters often seem to be projections of a white sensibility. However crucial Faulkner's projection theory was, it still left whites in control of blacks even if negatively. Thus, in much of Faulkner's work whites remained the primary focus.

With Lucas Beauchamp, however, Faulkner attempted to create a black man who refused to be the imaginary "other" for whites. As Lucas says to Zack Edmonds when he goes to fetch his wife Molly: " 'You thought that because I am a nigger I wouldn't even mind.' "[4] In one of those paradigmatic scenes of the black experience, one which echoes Frederick Douglass's confrontation with his white master, Lucas challenges not just a specific white man, but also aims to destroy the black image in the white mind.[5] He is willing to "kill" the self whites have tried to impose on him even if it means literally losing his life. By risking his life, Lucas achieves a kind of autonomy and becomes, as Douglass says, his "own master." And by refusing subsequently to say "sir" to any white man, by demonstrating his indifference to white opinion and by resolving to act even like a damn fool in pursuit of a buried treasure and with obdurate truculence in the face of a lynch mob in *Intruder in the Dust*, Lucas lives out that autonomy in his own fashion.

The problem is that in making Lucas so bullheaded, Faulkner renders him almost inaccessible to anyone or anything. "It was," writes Faulkner, "as if he were not only impervious to that blood, he was indifferent to it. . . . Instead of being at once the battleground and victim of two strains, he was a vessel, durable, ancestryless, nonconductive, in which the toxin and its anti stalemated one another, seethless, unrumored in the outside air."[6] Only at the end of "The Fire and the Hearth," when he buys his wife Molly a bag of candy as a reconciliatory gift, do we see a human gesture from Lucas; only then do we see a man concerned with more than establishing his superiority to others. The passage just quoted is significant for two reasons. First, we see Faulkner move beyond the agonized figures of mixed blood he had created earlier, as if to say, "I'll show you an autonomous black man, one without agony." The result, however, is a backwoods Nietzschean superman, serene in his indifference to most recognizable human motivations. Second, Faulkner seems to be predicting, if inadvertently, the way his oxymoronic, fictional rhetoric was to arrive at a standoff with itself. He was no longer able to energize his characters or the stories that contained them. In this sense, Lucas is the "vessel" of Faulkner's artistic decline. Having reached an almost inhuman pitch and height. Faulkner's voice began to stall rather than continue to soar.

Yet another sign that Faulkner went over the top with Lucas is that Lucas (like Sam Fathers) seems to lack any essential sympathy with black people outside his immediate family. He is a kind of Thoreauvian majority of one. Indeed, Roth Edmonds thinks of Lucas as one "*who fathered himself, intact and complete, contemptuous, as old Carothers must have been, of all blood black white yellow or red, including his own.*"[7] Thus Lucas is *in* but not *of* any community, not a subhuman projection of white fantasy but a superhuman projection of himself—and of Faulkner. What links Lucas and old Carothers is a metaphysics of blood, not a specific family tradition.

Indeed, there is a third figure linking yet subsuming Lucas and Carothers—Faulkner himself. The extraordinary effort of will in creating Lucas is a sign that Lucas is one of the many personae of the artist in Faulkner's oeuvre. Like Faulkner, whose original name was Falkner,[8] Lucas changes his name; and in doing so Lucas asserts his genealogical and psychic autonomy from the family while maintaining a tie with old Carothers. Only in this way can Lucas empower himself rather than be submerged in the family and racial nexus. With the descendant of slaves so with the descendant of slaveholders, the will to autonomy defeats the anxiety of influence. In other words, Faulkner's representation of an autonomous black character was based upon his own self-representation. His general experience having failed him, he fell back on the one character he knew—or imagined he knew—best.

Moreover, Lucas's gestures of defiance remain only gestures since they are acknowledged by no community of solidarity in which they can strike a chord and suggest group support or even action.[9] For a black man to choose his name is potentially of profound political importance, but Lucas's gesture has no political resonance and thus remains confined to the personal and private sphere. To put matters in a wider perspective, the problem of blacks under oppression in slavery or freedom was not a lack of individual courage in standing up to the white man. Rather, it was that circumstances allowed few opportunities for group defiance. Lucas has a distant, though fictionally inferior, descendant in Alex Haley's Kunta Kinte, but he bears hardly any resemblance to William Styron's—or history's—Nat Turner.

What I want to suggest at this juncture is that in "The Fire and the Hearth" Faulkner created his most autonomous black character, but had in a sense already reached a dead end with him. In going beyond his previous view that all blacks were shadowy projections of white fantasy, Faulkner imagined a black character who was self-created, but for that reason lacked vital links with the black community in which he lived.

FAULKNER AND GAVIN STEVENS

After completing a sizable chunk of what became *Intruder in the Dust*, Faulkner described his work in progress to Harold Ober: "the premise being that the white people in the South, before the North or the gvt. [sic] or anyone else, owe and must pay responsibility to the Negro. But it's a story; nobody preaches in it."[10] Rarely has an author been so off the mark about his own work, since the novel's political message is that the white South has the "privilege" of giving blacks equality and there is more than enough preaching in the book.

Intruder in the Dust was Faulkner's first novel to be adapted as a film and gave him the financial security he had long sought. It also helped establish a subgenre of Southern fiction—the racial thriller. These racial thrillers focus on a community in crisis, one in which a black man has been killed or is charged with murder or rape. The white community is split between the moderate but passive middle class and the "rednecks" who threaten not only to exact vengeance upon the black man but also to challenge the basic but tenuous structures of civilized life.

At the moral center of such novels is the relationship between an adult of good will, often a lawyer, and a younger relative. In the course of the novel, the two figures teach each other something essential—the mentor educates the younger person into the ways of the world, while the younger person reminds the mentor of an intuitive justice to which the adult world has grown indifferent. There is no political action per se. Poor whites are potential mob members, the black community is largely passive, and the middle-class white community puts its faith in the court system. In general such novels are moral psychodramas for moderate, well-intentioned white readers who can have their essential moral decency reaffirmed and in turn can look down their moral noses at the backwardness of poor whites.[11]

Intruder in the Dust is the story of how a sixteen-year-old white boy, Chick Mallison, becomes aware that a black man, Lucas Beauchamp, is neither subhuman nor an object of benevolence, but a person of strength, will, and not a little contrariness. Yet on another level, Lucas does function as a kind of object throughout most of the novel. Although he orchestrates much of the action, he is confined to jail. While Uncle Gavin dithers and a mob of rural whites gathers in anticipation of a lynching, Chick organizes a digging party to exonerate Lucas. In sum, Chick and Gavin take over the novel from Lucas and make it theirs for most of its duration.

There has been considerable critical discussion of the resemblance between Gavin's and Faulkner's political views. There is no doubt that Stevens's pronouncements sound much like Faulkner at his most political. For what it is worth, Faulkner told Malcolm Cowley that Stevens "was not speaking for the author, but for the best type of liberal Southerners. . . . If the race problems were just left to the children . . . They'd be solved soon enough."[12] Leaving aside a certain slipperiness here (Is Faulkner praising Stevens or putting him down?) and also a marked sentimentality about the natural sense of justice possessed by children, it is safe to say that Chick's action and Stevens's opinions mirror the split in Faulkner's own mind between an uneasiness with and a desire to preserve the racial status quo. (This split was earlier apparent in the dialogue between Ike McCaslin and McCaslin Edmonds in "The Bear.") Although gestures of defiance or repudiation attracted Faulkner's fictional interest, he always seemed to undermine or blunt their force, whether in *Go Down, Moses* or in *Intruder in the Dust*.

Stevens's position runs as follows. The South's "homogeneity" must be defended against outside interference, since that homogeneity is the source of everything of "durable and lasting value." Meddling by outsiders is also wrong because white Southerners must have the "privilege of setting him ["Sambo"] free," something that will not be accomplished by "next Tuesday." When Chick objects—and rightly so—that this sounds like an excuse for continued injustice, Stevens says: " 'I only say injustice is ours, the South's. We must expiate and abolish it ourselves.' " Above all, this must be done to heal the internal divisions in the country, faced as it is by the Soviet challenge.[13]

There are several things to say about Stevens's position. By emphasizing white guilt and responsibility, Stevens implicitly affirms white moral superiority. This is a familiar form of white Southern casuistry, a kind of "fortunate fall," which reminds us that guilt is an emotion of the powerful, not the powerless. The problem is that Stevens uses it to reinforce rather than undermine white pride. Similarly, Stevens transforms another valid moral insight—white Southerners should initiate change themselves, not let others thrust it upon them—into a moral luxury. The insight is not matched by any awareness on Stevens's part that blacks must also change their ways of being and acting. For the only way an oppressed people can become the psychological equal of their oppressors is by self-liberation. Conceptually and existentially, no person or group can be freed by someone else, particularly by its oppressors.

Finally, Faulkner's letter to Ober in which he writes that white people "owe and must pay responsibility to the Negro" should be contrasted with Stevens's claim that white Southerners have the "privilege" of setting blacks free. The important point is that the letter deploys the metaphor of debt and obligation, a figure later used to great effect by Martin Luther King, Jr., in his "I Have a Dream" speech of 1963, while Stevens's rhetoric makes it sound as though making good on past discrimination would be a gift from the powerful to the powerless. But a gift can be a way of confirming a relationship of inequality,[14] while to demand that a contract be fulfilled is to assert (potential) equality. Whether Faulkner was aware of the shift in language between the letter and the novel, the author's implied contractarian conception was belied by the lawyer's paternalism.

With this in mind, we can see how Stevens's position functions vis-à-vis Chick's action. On one level, Stevens's position does undermine Chick's action, yet at another level Chick, as a Southerner, might be seen as taking just the sort of steps that Gavin approves of rather than leaving things to outsiders. Indeed, as Stevens delivers his breathless peroration while speeding through the countryside, the two positions gradually merge: strophe and antistrophe form the choral comment. And this suggests that Gavin is Chick's fate, the man he will become. Once having realized that Lucas is not just a "nigger," Chick's education is rounded off by Gavin's adult wisdom. Chick is implicitly incorporated into the dominant white order.

Finally, then, Stevens's monologue and Chick's action push Lucas and the murder mystery to the novel's periphery. The aesthetic and political problem with Stevens's pronouncements is that they are directed at the wrong person. Their proper recipient is Lucas. By having Stevens deliver them to Chick, Faulkner reinforces Stevens's contention that the moral problems of the region concern whites more than blacks and that blacks implicitly are incapable of becoming full partners in the essentially political dialogue. Put another way: Stevens's ideas demand an answer within the novel, not from liberal critics outside its confines.

And yet Stevens receives an oblique answer of sorts. It comes from Lucas in the form of a challenge to the paternalistic "gift" relationship which traditionally links the two races. But that answer is in the form of a social gesture rather than political action or dialogue. To it we will now turn.

The Use and Abuse of Gifts

Faulkner's fictional world offers rich materials for analyzing the relationship among the political, social, and private realms. Although he presents us with no straightforward mimetic portrayal of the South (whatever that might be), his South exemplifies some of the important dimensions of the region's racial order. By examining Lucas's position at the center of certain crucial social transactions, we can understand much about the way the society and polity function in his fictional world and in historical actuality.

To develop this claim, some conceptual points should be made. In Faulkner's South blacks are quintessentially private, laboring beings who have no place in the public realm. They do, however, share a social realm with whites.[15] Moreover, in the particular case of the South, the distinction between the legal and social orders was only fitfully maintained. Put concretely: what should have been left to informal rules of social intercourse was legally proscribed; a black man, for example, could not socially associate with a white woman nor might he legally marry her. What should have been the outcome of a personal decision within a social order was forbidden by law.

With this in mind we can better characterize and delimit Lucas's freedom and autonomy. If we define freedom in terms of legal status, personal character, and access to political participation, we can see that Lucas is autonomous psychologically but he is not fully free in the other two senses.[16] In the "Lucas" stories freedom as equal status before the law is nonexistent since Lucas lives in a society that allows paternalistic gifts between whites and blacks, oppressor and oppressed, but does not institutionalize a mutual recognition of rights and duties among equals.

Lucas implicitly recognizes this when he wonders: " 'How to God . . . can a black man ask a white man to please not lay down with his black wife? And even if he could ask it, how to God can the white man promise he wont?' "[17] This crucial passage from "The Fire and the Hearth" can be unpacked to suggest that black-white relationships are regulated by gifts and favors rather than by rights and mutual obligations. Lucas's question is both poignant and cogent, not simply because he is not supposed to make such a request but also because such a humiliating request is the only one he *can* possibly make. His wife, the exchange object in the patriarchal order, has been stolen from him by Zack Edmonds, but Lucas lacks the legal standing to demand her return. In an order of reciprocity, one person can demand that another recognize his/her rights to property. But as a black man Lucas can only "ask" for a "promise." All this is a way of saying that Lucas has no rights, since rights exist by virtue of a contract among equals or as a gift from God or nature but not by virtue of a "free"gift from another person.

Thus we can see the way in which Faulkner's world—and by implication the South—can be understood in terms of the social and legal transactions at its center. (Such transactions both mirror and determine the depth of psychological relationships binding and separating blacks and whites.) For example, the relationship between Thomas Sutpen and his son Henry in *Absalom, Absalom!* or between Carothers and his white male heirs is cemented by the socially customary, though not legally obligatory, gift of property and name. But the relationship between Sutpen and Charles Bon or between Carothers and his black descendants is marked by a purely "free," even capricious gift that the white giver can always refuse to give. Quentin and Shreve imagine Bon asking for recognition from Sutpen. But however personally important such recognition would have been, it could never have become a social or legal fact. Analogously, Lucas's black relatives either refuse or accept Carothers's gift of money, but in either case it is a free gift and thus an insult since it lacks either a social or personal dimension. Money is impersonal, not personal, property. Finally, the pathos of Lucas's position is that he wills to act as though he has a right to recognition as an equal, although his de facto position is that he has no such right. He has no real birthright. Still, his "will" is a match for old Carothers; and in this sense he is Carothers's true heir.

"The Fire and the Hearth" is organized around the dialectic between gift and theft. Lucas's family lives on the Edmonds's land, which is a gift, yet Lucas treats it as rightfully his. He wastes his time and almost loses his wife by trying to find buried gold, an imaginary and disruptive gift of unknown provenance.[18] Lucas allows Molly to be a substitute mother for Zack's newborn, but this gift is transformed into a theft until Lucas asserts his property rights which he must, however, fight for. Zack gives Lucas back his wife, but Lucas refuses to recognize it as a gift since he has faced down Zack and earned recognition through the threat of violence. Finally, Lucas reestablishes his relationship to Molly, after his obsession with the gold has threatened their marriage, by buying her a gift of candy. By this we are reminded that wives are related to husbands by and as gifts: as whites are to blacks, so husbands are to wives. The truth underlying the gift relationship in such a society is the power to steal with impunity or to exercise control.

In *Intruder in the Dust* the focus falls on the dialectic between gifts and exchanges of services among equals. It proceeds in a dizzying fashion. Lucas saves Chick's life and gives him a meal. When Chick treats this as an exchange of services by offering to pay seventy cents, Lucas rejects the offer and Chick feels humiliated. He tries to even the score by sending a dress to Molly, a compensatory exchange disguised as a gift. But Lucas reciprocates by sending Chick a bucket of molasses, ostensibly in exchange but in fact a gift that maintains his superiority as a gift-giver. As the plot thickens, however, Lucas needs a favor, or a gift. He shrewdly chooses the one person who owes him one, Chick, and commissions him to organize the digging party. Thus, Lucas subtly shifts the nature of the transactions from a battle of gifts to an exchange of services among equals. Having saved Chick's life, Lucas asks now to be saved by him. By finally allowing Chick to pay him back, Lucas maintains his life and his superiority.

With all this in mind we can look once again briefly at Stevens's pronouncements. Stevens asserts the white Southern "privilege" of freeing black people, of freedom as a gift. But Lucas's manipulation of both the gift and the exchange of services parodies Stevens's paternalism and thereby renders it ludicrous. No one can give Lucas anything, even if he thinks he can.

Indeed, the fictional climax to *Intruder in the Dust* comes when Lucas refuses to accept Stevens's legal work on his behalf as a gift. When the lawyer refuses to accept Stevens's money from Lucas, Lucas still insists that he be charged something. Stevens finally accedes. But of all things, Lucas now wants something else which will legally confirm that an exchange of services rather than a gift has been at issue. The novel's last words, Lucas's last words, are: " 'My receipt.' "[19] By making that demand, Lucas finally comes out on top, first as a gift-giver and then as an equal, receiving contractual acknowledgment.

Yet the ultimate limitations must be recognized. Although Lucas creates a space of personal autonomy and social leverage, his manipulative gestures of defiance never attain the status of political action (or talk).[20] They issue from an individual rather than from a community and are directed toward individuals rather than toward the political order. The black community is literally in hiding throughout most of *Intruder in the Dust*. Both Faulkner and Lucas were creatures of worlds that allowed no political or public role to black people. We cannot imagine Faulkner, or Lucas for that matter, imagining the ways in which gestures of defiance might be transformed into acts of political transformation. That did not begin to change until 1955.

Notes

1. Faulkner's career is most thoroughly traced in Joseph Blotner, *Faulkner: A Biography* (New York: Random House, 1974), and David Minter, *William Faulkner: His Life and His Work* (Baltimore, Md.: The Johns Hopkins University Press, 1980).

2. See Faulkner, *Essays, Speeches and Public Letters*, ed. James Meriwether (New York: Random House, 1965); Lee Jenkins, *Faulkner and Black-White Relations: A Psychoanalytic Approach* (New York: Columbia University Press, 1981); and Eric Sundquist, *Faulkner: The House Divided* (Baltimore, Md.: The Johns Hopkins University Press, 1983), the latter two excerpted in this volume. In general Faulkner falls into the mainstream of white "democratic" views of blacks, tracing back to Lincoln and Jefferson. This position contends that white superiority derives from intellectual rather than moral or emotional capacities.

3. Sundquist is particularly stimulating on this topic.

4. *Go Down, Moses* (New York: Modern Library, 1942), 53. All subsequent quotations from "The Fire and the Hearth" are from this edition.

5. My analysis here draws upon the Hegelian discussion of the master-slave confrontation. An account of Douglass's fight with his master Covey can be found in his *A Narrative of My Life* (Garden City, N.Y.: Doubleday Anchor, 1963).

6. *Go Down, Moses*, 104.

7. Ibid., 118.

8. See Blotner, ed., *Selected Letters of William Faulkner* (New York: Random House, 1977), 212 for Faulkner's account of his changing the spelling of his family name.

9. See Eugene Geneovese, *Roll, Jordan, Roll* (New York: Vintage Books, 1976) for this point about the difference between individual and collective resistance.

10. *Selected Letters*, 262.

11. Novels that might be designated racial thrillers would include Harper Lee, *To Kill a Mockingbird*, Jesse Hill Ford, *The Liberation of Lord Byron Jones*, and Madison Jones, *A Cry of Absence*. It should be noted here that Jones's novel is much more condemnatory of the respectable, white middle class.

12. Malcolm Cowley, *The Faulkner-Cowley File: Letters and Memories* (New York: Viking Press, 1966), 110.

13. *Intruder in the Dust* (New York: New American Library, 1949), 110, 102, 132. All quotations from *Intruder in the Dust* are taken from this edition.

14. The classic discussion of the gift relationship is found in Marcel Mauss, *The Gift*. A stimulating recent discussion in a literary context is Lewis Hyde, *The Gift* (New York: Vintage Books, 1983). I have made no attempt to apply Mauss or Hyde in any exact way. Indeed, my contention would be that the gift relationship is not preferable per se to a contractual exchange of services and certainly not in societies based upon contractual relations among legal equals. My discussion is not meant to imply that any society entirely excludes the other sort of transaction nor that all gifts are covert efforts to dominate the receiver.

15. My analysis here derives from Hannah Arendt's *The Human Condition* (Garden City, N.Y.: Doubleday, 1958) and from the Hegelian distinction between state and civil society.

16. I will develop this formulation of the three dimensions (or types) of freedom in a study of the civil rights movement now in progress.

17. *Go Down, Moses*, 59.

18. It is also interesting to note that the action in both "Lucas" stories has to do with something that is allegedly buried and must be found and exhumed.

19. *Intruder in the Dust*, 158.

20. I have explored this theme of gesture versus political action further in "A Fable: Faulkner's Political Novel?" *Southern Literary Journal* 17, no. 2 (Spring 1985): 3–17.

The Priest Line

[The Old Aristocracy: Boss Priest, Ned McCaslin, and Bobo Beauchamp]

Walter Taylor*

Americans, Ralph Ellison commented in 1958, create their self-image in terms of "a joke at the center of the American identity." That joke was a masking joke: a ritual of disguise whose central figure was "a smart man playing dumb." Ellison saw the principle operating in our great men. Franklin had "allowed the French to mistake him for Rousseau's Natural Man"; "Lincoln allowed himself to be mistaken for a simple country lawyer." It had descended to his contemporaries. "Hemingway poses as a non-literary sportsman, Faulkner as a farmer." It was so deeply embedded in the American grain, Ellison concluded, that "America is a land of masking jokers."[1]

For Ellison that fact explained a great deal about black and white Americans. Since colonial times, the joke that mask concealed was frequently an ethnic joke: "Americans began their revolt from the English fatherland," he pointed out, "when they dumped tea into the Boston harbor, masked as Indians." Codified, these white rituals eventuated in the minstrel show. Despite "its ringing of banjos and rattling of bones, [and] its voices cackling jokes in pseudo-Negro dialect," the "role" of the minstrel show did not "grow out of the Negro American sense of the comic"; it grew "out of the white American's Manichaean fascination with the symbolism of blackness and whiteness." In such performances blacks were "caught up associatively in the negative side of the basic dualism of the white folk mind, and . . . shackled to almost everything it would repress from conscience or consciousness." The minstrel show thus "constituted a ritual of exorcism." In it "the specific rhetorical situation . . . [involved] the self-humiliation of . . . [a] 'sacrificial' figure," and "one of the powerful motives at work in the audience" was "a psychological dissociation from this symbolic self-maiming."[2] For Ellison, the dynamics of the minstrel show were like the dynamics of a lynching: by

*Reprinted with permission from *Faulkner and Race: Faulkner and Yoknapatawpha*, ed. Doreen Fowler and Ann J. Abadie (Jackson: University Press of Mississippi, 1987), 111–29. Original title: "Faulkner's *Reivers:* How to Change the Joke without Slipping the Yoke."

245

projecting its own darker motives onto this black figure, the minstrel's audience purged itself—through laughter at his "self-maiming" rather than by executing him.

This was "the joke at the center of the American identity": but for Ellison there were alternative versions of that joke. Black Americans could "slip the yoke" of bondage if they could find ways to "change the joke" that supported it, and Ellison had a tale about a "very dark Southern friend" of his to illustrate his point. His friend had been bargaining with a white businessman who complained of his "recalcitrance" in finalizing the deal. The complaint prompted this dark Southerner to what Ellison pointedly called a "laughing reply." The reply was "I know, you thought I was colored, didn't you?"[3]

Let us pause here to belabor the obvious. In this anecdote the white businessman starts with the notion that the joke is on Ellison's friend: that because he is black this man will have to act out the "self-maiming" clown role, which means he will settle for less in the deal. But when Ellison's friend remains laughingly recalcitrant, the joke turns around. The white businessman realizes the clown mask has obscured his vision: that the joke is on him for assuming this "very dark" man was also "colored." Change the joke and slip the yoke. But there were other ways of doing that, and Ellison had suggested one in 1952 in *Invisible Man* through the deathbed speech of his protagonist's grandfather, a "quiet old man who never caused any trouble": "Son, after I'm gone I want you to keep up the good fight. I never told you, but our life is a war and I have been a traitor all my born days, a spy in the enemy's country ever since I give up my gun back in the Reconstruction. Live with your head in the lion's mouth. I want you to overcome 'em with yeses, undermine 'em with grins, agree 'em to death and destruction, let 'em swoller you till they vomit or bust wide open."[4]

Ellison's old man advises his son to accept the "joke at the center of the American identity" as a condition of black American life; but he also shows him one way to use that joke. The old man's "mask of meekness," he commented, "conceals the wisdom of one who has learned the secret of saying the 'yes' which accomplished the expressive 'no.' " A dangerous game, but a "spy in the enemy's country" must obviously wear a disguise. And this is no passive response. The old man puts on his mask to "overcome"; he plans the "death and destruction" of his enemies. This too was "the joke at the center of the American identity," and Ellison thought its significance for relations between the races was profound: "It is across this joke," he concluded, "that Negro and white Americans regard one another."[5]

I know of no evidence that, when some three years later Faulkner sat down to write *The Reivers*,[6] he had read Ellison's essay. I rather think he had not.[7] But through a long career, Faulkner had been fascinated by "the joke at the center of the American identity." In Simon Strother of *Flags in the Dust* (1927), Ringo Strother of *The Unvanquished* (1938), and Lucas Beauchamp of *Go Down, Moses* (1942), this figure had provided Faulkner with memorable characterizations. Now he was ready to make the masking joker a focal point of his new novel, and the result was a work that, I believe, ranks rather high in his canon artistically. It was also a paradigm of the paternalistic ethic of Faulkner's youth.

Raised in a family that styled itself aristocratic, Faulkner inherited the world of noblesse oblige, the neofeudal code effected by Southern aristocrats. Their paternalist lifestyle was predicated on a trifurcated population with two underclasses, one white, and one black, presided over by a minority of affluent aristocrats. In this world noblesse oblige was not merely the aristocrat's code of honor, it was also his rationale. It was important to the aristocrat's conscience to preside over the welfare of his black and white dependents, who were, he insisted, irresponsible and in need of his protection; but it was just as important to have irresponsible dependents to protect, in order to justify his lifestyle—in order, that is, to rationalize his monopoly of the land and, in the case of the blacks, the fact that he had enslaved them and extended their bondage as sharecroppers.

During Faulkner's youth, that world was under siege by poor-white voters led by James Kimble Vardaman, whose racism signalled the hardening of a stone age of Jim Crow; the force of that threat is revealed in the fact that Faulkner's aristocratic grandfather, former state senator John Wesley Thompson Falkner, found it necessary to ally himself politically with the "White Chief," as Vardaman was called. I believe that the tensions of those years played a significant role in Faulkner's career.[8] During the major phase of that career Faulkner set out, in Robert Penn Warren's happy phrase, to do "a more difficult thing" than Joyce's Dedalus: "To forge the conscience of his race, he stayed in his native spot and, in his soul, in images of vice and virtue, reenacted the history of that race."[9] No modern writer has engaged himself in a more deeply motivated, or a more agonized, struggle to come to grips with the realities of his homeland; and in 1954, when *Brown* v. *the Board of Education* made the question of the "real" South once more a national issue, Faulkner responded as his code of noblesse oblige demanded: in a series of interviews and lectures he took on himself the task of spelling out what he saw as the "moderate" position on integration. This position was not always so moderate; often it consisted of firing off invective at those he considered extremists of both persuasions. But there was no denying Faulkner's sincerity, or the price his stand cost him in pain. And a great deal of that pain was personal. A long-standing criticism from many Southerners was that, by emphasizing the South's failures in his novels, he had helped deliver it into the hands of outsiders who did not understand; now he was receiving the same criticism from Southerners about his statements on the "moderate" position, some of it from his own family.[10] As Faulkner began *The Reivers*, there were thus pressures on him to write something affirmative about the South. And as he composed the novel, daily headlines made it plain that the time for that was running out, that an era was coming to an end. Not long after his final novel was published, the new era exploded in a bloody riot [when the black James Meredith attempted to enroll at the University of Mississippi]. . . .

Faulkner took care in the early going to separate Lucius Priest, his narrator, from certain political attitudes. Lucius identifies the imperious whorehouse landlord Mr. Binford as a "Republican" and a "Conservative," and proceeds to offer an economic-determinist assessment of the entire political spectrum: "a Republican is a man who made his money; a Liberal is a man who inherited his; a Democrat is a barefooted Liberal in a cross-country race; a Conservative is a Republican who has learned to read and write."[11] But *The Reivers,* from the beginning, articulates a more conservative politics than Republicanism, and in this it is also personal. The Priest family, a branch of the McCaslin family of *Go Down, Moses,* resembles the Faulkner family pointedly. Old Carothers McCaslin is a family patriarch on the order of Colonel W. C. Falkner. "Boss Priest," Jefferson banker and grandfather of the novel's narrator, recalls Faulkner's banker grandfather, J. W. T. Falkner. Mr. Maury Priest, Lucius's father, runs a livery stable, as did Faulkner's father, Murry C. Falkner. Like the Falkner children, the young Priests are presided over by a servant known as "Mammy Callie"; and the Priests, like the Falkners, are served by a black retainer known as "Uncle Ned." As the novel opens, aging Lucius explains to his own grandson about his 1905 introduction to what he calls "Non-virtue" (p. 54). While Boss, Mr. Maury, and his mother are out of town, Lucius and Boon Hogganbeck, a hand at the livery stable, steal Boss's Winton Flyer auto for a trip to Memphis; on the way they discover a stowaway in the person of "Uncle Ned" McCaslin, who as old Carothers's black grandson is also Lucius's kinsman. In Memphis, while Boon takes Lucius to visit Everbe Corinthia, his girlfriend who is also an employee of Miss Reba's whorehouse, Ned swaps the Winton Flyer for a racehorse named Coppermine—the first stroke in an involved scheme through which he hopes to win the Winton back by betting on the horse and, in the process, buy back his cousin Bobo Beauchamp from a Memphis loan shark. This bizarre scheme climaxes with Lucius racing the stolen horse in Parsham, Tennessee, when Boss unexpectedly appears to end the charade. By that time a chastened Lucius has had his fill of "Non-virtue" and is ready for punishment. "Do something about it," he tells Boss of his guilt. "Do anything, just so it's something" (p. 301). He receives, instead, an initiation into the adult world of the paternalistic gentleman.

Punishment, Boss knows, is the one reward no paternalist can receive. One of Mr. Maury's stable hands might be punished for unauthorized use of the stable's teams by being "fired": which means, in Lucius's words, "docked a week's pay (with vacation)" (p. 14). But there is no one above the paternalist, who is the sole judge of his own actions. "Live with it." Boss counsels Lucius. "A gentleman always does. A gentleman can live through anything. He faces anything. A gentleman accepts the responsibility of his actions and bears the burden of their consequences" (p. 302). The joke, Lucius thus learns, is on him. As an innocent, he had thought he could be purged of his guilt by punishment; now, knowledgeable in the nature of "Non-virtue," he must "live with it"—that is, he realizes he cannot be purged, and hence must assume total responsibility for his actions. Lucius is thus initiated into the cult of noblesse oblige, a godlike responsibility beyond which there is no appeal. And at the heart of the situation, for William Faulkner as for Ralph Ellison, lies "the joke at the center of the American identity." As Lucius bursts into tears over this discovery Boss offers his eleven-year-old grandson the paternalist's only consolation for his predicament: a toddy.

But the central comic image in *The Reivers* is not that of the bland paternalist embarrassed by the absoluteness of his power. It is that of the underclass whose dependent status validates the paternalist's protective role. The "joke at the center of the American identity" surfaces rather early in *The Reivers*. As Lucius begins to explain his confrontation with "Non-virtue," what comes to his mind is the story of an old black man: "I was in the position," he laments, "of the old Negro who said——" (p. 62).

Before dealing with *what* this old Negro said, let us once more pause to belabor the obvious. Why must Lucius invoke an "old Negro" to make his point? Why not, for example, a young Negro? Why not a young white man? For that matter, what sex is Lucius's "old Negro"? Is this an "old Negro" woman? For Lucius to make his point he must invoke an "old Negro" man, and that signals the presence of the masking ritual exemplified by the minstrel show: a ritual that according to Ralph Ellison is a white invention. We would, then, expect this "old Negro" to play the "self-maiming" clown, which he proceeds in a rather mild fashion to do, talking Faulkner's version of black idiom as he converses with his God about the joke God has played on him: his own Non-virtue. "Here I is, Lord," he says. "If you wants me saved, You got the best chance You ever seen standing right here looking at You" (p. 62).

That, of course, is funny, but it may not be quite as funny as it sounds. In Ellison's terms, such a joke would invoke a "ritual of exorcism." Those things that "the white folk mind . . . would repress from conscience or consciousness" would be projected onto this black figure, then purged through laughter. In the comic world of *The Reivers* those things come under the heading of Non-virtue, which is here revealed as a permanent condition of the old man's character. But Lucius's "old Negro" has managed to alter the terms of the joke. Without denying his non-virtuous nature, he has shifted the responsibility for it: he is open-minded on the subject, willing to change if his Lord is willing to intervene and bring the change about. The joke is thus not merely on the "old Negro"; it is also on the Lord, who, having created this old man's non-virtuous nature, must now take responsibility for it. In Ellison's terms, he has "overcome" his Lord "with yeses," and is undermining Him "with grins." Lucius's "old Negro" has thus maneuvered his Lord into a position very much like that of the paternalist who, faced with the dependency of a working class he is responsible for, must bear the burden of protecting it. This of course is something less than agreeing his Lord "to death and destruction." The "old Negro" has his Lord exactly where he wants

Him: if his Lord assumes responsibility for his Non-virtue, He thus absolves the "old Negro" of his own responsibility, and he is free to behave as he pleases. It is the Lord, in short, who now seems to need a toddy.

Lucius's "old Negro" story foreshadows the emergence of the novel's central comic figure. Ned McCaslin is the epitome of the masking joker; like Ellison's B. P. Rinehart he glides, chameleonlike, through a repertoire of roles, the most important of which is identified by Lucius as "Uncle Remus" (p. 182). Lucius identifies two more: "the spoiled immune privileged-retainer impudence of [Ned's] relations with Boon" and "the avuncular bossiness of those [relations] with me" (p. 128). To this list should be added, among many, the roles of the con man and the sweet-talking lover.

If Ellison's "ritual of exorcism" is operating here we should experience Ned as "self-maiming"—that is, as playing the clown when the laughter is at his expense. He is, in fact, one of the funniest characters in Faulkner, and as often as not the joke is on him. Ned is not the only source in *The Reivers* of malapropisms, a disease that is epidemic in the poor white as well as in the black community. But Ned is their fountainhead in the novel, the author of the richest and best. For Ned a sardine is a "sour dean" and unattached women are arrested for "fragrancy." In a snobbish mood about his McCaslin-Priest family, Ned insists that Boss needed "to put Colonel Sartoris back in his place he had done upstarted from." When someone tells him Memphis "is where the jack's at"—meaning, of course, where the money is, Ned replies, "In course they has jacks here. Dont Memphis need mules the same as anybody else?" When Lucius asks what blue laws are, Ned responds that he doesn't know either, "Lessen it means they blewed in all the money Saturday night" (pp. 286, 257, 117, 141–42, 140).

Here, of course, we laugh at Ned's ignorance, although the humor is rather bland; when he glides into his role as lover the humor descends to burlesque. Ned has had four marriages, Lucius reports, and his relation to his wife Delphine in 1905 is less than successful. Ned "was . . . often nowhere in range of any voice" around Boss's household, Lucius relates, "since one of them was his wife's" (p. 30). His marriage does not deter him from other amorous endeavors; he is a hard man to get out of any kitchen with a woman in it, and he is never satisfied merely to let nature take its course. "When I sugars up a woman," he tells a fat cook at the Parsham hotel, "it aint just empty talk. They can buy something with it too" (p. 219). If it is "money you talking about, Good-looking," he tells Miss Reba's maid Minnie, "I got it or I can get it." Ned has nothing against flattery either. Impressed with Minnie's gold tooth, he is ready to "let that tooth do its shining amongst something good enough to match it." To Ned, that would be, "like a dish of catfish or maybe hog meat if it likes hog meat better" (p. 118). But Ned plays the lover's role with more persistence than success. "Maybe," the cook advises Minnie, "that Mississippi sugar will spend where it came from, but it wont buy nothing up here in Tennessee. Not in this kitchen, nohow" (p. 220). The cook could have spared this advice to Minnie, who has already survived one encounter with Ned. "If all you got to depend on for appetite is me," Lucius hears her say when she carries Ned's food to the porch, "you gonter starve twice between here and morning." Soon Lucius and the others hear "a quick sharp flat sound" and Minnie reappears—"breathing a little quick," Lucius reports. "He like most of them." Minnie tells Miss Reba, "He got plenty of appetite but he cant seem to locate where it is" (p. 134).

Ned's misadventures as a lover veer toward low humor of which his Non-virtue is the butt; the same can be said of another side of Ned, his prejudices. Ned can be a snob about his own white family. Boss "had to buy that automobile." he tells Lucius, "to put Colonel Sartoris [who had recently purchased one] back in his place" (p. 117). He can sound like a racist on the subject of other blacks. "With a horse anything can happen," he tells Lucius of the upcoming race. "And with a nigger boy on him, it's twice as likely to" (pp. 263–64). Perhaps his failures with Minnie and the cook result from the fact that these women sense what Ned's wife Delphine already knows: Ned has a formidable streak of chauvinism. When Boon beats up Everbe for sleeping with the poor-white sheriff Butch Lovemaiden, Ned lectures Lucius, "Hitting a woman dont hurt her because a woman dont shove back at a lick like a man do; she just gives to it and then when your back is turned, reaches for the flatiron or the butcher knife." For Ned, this is useful knowledge. "That's why hitting them dont break nothing," he tells the boy; "all it does is just black her eye or cut her mouf a little" (p. 263).

Again, all this is meant to be funny, and again the laughter is at Ned's expense. Ned, in short, frequently does not know when the joke is on him, and his unconscious "self-maiming" is in the tradition of the minstrel burlesque. Still, Ned is aware of "the joke at the center of the American identity," and more than any other character in Faulkner he thrives on its nuances. Ned's conscious use of the interracial joke surfaces early in the Memphis trip when Lucius and Boon discover him beneath a tarpaulin in the rear of the Winton Flyer. "I wants a trip too," he tells them, and adds a half-jovial, half-challenging, "Hee hee hee" (p. 70).

That "Hee hee hee" is worth pondering. It is Ned's equivalent of the "laughing" statement of Ellison's dark friend: "I know, you thought I was colored, didn't you?" That is, it is Ned's signal that the interracial joke is in operation. The joke here is on Boon and Lucius: noblesse oblige demands that they cannot summarily dump a black McCaslin dependent this far from home, much less Ned, who is Lucius's blood kin. The incident suggests the second and third roles Lucius mentions ("spoiled immune privileged-retainer" and "avuncular bossiness") and foreshadows the "Uncle Remus" role that Ned glides into when it pleases him. The term "Uncle Remus," which is used by both Lucius and Sheriff Butch (p. 177), is somewhat misleading. In most ways Ned has little in common with Joel Chandler Harris's kindly, white-locked old man. Lucius's mother is alone in wanting to call Ned "Uncle." At age forty-five he "hadn't earned" the title, Lucius asserts, "even by just living long enough for the fringe of hair embracing his bald skull to turn gray, let alone white." Ned, in fact, "may not have wanted to be called Uncle," he points out (p. 30). And his "Uncle Remus" role is more like a composite of Uncle Remus and Brer Rabbit; the role Lucius is describing is the role of the masking joker.

This role is illustrated as Lucius, Boon, and Ned comfront a poor-white "mud farmer," a man who charges two dollars a passenger to pull the Winton Flyer through a bog he himself has created in the road. When this man flippantly remarks that "mud's one of our best crops," Ned plays the "old Negro" to express his irritation. "At two dollars a mudhole," he tells the man, "it ought to be your best" crop. The mud farmer, interested only in profit, wants no confrontation; but this is an interracial joke he cannot ignore, an impertinent response that implies extortion. "I dont know but what you're right," he replies, but then, as he orders Ned to hold the mule team's doubletree, he seems to be trying to put Ned in his place. "You look like a boy that knows which end of a mule to hook to," he says (p. 88).

Once more to belabor the obvious, the two men at this point appear to be even. Ned has used the interracial joke to call the mud farmer an extortionist and the mud farmer has used it to call Ned a boy, and by implication, a field hand—an insult to any "spoiled immune privileged retainer." But now Lucius, Boon, and Ned are faced with yet another mud hole, a "reserve patch" the mud farmer calls it, and that elicits a more complex response from Ned. "You means the Christmas middle," he says, and launches into a rather obtuse explanation of what that means. "It's how we done at McCaslin [plantation] back before the Surrender when old L. Q. C. was alive. . . . Every spring a middle is streaked off in the best ground on the place, and every stalk of cotton betwixt that middle and the edge of the field belongs to the Christmus fund, not for the boss but for every McCaslin nigger to have a Christmas share of it. That's what a Christmas middle is. Likely you mud-farming folks up here never heard of it" (pp. 89–90).

The joke is again on the mud farmer. He is not only being castigated for his extortion, but also for greed and for his poor-white ignorance of plantation ways—in particular for what is represented here as plantation charity toward blacks. Yet how can the mud farmer be sure that this is more than the garrulous rambling of a black eccentric—the "old Negro" figure whom Lucius invoked earlier? The mud farmer is forced to take notice. His response is appropriate and shows that he, too, is aware of the "joke at the center of the American identity." The man looks at Ned, and "after a while," Lucius reports, "Ned said, 'Hee hee hee' "—to which the mud farmer replies, "That's better. . . . I thought for a minute me and you was about to misunderstand one another" (p. 90). The fact is, they do understand one another perfectly. Ned can make his feelings known through the indirect route of the "old Negro" role and they are heard; but the mud farmer reclaims his own status by making Ned acknowledge that the role is a joke.

Ned uses this Uncle Remus mask in his first encounter with belligerent sheriff Butch Lovemaiden at black Uncle Parsham Hood's home, where the horse Coppermine is stabled. Here the stakes are higher. Ned is in alien territory where blacks without local connections are powerless. Butch, who claims to be investigating the horse race, has taken a fancy to Everbe, and is trying to provoke Boon into attacking him—a move which will allow Butch to jail Everbe's only adult white male defender. Ned, in his Uncle Remus role, appears blandly unaware of any problems as he comes on the scene. "Morning, Mr. Boon," he says. "You and Mr. Shurf want Lucius to bring the horse out?" By giving the title of "Mister" to both men—in other situations he gives it only grudgingly to either—Ned elevates both to a status above him; he then proceeds to manipulate them, asking about the horse to get both men's minds off Everbe. Butch is not so easily placated, launching into a tirade about "strange niggers" designed to intimidate Ned and ending with a compliment that contains an implied threat: "at least you got sense enough to recognize the Law when you see it." Ned's bland response invokes the interracial joke. "Yes sir," he says. "I'm acquainted with Law," and he adds ambiguously, "We got it back in Jefferson too" (p. 173). But before the ambiguities of that remark have time to sink in on Butch, Ned has changed the subject, asking Boon about the horse again. As the puzzled sheriff hesitates, Everbe has time to head for the stable, where Butch quickly follows her with Ned a few steps behind. Ned has thus managed to separate Butch from Boon, and to keep the two men apart he now allows the conflict between him and Butch to intensify. Lucius recounts the story:

> "We just sent for [the horse's] jockey," Ned said, "then you can see him work." Then he said, "Unlessen you in a hurry to get back to yourn."
> "My what?" Butch said.
> "Your law work," Ned said, "Back in Possum or wherever it is."
> "After coming all the way out here to see a race horse?" Butch said. "All I see so far is a plug standing half asleep in a lot."
> "I'm sho glad you tole me that," Ned said. "I thought maybe you wasn't interested" (pp. 176–77).

By gliding in and out of his Uncle Remus role, Ned thus manages to hover on the borderline of disrespect without suffering the consequences; and Butch, trying to decide whether he has been insulted, has no time to worry about Boon. As a calmer Boon approaches the stable, Ned's next move identifies Butch's real motives. Since Butch's reason for coming to Uncle Parsham's house is the horse, Ned tells Boon, "maybe what you and Miss [Everbe] better do is go on back to town now." Butch now has no choice but to order them to stay with him, a de facto admission of his designs on Everbe. Ned has thus used the interracial joke to strip Butch, publicly, and Butch's response proves he knows it. "Ha ha ha," he says. He says it "without mirth," Lucius reports, "without anything." And it is at this point that Butch labels Ned "Uncle Remus" (p. 177).

Ned's Uncle Remus mask is only a partial success with Butch, a stall to keep Boon out of jail; but it anticipates his final and most impressive effort at playing the "old Negro," when he is summoned by Boss Priest for a climactic confrontation with Boss, the aristocratic patriarch of Parsham, Colonel Linscomb, and the Chicagoan-turned-Memphian Mr. van Tosch, owner of Coppermine and former employer of Bobo Beauchamp. The atmosphere of this smug scene is heavy with moonlight and magnolias. The setting is old Parsham Place, Colonel Linscomb's home. It is "big," Lucius reports, "with columns and porticoes and formal gardens." Colonel Linscomb's office has a "special table" for his stud book, another for toddy mixings. Lucius remembers "a French window that opened onto a gallery above the rose garden . . . and honeysuckle too and a mockingbird somewhere outside" (pp. 281, 284). The Colonel is dressed in white linen, Boss in his Confederate gray.

For Ned, this confrontation is crucial; at stake is not merely his position with Boss but also the fate of his cousin Bobo. His response is a triumph of "old Negro" role playing. Ned's ploy here is to emphasize the distance between himself and these formidable white men. His first opportunity surfaces when Colonel Linscomb offers him a drink. Ned respectfully accepts the drink, then sets it on the mantel untouched; when Boss insists, he kills the drink at one swallow. Refusing to drink with his "betters" allows Ned to deal with Mr. van Tosch—"an alien, a foreigner," as Lucius points out (p. 287)—in the role of a dependent, a context in which his charade with the white man's horse seems almost reasonable. He begins by planting an idea in van Tosch's head. "Bobo," he says, "got mixed up with a white man." This Northerner, Lucius relates, "hadn't lived in our country long enough yet to know the kind of white blackguard a young country-bred Negro . . . would get involved with." He is appalled to learn, and the impact of this new knowledge is registered by an unconscious, "Ah." That "Ah" marks a pivotal moment for Ned. From that point van Tosch, facing the guilt of noblesse oblige for the first time, is his. When the Northerner asks, "But why didn't . . . [Bobo] come to me?" Ned reminds him that Bobo did. "You told him No," he says, and proceeds to hammer home the Southern facts of life. "You're a white man," he says. "Bobo was a nigger boy" (pp. 287, 288).

No wonder Ned declines to drink with these aristocrats. The greater the distance between him and them, the greater his advantage. When Boss tries to close this gap he only widens it. "Then why didn't he come to me?" Boss asks Ned. But the battle is already lost. "What would you a done?" Ned scolds. "If he had come . . . and told you, Dont ask me no questions: just hand me a hundred and a few extra dollars and I'll go back to Memphis and start paying you back the first Saturday I gets around to it?" The point hits home, and Boss, sensing defeat, can only plead his own kinship to Bobo: "I'm a McCaslin too." But this allows Ned to widen the gap further. "You're a white man too"—and as Ned continues, telling how his outrageous scheme was hatched in a Beale Street bar, an idea takes shape in Boss's mind which explains everything. "Now I'm beginning to understand," he announces. "A nigger Saturday night. Bobo already drunk, and your tongue hanging out" (pp. 288, 289, 290–91). This is exactly what Ned has been looking for, and as he admits that "With my people, Saturday night runs over into Sunday," he has these white aristocrats exactly where he wants them. Colonel Linscomb now joins the dialogue. That "nigger Saturday night," he tells Ned, runs over

> "into Monday morning too. . . . You wake up Monday morning, sick, with a hangover, filthy in a filthy jail, and lie there until some white man comes and pays your fine and takes you straight back to the cotton field or whatever it is and puts you back to work without even giving you time to eat breakfast. And you sweat it out there, and maybe by sundown you feel you are not really going to die; and the next day, and the day after that, and after that, until it's Saturday again and you can put down the plow or the hoe and go back as fast as you can to that stinking jail cell on Monday morning. Why do you do it? I don't know." (p. 291)

Ned does know, and because he knows, Colonel Linscomb's tirade signals the triumph of Ned's "old Negro" act. In Ellison's terms Ned's "self-maiming" ("With my people Saturday night runs over into Sunday") has afforded the Colonel an "exorcism" by means of which he projects his own guilt onto all blacks and purges it—this time not through laughter but through scorn. Ned now comes up with the one response that will cement the idea in Linscomb's mind. "You cant know," he tells the Colonel. "You're the wrong color. If you could just be a nigger one Saturday night, you wouldn't never want to be a white man again" (p. 291). That, of course, is precisely what Boss, the Colonel, and the initiate van Tosch want to hear, and one is tempted to add, in Ned's behalf, a raucous "Hee hee hee." More than any other character in Faulkner, Ned knows how to "overcome 'em with yeses, undermine 'em with grins." His role as "old Negro" reinforces these aristocrats' self-esteem in their own roles. He is, in fact, a godsend: a black oracle who articulates the theories of paternalism at the same time that he illustrates them. There are two worlds, Ned has shown these aristocrats, and there is something in them for everybody. For blacks, there is the jubilee of a "nigger Saturday night." For paternalists, there is the responsibility of caring for their black dependents, a duty that absolves not only their aristocratic lifestyle but also their responsibility of having enslaved those dependents in the first place. Ned has these white men exactly where he wants them, and by the time he has finished his tale a defeated Colonel Linscomb is ready to acknowledge that the joke, finally, is on them. "Let's all have a toddy," he says. He says this "briskly," Lucius reports (p. 293). Predictably, Ned allows this drink also to remain untouched.

But this, again, is something less than a commitment to "agree 'em to death and destruction." Ned may have changed the joke, but the last thing he wants to do is slip the yoke. The color line is his piece of cake, and he intends to have that cake and eat it too. Faulkner's facetious jacket blurb for *The Reivers* contains a kernel of truth. There is a sense in which his novel is a "Bible of free will and private enterprise" for the Western world. But Ned's characterization, created at the end of one era and on the threshold of another, raises questions of a different sort. It is most suggestive that Faulkner decided to set his [novel] in 1905. If a vigorous and intelligent black like Ned could thrive in that era—so Lucius's narrative implies—others could thrive as well. Faulkner is careful, moreover, to surround Ned with successful blacks like hard-working John Powell and dignified Uncle Parsham Hood. And in this stone age of Jim Crow, the only truly prejudiced white in the novel is Butch Lovemaiden, the sheriff who is more interested in making love than war.

Faulkner, three years younger than Lucius in 1905, had other memories of that era. The grandson of aristocratic J. W. T. Falkner could hardly have been unaware of the opinions of the family's political ally, White Chief James Kimble Vardaman, who thought that "the Negro" was a "lazy, lying, lustful animal" whose nature "resembles the hog's."[12] And with the rest of Oxford he had learned about Jim Crow the hard way when a mob took black Nelse Patton from the town jail, dragged his mutilated body to the square and left it hanging from a tree.[13] But one could learn rather little of all that from *The Reivers*, set two years after Vardaman's inauguration as Governor and three years before the lynching of [Nelse] Patton.

It is one thing to write comedy; it is another to ask readers to accept a mind-bending version of history orchestrated to sanctify the social outlook of an archaic class. A novel, for better or worse, affirms a world. By the way its vision is structured, by the way it praises virtue and blames evil, it sets up systems of values. In these ways, great books liberate us from our narrowness of vision; but lesser books, sometimes by their very persuasiveness, enforce that narrowness. For Ralph Ellison, there was another way to "slip the yoke" of the "joke at the center of the American identity." That was by stripping away all masks, black and white, until the human being behind them was visible. The "mode" of his protagonist was "confession, not concealment," he wrote, and his development was "a process of *rising* to an understanding of his human condition."[14] Faulkner, in works like *Light in August* and *Absalom, Absalom!*, had made the confessional the mode of his own protagonists, as he set out, Dedalus-like, to "forge the conscience of his race." Now, admitting that he did not "know the answer to the human condition," he had written one of his funniest books; and in doing so he had enlisted our humor in praise of a regressive society. Written at the end of one South, published on the threshold of another, Faulkner's mellow reminiscence beams the very loud political message that Jim Crow was not so bad. And the speaker of that message, the final face through which Faulkner regards us, is that of Ned McCaslin. Based on a white man's perception of "the joke at the center of the American identity," Ned does not represent black Americans in any significant way; he represents, rather, the distilled essence of the tradition that enslaved them.

From behind Ned's black face Faulkner's eyes look out at us. He stares at us a moment, then smiles and laughs a mellow "Hee hee hee." To which we can only respond by changing our own jokes. We can, perhaps, with

Butch Lovemaiden, mumble "Ha ha ha"—"without mirth," as Lucius tells us, "without anything." Or perhaps, with the mud farmer, we can stare at him a moment and say, "That's better. . . . I thought for a minute me and you was about to misunderstand one another."

Notes

1. Ralph Ellison, "Change the Joke and Slip the Yoke," in *Shadow and Act* (New York: Random, House, 1964), pp. 54, 55. The phrase "a smart man playing dumb" is Stanley Edgar Hyman's; Ellison's essay was written as a response to statements by Hyman about *Invisible Man* (1952).

2. Ibid., pp. 54, 47–48, 49.

3. Ibid., p. 54.

4. Ellison, *Invisible Man* (New York: Random House, 1952), pp. 13–14.

5. "Change the Joke and Slip the Yoke," pp. 56, 54. Faulkner consciously patterned *The Reivers* in some degree on *Huckleberry Finn*. See Joseph Blotner, *Faulkner: A Biography*, 1-vol. ed. (New York: Random House, 1984), p. 418. Ellison wrote of his own early experiences with Clemens's novel: "I could imagine myself as Huck Finn . . . but not, though I racially identified with him, as Nigger Jim, who struck me as a white man's inadequate portrait of a slave." The characterization, he thought, made blacks "uncomfortable." That was because, "writing at a time when the blackfaced minstrel was still popular, . . . Twain fitted Jim into the outlines of the minstrel tradition." It was "from behind this stereotype mask that we see Jim's dignity and human capacity—and Twain's complexity—emerge." He added this suggestive comment: "A glance at a more recent fictional encounter . . . that of Chick Mallison and Lucas Beauchamp in Faulkner's *Intruder in the Dust*, will reinforce my point. For all the racial and caste differences between them, Lucas holds the ascendency in his mature dignity over the youthful Mallison and refuses to lower himself. . . . Faulkner was free to reject the [white Southern] confusion between manhood and the Negro's caste status." See "Change the Joke and Slip the Yoke," pp. 58, 50. Lucas Beauchamp is, of course, a far more dignified and serious figure in *Intruder in the Dust* than he is in *Go Down, Moses*, or than Ned McCaslin is in *The Reivers*. Ellison voiced a more complex statement of his opinions on Faulkner in "Twentieth-Century Fiction and the Black Mask of Humanity." See *Shadow and Act*, pp. 41–43.

6. See Blotner, p. 691. Faulkner had conceived the germ of the plot as early as 1941 (Blotner, p. 418).

7. Faulkner's biographers and interviewers reveal rather little record of contact with, or comment on, black writers. In a rare statement on the subject in Japan in 1955 he claimed knowledge of Ellison, Richard Wright, and "others that don't have the talent of those two." Faulkner thought Wright had "a great deal of talent." But Wright had written "one good book and then went astray, he got too concerned in the difference between the Negro man and the white man and he stopped being a writer and became a Negro." Faulkner thought Ellison "has talent and so far has managed to stay away from being first a Negro, he is still first a writer." For that reason, apparently, Faulkner thought Ellison "will go far." See James B. Meriwether and Michael Millgate, eds. *Lion in the Garden: Interviews with William Faulkner, 1926–1962* (New York: Random House, 1968), p. 185.

8. I have discussed these questions at length in *Faulkner's Search for a South* (Urbana: University of Illinois Press, 1983), pp. 4–17.

9. Warren, "Faulkner: The South and the Negro," *The Southern Review*, 1 (Summer 1965): 529.

10. See *Faulkner's Search*, pp. 166–83. Also, Blotner, pp. 615, 616–18, and David Minter, *William Faulkner: His Life and Work* (Baltimore: Johns Hopkins University Press, 1980), pp. 235, 237.

11. Faulkner, *The Reivers* (New York: Random House, 1962), p. 109. Subsequent references to this work are cited in the text.

12. Albert D. Kirwan, *Revolt of the Rednecks* (Lexington: University of Kentucky Press, 1951), p. 146.

13. See *Faulkner's Search*, pp. 14–15; Blotner, pp. 31–32.

14. "Change the Joke and Slip the Yoke," p. 57.

APPENDIXES

[Faulkner's Holograph Genealogy]   William Faulkner*

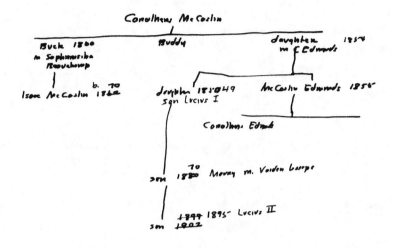

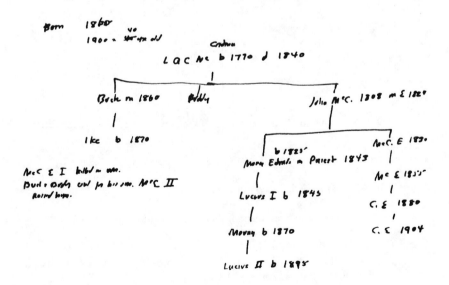

*University of Virginia MSS Accession #9817f; reprinted with permission from *William Faulkner Manuscripts* (New York: Garland Publishing, Inc., 1987), vol. 16, 241.

The McCaslin-Edmonds-Beauchamp Family

Robert W. Kirk with Marvin Klotz*

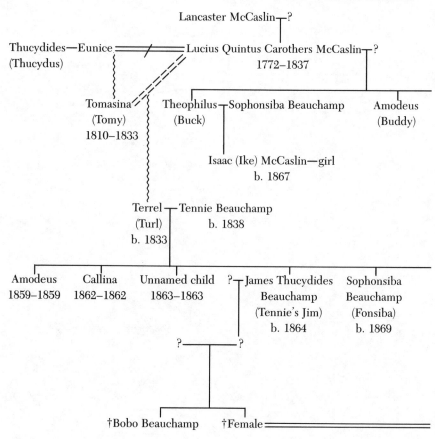

═╪═ denotes an illicit relationship.

════ denotes an incestuous relationship.

⌇⌇⌇ denotes the issue of an illicit or incestuous relationship.

†Grandchildren of Tennie's Jim.
[Ned William McCaslin (b. 1860) is said to be the son of a slave daughter
of Lucius Quintus Carothers McCaslin.]
See also Thomas J. Wertenbaker, Jr., "Faulkner's Point of View and the
Chronicle of Ike McCaslin," *College English*, 24 (1962): 169–178.

*Reprinted with permission from *Faulkner's People: A Complete Guide and Index to Characters
in the Fiction of William Faulkner* (Berkeley, Calif.: University of California Press, 1963), 316–
17. © 1963 the Regents of the University of California.

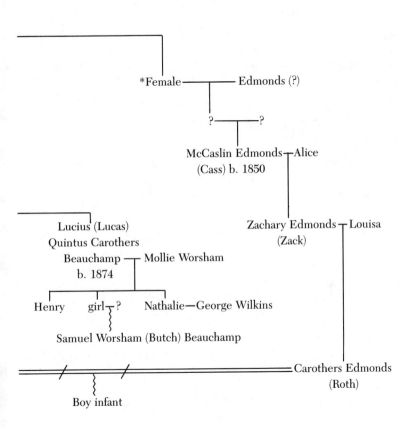

*Female————— Edmonds (?)

?————?

McCaslin Edmonds—Alice
(Cass) b. 1850

Lucius (Lucas)   Zachary Edmonds—Louisa
Quintus Carothers   (Zack)
Beauchamp —— Mollie Worsham
b. 1874

Henry   girl—?   Nathalie—George Wilkins

Samuel Worsham (Butch) Beauchamp

Carothers Edmonds
(Roth)

Boy infant

*It is not clear whether this McCaslin married an Edmonds, or whether she had a
daughter who did so.

[Family Members]   Harry Runyan*

THE BEAUCHAMP LINE

Beauchamp, Bobo.   One of the Yoknapatawpha County Beauchamps who worked for Mr. van Tosch in Memphis. He went into debt, stole van Tosch's horse Coppermine, and then traded it to Ned McCaslin for Mr. Priest's car, which Bobo gave to his creditor (*The Reivers*).

Beauchamp, Fonsiba (Sophonsiba).   The daughter of Tomey's Turl and Tennie. Born in 1869. At the age of seventeen she married a northern Negro and moved to a small farm near Midnight, Arkansas. Appears in "The Bear"; referred to in "The Fire and the Hearth" (*Go Down, Moses*).

Beauchamp, Henry.   The son of Lucas and Mollie Beauchamp. Born in 1898. Throughout his childhood he was a constant companion to Roth Edmonds ("The Fire and the Hearth" in *Go Down, Moses*).

Beauchamp, Hubert.   The owner of a large plantation twenty-two miles from the McCaslin lands. His sister Sophonsiba married Theophilus (Uncle Buck) McCaslin. Appears in "Was" and "The Bear" (*Go Down, Moses*).

Beauchamp, James.   A son of Tomey's Turl and Tennie and older brother of Lucas. Was known as Tennie's Jim. Born December 29, 1864. On his twenty-first birthday he fled north and disappeared. Later it was discovered that he went to Indiana. He died around 1938. A granddaughter of his had a child by Roth Edmonds. He was also the grandfather of Bobo Beauchamp. Appears in "The Old People" and "The Bear"; is referred to in "The Fire and the Hearth" and "Delta Autumn" (*Go Down, Moses*) and *The Reivers*.

Beauchamp, Lucas.   A son of Tomey's Turl and Tennie. Born March 17, 1874. His full name was originally Lucius Quintus Carothers McCaslin Beauchamp. Married Mollie Habersham (called Worsham in ["Go Down, Moses"]). Had three children, Henry (born 1898), an unnamed daughter (the mother of Samuel Worsham Beauchamp), and Nathalie. Lucas was arrested for the murder of Vinson Gowrie, but was freed through the activities of Chick Mallison and Eunice Habersham. Has a major role in "The Fire and the Hearth" (*Go Down, Moses*) and *Intruder in the Dust*. Appears more briefly in "The Bear." Is referred to in "Go Down, Moses," "Delta Autumn," and *The Reivers*.

Beauchamp, Mollie.   The wife of Lucas. She had been, according to "Go Down, Moses," from the Worsham family of Jefferson, but according to *Intruder in the Dust* she was from the Habersham family. She died sometime in the early 1940s. Has a major role in "The Fire and the Hearth" and "Go

*Reprinted with permission from *A Faulkner Glossary* (New York: The Citadel Press, 1964), 24–26, 56–57, 110–11, 128–29.

Down, Moses"; appears briefly in the early part of *Intruder in the Dust;* is referred to in "Delta Autumn."

Beauchamp, Nathalie.   The daughter of Lucas and Mollie Beauchamp. She married George Wilkins, a shiftless laborer, and moved with him to Detroit. Appears in "The Fire and the Hearth" (*Go Down, Moses*); is referred to (but not by name) in *Intruder in the Dust.*

. . . .

Beauchamp, Samuel Worsham.   The grandson of Lucas and Mollie Beauchamp. Known as "Butch." His mother died when he was born and Mollie raised him. At the age of nineteen he went to Jefferson and at once began getting into trouble. After being put in jail for robbing a Jefferson store, he escaped and fled north. He was electrocuted at the age of twenty-six in the Illinois state prison at Joliet for killing a Chicago policeman ("Go Down, Moses").

Beauchamp, Sophonsiba (Sibbey).   The sister of Hubert Beauchamp. She married Theophilus McCaslin in 1859. Was the mother of Isaac McCaslin. Appears in "Was" and "The Bear" (*Go Down, Moses*).

Beauchamp, Terrel.   Known as Tomey's Turl, he was the son of Tomasina, the daughter of a Negro slave woman Eunice and old Carothers McCaslin, and, in turn, the son of McCaslin as well. Hence, [Carothers] was both his grandfather and his father. Terrel fell in love with a slave named Tennie belonging to the Beauchamp family, so Uncle Buddy McCaslin played a game of poker with Hubert Beauchamp and won, thus winning Tennie. Terrel and Tennie were married in 1859. They had several children, three of whom lived: James, Fonsiba, and Lucas. Denied the name McCaslin, they took the name Beauchamp. Appears in "Was"; referred to in "The Fire and the Hearth" and "The Bear" (*Go Down, Moses*). There was in Jefferson around 1910 a fireman at the power plant named Tomey's Turl Beauchamp. He was thirty years old at the time. His relationship with the Beauchamp family is not known (*The Town*).

THE EDMONDS LINE

Edmonds, Carothers McCaslin (Cass).   The grandson of old Lucius Quintus Carothers McCaslin and the son of Carolina McCaslin. Born in 1850. He raised Ike McCaslin, and Ike turned over the McCaslin lands to him. He was the father of Zachary Taylor Edmonds. Appears in "Was," "The Old People," and "The Bear" (in *Go Down, Moses*). Is referred to in "The Fire and the Hearth" and "Delta Autumn" (*Go Down, Moses*), "A Bear Hunt," *The Town,* and (as McCaslin Edmonds) *The Reivers.*

Edmonds, Carothers (Roth).   The son of Zachary Edmonds and great-great-grandson of old Lucius Quintus Carothers McCaslin. He was born in 1898. He attended the state university at Oxford around 1920. The last white descendant of the family, he maintained the old McCaslin plantation. He fathered illegitimately around 1940 a child born to the granddaughter of James Beauchamp. Has a major role in "The Fire and the Hearth" and "Delta Autumn" (*Go Down, Moses*), and appears briefly or is merely referred to in "Go Down Moses," *Intruder in the Dust*, "Race at Morning," *The Town* and *The Reivers*.

Edmonds, Louisa.   The wife of Zachary Taylor Edmonds (*The Reivers*).

Edmonds, Sarah.   The maiden name of Grandfather (Boss) Priest's wife. She was born in 1854, and was probably a sister of Carothers McCaslin Edmonds (*The Reivers*).

Edmonds, Zachary Taylor (Zack).   The son of McCaslin Edmonds and father of Roth Edmonds. Appears in "The Fire and the Hearth" (*Go Down, Moses*) and *The Reivers* (where he is called McCaslin Edmonds's nephew). Charles Mallison, Jr., in *The Town*, calls McCaslin Edmonds Roth's father, and does not mention Zack.

The McCaslin Line

McCaslin, Amodeus (Uncle Buddy).   A son of old Lucius Quintus Carothers McCaslin and a twin of Theophilus (Uncle Buck) McCaslin. He was born around 1800 in Carolina. Some ten years before the Civil War he and his brother embarked on a project to free their slaves. When the war came he played a game of poker with his brother to see who would enlist and who would stay home. He won, so he became a sergeant in Colonel Sartoris's regiment. He was never married. He died around 1870. Appears in "Was" (*Go Down, Moses*) and "Retreat" (*The Unvanquished*), and is referred to in most of the other stories in *Go Down, Moses* [and some in *The Unvanquished*].

McCaslin, Delphine.   The wife of Ned William McCaslin and cook for Grandmother Priest (*The Reivers*).

McCaslin, Isaac (Uncle Ike).   The son of Theophilus McCaslin and Sophonsiba Beauchamp. He was born in 1867 and was raised by his cousin McCaslin Edmonds, to whom he gave the McCaslin lands. He married a Jefferson girl and moved to Jefferson, where he became a carpenter and opened a hardware store (where Jason Compson later worked). He was taught woodlore and hunting by Sam Fathers. He died in 1947. Appears in most of the stories in *Go Down, Moses*, "A Bear Hunt," "Race at Morning," and *The Reivers*. Is referred to in *The Hamlet*, *The Town*, and *The Mansion*.

McCaslin, Lucius Quintus Carothers.   The father of the McCaslin twins and a daughter who married an Edmonds. He was the first of the McCaslins in Yoknapatawpha County, arriving there from Carolina around 1800 (although in *The Reivers* the date is set at 1813). He fathered, through a Negro slave and her daughter, the branch of the family which became known as the

Beauchamps. He died in 1837. He appears in none, but is referred to throughout most of the stories in *Go Down, Moses* and in *The Reivers*. He is mentioned in *Intruder in the Dust*.

McCaslin, Ned William.   The Negro coachman for Grandfather Priest. He was born on the McCaslin lands in 1860 and claimed to be a grandson of old Lucius Quintus Carothers McCaslin (although the Negro descendants of McCaslin were known as Beauchamps). It was Ned who traded Grandfather Priest's automobile for the stolen racehorse. He died in 1934 (*The Reivers*).

McCaslin, Theophilus (Uncle Buck).   A son of old Lucius Quintus Carothers McCaslin and a twin brother of Amodeus (Uncle Buddy) McCaslin. He was born around 1800 in Carolina. He stayed at home during the war and let his brother enlist. Around 1859 he married Sophonsiba Beauchamp. They had one son, Isaac. Uncle Buck helped Bayard Sartoris and Ringo hunt down Grumby, the man who killed Granny Millard. He died around 1870, three years after his son was born. Appears in "Retreat" and "Vendée" (*The Unvanquished*), and in "Was" (*Go Down, Moses*), and is referred to throughout most of the other stories in *Go Down, Moses* and in *The Hamlet* and *The Reivers*.

THE PRIEST LINE

Priest, Alexander.   The baby brother of Lucius Priest (*The Reivers*).

Priest, Alison Lessep.   The wife of Maury Priest I and mother of Lucius (*The Reivers*).

Priest, Lessep.   A younger brother of Lucius Priest (*The Reivers*).

Priest, Lucius Quintus Carothers (Boss).   A distant relative of the Mc-Caslins, he came to Jefferson in 1865 from Carolina looking for his cousins. He married a granddaughter of old Lucius Quintus Carothers McCaslin named Sarah Edmonds in 1869. He was the father of Maury Priest I and was president of the Bank of Jefferson (*The Reivers*).

Priest, Lucius Quintus Carothers II.   The son of Maury Priest I and grandson of old Lucius Quintus Carothers (Boss) Priest and great-great-grandson of old McCaslin. He was eleven years old in 1905 and went on the escapade to Memphis with Boon Hogganbeck and Ned McCaslin and was the jockey in the race at Parsham. He narrates *The Reivers*.

Priest, Lucius Quintus Carothers III.   While his last name may not be Priest, he is the grandson of Lucius Quintus Carothers Priest II, and the "you" to whom the story of *The Reivers* is related. He speaks the first two words of the novel.

. . . .

Priest, Maury I.   The son of Boss Priest and father of the narrator of *The Reivers*. He ran a livery stable in Jefferson.

Priest, Maury II.   A younger brother of Lucius Priest (*The Reivers*).

Priest, Sarah Edmonds.   The wife of Boss Priest and grandmother of young Lucius. She was born in 1854 and was a granddaughter of old Lucius Quintus Carothers McCaslin (*The Reivers*).

A Chronology of *Go Down, Moses*   Meredith Smith*

The following chronology of Faulkner's novel *Go Down, Moses* has not been calculated by any one method. Each date has proven to be a problem in itself, requiring its own means of solution. The dates determined solely by the ledger entries in part 4 of "The Bear" are marked with an asterisk. Other dates have been calculated in relation to these dates, or from such evidence as the ages of characters or external events like wars and elections. Often the evidence is contradictory, suggesting two or even three possible dates for one event. These dates are footnoted in an attempt to resolve the contradictions. All page references are to the 1955 Modern Library reissue of the original text (New York, 1942), [which uses the same pagination as the Vintage Books edition].

1772*	Lucius Quintus Carothers McCaslin born in Carolina (p. 266)
1779*	Thucydus born to Roskus and Fibby (p. 266)
< 1797–1799 >	Twin boys (Amodeus and Theophilus) born to L. Q. Carothers McCaslin and his wife (pp. 4, 7, 164, 304)
1807*	Eunice bought (p. 267)
1809	Sam Fathers born (pp. 164, 215, 299, 350)
1809*	Eunice married to Thucydus (p. 267)
1810*	Tomasina ("Tomy" or "Tomey") born to Eunice (pp. 269, 270)
< 1812–14 >	Hubert Beauchamp born (pp. 303, 307) "Warwick" built by Hubert's father (p. 305) L. Q. Carothers McCaslin's wife dies—he is "long a widower" by 1832 (p. 270)
1830*	Percival Brownlee born (p. 264)
Dec. 25, 1832*	Eunice drowns (p. 267)
June 1833*	Tomey's Terrel born to Tomey; she dies (pp. 269–70)
June 27, 1837*	L. Q. Carothers McCaslin dies,[1] Roskus freed, Fibby freed (pp. 163, 266)
1838*	Tennie born (p. 271)
Jan. 12, 1841*	Roskus dies (p. 266)

*Reprinted by permission of the publisher from *Mississippi Quarterly* 36, no. 3 (Summer 1983): 319–28. © 1983 Mississippi State University.

Nov. 3, 1841*	Thucydus leaves plantation (p. 267)
Dec. 1841*	Thucydus sets up blacksmith shop in Jefferson (p. 267)
1843	Boon born (p. 228)
Aug. 1, 1849*	Fibby dies (p. 266)
1850	Cass born[2] (pp. 4, 10, 164, 272)
Early 1850s	Buck and Buddy establish $1,000 legacy for Tomey's Terrel (pp. 105–106)
Feb. 17, 1854*	Thucydus dies (p. 267)
June 1854	Tomey's Terrel comes of age, stays on plantation (p. 106)
Mar. 3, 1856*	Buck buys Percival Brownlee (p. 264)
Oct. 2, 1856*	Brownlee freed (p. 265)
Summer 1859*[3]	Buddy wins Tennie in poker game; Tennie and Tomey's Terrel marry (pp. 105, 271, 300)
Winter 1859*[4]	Amodeus McCaslin Beauchamp, son of Tomey's Terrel and Tennie, born and dies (p. 271)
1861	Civil War begins; Buck joins John Sartoris's regiment (pp. 234, 272, 350)
1862	Brownlee reappears as preacher (p. 292)
1862*	Daughter of Tomey's Terrel and Tennie born, dies (p. 272)
1863	Buck rides in and out of the Gayoso Hotel in Memphis while it is held by Yankees (pp. 233–34)
1863*	Another child born to Tomey's Terrel and Tennie and dies (p. 272)
1864 (or before)[5]	Cass orphaned (p. 272)
Dec. 29, 1864*	Tennie's Jim born to Tomey's Terrel and Tennie (p. 272)
1865	Buck returns from war (pp. 273, 350)
< 1865–1866 >	Buck and Sophonsiba marry (pp. 261–62, 301)
1866	Brownlee reappears, seen by Buck (pp. 292–93)
Oct. 1867	Ike born (pp. 196, 273, 274, 289, 301); two weeks later, Hubert seals gold pieces in cup (p. 301)
Early July 1869	Fonsiba born to Tomey's Terrel and Tennie (pp. 273, 274, 276)
1870[6]	First Buddy, then Buck die within the year; Cass

	takes responsibility for plantation (pp. 106, 114, 163, 274, 304)
< 1871–73 >	Sophonsiba makes Hubert dismiss his "cook" (pp. 302–303)
Jan. 19, 1873	Hubert removes the last gold piece from cup (pp. 305–306)
	Sometime the same year, Hubert replaces the cup itself (pp. 306, 308)
< 1873–77 >	"Warwick" burns; Hubert and Tennie's great-grandfather come to McCaslin farm to live (pp. 304–305, 307, 310)
Mar. 17, 1874[7]	Lucas Beauchamp born to Tomey's Terrel and Tennie (pp. 273–74, 281–82)
1875	Ike shoots rabbit (p. 176)
< 1874–1875 >	Zack Edmonds born (pp. 47, 55, 104, 114)
< 1876–77 >	Hubert dies (pp. 305–306)
1877 (or before)	Sophonsiba dies (p. 306)
Mar. 1877	Jobaker dies (pp. 172–75), Sam goes to live in Big Bottom
Nov. 1877	Ike goes for first hunt (pp. 175, 191, 192, 195, 196, 204)
Dec. 25, 1877	Ike receives gun from Cass (p. 205)
< 1877–78 >	Ike and Boon buy a wild pony when Ike is ten years old (pp. 232–33)
June 1878[8]	Ike tries to see Old Ben; finally succeeds (pp. 205–209)
1879	Boon shoots Negro (p. 230)
Nov. 1879	Ike kills first buck (pp. 209–10, 330, 350)
	Ash goes hunting (pp. 323–26)
	Ewell shoots buck from caboose of logging train (p. 319)
	Ike and Cass discuss mortality and immortality (pp. 186–87)
Nov. 1880	Ike kills first bear (pp. 210, 296)
Summer 1881	Ike and fyce corner Old Ben (pp. 295, 296, 297, 299)
	Sam captures Lion after doe, fawn, and colt found killed (pp. 209, 212–13)
	Cass and Ike talk about truth (pp. 296–97)

Nov. 1881	Lion participates in hunt; seven strangers watch (pp. 222–23) Lion sleeps with Boon (pp. 220–22)[9]
Nov. 1882	Hunters corner Old Ben, General Compson draws blood (pp. 224, 225, 226)
Dec. 1883	Ike and Boon go to Memphis (pp. 192, 226–35) Boon kills Old Ben, Lion dies, Sam dies (pp. 191–92, 226, 246–54)
Winter 1883–84	Ike reads ledgers on farm (pp. 268, 273) Hunters incorporate and lease hunting rights on land (p. 315)
Nov. 1884	Hunters go farther into woods to hunt (p. 316)
Jan. 1885	Boon made town marshal (pp. 316–17)
Spring 1885	De Spain leases timber rights (p. 316)
Summer 1885	Ike revisits land, sees snake, sees Boon at gum tree (pp. 316, 327–28, 330)
Dec. 29, 1885	Tennie's Jim disappears night of his twenty-first birthday; Ike follows him to Jackson, Tennessee, with his third of the legacy, does not find him (pp. 105, 273, 276)
Jan. 12, 1886*	Ike returns from fruitless trip to Jackson (p. 273)
1886	Cass hears Percival Brownlee proprietor of brothel (p. 293)
July 1886	Fonsiba leaves with husband (pp. 274, 276)
Dec. 11, 1886	Ike finds Fonsiba and husband in Arkansas, deposits money in bank for her (pp. 276–80)
1887[10]	Tomey's Terrel dies (pp. 106, 270–71)
Oct. 1888	Commissary scene between Ike and Cass on Ike's twenty-first birthday (pp. 254–55, 289, 292, 293, 351) Ike unseals Hubert's legacy (pp. 306–307) Cass brings money to Ike's bungalow, Ike forced to accept loan (p. 308)
Oct. 1889	Ike, earning money as a carpenter, tries unsuccessfully to pay back loan (p. 310)
< 1889–90 >	Ike marries (p. 311)
Mar. 17, 1895	Lucas comes of age, claims inheritance (pp. 107, 281–82)

< Mar. 17, 1895–	
Mar. 17, 1896 >	Lucas marries Mollie (pp. 35, 101, 110)
< 1890–1897 >	Cass Edmonds dies (pp. 73, 110)
Winter 1897–98	Henry born to Lucas and Mollie (pp. 45, 111)
Mar. 1898	Roth born; his mother dies (pp. 36, 45–46, 110, 118, 121)
Autumn 1898	Lucas and Zack fight (pp. 46–49)
< 1898 or later >	Tennie dies (p. 271)
Summer 1905	Roth rejects Henry (p. 111)
1917	George Wilkins born (pp. 40, 123)
< 1917–18 >	Roth fights in WWI (p. 338)
1921	Zack dies (p. 116) Lucas sets up still (pp. 35, 65)
Spring 1923	Nat born to Lucas and Mollie (pp. 73, 117, 123)
< 1937 or before >	Ike's wife dies (pp. 3, 352)
Nov. 1939	Roth meets girl, granddaughter of Tennie's Jim (p. 358)
Jan. 1940	Roth takes girl to New Mexico for two weeks (pp. 337, 358)
July 1940	Samuel Worsham Beauchamp executed; probable date for present action in "Go Down, Moses"[11]
Oct. 1940	George and Nat secretly married, or document forged with this date (p. 72); Roth's baby born (p. 358)
Nov. 1940[12]	Ike hunts with Roth, girl arrives with hers and Roth's baby (pp. 335, 338–39, 340, 344, 350, 353)
Feb. 1941	Rider and Mannie married (pp. 137, 138, 139)
Spring 1941[13]	Lucas and George get caught by sheriff with stills; trial (p. 62)
Summer 1941	George buys new still with money Lucas has given him (p. 75)
Aug. 1941	Mannie dies (pp. 137, 138) Salesman comes with divining machine (p. 78) Mollie asks for divorce (p. 102)
Sept./Oct. 1941	Mollie leaves with machine, she and Lucas go to court for trial, Lucas changes his mind (p. 125)
Spring 1942	George and Nat's child expected (p. 123)

Notes

1. There are contradictory passages about Carothers McCaslin's death. On p. 163, the narrator states that he had lived to be eighty years old. However, p. 266 provides an exact date of birth and death as recorded by his son and seems to be more reliable. The passage on p. 163 is puzzling, for it also suggests that Buck and Buddy lived to be eighty, which does not accord with other evidence provided in the text, such as that on p. 106.

2. Cass's birthdate is given several times as 1850, and he is definitely nine years old in the present time of "Was." However, there is a problem in determining what time of year he was born. The narrator states consistently that Cass is sixteen years older than Isaac, who is born in October 1867. Cass would have to have a birthday later in the year than Isaac's in order to be sixteen years older. Late October would account for the age difference and would be a logical choice if "Was" occurred in that month. However, there is every indication that the present action of "Was" is meant to take place in the summer (see note 3). These conflicts then cannot be resolved.

3. The time of year for this chapter seems to be summer. Several clues are given—all rather subtle. Mr. Hubert sits in the spring-house with his boots off and his feet in the water, supposedly cooling off. Later, Cass mimics him and thinks that soon (late afternoon or evening) it would be cool enough for a race (p. 13). After dinner, Hubert and Buck sit out on the front gallery (p. 12). Finally, Miss Sophonsiba offers to show Buck her garden (p. 14), probably in full bloom in summertime.

4. This date deserves some attention. If "Was" takes place in the summer months of 1859 and Tennie has her baby the same year, she was either pregnant at the time of the card game and the hunt for Tomey's Terrel—making the forced separation of the two more significant—or the baby was born prematurely. (The baby's sex is stated as male. For the sex of the child to be evident, the date of its birth should be at least four months after its conception.) If the story is set in October (see note 2), Tennie would definitely have been pregnant during the present action of "Was."

5. There is no definite date given for Cass's parents' deaths. However, we know he was an orphan by this time, living with Buddy while Buck was in the Confederate Army.

6. The determination of the date of Uncle Buck's death is one of the most difficult chronological problems in Go Down, Moses. Whether he died in 1870 [Rosemary Stephens, "Ike's Gun and Too Many Novembers," Mississippi Quarterly, 23 (Summer 1970) and Stanley Sultan, "Call Me Ishmael: The Hagiography of Isaac McCaslin," Texas Studies in Language and Literature, 3 (Spring 1971) offer this date for Uncle Buck and Buddy's deaths], 1873 [Albert J. Devlin, "Faulknerian Chronology: Puzzles and Games," Notes on Mississippi Writers, 6 (1973), and T. J. Wertenbaker, "Faulkner's Point of View and The Chronicle of Ike McCaslin," College English, 24 (December 1962) give this date], or 1879 [Edmond Volpe, A Reader's Guide to William Faulkner (New York: Farrar, Straus & Giroux, 1964] is important to our understanding of his relationship with his son Isaac. The problem arises from inconsistencies in the text. However, a logical decision is possible by weighing the importance of each passage containing an indicative reference.

Edmond Volpe's date of 1879, as Devlin points out, is impossible. If Uncle Buck had been living when Ike was twelve years old, we must assume Ike would not have needed Cass as a guardian; or at least the fact that his father was still alive would be apparent. Volpe bases his conclusion upon one passage, on p. 163, where the narrator states that Ike "would live to be eighty, as his father and his father's twin brother and their father in his turn had lived to be." However, this passage must be scrutinized. Although Ike might live to be eighty years old, his grandfather died at sixty-five, according to ledger entries. All the evidence points to an earlier date for Buck and Buddy's deaths as well. On p. 106, the narrator states that "Amodeus and Theophilus were dead too, at seventy and better."

We know that Uncle Buck was "nearing seventy" when Ike was born in 1867. After Uncle

Buck has made his last ledger entry in 1869 (p. 273), the narrator proceeds: "for the boy himself was a year old, and when Lucas was born six years later, his father and uncle had been dead inside the same twelve-months almost five years. . . ." (p. 274). This passage does not provide a solution to the problem. It refers to the year 1869 when Fonsiba was born, suggesting 1870 as the year for Buck and Buddy's deaths, and 1875 as the year for Lucas's birth. However, the date for Lucas's birth given in the ledgers and in other chapters is March 17, 1874 (p. 281). The confusion arises only if the reader imposes another date into the passage, ignoring its internal consistency. The date presented for Uncle Buck's and Buddy's deaths in this passage is 1870. Faulkner makes a specific reference here to Ike's age in relation to his father's death as well as to the impossibility of Lucas's ever remembering Buck and Buddy. If we accept this relationship with Ike as the heart of Uncle Buck's function in the novel, this passage seems the most accurate indicator of Faulkner's intention. The twins would have been about seventy or seventy-one if we accept 1799 as their birthdate (pp. 7, 164), dying at "seventy and better" (p. 106). We know Uncle Buck was very ill when he made his last ledger entry in 1869 (p. 273).

There are other contradictions which complicate this problem. The most difficult statement to reconcile with this date appears on p. 304 where Buck, described as "almost seventy-five years," says " 'Go get that damn cup. Bring that damn Hub Beauchamp too if you have to.' " If we accept 1799 as Buck's birthdate, this passage would have to take place in 1873, or 1874, before his birthday. However, if Buck's age were not mentioned the passage could be placed earlier. Hubert started removing the gold pieces from the cup soon after they were placed there in 1867. Buck could have been suspicious at any time about Hubert's financial situation and could have made such a demand. The only contradiction here is Uncle Buck's age right before he died, which has been given three times, three different ways (pp. 163, 106, 304). Therefore, this fact seems the least reliable of all the evidence Faulkner provides us.

Another apparent contradiction is the passage on pp. 272–73 discussing the $1,000 to Tomey's Terrel, later changed to $1,000 for each of his children by Buck and Buddy: "it would be another two years yet before the boy, almost a man now, would return from the abortive trip into Tennessee with the still-intact third of old Carothers' legacy to his Negro son and his descendants, which as the three surviving children established at last one by one their apparent intention of surviving, their white half-uncles had increased to a thousand dollars each. . . ." (pp. 272–73). This passage suggests that Buck and Buddy lived to see the three children survive. If this statement is to be read literally, their deaths would have to be after 1874, when Lucas was born. Ike would have been almost seven years old at this time and Hubert Beauchamp would have already died. We know that Buck dies before Hubert comes to live with his sister and Isaac, presumably in 1873. Therefore, a more logical interpretation of this passage is a broader one. Buck and Buddy could have lived to see James and Fonsiba, the record of whose birth is the last ledger entry Buck makes, survive before their own deaths in 1870. Their decision then was not that the $1,000 legacy would now be increased to $3,000; but that each of Tomey's Terrel's children, however many might survive, would be given the legacy in the amount their father refused. With this latter interpretation, they would not have had to have lived to see Lucas's birth.

There are two passages which suggest a later date, after Lucas's birth. The problem suggested is whether Lucas actually remembers Uncle Buck and Buddy "in the living flesh" (p. 39). Zack tells his son Roth on p. 114, " 'You think that because Lucas is older than I am, old enough even to remember Uncle Buck and Uncle Buddy a little . . . is not reason enough for him not to want to say mister to me?' " The other passage, on p. 39, is told by the narrator through Lucas's consciousness. Lucas is proudly thinking about himself as the "oldest living McCaslin descendant still living on the hereditary land, who actually remembered old Buck and Buddy in the living flesh." There are several reasons implicit in these passages for the reader to doubt their factuality. "Remember" is used in an abstract sense. Unless we accept that Buck lived until Isaac was about nine or ten years old, Lucas, six and a half years Ike's junior, could not possibly have "remembered" Uncle Buck and Buddy. He more likely remembered "about" them from stories told him by his parents. The "fact-givers" must be examined in both cases. Zack tells Roth that

Lucas remembers Uncle Buck and Buddy either because Lucas has convinced him of it (he was even younger and would have no reason to know the exact date of their deaths; Lucas might have bragged to the younger boy to gain a "one-uppance" when they were childhood playmates) or because he wants Roth to believe it to understand his and Lucas's relationship. The other passage is centered upon Lucas's pride in his heritage. Lucas might have convinced himself that he remembers Uncle Buck and Buddy to add to his feeling of superiority and pride. These passages are not necessarily contradictions in fact, only in interpretation.

The most logical date for the death then is 1870. This date confirms that Isaac had almost no relationship with his father, was little more than an infant when Buck McCaslin died. Understanding how slight this relationship was is essential to an understanding of the mature Ike.

7. There is a contradiction in these two pages. On p. 274 the narrator states that Lucas is born six years after his sister Fonsiba (whose birthdate is recorded as 1869). Lucas would then be born in the year 1875. However, the second passage again gives more complete information, with a ledger entry with a specific date. The second passage thus seems to be the accurate one. There are many references to Lucas's age, his coming of age and other dates given in "The Fire and the Hearth" which substantiate this latter date.

8. There is a problem here only in the date on the gun Ike is using. It is a Christmas gift with the date 1878 engraved on it; yet he is using it in the summer of 1878. Rosemary Stephens ("Ike's Gun and Too Many Novembers") feels the contradiction arises from the 1878 date, assuming it is dated on Christmas day 1878. However, it is never stated in the narrative that the date on the gun is Christmas 1878. Although the gun was a Christmas gift, it easily could have been engraved afterwards, in the early months of 1878 before that summer when Isaac takes it with him to the Big Bottom.

9. Isaac states that Lion sleeps with Boon the second November he is in camp and sleeps with him "all the nights of the next November and the next one" (p. 222). Since Lion dies the next December after leading the hunt for Old Ben, Rosemary Stephens feels that too many Novembers are listed, unless Boon actually slept with Lion the first November he was in camp. However, there is never any statement in the narrative that Boon did not sleep with Lion that first November; no one *knew* until the second. The number of Novembers Isaac lists is not meant to be a chronological count of the hunts ahead—it is dreamlike and consistent with Ike's feeling about the endless nature of the hunt. He could have added five more Novembers and not have meant them literally.

10. Here again there are two possible dates offered. The first passage states that Tomey's Terrel died after Carothers McCaslin had been dead for fifty years, putting his death in 1887 or afterwards. The second passage states that he was still alive when Ike was ten years old (1877), suggesting that he died soon afterwards. Since these two passages do not have to be mutually exclusive, I must take the later date, which does not force a contradiction.

11. One possibility for establishing the date would be to use the census taken as a clue. Since the census is taken every decade, this story could take place in 1940. This date would place "Go Down, Moses" chronologically before "The Fire and the Hearth." There is no definite clue in "Go Down, Moses" linking it with the overall chronology of the novel. The only facts on which a speculation can be based are the relationships described—Samuel Worsham Beauchamp is Mollie's grandson by her daughter (whom I believe to be her second child). Miss Worsham believes that this daughter is Mollie's oldest, but she seems to misunderstand a number of other important facts about Mollie, and her word cannot be taken as totally reliable. The daughter seemingly bears Sam out of wedlock, the father deserts her, and she dies in childbirth. Although Faulkner never states that they are not married, there is no mention of marriage, and Sam's surname is Beauchamp. The mother's death in childbirth would have been more probable if she had been very young. Determining her date of birth would help determine the present time of this chapter. If Sam's mother were Mollie's second child, she could have been conceived when Mollie returned to Lucas after spending six months at the big house nursing Roth—fall 1898. She would then have been born in 1899. If she was young when she

conceived Sam, her age could be speculated to be anywhere from fifteen to seventeen at the time of childbirth. If this group of guesses can be accepted, depending on his mother's age at the time of his birth, Sam would be born between 1914 and 1916. The year of his banishment from the plantation would thus fall between 1933 and 1935, his arrest and escape in Jefferson between 1934 and 1936. The present time would then be July 1940, 1941, or 1942—the first date consistent with the census clue, the final date serving more effectively as an epilogue because of its sequential relationship to the events in "The Fire and the Hearth." I personally find the year 1940 the most logical time for the present action with the information given.

12. The date for the present events in "Delta Autumn" is difficult to determine. There are many references to the fact that Isaac has been hunting for sixty years and that he is over seventy years old. Both of these facts place the date after 1937. Roth is "just forty" according to Isaac, moving the date to at least 1938. It has been "twenty-odd" years since Roth fought in World War I, again suggesting a date after 1938. The final clue, which narrows the possibilities considerably, is Roth's contemptuous question (p. 338). " 'After Hitler gets through with it? Or Smith or Jones or Roosevelt or Willkie or whatever he will call himself in this country?' " The election between Roosevelt and Willkie was November 5, 1940, so the names would still be more probably recalled that November. This year seems to be the logical choice for the present action of this chapter, although 1941 is also a possibility.

13. The year 1941 is decidedly the date for the present action in "The Fire and the Hearth." There are many references to Roth's age as forty-three (pp. 45, 118, 121) and Lucas's as sixty-seven (pp. 33, 42, 61, 79, 102, 118, 121, 122). Both Roth and Lucas have March birthdays, so the story should be after March 1941. Lucas and Mollie have been married forty-five years (pp. 35, 101), also placing the action in 1941. The month or season within the years is determined by the farm calendar. Before the incident with the stills, Lucas needs to finish planting his crop (spring). After the trial, there is nothing to do but watch the "cotton and corn springing up" (p. 75 [summer]). When Mollie asks for the divorce, Roth tells her that Lucas does not have anything to do now that it is late summer. When Mollie finally leaves with the divining machine herself, the first frost has fallen and the cotton is ginned and baled (p. 125 [late fall]). The story is written in a chronological sequence with few flashbacks. The chronology in this chapter is the most straightforward in the novel.

[The Poker Game in "Was"]   Robert L. Yarup*

Uncle Buddy devises the strategy of the game on the performance of his opponent in the preliminary match between Buck and Hubert, which is scouted by Cass under the orders of Buddy ("Watch him. . . . Watch Theophilus")[1] and microscopically detailed to him. The original stakes were five hundred dollars against Sibbey with the loser buying either Tennie or Turl for three hundred dollars. In a game of five-card draw, Buck draws two cards; Hubert draws one. Hubert looks "quick" at his hand and asks Buck if he helped "them threes" (Go Down, Moses, p. 24). Buck says no, and Hubert triumphantly replies that he did and reveals three kings and two fives.

In setting up his adversary, the experienced gambler would observe the prominence of the ruling king and of threes in the game. Of the three participants, the dealer Cass will play a crucial role in the return match. There are three discards, face down, naturally, and given importance as Cass carefully recounts Hubert flipping his discard "onto the two" (p. 24) which Uncle Buck had discarded. Hubert first thinks that Buck has three of a kind, and by the nature of his "quick" (p. 24) decision in drawing one card, it is apparent that Hubert draws on two pair, kings and fives, and draws a third king. Faulkner emphasizes this probability by thematic design, for it is this third king that wins his "freedom" (p. 23) from Sophonsiba, the "lucky queen" (p. 11) who will now rule over her "buck bee" (p. 11). He has also won the three hundred from Buck for Tennie. Thus psychologically imbedded in Hubert's mind, threes are a winning combination for him, his third king securing the promise of "a little peace and quiet and freedom" (p. 23) that he could not achieve in his midnight race (p. 6).

Following Cass's report, Uncle Buddy wants to know where Tomey's Turl is and what he had to say about the game. Buddy's "Hah" (p. 25) signals a satisfying readiness to join in the pursuit.

Hubert and Uncle Buddy's game shifts from five-card draw to five-card stud, which recalls Hubert's pair of fives in the first game. Buck's freedom is again at stake, and the continuity with the first game is further established by Hubert's comment that he will retain the three hundred dollars for Tennie even if he loses. An expediently devised McCaslin propriety demands the third participant be someone other than young Cass, and "animal mule or human" (p. 27) is beckoned from the dark to deal. The threes which flood the first game mysteriously pervade the second.

Hubert's first king develops the continuity from his winning three kings in the first game, and he confidently repeats the bet: "Buck McCaslin against Sibbey's dowry" (p. 27). His first three reinforces the continuity; his second three is not only reminiscent of his pair of fives but also of his pair of kings to which he drew a third king in his winning hand. But the final ace breaks the continuity, and Buddy's corresponding five, securing the possibility of a

*Reprinted with permission from The Explicator 41, no. 4 (Summer 1983): 43–45.

straight, stands now in opposition to Hubert's king. If Hubert's draw was a five instead of a king in the first game as previously noted, Uncle Buddy's five would be equally devastating to his confidence. Apparently shaken for the first time (note his "quick" decision and movement in the first hand), "he didn't look at anything or move for a whole minute" (p. 28) as he watched Uncle Buddy look at his hole card. Hubert checks, but another reversal occurs when Buddy bets "them two niggers . . . against the three hundred dollars Theophilus owes you for Tennie, and the three hundred you and Theophilus agreed on for Tomey's Turl" (p. 28). The ace signals now not only a change in luck, breaking the potential for duplicating a full house and winning combination as his king lay dormant under the ace among his three treys, but also points to a vivid distinction between his first and second opponents, reminding that "a man playing cards with Amodeus McCaslin ain't gambling" (pp. 26–27). Trapped into giving "a nigger away" (p. 28) or buying one for three hundred dollars, Hubert turns his face down card over, which is a three, his third three, and he ponders the possibility of Uncle Buddy having the fourth three needed to fill his inside straight.

With his game in reverse, his confidence waning, and his mind inundated with threes, now covering all possible loopholes, he thinks of the possibilities of foul play: "and you just shuffled and I cut afterward" (p. 29). After contemplating what his loss will cost him by calling Buddy's hand, "And I will have to buy that nigger" (p. 29), he asks, "Who dealt these cards, Amodeus?" (p. 29). Even though the odds are forty-two to one against it, what psychology would bet against the probability that Uncle Buddy's hole card is a three, especially after the light shines on the dealer? Just as in Turl's race against Hubert's crack "Walker dogs" (p. 10), this "wasn't any race at all" (p. 15).

Now, what this observer wants to know is what effect did the mysterious hole card (mysterious only because it is never revealed) have on the psychology that arranged for Tennie and Tomey's Turl to have three children after their first three children died in infancy, the first named after the man who, so to speak, set them free?

Note

1. William Faulkner, "Was," *Go Down, Moses* (New York: Random House, 1942), p. 6. All subsequent citations from "Was" are to this edition.

INDEX

Only substantial references are indexed. Works and characters appear under the author's name except in the case of Faulkner where they are listed separately *in italics*. Only significant notes or matters of significant bibliographical import in notes are included; material in the Appendixes has not been indexed.